M000192012

HERSTORIES ON SCREEN

KATHLEEN CUMMINS

HERSTORIES ON SCREEN

Feminist Subversions of Frontier Myths

WALLFLOWER

NEW YORK

Wallflower Press is an imprint of Columbia University Press
Publishers Since 1893
New York   Chichester, West Sussex
cup.columbia.edu

Copyright © 2020 Columbia University Press
All rights reserved

Library of Congress Cataloging-in-Publication Data
Names: Cummins, Kathleen, author.
Title: Herstories on screen : feminist subversions of frontier
myths / Kathleen Cummins.
Description: New York : Wallflower Press, 2020. | Includes
bibliographical references and index.
Identifiers: LCCN 2019049409 | ISBN 9780231189507 (cloth) |
ISBN 9780231189514 (paperback) | ISBN 9780231851299 (ebook)
Subjects: LCSH: Feminist films—History and criticism. | Feminism and motion
pictures. | Women in motion pictures. | Frontier and pioneer life—In motion
pictures. | Motion pictures and women. | Women in the motion picture industry. |
Women motion picture producers and directors.
Classification: LCC PN1995.9.W6 C86 2020 | DDC 791.43/6522—dc23
LC record available at https://lccn.loc.gov/2019049409

Columbia University Press books are printed on permanent and durable
acid-free paper.
Printed in the United States of America

Cover design: Milenda Nan Ok Lee
Cover photo: © Photofest

CONTENTS

ACKNOWLEDGMENTS

THIS BOOK has been in the works for a number of years, and a number of people were fundamental to its completion. First, I am indebted to Dr. Kathryn McPherson, a brilliant teacher who generously shared her invaluable wisdom and insight about feminist writing. From the very beginning, Kate has championed my work, and she has been a great source of inspiration and encouragement, especially through difficult times. I am also thankful for the financial support I received from the Graduate Program in Gender, Feminist & Women's Studies at York University and the Faculty of Animation, Arts and Design at Sheridan College, which enabled me to travel to conferences where I presented aspects of this book. I am also very indebted to editors Yoram Allon and Ryan Groendyk of Wallflower, who took a leap of faith with this project, which I will never forget. And finally, I wish to say a mammoth thank-you to Lou Mersereau, my partner in life and father to our two lovely and supportive daughters, Teresa and Louisa. Having read countless drafts, Lou has been a steadfast source of strength, patience, and encouragement. This book is dedicated to Lou, Louisa, and Teresa.

INTRODUCTION

Herstories in the Counter Narrative Tradition

*The myths governing the cinema are no different from those
governing other cultural products: they relate to a standard
value system informing all cultural systems
in a given society. . . . It is possible to use icons
(i.e. conventional configurations) in the face
of and against mythology usually associated with them.[1]*

—Claire Johnston

*I think we need to do more than try to document history.
I think we need to probe. We need to have the freedom to
romanticize history, to say, "what if," to use history
in a speculative way and create speculative fiction.
I think we need to feel free to do that.[2]*

—Julie Dash

HERSTORIES ON SCREEN: *Feminist Subversions of Frontier Myths*
is a transnational qualitative study that examines ten long-
form dramatic narrative English-language films directed by
women, produced between 1979 and 1993. These films tell stories of
female emancipation and resistance in former white-settler nations—
Canada, the United States, New Zealand/Aotearoa, and Australia. Set
in rural landscapes that represent or evoke iconic national frontier
spaces, the films take place across a wide temporal range, from the
mid-nineteenth century to the late twentieth-century. Though a few
of these films are set in contemporary times, all of them aim to

subvert tropes strongly associated with frontier myth-histories (e.g., the Western) and hence challenge dominant narratives that have rendered invisible and irrelevant the voices, experiences, and stories of women across the axes of race, sexuality, class, and age. Examined collectively, the films can be seen as representing a kind of transnational feminist film wave in which women filmmakers told herstories on the big screen. The term *herstory* is apt for this study because the issues and discourses that permeate these films reflect the key debates that animated what is commonly referred to as second-wave feminism or the "women's movement" of the 1960s and 70s. An expansion of the fight for suffrage waged by first-wave feminists of the late nineteenth century, the often oversimplified second-wave women's movement comprised a diverse range of struggles focalized on gender equity, reproductive rights, the nature of gender, and the role of the family. Born out of the second wave, the herstory term means "history considered or presented from a feminist viewpoint or with special attention to the experience of women."[3] This study renders visible the various feminist discourses that emerge across this body of work illuminating the range of possibilities for expressing feminist politics within popular forms such as the narrative feature film. In this sense, the films are what French philosopher Jean-François Lyotard called "little narratives," or metanarratives that call attention to themselves, a defining feature of postmodern and postindustrial societies. These kinds of narratives are in contrast to the grand narrative or "emancipative narrative," a defining feature of the modern age that Lyotard was the first to identify as a method deployed by societies to legitimize knowledge or make sense of history (interconnecting a series of events in a linear structure), and are, hence, tied up with power and domination.[4]

Table I.1 summarizes the ten films featured in this study. The appendix gives more extended summaries of the films, and chapter 1 contains detailed plot synopses.

The scope of this study is defined by the following factors. First, the study focuses specifically on films that were directed by women. Second, the films all hail from former frontier white-settler nations and are all in the English language. Third, all the films are narrative feature films with the intent to reach a large audience. Fourth, the selected ten films are all deemed landmark feminist texts and represent

TABLE I.1 The Films

Country	Film Title	Director	Year of Release
Australia	*My Brilliant Career*	Gillian Armstrong	1979
	Bedevil	Tracey Moffatt	1993
Canada	*My American Cousin*	Sandy Wilson	1985
	Loyalties	Anne Wheeler	1987
	The Wake	Norma Bailey	1986
New Zealand/	*Mauri*	Merata Mita	1988
Aotearoa	*The Piano*	Jane Campion	1993
United States	*Daughters of the Dust*	Julie Dash	1991
	Thousand Pieces of Gold	Nancy Kelly	1991
	The Ballad of Little Jo	Maggie Greenwald	1993

Source: Author's own data.

significant watershed moments in women's cinema. Finally, all the selected films deploy or subvert (or both) tropes of popular frontier myth-history narratives.

LA POLITIQUE DES (FEMME) AUTEURS

The focus on women directors is rooted in a historical critical tradition in which authorship of a film has been largely attributed to the director rather than to other key contributors such as the producer or screenwriter. The concept of the director as author has been around since the 1920s, but it became entrenched in film criticism largely through the French film journal *Cahiers du cinéma*, whose founder, André Bazin, famously coined the phrase *la politique des auteurs* in 1957. The original *Cahiers* group argued that authorship in the cinema was located not in the story but in the director's use of style, mise-en-scène, and filmmaking practices.[5] The auteur theory and model was later propagated by American film critic Andrew Sarris in the 1960s. These theorists and critics took up Alexandre Astruc's idea of *la caméra-stylo*. Astruc argued:

> Direction is no longer a means of illustrating or presenting a scene, but a true act of writing. The film-maker/author writes with his camera

as a writer writes with his pen. In an art in which a length of film and sound-track is put in motion and proceeds, by means of a certain form and a certain story (there can even be no story at all—it matters little), to evolve a philosophy of life, how can one possibly distinguish between the man who conceives the work and the man who writes it? Could one imagine a Faulkner novel written by someone other than Faulkner? And would *Citizen Kane* be satisfactory in any other form than that given to it by Orson Welles?[6]

With regard to authorship and women, the female film auteur has been glaringly nonexistent, with a few notable exceptions. In truth, film canon lists today remain male dominated. A list by the American Film Institute (AFI), the "100 Greatest American Films of All Time," has no female directors at all. Only six of the films are (white) female-driven narratives, and only three are black male-driven narratives. This is perplexing because the AFI claims to provide "leadership in film and television and is dedicated to initiatives that engage the past, the present and the future of the moving image arts."[7] In Canada, the federally funded nonprofit Reel Canada published its "150 Canadian Films" list, in which 18 percent of the films were directed by women; 7.3 percent were directed by women of color. Twenty-four percent of the films were female-driven narratives; sixteen featured indigenous women or women of color.[8] Reel Canada claims its project "promotes the power and diversity of Canadian film."[9] On an international scale, however, in the "Greatest 100 Films of All Time" list published by the British Film Institute (BFI), only two of the films were directed by women, both of whom were white. Only twelve out of one hundred films were female-driven narratives, and only one, *Imitation of Life*, featured a woman of color: Juanita Moore, in a costarring role opposite a white woman. The BFI states that its "poll has come to be regarded as the most trusted guide there is to the canon of cinema greats, not to mention a barometer of changing critical tastes."[10] Feminist film theorist and historian Janet Staiger called this exclusionary practice the "politics of admission." She argued that canonical lists tellingly "tended to suppress historical, class and social issues."[11] Also relevant here is feminist art historian Linda Nochlin's question posed in 1971, "Why have there been no great women artists?"[12] Almost fifty years later, canonical film lists force us to ask, Why have there been no great women directors?

In recent years, multiple studies have revealed sobering and disturbing statistics about gender and racial inequity in the film and television industry. In short, the film industry is in a gender crisis, a state of emergency, if you will. The "Celluloid Ceiling" report concluded that in 2018 women accounted for 8 percent of directors in the top 250 Hollywood theatrical releases.[13] Because of these statistics and other gender equity reports, in 2015 the American Civil Liberties Union instigated "a campaign demanding that our government launch an investigation into the systemic failure to hire women directors at all levels of the film and TV industry in violation of state and federal civil rights laws."[14] The European Women's Audiovisual Network's pan-European study "Where Are the Women Directors?" also concluded that the "vast majority of the funding resources (namely 84%) go into films that are NOT directed by women."[15] The 2019 "On Screen Report" study by the Canadian organization Women in View concluded that "women—especially women of colour and Indigenous women—remain significantly underemployed on Canada's publicly funded film and television productions." Out of a total of 267 film projects funded between 2015 and 2017, 12 contracts went to indigenous women—6 for writing and 6 for directing.[16] During the time period of this study, 1979–1993, no indigenous women directed a dramatic feature-length film in Canada or the United States. The Screen Australia study "Women Working in Key Creative Roles" concluded that between 1970 and 2014, 16 percent of feature films had a female director and 21 percent had a female screenwriter.[17] Studies show that in New Zealand/Aotearoa, women are well represented in documentary films but underrepresented in dramatic features. Merata Mita remains, as of 2019, the only Maori woman to direct a narrative feature film, *Mauri*. Deborah Shepard, a New Zealand writer and film scholar, commented that "since 2000 women have lost ground and film production and experimentation has declined, knocked back by the backlash against feminism, by recession and fiscal cutbacks caused by the global financial meltdown of 2008–9 and a change in political parties."[18] Shepard's remarks about backlash could be applied to all the nations featured in this study.

A SELECTIVE TRADITION

The second factor that defines the scope of this study is nation. The films all hail from former frontier white-settler nations (Australia, Canada,[19] New Zealand/Aotearoa, and the United States) and are all in the English language. In many ways these four nations share a similar origin story of white Anglo-Saxon settler expansionism, what Marxist cultural theorist Raymond Williams calls a "selective national tradition." In his examination of how selective traditions work within a society Williams argues:

> From a whole possible area of past and present, in a particular culture, certain meanings and practices are selected for emphasis and certain other meanings and practices are neglected or excluded. Yet, within a particular hegemony, and as one of its decisive processes, this selection is presented and usually successfully passed off as 'the tradition', 'the significant past'. What has then to be said about any tradition is that it is in this sense an aspect of contemporary social and cultural organization, in the interest of the dominance of a specific class. It is a version of the past which is intended to connect with and ratify the present. What it offers in practice is a sense of predisposed continuity.[20]

Hollywood Westerns, pioneer narratives such as Laura Ingalls Wilder's *Little House on the Prairie* novels (1932–1943), and Australian "kangaroo" Westerns are prime examples of narratives that work in the selective tradition. However, it is the Hollywood Western, a decidedly masculine genre, that is perhaps the most iconic and influential of all popular frontier stories. Examining the rise of the Western, historian Richard Slotkin argued:

> According to this myth-historiography, the conquest of the wilderness and the subjugation or displacement of the Native Americans who originally inhabited it have been the means to our achievement of a national identity, a democratic polity, an ever-expanding economy, and a phenomenally dynamic and "progressive" civilization.[21]

Slotkin called this a "mythology of violence" and considered it to be intrinsic to selling the war in Vietnam.

The invocation of the Indian war and Custer's Last Stand as models for the Vietnam war was a mythological way of answering the question, *Why are we in Vietnam?* The answer implicit in the myth is, "We are there because our ancestors were heroes who fought the Indians, and died (rightly or wrongly) as sacrifices for the nation." There is no logic to the connection, only the powerful force of tradition and habits of feeling and thought.[22]

Historian Elizabeth Furniss argued:

Historians Eric Hobsbawm and Terence Ranger have shown how these selective historical traditions have been creatively "invented" by colonial governments to promote nationalism and to legitimize the process of colonization and the subjugation of Indigenous peoples. The real power of a selective tradition, however, exists in its eventual colonization of popular consciousness: when it becomes transformed into a set of unquestioned, taken-for-granted historical "truths" that define conventional historical understandings among members of a society.[23]

THE POWER TO NARRATE

These films aimed to counter this selective tradition by using "icons in the face of and against mythology usually associated with them."[24] The filmmakers' choice and determination to work in the narrative feature film format can be seen as a political act, intended not only to break through the "celluloid ceiling" but also to destabilize, question, and reimagine popular frontier myth-history narratives (truths) through a feminist lens. By working in the narrative feature tradition, these filmmakers demanded what pioneering postcolonial theorist Edward Said called "the power to narrate."

The power to narrate, or to block other narratives from forming and emerging, is very important to culture and imperialism, and constitutes one of the main connections between them. Most important, the grand narratives of emancipation and enlightenment mobilized people in the colonial world to rise up and throw off imperial subjection; in the process, many Europeans and Americans were also stirred by these stories and their protagonists, and they too fought for new narratives of equality and human community.[25]

LANDMARK WOMEN'S FILMS

The selected ten films in this study are all deemed landmark feminist texts and represent significant watershed moments in cinema in which women "fought for new narratives of equality and human community." Gillian Armstrong's *My Brilliant Career* was the first narrative feature film to be directed by a woman in Australia in forty-six years, and it opened doors for other women filmmakers.[26] The film also helped revive Australian cinema in the 1970s.[27] Tracey Moffatt became the first Aboriginal Australian woman to direct a narrative feature film with *Bedevil*,[28] helping to pave the way for indigenous women filmmakers.[29] Sandy Wilson's directorial debut, *My American Cousin*, won numerous Genie Awards (the Canadian Oscars) for Best Picture, Best Achievement in Direction, and Best Screenplay. The film was also picked up for distribution by a big Hollywood distributer, 20th Century Fox, rare for a Canadian film.[30] Norma Bailey's *The Wake* was one of the first and only programs in Canada to feature Métis women in prominent roles. Métis are people of mixed European and indigenous ancestry, one of the three recognized Aboriginal peoples in Canada.[31] The film won numerous awards, including Canadian Gemini Awards (television) for Best Writing, Best Dramatic Series, and Best Actress (for Victoria Snow).[32] Anne Wheeler's award-winning *Loyalties* was honored for its nonstereotyped representations of indigenous women.[33] It should be noted, however, that Bailey and Wheeler are white women. Merata Mita's *Mauri* was the world's first narrative feature film directed by an indigenous woman,[34] and it is credited with developing Maori cinema.[35] Mita herself has been heralded as "the grandmother" and "an icon" of indigenous cinema.[36] *The Piano* won three Academy Awards, and Jane Campion is the second of only four women to be nominated in the Best Director category.[37] Campion was the first, and currently is the only, woman to be awarded the Palme d'Or at the Cannes Film Festival, an award that she shared with a male director.[38]

The Piano is now listed in the U.S. National Society of Film Critics list "100 Essential Films of All Time."[39] Julie Dash's *Daughters of the Dust* was the first narrative feature film with a theatrical release to be directed by an African American woman.[40] In 2004, the Library of Congress declared *Daughters* to be a National Treasure.[41] Nancy Kelly's *Thousand Pieces of Gold* received wide acclaim from high-profile film critics. Michael Willington of the *Los Angeles Times* favorably compared the film to the "lucid lyricism of a John Ford, a Budd Boetticher, a George Stevens."[42] Roger Ebert called Rosalind Chao's performance Oscar-worthy.[43] *The Ballad of Little Jo* was "the first Western written and directed by a woman since the silent era."[44] The film also received high praise from critics. Stephen Holden of the *New York Times* wrote, "It isn't every day that a movie reimagines the Old West in a vision as acute and provocative as Maggie Greenwald's astonishing film 'The Ballad of Little Jo.'"[45]

THE PERFECT STORM

This selection of ten films directed by women represents a feminist film wave of sorts. Most film waves occur because a group of filmmakers, usually politicized young males, aim to reinvent cinema or combat Hollywood domination and American imperialism within a particular time and place. For example, Italian Neorealism was born out of the harsh economic and culturally oppressive conditions in postwar Italy. Historically, film waves have been grounded in national or domestic cinemas, working within isolated film production contexts. The women filmmakers in this study were also strongly politicized and also aimed to counter the dominant cinema, both Hollywood and their own domestic cinemas, which had historically excluded female voices and women's stories. Like all film waves and movements, a certain set of political, cultural, institutional, and national conditions had to be in place for this to happen, and most of these conditions evolved out of, and were cultivated by, the second-wave women's movement. In her seminal book *Women's Pictures: Feminism and Cinema*, Annette Kuhn argued that there are two ways to ensure the development and survival of a feminist counter-cinema: "one, to work on dominant structures by attempting to open them up to new matters of form and expression, and two, to build oppositional institutions independently of dominant cinema."[46] The films in this study seem to have benefited from the implementation of both approaches.

Collectively these ten films can be seen as the outcome of a perfect storm in which a number of imbricating factors occurred simultaneously. One of the main factors was the advocacy of second-wave feminists who argued for women's storytelling and female authorship as a means of achieving gender parity and equity. Feminists implored women to claim ownership and authorship of their own narratives. Feminists argued that the oppression of women was rooted in the suppression of female and feminine narratives in service of the modern "master narrative." A construction of Modernity, both historical and imagined, the modern master narrative was constructed by, and for, a universal male human subject who had been normalized as an active, rational, and public figure. This master narrative was linear and rigidly structured around such binary divisions as masculine/feminine, active/passive, and civilized/uncivilized. Privileging the male voice and the silencing and marginalization of women was essential to the fulfillment of male subjectivity. Feminists urged that by (re)claiming authorship, women could (re)construct new mythologies and histories through a female lens, bringing women into focus as historical subjects and validating the female voice. There was, however, no consensus on how that female lens should be constructed. Across this scholarship and activism, feminists were divided over the concept of difference across the axes of race, ethnicity, class, and sexuality.

A key outcome of second-wave feminist advocacy for women's storytelling was the rise of state investment in domestic film and television production. Governments have always seen media as a key discursive tool in reconstructing and reimagining national identity and national pride (nationalism); this was particularly evident during World War II. By the 1970s, former British white-settler nations aimed to reimagine their identities through a postcolonial liberal democratic lens, shaking off ties with the British Empire, the dark history of chattel slavery, the assimilation and dislocation of indigenous peoples, racial segregation, class divisions, labor exploitation, and gender inequality. The state aimed to foster local and national talent, which had been untapped as a result of the dominance of Hollywood and British cinema. In tandem with the national cinema movement came the global rise of independent cinema and an emerging international film festival circuit cultivated by the Sundance Film Festival and the Toronto International Film Festival. These festivals would provide an important and high-profile exhibition platform for auteur-driven and non-Hollywood films, most of which were produced within the national cinema context. Part of this state investment in national cinemas included implementing film and television training programs with the aim of nurturing new voices and creating new auteurs. During the 1970s and 1980s, a number of national film training and financing programs were put in place to address issues of gender and racial inequity in the film and television industries in Canada, Australia, New Zealand/Aotearoa, and, to a lesser extent, the United States. These programs can be seen as an attempt by former white-settler frontier colonies to reinvent themselves as postcolonial states with an identity rooted in free speech, freedom of expression, equity, and diversity.

In Australia, the grassroots organization the Sydney Women's Film Group (SWFG),[47] formed in 1971, put enormous pressure on the Australian Film Commission to train women and fund their films. In 1975–76, the Australian Film Commission Women's Film Fund was established to help support women's filmmaking.[48] Gillian Armstrong was one of the first female graduates of the Australian Film and Television School (AFTS) (now the Australian Film Television and Radio School, or AFTRS) in 1974.[49] Both Armstrong and Tracey Moffatt received funding through the Australian Film Commission for their early films.[50] Moffatt received funding from the Women's Film Fund for her award-winning *Nice Coloured Girls* (1987), which received worldwide recognition.[51] Though a native of New Zealand/Aotearoa, Jane Campion was also one of the AFTS's alumni, graduating in the mid-1980s. Four of Campion's AFTS short films were shown at the Cannes Film Festival in 1985, with *Peel* winning the Palme d'Or for Best Short Subject Film. Campion's feature films *Sweetie* (1989) and *An Angel at My Table* (1990) both received financial backing from the Australian Film Commission.

With regard to indigenous filmmaking in Australia, the human rights legislation brought in by the Whitlam Government in 1975[52] helped usher in the Film Unit of the Australian Institute of Aboriginal Studies[53] and the Central Australian Aboriginal Media Association (CAAMA).[54] The release of two state-commissioned reports addressing public and commercial media organizations and their treatment of indigenous people also ignited change. These were the report of the Royal Commission into Aboriginal Deaths in Custody in 1991 and the Australian Film Commission report *Promoting Aboriginal and Torres Strait Islander Involvement in the Film and Television Industry* in 1992 by Shirley McPherson and Michael Pope.[55] On the recommendation of the latter report, the Australian Film Commission established the Indigenous Branch in 1993, which coincided with the release of Moffatt's *Bedevil*.

In New Zealand/Aotearoa, Merata Mita and Jane Campion benefited from various domestic film initiatives. *Mauri* received support and financing through the New Zealand Film Commission, established in 1978.[56] According to film historian Emiel Martens, though the founding documents of the New Zealand Film Commission "neglected New Zealand/Aotearoa's bicultural identity, from the late 1980s the Commission started to acknowledge a commitment to Maori filmmaking."[57] Mita's previous social justice documentaries, such as *Patu!* (1983), were funded by the Auckland Co-op Alternative Cinema, which helped produce independent, experimental, and documentary films by local filmmakers.[58] Though Campion had primarily worked within the Australian film industry context, earlier in her career she did receive $100,000 in development funds from the New Zealand Film Commission for an adaptation of Jane Mander's classic 1920 novel *The Story of a New Zealand River*.[59] Campion's involvement with this project has been the topic of much controversy because *The Piano* shares a number of similarities with Mander's novel. Campion, however, has always asserted that the screenplay for *The Piano* was original, not an adaptation of Mander's work.[60] There has also been some question as to whether *The Piano* qualifies as a New Zealand film because Campion had been trained and was professionally based in Australia. That said, the film has been embraced by the New Zealand film industry as a national film. Alistair Fox, however, argued that *The Piano* works as a New Zealand film because of its depiction of white settler history and culture.[61] Hilary Radner asserted that *The Piano* is working in the New Zealand Heritage Film tradition.[62]

In Canada, Anne Wheeler, Norma Bailey, and Sandy Wilson all received state support for their work, helping them launch and sustain their filmmaking careers. All three filmmakers gained film production training, experience, and financing through the National Film Board of Canada (NFB), particularly Studio D.[63] Studio D was the first fully state-funded women's film unit in the world.[64] *The Wake*, as part of the *Daughters of the Country* dramatic miniseries, was fully funded and distributed by the NFB.[65] *Loyalties* received funding from the Alberta Motion Picture Development Corporation,[66] Telefilm Canada,[67] and the Canadian Broadcasting Corporation (CBC), the national public broadcaster. *My American Cousin* also received funding through Telefilm Canada and the CBC. All of these films were made after the advent of the Canadian Broadcast Development Fund. Established in 1984 and administered by Telefilm Canada, the fund was set up to make available "a solid core of attractive Canadian programming in all categories."[68]

Though the United States has never had a state-funded national cinema, American independent filmmakers have historically found support from grants and fellowships provided by the National Endowment for the Arts (NEA).[69] In 1965 the United States Congress created the NEA as an independent federal agency "that funds, promotes, and strengthens the creative capacity of our communities by providing all Americans with diverse opportunities for arts participation."[70] Julie Dash managed to cobble together various NEA grants and fellowships, but she found most of her financing for *Daughters of the Dust* through PBS as part of its *American Playhouse* series.[71] Dash credits the director of program development for *American Playhouse*, Lynn Holst, for helping her finish the film after every Hollywood studio passed on the project.[72] Financially supported by the NEA, PBS created the *American Playhouse* series (1982–1994) with the intent to foster independent American feature film production "to counter the perception that PBS cared more about British imports (e.g., *Mystery*) than productions by and about Americans."[73] *American Playhouse* produced original American content with high production value intended for a competitive theatrical feature film market while also reflecting distinct American voices across the axes of gender, class, race, sexuality, generation, and region. Of 181 *Playhouse* productions to date, more than 40 were released theatrically as narrative feature films.[74] *Thousand Pieces of Gold* (1991) was also a *Playhouse* production.

Additionally, high-profile U.S. film schools such as the UCLA School of Theater, Film and Television; the American Film Institute; and the Sundance Institute help unknown filmmakers produce their first feature films through grants and industry support (e.g., festival exposure, promotion). The AFI began in 1965 as a presidential mandate to establish film as essential to American identity, to elevate the nation's greatest art form to its deserving place in history with the mission to preserve the heritage of the motion picture, to honor the artists and their work, and to educate the next generation of storytellers.[75] Julie Dash is a graduate of the American Film Institute and UCLA, where she made her award-winning short *Illusions* (1982), a film that explores racial and sexual discrimination in Hollywood. UCLA is also the birthplace for the L.A. Rebellion, an African American film movement, in which Dash was a key player.

The Ballad of Little Jo and *The Piano* are the only films among the ten that did not receive state funding. *Ballad* was financed by the film branch of PolyGram Filmed Entertainment, an Anglo-Dutch company based in London. Founded in 1980, it became a European competitor to Hollywood, focusing on British and art-house fare.[76] *The Piano* was fully financed by CiBy 2000, a French film production and distribution company that focused on art-house and independent films. *The Piano*, however, was set and filmed in New Zealand/Aotearoa and employed a local crew. Remarkably, the executives at CiBy 2000 gave Campion and her producer, Jan Chapman, complete artistic control, rare for any director, much less a woman who had never worked with Hollywood stars such as Holly Hunter and Harvey Keitel.[77]

METHODOLOGY

This study deploys a transnational lens in order to render visible women's filmmaking activity and feminist mobilization that would not be as apparent through a national lens. Transnational feminism as a method is not necessarily stable and includes a range of theoretical approaches from many disciplinary and interdisciplinary perspectives. I use the term *transnational* as a tool for highlighting this body of women's films that crossed national borders, as well as binational categories such as Maori cinema. Women's filmmaking has historically fallen under the radar in national cinema studies and has often been excluded from national film canons, which tend to focus more on filmmakers with a larger body of narrative feature film work. This is particularly true of filmmakers who are women of color or identify as indigenous and a number of the women filmmakers in this study, despite their status as trailblazers and "iconic."

The purpose of this study is not only to spotlight a wave of women's and feminist work but also to tease out the different feminist discourses that filter across and animate these films. Though these filmmakers and their films share some similarities, as stated earlier, this study is not motivated by a desire to construct a monolithic narrative about global sisterhood within a coherent "feminist cinema." Commonalities as well as differences come to the surface across the axes of race, ethnicity, class, sexuality, and ability. Feminist philosopher Denise Riley cautioned scholars away from writing a "master narrative of womanhood" because, she argued, "women" was an unstable category, and also because it mimicked patriarchal structures.[78] African American feminist historian Elsa Barkley Brown advocated for multivoiced models, what she called a "polyrhythmic" dialogue for examining different and even dissonant narratives from the past. Barkley Brown argued that African American jazz, memory-story quilts, and *gumbo ya ya* ("everyone talking at once") speech patterns could serve as models for a new kind of narrative that allowed for different voices and multiple rhythms to be played and heard simultaneously.[79]

> History is also everybody talking at once, multiple rhythms being played simultaneously. . . . As historians we try to isolate one conversation and to explore it, but the trick is then how to put that conversation in a context which makes evident its dialogue with so many others—how to make this one lyric stand alone and at the same time be in connection with all the other lyrics being sung.[80]

Across these films, women's voices and perspectives are brought to the forefront, not just the directors' voices but also the characters' voices. The discourses are rooted in feminism—although they collectively do not construct a monolithic feminist discourse. What discourses speak through these voices and stories? This study's aim is to illuminate how these films and the varying and sometimes unharmonious voices construct a multivoiced, polyphonous dialogue around some of the key issues, namely, female subjectivity, that animated feminist activism during the time period in which they were produced. These issues included female authorship and voice, the female gaze in film, and the objectification of women in the cinema. These key issues animate this study and the chapter organization.

The primary methods of textual analysis used in this study are formal and cultural analyses. "Formal analysis dissects the complex synthesis of cinematography, sound, composition, design, movement, performance and editing."[81] It is through this complex synthesis that we can examine how the films construct meanings, both explicit and implicit. Careful shot-by-shot analysis is deployed to foreground the filmmakers' use of cinematic language (the visual and sound regimes) and their construction of a feminist aesthetic and how that aesthetic reinforces the films' content (plots and characters). The other method of analysis deployed is rooted in cultural studies. The theoretical frames used in this study are feminist film theory, antiracist and postcolonial theory, and queer theory. Because this study focuses on clarifying how these different female-authored texts deploy or subvert frontier tropes, analysis is constructed through an intersectional lens of inquiry. The key questions in this study are as follows: What differing conclusions do these ten films come to about the role of gender and the place of *all* women in the construction of frontier myth-history narratives? What does this body of work tell us about the range of possibilities for expressing feminist politics within popular forms such as the narrative feature film?

To answer these questions, the study is organized into three chapters: chapter 1, "Women's Storytelling—Narrative, Genre, and the Female Voice"; chapter 2, "Debunking the Cult of True Womanhood/ Motherhood on the Frontier"; and chapter 3, "Feminist Symbolic Frontier Landscapes." Each chapter examines how each of the ten films destabilizes or re-visions dominant frontier history-myth narratives rooted in white-settler masculinist expansionism.

Chapter 1 examines the filmmakers' deployment of narrative and genre conventions to construct their counter feminist narratives about women in frontier spaces. Though all the films are constructed through a female lens or gaze, they do not collectively depict a monolithic, coherent feminist model of narrative. The key question for this chapter is, How are the filmmakers' differing reimaginings of frontier myth-histories shaped by form and aesthetics? As these films evoke the key debates around narrative and voice within second-wave feminism, the chapter provides a summary of this literature. To clarify how each film deploys genre to subvert tropes of frontier myth-histories, the chapter provides an overview of the history and conventions of the Western and melodrama, particularly the female melodrama and the Gothic. After these summaries, the chapter examines through close textual analysis how the films' deployment of narrative and genre shape their stories and differing feminist discourses. The films are primarily working within and across two narrative models: revisionism and deconstruction. The revisionist films—*My American Cousin*, *My Brilliant Career*, *The Ballad of Little Jo*, *Thousand Pieces of Gold*, and *The Piano*—foreground the female voice through empowered young women and adhere to the conventions of the popular cinema more closely. *Daughters of the Dust*, *Mauri*, and *Bedevil* are working in the deconstruction model and adhere to counter-cinema aesthetics, privileging the voices and experiences of subaltern women; *subaltern* is a postcolonial term for marginalized and displaced peoples within an imperial colony. Interestingly, the social realist films, *Loyalties* and *The Wake*, straddle both narrative models to foreground the legacy of colonialism in contemporary indigenous communities.

Chapter 2 examines the films' deployment or subversion of one of the central gendered tropes of frontier myth-history narratives, particularly the Western, what historian Elizabeth Thompson calls the pioneer woman archetype.[82] Rooted in the Victorian (British) "angel in the house" figure, the pioneer woman archetype has been upheld as the ultimate ideal of white (Anglo-Saxon) femininity in white-settler nations. Though this archetype does not appear in all these films, her (white) shadow ghosts their frames. All of these films seem to answer Virginia Woolf's 1942 call to action to "kill the angel in the house," though they do so in differing ways, particularly across the axis of race. The key question that animates this chapter is, How do the films deploy and subvert the trope of the "good pioneer white woman" and, through that subversion, how far do they interrogate gender and women's oppression in white-settler frontier societies? To answer this question, the chapter provides a summary of some of the key second-wave literature about womanhood and motherhood, including their depiction in the cinema and the maternal melodrama. Two different narratives about frontier womanhood are reflected across this corpus of films. The subaltern womanhood/motherhood narratives feature subaltern women who embrace motherhood and the maternal as a key method of resistance against colonial powers of oppression. These films are *Daughters of the Dust*, *Mauri*, *Bedevil*, *The Wake*, and *Loyalties*. The angel on the frontier counter-narratives feature a rebellious daughter figure who resists domesticity and the traditional role of nurturing wife and mother. These films are *My American Cousin*, *My Brilliant Career*, *The Ballad of Little Jo*, *Thousand Pieces of Gold*, and *The Piano*.

Chapter 3 examines the films' construction of feminist "symbolic settings" in their counter-narratives of feminist agency and resistance. Like the Western, all these films feature violence, albeit on varying levels of seriousness and graphicness. Violence in frontier myth-history narratives has historically been depicted as deadly physical violence enacted in male public spaces. Though women are not the intended targets of violence, they sometimes get caught in the cross fire. Because most of these films are working in the realm of melodrama, much of the violence is familial, gendered, and often sexual. Most of the films feature rape, attempted rape, the threat of rape, or sexual exploitation. Across these films, domestic and sexual violence is deployed as a weapon of power and oppression, either as a means of control or as punishment for female transgressions. The perpetrators of the violence are usually white male figures of authority who police white-settler spaces. The key question here is, How do the filmmakers represent violence as a tool of gender oppression in their symbolic frontier landscapes? There are two differing narratives. The decolonizing symbolic frontier landscape narratives include *Mauri*, *Daughters of the Dust*, *Bedevil*, *Loyalties*, and *The Wake*. These films spotlight the colonial violence enacted upon subaltern peoples through economic exploitation, appropriation of their lands, forced migration, and enslavement. The female transgressive symbolic frontier landscape narratives include *My American Cousin*, *My Brilliant Career*, *The Ballad of Little Jo*, *Thousand Pieces of Gold*, and *The Piano*. Across these films, the frontier space functions as a wasteland where "bad girls" are sent, although at times it can offer possibility for female independence.

1

WOMEN'S STORYTELLING—NARRATIVE, GENRE, AND THE FEMALE VOICE

THE TEN FILMS in this study re-vision or deconstruct the frontier myth-histories of English-speaking Canada, the United States, New Zealand/Aotearoa, and Australia through a female lens. As discussed in the introduction, these four nations are bonded by a "selective national tradition,"[1] focalized around a violent origin story of white settlement and expansionism in which an Anglo-Saxon Protestant male hero struggles for supremacy over untamed frontier spaces and indigenous peoples, leading to their dispossession and displacement. This chapter examines these ten films through the lens of narrative and genre in order to render visible the differing methods the female directors deployed to construct their herstories on the big screen. These differing methods result in diverging discourses not only about feminist aesthetics but also about the role of women and gender in white-settler frontier societies. The films evoke some of the key questions that divided feminists during the second-wave women's movement, such as What constitutes a feminist text? and What is its method of production? During the second-wave women's movement, feminists argued that women's storytelling and female authorship were vital in the struggle for female emancipation and gender equity. Divisions among feminists emerged around two imbricating axes: language and identity. Permeating these debates were two questions: Who is speaking, and to whom? and In what language are they speaking?

Across various disciplines, feminists advocated for rendering visible women's voices in history, culture, politics, law, literature, the arts, etc. Feminist historians, aligned with the new social history movement, advocated for women's history from below and aimed to recuperate the lost and suppressed voices of women. Women's history scholars from the 1980s such as Carroll Smith-Rosenberg and Christine Stansell resurrected female voices from the archives in order to foreground the construction of femininity across class and ethnicity.[2] Natalie Zemon Davis and Joan Scott, however, challenged the gendered nature of mainstream historiography and argued that projects attempting to recuperate historical women's voices were problematic. Davis destabilized the grand historical narrative by deploying an interdisciplinary method that used unofficial sources, such as folk history and ethno-cultural accounts of the peasantry.[3] Deploying poststructuralist theory, Scott advocated for gender history rather than women's history, arguing that gender categories are constructions of language and their definition varies across space, time, and culture.[4] These two methods within feminist historiography are reflected across this corpus of women's films. For the most part, the films adhere to the recuperation of historical women's voices, except for *Mauri* and *Bedevil*, the films by the two indigenous filmmakers.

Many second-wave feminists located female oppression in language and were primarily concerned with how male/masculine language suppressed the female/feminine voice. Feminist poet and scholar Adrienne Rich identified a male tradition and argued that it was not enough for women to just write their stories; they must write with new eyes and refrain from writing with a male voice and for a male reader, (re)constructing a woman-centered language.[5] Feminist anthropologist and activist Gayle Rubin argued that women must rewrite the psychoanalytic oedipal story of the family because it is a story that renders women powerless and incomplete, as both cultural and historical subjects, because of women's lack of the phallus, the patriarchal symbol for power.[6] Rich's "Compulsory Heterosexuality and

Lesbian Existence" expanded on Rubin's work by arguing that a key way patriarchy has oppressed women is through enforced hetero-sexuality. Rich argued:

> Whatever its origins, when we look hard and clearly at the extent and elaboration of measures designed to keep women within a male sex-ual purlieu, it becomes an inescapable question whether the issue feminists have to address is not simple "gender inequality" nor the domination of culture by males nor mere "taboos against homo-sexuality," but the enforcement of heterosexuality for women as a means of assuring male right of physical, economic, and emotional access. One of many means of enforcement is, of course, the render-ing invisible of the lesbian possibility, an engulfed continent which rises fragmentedly into view from time to time only to be submerged again.[7]

Rich advocated for a vision of "lesbian existence" that went beyond sexual intimacy to a political and emotional bond between women, es-pecially in regard to resistance against "male tyranny." Rich envisioned lesbianism as "a direct attack on male right of access to women."[8]

Deploying poststructuralist theory, the French feminists refuted the mind/body split, rejecting patriarchy's dependence on reason and binaries, and (re)envisioned women's emancipation through a fleshly abject (female) body, particularly the reproductive maternal body. Literary critic and philosopher Hélène Cixous advocated for a femi-nine language to be written in white ink from a bisexual worldview.[9] Philosopher and linguist Luce Irigaray introduced her famous two-lips speaking metaphor, in which her autoeroticism allowed for re-discovery of the self through an embodied voice.[10] Literary critic and philosopher Julia Kristeva argued that female subjectivity is possible only as a pre-subject, through a messy journey back to the body of the m(other), the site of the pre-oedipal plot.[11] Theorist and author Monique Wittig proposed moving away from psychoanalytic theory because it is embedded in dominant discourses of binary divisions.[12] In Wittig's *Le Corps lesbian*, a collection of poems, "*j/e* (I) and *tu* (you) violently tear each other to pieces in the process of love. The slashed pronoun *j/e* enacts women's violent entry into language."[13] Wittig advocated for lesbian desire and sexuality as a means of feminist agency and resistance. In her seminal "The Straight Mind," Wittig argued:

> For heterosexual society is the society which not only oppresses lesbians and gay men, it oppresses many different/others, it oppresses all women and many categories of men, all those who are in the position of the dominated.[14]

Out of the groundbreaking work of Rubin, Rich, and Wittig emerged queer theory, a body of scholarship that would challenge not only the construction of sexuality and desire but also gender identities and scripts. Queer theory is more aligned with what is commonly called third-wave feminism, but it warrants referencing in this overview because some of these films were produced on the cusp of the third-wave period and do evoke some of this scholarship. Though it is somewhat problematic to adhere to strict divisions between the so-called waves of feminism, the third wave is generally thought to have been started in the mid-1990s by a generation of women raised by second-wave mothers (e.g., Gen X) and was more diversified, with an intense focus on gender identity, sexuality, and race. Some examples of third-wave feminists are Eve Ensler, creator of *The Vagina Monologues* (1996); Queen Latifah; and the American feminist punk movement the riot grrrls. Queer theorists problematized and destabilized a heterosexual worldview rooted in the binary gender identities of female and male. For feminists using queer theory, a key inquiry was Who is the "she"? Expanding on the work of the French feminists, particularly Wittig and Irigaray, as well as Simone de Beauvoir's groundbreaking classic *The Second Sex*, gender theorist and philosopher Judith Butler turned her lens away from women's voices to subversive voices of difference that destabilize naturalized dualistic notions of gender identity and heterosexuality. Butler argued that gender identity, maintained through the naturalization of sexual difference, is in fact a volatile identity constructed by discourse and dependent on the compulsory mimicry and repetition of prescribed or ritual performances of femininity and masculinity articulated by and through the lived social body. Butler identified oppression through these naturalized scripts, or stories, inscribed through psychoanalytic descriptions of femininity as masquerade. Butler argued for gay and lesbian voices because they tell a different kind of story, such as those told by drag-queen artists who parody femininity and masculinity. They embody a queer world-view. These parodist texts deconstruct and foreground the imitative structure of gender as well as its contingency, and they have proven effective in demonstrating how discourse and culture are inscribed on and through the body.[15] A number of these films evoke queer literature, particularly Wittig's concept of a heterosexist gaze and Butler's idea of gender masquerade. On some level, many of these films destabilize heterosexuality by foregrounding female desire within homosocial spaces and relationships (*Daughters of the Dust*, *The Piano*, *Loyalties*, *The Wake*) or obscuring the gender binary (*The Ballad of Little Jo*, *Bedevil*, *My Brilliant Career*).

In the area of cinema, second-wave feminist film scholars argued that the Hollywood cinema subjugated women by reproducing a language (master script) based on sexual difference.[16] In 1975, deploying poststructuralist and psychoanalytic theory, feminist film theorist Laura Mulvey famously advocated for a new "language of desire" in the cinema in order to combat patriarchal discourse and power constructed through a male gaze.[17] Mulvey identified narrative construction and visual spectacle (pleasure) as key devices to subjugate the female and the feminine, a powerful psychoanalytic script for the patriarchal unconscious, structured on an active male/passive female binary model.[18] A decade later, expanding on Mulvey and literary critic Silvia Bovenschen, film theorist and literary critic Teresa de Lauretis advocated for a new feminist vision in the cinema, what she referred to as *de*-aesthetics, and looked to the counter-aesthetics of the avant-garde cinema as a model for women's filmmaking.[19] Feminist film theorists Mary Ann Doane and Sandy Flitterman-Lewis saw the potential in the Hollywood woman's films for the expression of female desire and the foregrounding of the instability of patriarchy, although they did not advocate for the popular cinema as rich terrain for feminist re-visioning.[20] Feminist film theorist Claire Johnston, however, argued in favor of popular cinema, and as early as 1973.

> At this point in time, a strategy should be developed which embraces both the notion of film as a political tool and film as entertainment.

For too long these have been regarded as two opposing poles with little common ground. In order to counter our objectification in the cinema, our collective fantasies must be released: women's cinema must embody the working through of desire: such an objective demands the use of the entertainment film.[21]

For the most part, second-wave feminist film scholars were suspicious of the popular cinema, particularly Hollywood, and upheld the merits of the avant-garde and documentary. Despite this tendency within feminist film criticism, ordinary women still flocked to popular films, particularly melodramas. The films in this study seemed eager to tap into that audience, and most take up Johnston's call to action.

Antiracist feminists took issue with Mulvey's racial blind spot with regard to female spectatorship. Cultural critic and activist bell hooks argued, "Mainstream feminist film criticism in no way acknowledges black female spectatorship. It does not even consider the possibility that women can construct an oppositional gaze via an understanding and awareness of the politics of race and racism."[22] Film historian and theorist Jane Gaines argued that the psychoanalytic model "works to block out considerations which assume a different configuration, so that, for instance, the Freudian-Lacanian scenario can eclipse the scenario of race-gender relations in Afro-American history." Gaines cautioned that the psychoanalytic model "inadvertently reaffirm[s] white middle-class norms."[23] Sociologist Patricia Hill Collins re-visioned the mobilization of black feminist knowledge and consciousness through black women's writing and activism, which she argued had produced a specialized knowledge operating outside white elite regimes.[24]

Anticolonial feminists advocated for a decolonizing gaze as a means of rendering visible the impact of nationalism, imperialism, modernity, and globalization on subaltern people. Deploying post-structuralism, literary critic and theorist Gayatri Spivak demonstrated the impossibility of speaking of, or for, the subaltern woman. Spivak's work located the material oppression of the subaltern woman in Western discourse. Pointing to the British abolishment of the practice of sati, Spivak unpacked the colonial discourse of white men saving brown women from brown men's cultures and customs as a linguistic device to disavow the other through gender. Spivak located her analysis in the exchange of meaning between speaker and listener, arguing that it is not only the speaking subject that matters; it is also hearing that completes the speech act. Spivak did not see access for the subaltern woman to Western narrative structures as the solution to her voice oppression, because then she would be forced into a position of identification with her oppressor.[25] Antiracist feminist scholarship is evoked throughout these films, particularly in *Daughters of the Dust*, *Mauri*, *Bedevil*, *The Wake*, and *Loyalties*, because all these films deploy a decolonizing gaze.

These key debates about women's storytelling, language, female authorship, and the female voice are felt throughout these ten films. Indeed, the differences among these films are most pronounced across the same axes that divided feminist scholars and activists: language and identity. Though all the films are grand counterfeminist narratives framed through a female lens, foregrounding gender relations as the key power dynamic, they reimagine or destabilize the tropes of frontier myth-histories through differing methods of construction. The films are primarily working within two narrative models, revisionism and deconstruction. Working in the revisionist model are *My Brilliant Career*, *My American Cousin*, *Thousand Pieces of Gold*, *The Ballad of Little Jo*, and *The Piano*. Revisionism is a mode that does not dismantle traditional classical narrative structures and genre conventions but rather re-visions those structures and conventions through a new and different lens; it does not aim to find a new language. Working in the deconstructionist mode are *Mauri*, *Daughters of the Dust*, and *Bedevil*. These films deploy an oppositional and decolonizing gaze to tell stories from a subaltern point of view. Deconstruction is directly focused on challenging traditional language structures, and it aims to render master scripts (white or colonial or both) irrelevant. *Loyalties* and *The Wake* tell stories through a Canadian indigenous point of view but are primarily revisionist. Though both films generally adhere to popular narrative and genre codes, it is through a social realist approach strongly aligned with documentary filmmaking.

The two genres the films are working in are the Western and melo-drama. The rationale for this study's focus on the Western as a genre is due to the fact that it is largely regarded as the dominant frontier myth-history narrative, primarily as a result of Hollywood's global reach. To clarify, though these films deploy and subvert tropes of fron-tier myth-histories and are set in a frontieresque landscape, both co-lonial and postcolonial, only two are traditional Westerns, *The Ballad of Little Jo* and *Thousand Pieces of Gold*. The films' plots and charac-ters are, however, primarily focalized around family issues, romance, and gender relations, the mainstay of the melodrama, historically a female genre. In order to fully examine how these films deploy genre codes and conventions, it is helpful to establish how this study deploys genre as a lens for feminist analysis.

Film scholars have historically identified genre films as a reflection of a society's cultural values and customs, embedded in familiar ico-nography and tropes. Andrew Tudor argued, "Genre notions—except the special case of arbitrary definition—are not critic's classifications made for special purposes; they are sets of cultural conventions. Genre is what we collectively believe it to be."[26] Repetition is key to the familiarity, which is the core reason genre films are so accessible and hence popular. Barry Keith Grant argued, "Stated simply, genre mov-ies are those commercial feature films which, through repetition and variation, tell familiar stories with familiar characters in familiar situations."[27] These stories of familiar characters are usually associ-ated with themes and situations that are constructed along a binary system such as good and evil or virginal and fallen. Patrick Phillips argued, "It is possible to identify the binary structure of a Hollywood genre and, in the process, not just list the typical thematic issues with which it deals but locate the 'ideological work' of that genre, the par-ticular myths it constructs and perpetuates."[28] And yet, as a number of genre film scholars have argued, genre itself has proven to be much more flexible and changeable than it seems. As grand counter-feminist narratives, these films embraced that flexibility to destabilize binary gender divisions, the ideological work made familiar, by re-visioning and deconstructing those myths.

THE WESTERN: THE (WHITE)
MALE MELODRAMA

The origins of the Hollywood Western predate the birth of cinema (1896) and can be traced back to New World narratives of the fifteenth century. The Western's frontier setting, heroes, iconography, and tropes were established by a variety of forms, such as the novels of James Fenimore Cooper (1820–1850s), the dime-store novels of the 1860s (e.g., Zane Grey), the late nineteenth-century Romantic paintings of Frederic Remington, and *Buffalo Bill's Wild West Show*, which ran from 1870 to 1920. Historian R. L. Wilson argued that by the turn of the twentieth century, Buffalo Bill was one of the most recognizable celebrities in the Western world, his shows having toured the United States, Canada, Britain, and Europe for decades.[29] Perhaps as a result of this exposure, the Western has not been an exclusively American form. The French, as early as 1912, were making Westerns.[30] In the 1960s, German Westerns and Italian spaghetti Westerns made their appearance. Interestingly, though these Euro-Westerns deployed the tropes of the American frontier, they were culturally, ideologically, and linguistically *not* American. Perhaps the appeal of the Western to other cultures and nations is rooted in its richness as a myth-making system. Film historian and theorist Douglas Pye argued:

> The Western is set on the frontier at a time when forces of social order and anarchy are still in tension; the "formula," to use Cawelti's term, is an adventure story with its apotheosis of the hero who stands between opposing forces in a symbolic landscape; the plot generally involves some form of pursuit, almost inevitably ending in a moment of transcendent and heroic violence; the characters can be divided into three main groups: the townspeople or settlers; hero or heroes; villain or villains.[31]

Film critic J. Hoberman claimed, "Like baseball, the western is a sacred part of America's post-Civil War national mythology, a shared language, a unifying set of symbols and metaphors, and a source of (mainly male) identity."[32] Film historian David Lusted referred to the

Western as "male melodrama" because it is a genre "that deals with problems of homosocial identity." Lusted argued:

> The Western can be seen as a male action genre exploring chang-ing expectations and notions of masculine identity through fantasy, dramatizing the psychic and emotional conflicts within and between men.[33]

With regard to masculinity, literary critic Jane Tompkins argued:

> The Western doesn't have anything to do with the West as such. It isn't about the encounter between civilization and the frontier. It is about men's fear of losing their mastery, and hence their identity, both of which the Western tirelessly reinvents.[34]

Conflicts and resolutions in a Western are structured around a set of binary divisions that represent universal themes such as community and individualism, law and lawlessness, civilized and uncivilized, East and West. These conflicts are always resolved through violence. This violence is often conflated with expressions of masculine identity and misogyny but also with white supremacy and the subjugation of nonwhite others, primarily indigenous peoples. Indigenous peoples in Westerns most often represent savagery, the uncivilized, and the vanishing race. According to historian Richard Slotkin, who has specialized in analyzing the role of the frontier in the formation of American culture and national identity, the defining characteristic of the Western was the "subjugation or displacement of the Native Ameri-cans" through violence.[35]

Joanna Hearne, a film historian and theorist who specializes in indigenous media, argued that the vanishing Indian was a common trope of the sympathetic Western and was as damaging as the savage stereotype. Hearne argued:

> Emerging from this ideology of the vanishing Indian that drove both policies and popular representations in the early twentieth century, many Westerns simply omit any images of Native families or

children, focusing instead on white settler families threatened by groups of (exclusively male) Indian warriors.[36]

At the center of the story and the violence is a (white) male hero (cowboy or gunslinger), a nomadic, rugged individual who battles adversaries alone. Feminist film theorist and historian Susan Hayward argued, "He never really wants to accept civilization, as embodied by the woman (who brings with her from the east the notion of community, family and so on). Rather he is always desiring to be on the move in the Wild West."[37] Film historian Michael Coyne, who specializes in American cinema, attested that this white male hero was almost always an Anglo-Saxon Protestant; a Catholic hero was a rarity, and the Western itself "sanctified Protestantism."[38]

Women have occupied a curious position in Westerns, what Tompkins described as a "women-less milieu."[39] Anthony Mann, a director of many Hollywood Westerns, once famously said, "Without women a Western wouldn't work."[40] Tompkins argued that women in Westerns serve one purpose, to "legitimize the violence men practice in order to protect them."[41] Perhaps this is what Mann was alluding to. Generally, women work in Westerns as signs across two binaries: Madonna/whore and white-settler/indigenous. The Madonna figure is the settler wife/mother or the daughter, who Hayward argued "had to be kept virginal at all costs."[42] The settler wife represents the Victorian "angel in the house" figure, rooted in the cult of true womanhood and deemed the ultimate ideal of femininity (she was known for four traits: piety, purity, submissiveness, and domesticity).[43] The teacher figure is a variation of the virginal daughter because she is usually unmarried and a *lady*. In contrast, the saloon girl or prostitute inhabits masculine spaces and is ruined or fallen. Because of her association with outlaws, the saloon girl is often more vulnerable to male violence. In many ways the saloon girl serves in a role similar to that of the femme fatale in thrillers, gangster pictures, and film noirs. Racially and ethnically, the saloon girl is often foreign, meaning not Anglo-Saxon Protestant, though she is rarely indigenous or African American. For the most part, African American women have been rendered completely invisible in the Western genre.[44]

Not surprisingly, feminist scholarship has been largely uninterested in or dismissive of the Western. Film theorist and historian Pam Cook, however, identified a number of female-driven Westerns, such as *Johnny Guitar* (1954), and identified the figure of the gender-bending heroine, who transgressed social conventions by rejecting traditional feminine clothing and the role of wife or mother.[45] Cook argued:

> Feminine in her white dress, masculine in black shooting gear, she moves between tomboy and mother figure with ease, demonstrating and maintaining a level of control allowed to very few women. But the film's feminism goes deeper than this, extending to a criticism of the Western's male values. Destructive masculine drives have gone out of control, creating a world dominated by death, betrayal, and revenge.[46]

Cook's analysis is significant here because it highlights a tradition in the Western in which women are front and center, albeit in a delimited way. Though Cook argued that the real women of the West, such as suffragettes, farmers, and professional women, were rarely featured as heroines in Westerns, "the search for realism is perhaps rather self-defeating in a genre that is more concerned with myth than historical accuracy."[47] All of these strong frontier heroines to whom Cook refers, however, have been white women.

Indigenous women have been the most misrepresented and silenced figures in the Western, not including African American women, and when they do appear it is usually in the form of racist and sexist stereotypes: the Indian princess and the squaw. Antiracist feminist film historian Maryann Oshana argued that the Western's representation of indigenous women was instrumental in rendering indigenous peoples as an inferior race.[48] The indigenous woman does not belong to the civilized world, and she is never saved, although she may be martyred. She rarely has a speaking role or dramatic agency, and she is often relegated to the background in scenes in which Indian tribes make an appearance. In her seminal article "The Pocahontas Perplex," American historian and museum curator Rayna Green, who specializes in indigenous women's history and culture, argued that the indigenous woman is caught between a rock and a hard place. "Her nobility as a Princess and her savagery as a Squaw are defined in terms of her relationships with male figures. If she wishes to be called a Princess, she must save or give aid to white men."[49] Green traces the story of Pocahontas and John Smith back to old European folklore, dating back to fourteenth-century Scotland. Green argued:

> In one of the best known old Scottish ballads, "Young Beichan" or "Lord Bateman and the Turkish King's Daughter," as it is often known in America: a young adventurer travels to a strange, foreign land. The natives are of a darker color than he, and they practice a pagan religion. The man is captured by the king (Pasha, Moor, Sultan) and thrown into a dungeon to await death. Before he is executed, however, the pasha's beautiful daughter—smitten with the elegant and wealthy visitor—rescues him and sends him homeward. But she pines away for love of the now remote stranger who has gone home, apparently forgotten her, and contracted a marriage with a "noble" "lady" of his own kind. In all the versions, she follows him to his own land, and in most, she arrives on his wedding day whereupon he throws over his bride-to-be for the darker but more beautiful Princess. In most versions, she becomes a Christian, and she and Lord Beichan live happily ever after.[50]

In *The Lay of the Land*, feminist literary critic and activist Annette Kolodny analyzed the deployment of the indigenous woman figure by (white) male writers as a kind of emblem for a land. Kolodny argued:

> Not until the end of the seventeenth century, when the tragic contradictions inherent in such experience could no longer be ignored, were the Indian women depicted more usually as hag-like, ugly and immoral.[51]

Indigenous film scholar M. Elise Marubbio, who has written extensively on the representation of indigenous people in film and popular culture, identified the celluloid maiden, a tragic hybrid figure, a conflation of the Indian princess and the sexualized maiden. Marubbio argued:

> The reliance of mainstream culture on these myths and various depictions of the Celluloid Maiden during different eras maintains the racialized Other as an exotic or erotic danger to a homogenous national identity.[52]

Indigenous women have been historically represented as a threat in the Western, even when they are depicted as sympathetic characters.

Despite its seeming rigidity, the Western has proven to be a fairly adaptable genre. Hayward argued that the Western has an anti-oedipal structure because the hero rarely ends up with the girl.[53] Pye argued, however, that Westerns are structured and resolved in the typical romance plot.[54] Because of this flexibility as a genre, the Western has been re-visioned and reimagined many times across different historical, political, industrial, and national contexts. The modern Western, or psychological Western, emerged in the 1940s with William Wellman's *The Ox-bow Incident* (1943). By the 1950s, this more serious and complex Western was constructed through a more hard-edged critical lens in which morally divided heroes are driven by revenge and there is graphic violence, as in Anthony Mann's *The Naked Spur* (1953).[55] The pro-Indian or sympathetic or antiestablishment Westerns first appeared in the 1950s, with Delmer Daves's *Broken Arrow* (1950), and continued into the 1990s. These films depicted Indians as more complex characters and foregrounded their unfair and oppressive treatment by whites. John Ford's *Cheyenne Autumn* (1964), Sydney Pollack's *Jeremiah Johnson* (1972), and Arthur Penn's *Little Big Man* (1970) aimed to critique Manifest Destiny and the white man's ways, though the plots revolve around a sympathetic white male hero who is adopted by a tribe.[56] These Westerns were not, however, constructed through an indigenous gaze. Joanna Hearne argued:

> The prominence of revisionist Indian Westerns is one example of the way public appetite for images of Indians both covered over and enabled Indigenous expression. In appropriating images of Indians for counterculture messages, revisionist Westerns obscured

the specificity and voices of individual tribes and a thriving pan-Indian political movement. *A Man Called Horse, Tell Them Willie Boy Is Here*, and *Billy Jack*, for example, elide and blur distinct tribal beliefs and narratives, instead adopting the sexualized captivity narrative and (in the latter two films) outlaw and vigilante figures as defining plot structures and central metaphors for Native-white relationships.[57]

The indigenous woman was also often deployed as a plot device or sexual object for male viewing pleasure in these revisionist Westerns. Marubbio asserted that the role of the celluloid maiden in counter-cultural Westerns was still rooted in the Indian princess/squaw binary construct. Oshana also argued that the sympathetic pro-Indian Westerns were still rife with sexist tropes.

> In all these sympathetic films of the fifties and sixties there was no major breakthrough in the roles of Indian women. The women's image has remained consistently backward and static. The roles for women are clearly defined: if they are not being raped or murdered, they are usually shown as slaves, household drudges, or bodies en masse in camps and caravans. Women are most often portrayed as victims, convenient objects for men to rape, murder, avenge or ridicule.[58]

As mentioned previously, the emergence of the international Western took the genre outside of its American context, demonstrating its adaptability and its power as a potent myth-making form.[59] Produced during the Soviet era, Red Westerns (*Osterns*) featured an indigenous warrior as the central hero. Vincent Bohlinger argued:

> *White Sun of the Desert*, in fact, adheres very closely to what Will Wright describes as the "classical plot" of Westerns: "the story of the lone stranger who rides into a troubled town and cleans it up" while "winning the respect of the townsfolk." The film's particulars, even when altered to reflect the cultural aspects of the Soviet Union, map perfectly onto the syntax of the American Western.[60]

India produced curry Westerns, which featured musical numbers. According to Madhuja Mukherjee, *Sholay* can be "read as a self-conscious reworking of post-war Hollywood Westerns in terms of its visual-scape, iconography, characterization and ideological implications."[61] German Westerns, produced between 1962 and 1986, were immensely popular. The German film adaptation of Karl May's romantic vision of the West, *Der Schatz im Silberseel/Treasure of Silver Lake*, was an overwhelming commercial success throughout Europe. Directed by Harald Reinl, *Treasure of Silver Lake* "became the most successful German production since the war, was distributed internationally (released in sixty countries), and did extremely well throughout Europe. . . . Its success was ultimately responsible for the avalanche of European (later mostly Italian) Westerns, some of which would eventually capture the American market."[62] Spaghetti Westerns are perhaps the most well-known of the international Westerns, partly because of the use of American actors such as Clint Eastwood. Cultural historian Christopher Frayling, who specializes in popular culture, argued that spaghetti Westerns were known for expressing subversive political ideas and the destabilizing of masculinist tendencies.[63] Film historian Marcia Landy argued that Sergio Leone's films

> interrogate masculinity and its discontents, its complicity with violence and power. . . . [They] orchestrate the problematics of language, patriarchy, subalternity, masculinity, the family, social power, and the clash between rural and urban life and between tradition and modernity.[64]

Despite these re-visionings and reimaginings that took place across different industrial, national, and political contexts, many theorists and critics still see the Western as Tompkins's "women-less milieu" and the "antithesis to melodrama and domesticity."[65] However, Pam Cook argued:

> While teaching a course on John Ford and the western, I was struck by the similarity of many classical western narratives, with their emphasis on circularity, digression, and delay, to the structure of

classical women's pictures. The choices facing the western hero, between love and duty, family life, and a wanderer's existence are not that different from those encountered by women's picture heroines. In several of Ford's classical westerns, the expressive use of music and mise-en-scène to heighten emotional affect can only be described as melodramatic—indeed, I would suggest that a comparative analysis of *My Darling Clementine* (1944) and *Written on the Wind* (1957) would produce interesting results in terms of generic cross-fertilization. In his study of *Stagecoach* (1939), Edward Buscombe examines the way that the film was marketed using Claire Trevor's costume and hairstyle, one of the strategies employed in promoting women's pictures.[66]

MELODRAMA: THE WOMAN'S PICTURE

The term *melodrama* is quite broad and includes a range of media and narratives. The melodrama originated in medieval morality plays and the oral tradition and was developed in the nineteenth century by the French in the form of the sentimental novel, focalized around familial relations, thwarted love, and forced marriages. Deploying psychoanalytic and Marxist theory, film historian and theorist Thomas Elsaesser and literary critic Peter Brooks did groundbreaking work in the 1970s on melodrama. They advocated for melodrama as an important form warranting serious critical attention.[67] Elsaesser's seminal "Tales of Sound and Fury: Observations of the Family Melodrama" traced "the melodramatic imagination across different artistic forms and epochs" and the "structural and stylistic constants in one medium during one particular period (the Hollywood family melodrama between roughly 1940 and 1963)."[68] Elsaesser asserted that Hollywood melodramas have a "myth-making function, insofar as their significance lies in the structure and articulation of the action, not any psychologically motivated correspondence with individualized experience."[69] According to Elsaesser, the melodrama can trace its genealogy back to "the late medieval morality play, the popular *gestes* and other forms of oral narrative and drama like fairy tales and folk songs."[70] Elsaesser's analysis of Douglas Sirk's use of visuals in *Written on the Wind* (1956) speaks to Brooks's point about grand gesture over the spoken word and to Elsaesser's point about melodrama's myth-making abilities. According to Elsaesser, Sirk was particularly critical of the hollowness of the American Dream, and all that went with it, and expressed these political ideas in his use of mise-en-scène and montage.

> A yellow sports car drawing up the graveled driveway to stop in front of a pair of shining white Doric columns outside the Hadley mansion is not only a powerful piece of American iconography, especially when taken in a plunging high-angle shot, but the contrary association of imperial splendor and vulgar materials (polished chrome-plate and stucco plaster) create a tension of correspondences and dissimilarities in the same image, which perfectly crystalizes as the decadent affluence and melancholy energy that give the film its uncanny fascination.[71]

Brooks considered melodrama the quintessential modern form, what he called *"le genre serieux."*[72] Brooks saw theatrical melodrama as a form that is highly expressive of social fears and desires focalized around modernization and the alienation of the individual. Susan Hayward argued:

> Melodrama does two things in relation to the social changes and the advent of modernization. It attempts to make sense of modernism, and that of the family. To take the first point, modernism exposed the reality of the decentered subject caused by the alienation under capitalism and technological depersonalization. Melodrama becomes an attempt to counter anxieties produced by this decentering and the massive scale of urban change—hence the "moral polarization and dramatic reversals" that structure this genre. . . . Bourgeois values are felt to be under threat—perhaps because they never had time to become fully established (unlike feudalism)—and viewed in this light, the melodrama is quite paranoid. Thus, for the bourgeoisie the social, which to them means firmly Victorian morality and what assails it, must be expressed through the personal.[73]

Brooks argued that melodrama's potential for political expression is due primarily to its flexibility and adaptability, rooted in the genre's seemingly simple means of expression, its "text of muteness." Melodrama's ability to construct meaning through signs allows it to function on a mythical level.[74] "The desire to express all seems a fundamental characteristic. Nothing is left unsaid. Characters utter the unspeakable."[75] A drama of the ordinary for the illiterate masses, melodrama depended on grand gesture, histrionic acting, and emotional excess rather than on the spoken word; Brooks saw this as a way for stories to speak covertly. All of these qualities outlined by Brooks explain why melodrama was a natural fit for narrative cinema, whose language was essentially a visual one, established early on in the silent film era. Indeed, the founding father of cinematic language was D. W. Griffith, a director who worked primarily in melodrama.

The Hollywood melodrama is also a broad genre, encompassing a wide range of subgenres (film noir, thriller, musical) and narratives, which according to Susan Hayward can be organized into two categories: masculine and feminine.[76] This study focuses on the feminine category, which encompassed female melodrama and *woman's films*, which featured female-driven plots set in the domestic realm (the female sphere). Many were based on female-authored novels and plays, though they were always directed by men (e.g., Alfred Hitchcock, Max Ophüls). The heyday of the woman's film was in the 1930s and 1940s. Themes often centered on illness, motherhood, romantic love, paranoia, hysteria, female sacrifice, and female transgression.[77] Marcia Landy argued that melodrama is a form focalized around female victimization.

> Seduction, betrayal, abandonment, extortion, murder, suicide, revenge, jealousy, incurable illness, obsession, and compulsion— these are part of the familiar terrain of melodrama. The victims are most often females threatened in their sexuality, their property, and their very identity.[78]

Second-wave feminists were drawn to the woman's film primarily because it was the one genre that explicitly addressed a female spectator and was seemingly a vehicle and outlet for female desire. The foundational second-wave feminist studies on melodrama conducted by Pam Cook, Claire Johnston, Laura Mulvey, Christine Gledhill, Mary Ann Doane, E. Ann Kaplan, Annette Kuhn, and others were instrumental in establishing feminist film theory as a major branch of film scholarship.[79] However, despite the overwhelming femaleness of the woman's film, the general consensus across this scholarship was that the genre duped women viewers into identifying with a female protagonist who was disempowered and whose gaze was disavowed. In *The Desire to Desire: The Woman's Film of the 1940s*, Doane argued that though the female protagonists in the woman's film seemingly have agency, they suffer in one form or another, whether from broken hearts, mental illness, or disease. Doane identified the suppression of female subjectivity through an overidentification of the female spectator with the images on the screen. Doane concluded that the processes of subjectivity in the woman's film produces incoherence and instability, a paradoxical process that involves the simultaneous construction and disavowal of a powerful female gaze.[80]

Some feminists argued in favor of the woman's film as a potentially empowering form for women, exemplified in the very rare films directed by female filmmakers such as Hollywood pioneer Dorothy Arzner. In many ways, female authorship has been historically tied to the woman's film and female melodrama, for obvious reasons: for the most part these were the kinds of films women directors would have been assigned by male studio executives and producers who aimed to target female audiences. Dorothy Arzner remains an intriguing case study for feminist film scholarship as a female director who worked primarily in woman's films and female melodrama during the heyday of the Hollywood studio system (1920s–1940s). Groundbreaking second-wave film scholarship resurrected Arzner as a lost and forgotten female Hollywood director and set out to understand how her work differed, if at all, from that of her male counterparts working in woman's films and female melodrama. Arzner became the litmus test to see if female authorship could actually exist in the popular cinema. Feminists have been divided over Arzner, at times reluctant to claim her work as feminist, albeit fascinated with her

collaborations and friendships with female stars such as Joan Craw-
ford (*The Bride Wore Red*), Katharine Hepburn (*Christopher Strong*),[81]
Rosalind Russell (*Craig's Wife*),[82] and Maureen O'Hara (*Dance, Girl,
Dance*),[83] not to mention her (closeted) lesbian identity/persona. Claire
Johnston argued:

> In general, the woman in Arzner's films determines her own iden-
> tity through transgression and desire in search for an independent
> existence beyond and outside the discourses of the male. Unlike
> most other Hollywood directors who pose "positive" and "inde-
> pendent" female protagonists (Walsh, Fuller, Cukor and Hawkes,
> for example), in Arzner's work the discourse of the woman, or
> rather her attempt to locate it and make it heard, is what gives the
> system of the text its structural coherence, while at the same time
> rendering the dominant discourse of the male fragmented and
> incoherent.[84]

Kaplan argued that though Arzner's female heroines, such as Cynthia
in *Christopher Strong* (1932), may reject patriarchal language, they pay
for it through either punishment or death. Kaplan argued:

> The film shows the need for Cynthia to be contained, and finally
> punished, for her transgressions. Significantly, like Marguerite
> Gautier in Cukor's *Camille*, Darrington is not ultimately constrained
> by outside forces so much as through her internalization of patriar-
> chal values. She makes herself victim by refusing to fight for what
> she wants, conceding to the rules of the symbolic order that prohibit
> breaking up the "happy family." Prior to this, she also conceded that
> being a mother should take precedence over career, this choice again
> not really being something over which she has control so much as
> one constructed for her by patriarchy. The film accepts her suicide
> as the proper thing for a woman to do in her situation and does not
> challenge the patriarchal discourse that leads to this conclusion.[85]

Judith Mayne's seminal work applies a lesbian reading of Arzner's
films. Though Arzner was a lesbian, her films were never explicitly
about lesbian love; this would have been impossible in the Hays Code

era.[86] However, Mayne argued that Arzner's depictions of (heterosexual) romance and female friendships are informed by a lesbian sensibility. Mayne argued:

> Female friendships acquire a resistant function in the way that it exerts a pressure against the supposed "natural laws" of heterosexual romance. Relations between women and communities of women have a privileged status in Arzner's films. . . . There is an erotic charge identified with those communities.[87]

Perhaps where there is agreement is in Arzner's status as a trailblazer and her ability to destabilize a heterosexist male gaze.

Patricia White's book *Uninvited: Classical Hollywood Cinema and Lesbian Representability* expands upon Mayne's idea of an "erotic charge" in the woman's film. White examined the construction of an erotically charged desiring female gaze between women in Hollywood melodramas even when the films were not explicitly about lesbianism, as in *Rebecca* (1940). Of course, as White discussed, Hollywood was very restricted in how lesbianism could be in fact depicted on the screen, largely as a result of the Hays Code. White argued that Hollywood implied lesbian desire through female looking relations in which a female (erotic) figure is the object of female desire (spectator and character) on the part of asexual supporting characters (dykey) and cross-dressing female stars (Greta Garbo, Katharine Hepburn). White argued:

> The construction of lesbianism occurred primarily within, rather than despite, the movies' highly *visible* and regulated constructions of femininity, and through their appeal to female audiences. Hollywood's conscious, varied, and inventive attempts to represent and appeal to female subjectivity and desire, particularly through the production of "women's pictures" and through their ancillary promotional discourses, inevitably introduced the potential for lesbian inference.[88]

Antiracist scholars advocated for the power of melodrama to express the trauma of racial violence and oppression. Expanding on

Brooks, bell hooks identified the potential for an oppositional gaze in melodramatic forms through her analysis of the race movies directed by Oscar Micheaux, one of the very few African American film-makers working in the 1920s and 1930s.[89] Hooks argued that Micheaux addressed black spectators in impassioned narratives that could express the unspeakable black desire in a white man's world. Hooks argued:

> Calling into question the Western metaphysical dualism which associates whiteness with purity and blackness with taint, the subtext of Micheaux' seemingly simple melodrama interrogates internalized racism and the color caste system.[90]

Jane Gaines examined Micheaux's deployment of melodramatic structures in her analysis of his portrayal of the lynch mob in the race movie *Within Our Gates/La Negra* (1920), the antithetical to Griffith's *Birth of a Nation* (1915). Gaines argued:

> Melodrama elevates the weak above the powerful by putting them on a higher moral ground. Micheaux's spectacle of lynching, then, was rhetorically organized to encourage the feeling of righteous indignation in the black spectator.[91]

In his analysis of Billy Woodberry's African American *Bless Their Little Hearts* (1982), film theorist and critic Chuck Kleinhans examined the realist melodrama as a political tool "used by artists seeking to depict the unrepresented and misrepresented." Kleinhans argued:

> This realist melodrama form avoids irony and self-reflection. It cannot claim the sophistication of playing stylization against content to achieve the ironic distanciation claimed for Sirk, for example, but in its plain frankness, in its direct validation of the everyday and everyday desires, it speaks powerfully and directly of that which is unrepresented, misrepresented, and underrepresented in the dominant culture's depiction of the exploited.[92]

Feminist film and media theorist Jane Shattuc argued for "the affective power of the melodramatic text" in her analysis of Steven Spielberg's adaptation of Alice Walker's *The Color Purple* (1985).[93] Shattuc took issue with "feminist criticism's refusal to own up to the political power of affect in melodrama (even in its conservative 'happy ending' form) and, in particular, the racial implications of such a denial for the reception of *The Color Purple*."

> *The Color Purple*, both as a novel as well as a film, follows the utopian tradition of the black bourgeois uplift literature tradition. The film traces the classic slave narrative structure as Celie is liberated from patriarchal enslavement while simultaneously becoming literate. Jacqueline Bobo offers strong evidence of the positive ideological influence that the film had on black women. They were "moved" by "the fact [that] Celie eventually triumphs in the film." She chronicles how they "cried," "became angry," and finally "became proud" of Celie's liberation. Bobo concludes that "Black women have discovered something progressive and useful in the film." This discovery was made through the emotive power of identification with the film's Utopian logic.[94]

A few of the films in this study are working in the paranoid woman's film genre, also known as the Gothic woman's film, and are working on the periphery of the horror/thriller genre. Both horror and the thriller originated in the late nineteenth-century Victorian Gothic novel, as well as early antecedents such as Mary Shelley's *Frankenstein* (1818) and Dr. Polidori's *The Vampire* (1819).[95] Discussing Hitchcock's *Rebecca* (1940) and *Gaslight* (1944), Susan Hayward pointed out that in "both films the woman is trapped in the house. Doane discusses these films as 'horror-in-the-home' melodramas where marriage and murder are brought together in the female protagonist's mind."[96] Barry Keith Grant argued that the "beast in the boudoir" figure stands as the generic image for the horror genre as a whole, "for the sexual tensions that resonate in this scenario vividly evoke the genre's dominant themes." Grant argued:

> Probably the most common image in horror movies, whatever the sub-genre—from *The Cabinet of Dr. Caligari* (1919) to *Candyman* (1992), and even before that in Gothic art (perhaps most notably Henry Fuseli's *The Nightmare* [1781])—is what Harvey Roy Greenberg . . . calls the beast in the boudoir. Most often in such scenes (but not always), the monster is coded as male, the victim female. Typically, her vulnerability and sexuality are heightened because she is a comely maiden wearing a night-gown or a wedding-dress or some other light-coloured garment.[97]

The key issues that have dominated film scholarship on horror have been about perverse and repressed sexuality in the nuclear family. Grant argued that "horror is a genre preoccupied with issues of sexual difference and gender," even when difference is not foregrounded explicitly.[98] A number of feminist film scholars have identified the potential of horror to express ideas about gender, if only in isolated moments. Film theorist Linda Williams argued that the female look in horror films (*Phantom of the Opera*, *Peeping Tom*, *Psycho*) is privileged because the object of the gaze shifts from herself to the monster, also an othered figure of difference. The woman looks, but this looking has power only if the woman's sexual desire is disavowed.[99] Film theorist Barbara Creed famously drew on Julia Kristeva's seminal essay "Power of Horror" to explore how the horror film is a psychoanalytic scripting of the abject monster-mother. According to Kristeva, this maternal abjection has no respect for borders, positions, and rules disturbing identity, system, and order. Creed argued that this maternal abjection is reflected in the horror genre, particularly the Hollywood cinema.[100] Film theorist Carol Clover famously identified the opportunity for disruption of gender identity in horror. Disputing Mulvey's binary model, in which the female spectator is forced to assume a transvestite position of identification, Clover identified the fluidity of point of view and gender identification in horror, represented by the masculine figure of the final girl (the last girl standing). Clover pointed out that these final girls are not feminist figures because they must suppress sexual desire in order to survive.[101] These scholars identified the potential for horror to produce the power of vision in female figures, collapsing the female object/male subject binary.

However, to be clear, the films in this study are not really working within the horror genre in the strict sense of the word. Rather, a number of the films (especially *The Piano*, *Loyalties*, and *Bedevil*) deploy and subvert some of the iconic tropes of horror.

THE DECONSTRUCTING NARRATIVES

First, Second and Third cinema are all Cinemas of the Modern Nation State. From the Indigenous place of standing, these are all invader Cinemas.[102]

—Maori filmmaker Barry Barclay

The films in this study that tell herstories deploying deconstruction as a storytelling method are *Daughters of the Dust*, *Mauri*, and *Bedevil*. All three films tell stories from the point of view of subaltern people, primarily women. Julie Dash, Merata Mita, and Tracey Moffatt depict frontier spaces that are rife with the dislocation, disenfranchisement, and capitalist exploitation of subaltern peoples; racist violence is a key weapon deployed by colonial powers. The lone white male hero of the Hollywood Western is a marginal figure and often takes the form of a predatorial villain. Though all the films are set in frontier spaces, they are focused on families and domestic issues, working within and against the conventions of the woman's film, including the Gothic melodrama. A key theme throughout these films is saving the subaltern family or community. Through their subversions of the frontier myth-histories, these three films highlight gender oppression as a key colonial and racist tool of power.

The filmmakers, all women of color, deploy many of the strategies advocated by antiracist and anticolonial feminists to destabilize sexist and racist tropes of popular frontier myth-histories. Evoking the work of Elsa Barkley Brown, who advocated for a method of historiography that embraces highly symbolic qualities and narrative patterns as reflected in African American patchwork quilts and jazz, these films embrace a multivoiced, nonlinear narrative structure foregrounding subaltern female voices that speak to a subaltern female spectator. Oral storytelling is featured across these films, the primary narrator being a subaltern woman. The primary role of the female subaltern storyteller is to reconstruct and preserve subaltern history, language, and cultural identity with the aim of healing and allaying the suffering of colonial oppression and exploitation. Deploying mythic structures and rituals, the female narrators tell stories using gesture, music, song, dance, symbolic objects, and iconography. Evoking the decolonizing work of Spivak and hooks, the films speak to a subaltern viewer and listener, one who knows the myths and practices of these rituals, through an oppositional gaze. On the power of looking in the black community, hooks argued that

> all attempts to repress our/black people's right to gaze had produced in us an overwhelming longing to look, a rebellious desire, an oppositional gaze. By courageously looking, we defiantly declared, "Not only will I stare. I want my look to change reality." Even in the worse circumstances of domination, the ability to manipulate one's gaze in the face of structures of domination that would contain it, opens up the possibility of agency.[103]

Through this method, the filmmakers are able to foreground subaltern female desires and dismantle racist Western frontier tropes of subaltern and colonized women as silent and invisible.

DAUGHTERS OF THE DUST

The Griot[104] will come to a birth, wedding or funeral and over a period of days will recount the family's history, with the stories going off at a tangent, weaving in and out. I decided that Daughters of the Dust *should be told in that way.[105]*

I want to touch something inside each black person that sees it, some part of them that's never been touched before. So I said, let me take all of this information that I have gathered and try

*to show this family leaving a great-grandmother in a very
different way. And that was when I realized that I could not
structure it as a normal, Western drama. It had to go beyond
that. And that's when I came up with the idea of structuring
the story in much the same way that an African griot
would recount a family's history.*[106]

—Julie Dash

Daughters of the Dust is set on St. Simons Island, off the Georgia coast, at the turn of the twentieth century. The plot centers on a last supper before the Peazant family prepares to leave for the mainland in search of a better life. With her Sea Islands setting, Julie Dash destabilizes a central tenet of the American frontier myth-history, that it is set in the West. The Sea Islands are situated off the East Coast of the United States, rather than in the West, and the Peazant family is headed north, subverting the Western's central East/West dichotomy. Focalizing the film's conflicts around family turmoil, Dash deploys and subverts the codes of the maternal melodrama and the Gothic woman's film to tell a story about the haunting legacy of slavery for African American families and communities.

The structure of *Daughters* is cyclical and told in the African griot oral tradition. This was Dash's way to "touch an audience" by taking them back "inside [their] collective memories."[107] Unlike a conventional film narrative, *Daughters* does not have a three-act structure with a central protagonist. Multiple story lines are presented from the points of view of various narrators and storytellers, collectively weaving together Dash's episodic narrative. These storytellers are all descendants, *daughters*, of Great-Great-Grandmother Nana Peazant (Cora Lee Day), the family matriarch, who refuses to migrate north with her children. Nana is a very old woman and chooses to stay on the island, to be buried with "the old souls." The separation of the Peazant family from their Gullah roots and Nana is the source of much dramatic tension. The different storytellers tell of various chapters in the Peazant family history, and all are spoken through a subaltern female voice using highly poetic language. In some sense, *Daughters* can be seen as working within the epic poem form.

The Unborn Child (Kai-Lynn Warren), a spirit from the future, tells the story of her parents, Eula (Alva Rogers) and Eli (Adisa Anderson), and their troubled marriage.

> My story begins on the eve of my family's migration north. My story begins before I was born. My great-great-grandmother, Nana Peazant, saw her family coming apart. Her flowers to bloom in a distant land. And then, there was my ma and daddy's problem. Nana prayed and the old souls guided me into the New World.

Only Nana Peazant can see the Unborn Child, who she has called forth to solve and heal Eli and Eula's problem. The Unborn Child's parents are coming apart because her mother was raped by a white man (which occurred before the film begins), and it is unknown who fathered the baby she is now carrying. Understandably, Eli is tormented by his wife's rape and by the prospect that the child she is carrying may have been fathered by a white man. Eli is also angry because Eula refuses to reveal the identity of her rapist. Eula knows that if Eli discovers her rapist's identity he will seek vengeance, no doubt leading to more tragedy. Eula's cousin Yellow Mary warns, "There's enough uncertainty in life without having to sit at home wondering which tree your husband's hanging from. . . . Don't tell him anything."

Eula's rapist functions as a ghost or bogeyman, an invisible but ever-present threat who lurks on the edges of Dash's African American frontier, someone who cannot ever be named. Indeed, whites in general ghost Dash's frame; though we know they are around, they never make an appearance on-screen. The tension is constructed around whether Eli and Eula will be able to save their marriage and whether Eli can ever accept the Unborn Child as his own.

Iona's story revolves around forbidden romance. Iona (Bahni Turpin) is in love with St. Julien Lastchild (M. Cochise Anderson), a member of the Cherokee Nation, but is set to leave with her family for the mainland. One of the most lyrical moments in the film is Iona's reading of a poetic love letter St. Julien has written to her, urging her to remain on the island with him. Iona is torn between her love for St. Julien and her loyalty to her family, especially her embittered mother, Haagar (Kaycee Moore), who sees no future in staying at Ibo Landing. Haagar has come to hate the islands because of what they represent, including a traumatic history of slavery, and Nana's "old salt water" ways. In the end, Iona must choose between St. Julien and the islands, and her mother.

Yellow Mary (Barbara O) tells her story of maternal loss and sexual exploitation. Traveling with a female companion, Trula (Trula Hoosier), Yellow Mary has returned to the islands after some time away. She is a character shrouded in mystery. Though she has been invited to partake in the Peazants' last supper, it is not clear by whom. Yellow Mary is the "prodigal daughter," whose return is met with suspicion and disdain by most of the Peazant family. It is implied that both Yellow Mary and Trula are mainland prostitutes. Despite her mysterious persona and her black-sheep status in the family, Yellow Mary is a very sympathetic character who has suffered greatly. Yellow Mary's story reveals a tragic reality.

> My baby was born dead, and my breasts were full of milk. We needed the money, so I was hired out to a wealthy family . . . some big, supposed to be, "muckety-mucks," off Edisto Island. High-falutin' buckra. When they went to Cuba, I went with them. I nursed their baby, and took care of the other children. That's how I got "ruint." . . . I wanted to go home and they keep me . . . they keep me. So, I "fix" the titty . . . they send me home.

Many of her relatives, however, do not seem to give Yellow Mary much sympathy. The only Peazants who do accept Yellow Mary and offer her any understanding are Nana and Eula, who has also been "ruint" at the hands of white men. Yellow Mary is a divisive character who brings forth painful memories and historical truths about the experience of many young female black slaves, who had the double burden of being exploited for their reproductive and sexual labor. These are memories that many of the Peazants do not want to bring up. Yellow Mary, however, is not afraid of speaking and facing the truth about who she is and what she has become. This is why she clashes with many of the other characters. In the end, Yellow Mary does not want to disrupt; she wants only peace and a new start in life.

Viola (Cheryl Lynn Bruce) is a Christian missionary and spinster who, like Yellow Mary, has returned to the islands from the mainland after some time away. In contrast to Yellow Mary, Viola speaks highly of the mainland and all its opportunities and modern ways. Though Viola may be modern, she is a religious zealot with an uptight schoolmarm persona. Accompanying Viola on her return home is Mr. Snead (Tommy Redmond Hicks), a professional photographer, who Viola has hired to document her family's historic journey to the mainland. Though they are traveling companions, the relationship is strictly business. On their boat trip to Ibo Landing, Viola reminisces with Yellow Mary about the past, providing us a history lesson in the process.

> VIOLA: "Yellow Mary, look!" *Viola points to an old shanty house on a small island.* "Uncle Spikenard lived there. Do you remember him?" *Yellow Mary does not reply.* "I guess not, I was just a young Miss too, then. He was from Africa, and just after the war, he moved from the plantation to the little house on the waterfront. Remember how Uncle Spikenard used to get angry, he'd talk funny so the children couldn't understand him? He'd speak in African words and sounds. You know, Uncle Spikenard told me, just before the war they'd keep boatloads of fresh Africans off some secret islands around here."
>
> MR. SNEAD: "Viola, our government banned the transporting of Africans for slavery fifty years before the Civil War."
>
> VIOLA: "Not back off these islands. Noooo! Just before the war, they were still running and hiding salt water Africans, pure bred, from the Yankees."

Viola's story is not personal. As a storyteller she keeps her distance, as would a schoolteacher. Later it will be revealed that Viola does harbor great pain, which she keeps at bay with Christianity. For Viola, Christian stories are her armor and means of survival as a black woman in a white man's world.

Nana as a storyteller tries to instill the importance of the Peazants' history of African diaspora and slavery into the younger generations before they leave. Nana tells the story of slavery—a large historical story. Nana believes that calling on the old souls is a key strategy for resisting the racist oppression, exploitation, and violence that her descendants (flowers to bloom) will inevitably meet in the promised land. Like an African griot, Nana narrates the past through various rituals and myths rooted in West African history, culture, and religion, such as hoodoo (voodoo). Nana's stories are highly poetic and iconographic. She serves as a kind of poet for her people, one who sits on a throne of sticks. Nana says:

> Our hands scarred blue with poisonous indigo dye that built up all those plantations from swampland. Our spirits numb from the sting of fever from the rice fields. Our backs, bent down forever with the planting and the hoeing of the Sea Island cotton. I was an elder. And, many years ago, as I lay in my mother's arms, I saw Africa in her face.

In figure 1.1, Nana is surrounded by her many daughters as she passes on painful stories from the past.

At the end of the film, the Unborn Child offers us resolution, though it is bittersweet.

FIGURE 1.1 Nana Peazant (center), Viola (right top corner), Eula, and her mother, Hagaar (left corner), *Daughters of the Dust*.

And so, on the 19th day of August, 1902, they left these islands and set out for the North, having said farewell, perhaps never to see us again. My Momma and Daddy stayed behind with Yellow Mary. Some say Eli got himself all involved with the anti-lynching issue. Some say Eula saw too much of herself in Nana Peazant, and wanted her children born on this island. They say Mama was always peculiar and Nana's roots and herbs set she off. All I know is, I was born before Nana passed on. We remained behind, growing older, wiser, stronger.

In this way, a young female spirit guides us through the film's plot toward an African American future. Dash's female multivoiced narration weaves a story that is about both the Peazants' family struggles to remain together, despite their differences and conflicts, and the struggles of African Americans to maintain a connection to their distinct culture, language, and history. Here, family conflicts and domestic troubles are not rooted in the psychological or psychoanalytic structures of the woman's film, as Doane argues, but rather in colonial and racist constructs such as slavery.

MAURI

I can unite the technical complexity of film with a traditional Māori philosophy that gives me a sense of certainty, an unfragmented view of society, an orientation towards people rather than institutions. I have an enormous responsibility to them and their descendants. I'm actually in the position of the person who carried the oral tradition in older times. It's similar to the way the Whaikoreo and the stories that are told on the Marae keep history alive and maintain contact with the past. Carrying on a tradition means redeeming the past, redeeming the culture.[108]

—Merata Mita

Set on a 1950s New Zealand/Aotearoa frontier, Mita's *Mauri* centers on a large Maori family, the Rapanas. *Mauri* works in the social realist tradition, deploying nonprofessional actors, including Maori activist Eva Rickard in the role of a *kuia*, elder.[109] Mita's cyclical narrative opens with a birth scene and ends with a death and a rebirth. There are three imbricating story lines in *Mauri*, which pivot around Kara Rapana, the matriarch who struggles to keep her family together in the face of broken land treaties, racial hatred and violence, and the lure of urban gangs. The first story line revolves around Paki, a male fugitive from the law who has assumed the identity of Kara's deceased nephew, Rewi Rapana. Paki/Rewi (Anzac Wallace) is a haunted and hunted man who has lost all sense of his Maori identity; he has even stolen Rewi's sacred totem from his dead body, committing a crime in the Maori spirit world. Mita constructs dramatic tension around whether Paki/Rewi will find spiritual salvation. A second story line centers on Remari (Susan D. Ramari Paul), a young Maori woman who is romantically involved with and attached to two men, Paki/Rewi and Steve Semmens (James Heyward), a Pakeha (white settler). Though Steve genuinely loves Remari, he also feels loyalty to his unstable racist father, Mr. Semmens (Geoff Murphy), who has swindled the Rapanas out of their land. A third story line focuses on Kara's other nephew, Willie Rapana (Willie Raana), a gang leader who is on the run from both the law and rival gangs. Through the male characters Paki/Rewi and Willie, Mita foregrounds the marginalization and criminalization of indigenous men in colonial white-settler societies. Awatea (Rangimarie Delaware) is Kara's great-granddaughter, who makes various appearances throughout the narrative, observing the adults around her and trying to make sense of the world. In figure 1.2, Kara, seated with a Maori elder, teaches Awatea how to weave her first Maori *kete* (basket).

Mita's narrative follows the conventions of melodrama in which all story lines are focalized around a multigenerational family in crisis. As in Dash's *Daughters*, the family stands in for the larger community. The problems the characters face mirror the issues faced by the Maori as a colonized, disenfranchised people. Mita draws a parallel between the loss of Maori land (the Rapanas' land) and the loss of Maori youth to urban gangs (Willie), as well as the erosion of cultural identity (Paki). Though it is the 1950s, Maori communities are still fighting the Pakeha (white-settler) government for

FIGURE 1.2 Kara (center), Awatea, and Maori elder, *Mauri.*

land rights and racial equity. These problems create much conflict within and for the Rapana family, who must face a traumatic past and an unknown future, represented by Kara's great-granddaughter, Awatea. With regard to the Western, Mita renders the Pakeha/white-settler characters as peripheral figures. The only sympathetic white character is Steve Semmens, Remari's well-intentioned lover.

Mita's storytelling methods are rooted in Maori myth and ritual, depicted in the film's soundtrack and iconography. Kara is her community's and the film's oral storyteller, and she aims to preserve Maori culture, history, and language (*Te Reo Māori*) through the performing of ancient Maori rituals and *waiata* (traditional ancestral Maori songs, chants, and laments).[110] Mita exemplifies this Maori method for "redeeming the past, redeeming the culture" in the opening birthing sequence of the film.

> SHOT: *Medium-close angle on Diane, a young Maori woman in labor. She leans against the broad shoulder of Paki/Rewi. Maori chanting is heard on the soundtrack.* Kara says, "How are you doing, Diane?"

Diane moans as she labors. Kara guides her with "Push, that's it, push. It's nearly here."

SHOT: *Medium angle on a Pakeha/white medical doctor who observes as Kara guides the labor. Kara says to the doctor, off-screen,* "You can come . . ."

SHOT: *Wide three-shot on Kara, laboring mother, and Paki/Rewi. Kara continues with* "and give me a hand with the delivery." *The doctor enters the frame, a bit bewildered. Kara says,* "Hold it. Slowly." *Maori chanting continues on the soundtrack.*

SHOT: *Medium-close angle on the laboring mother. Kara exclaims,* "Oh, oh!"

SHOT: *Close angle on Kara's hands. The doctor says, off-screen,* "Scalpel." *Kara stops the doctor. Her hand places a seashell in the doctor's hand instead of a scalpel. She says,* "No, use this." *The doctor's palm remains open, holding the seashell. Kara explains,* "It has cut the cords of generations." *Maori chanting continues.*

SHOT: *Medium-long shot on Willie donning a black leather jacket as he enters the doorway of a hospital room. He smiles broadly. Newborn baby sounds are heard off-screen. Willie's fellow gang members enter the frame, surrounding him. They all look on as Diane holds her baby. Willie exclaims,* "Just in time!"

SHOT: *Close angle on the swaddled newborn baby. The Maori waitia is emphasized on the soundtrack. Characters off-screen speak to each other in Maori.*

CUT TO: Title: *Mauri.*

The word *Mauri* translates into "life force" or "spirit." This life force is the glue that keeps the Maori community and the Rapana family together, and it is continually under threat. The newborn child symbolizes this life force, which has to be brought into the world in a culturally specific Maori way. Willie's words, "Just in time," suggest that this child's birth is timely, promising hope for the future. The cutting of the umbilical cord with the seashell in some sense represents Mita's Maori filmmaking itself: bringing something to life with Maori tools, Maori storytelling traditions. Kara's handing the seashell to the Pakeha doctor renders him a helpmate and functions as a teaching moment in Maori culture and history, through gesture and iconography.

BEDEVIL

My work has an uncool emotion and heat to it, my narratives
have glaring clichéd aspects. People feel that they've seen it
before—but I'm giving it to them all over again with my slant
on it. People recognise the "clichés" and don't seem
to mind them.[111]

—Tracey Moffatt

Bedevil is set on a postcolonial Australian frontier and spans four decades (1950s–1990s). The nonlinear, nonchronological film is structured by a series of ghost stories, told from disparate points of view,
that tell of community and family breakdown, land dispossession,
and the dislocation of Aborigine and Torres Strait Islander peoples.
These stories are told by a diverse range of individuals from across
the axes of gender, race, ethnicity, sexuality, and age. Hence, Moffatt
does not feature or privilege female voices in her narrative. The film
evokes Joan Wallach Scott's idea of gender analysis rather than the
woman's stories model. Working within and against the Gothic melodrama, Moffatt deploys silent gestures and highly mythic rituals to tell
stories of trauma and loss. Deploying the signature hyperreal aesthetic
Moffatt developed as an art photographer, she constructs an uncanny
and eerie story about the horrors of colonialism.

There are two ways Moffatt deploys storytellers in *Bedevil*. First,
Moffatt has her storytellers address the camera as if they were documentary subjects answering questions from an off-screen interviewer.
By breaking the fourth wall, Moffatt draws attention to the cinema apparatus, disrupting viewers' expectations of realism or conventional
storytelling associated with the popular cinema. Through this device
Moffatt foregrounds the storytelling process and the construction of
the gaze in cinema. By having the storytellers speak to an off-camera
interviewer/filmmaker, Moffatt draws attention to her own gaze, that
of an indigenous woman. This evokes the traditional and colonial
representation of indigenous people in Australian ethnographic films,
in which the gaze has been historically constructed by and through a

white male lens. Moffatt's work also reflects the work of film scholar Bill Nichols, who aligned ethnography with pornography. Nichols equated the two forms because both depend on a controlling gaze that silences and objectifies the primary actors. Nichols argued:

> Both pornography and ethnography promise something they cannot deliver: the ultimate pleasure of knowing the Other. On this promise of sexual or cultural knowledge they depend, but they are also condemned to do nothing more than make it available for representation.[112]

Moffatt's film is neither an ethnographic film nor a genre film. Rather, Moffatt deploys the tropes from ethnography and the Gothic thriller to render visible the colonial demarcation of the Australian frontier as a haunted space. This is similar to Dash's frame, in which whites lurk in the shadows. However, Moffatt is careful not to represent indigenous people as victims and whites only as threats. Moffatt breaks down the white-settler/indigenous binary division. The real threat here is colonial expansionism.

The second way the storytellers work in *Bedevil* is by foregrounding dissonance and incoherence. As Dash does in *Daughters*, Moffatt foregrounds oral history by deploying a diverse range of storytellers. Unlike those of Dash and Mita, however, Moffatt's storytellers represent a diverse range of Australian identities across the axes of gender, race, class, sexuality, and ethnicity. Moffatt herself identifies as Aborigine and Irish and was raised primarily in a white-settler foster home. Moffatt's construction of these diverse points of view and voices critique the idea of coherent monolithic identities and harmonious multiculturalism; Moffatt's frontier encompasses neither of those things and is at times confusing, disturbing, and unsettling. Moffatt deploys tropes of the Gothic melodrama and woman's film to critique and reconstruct the frontier experience.

In the segment "Mr. Chuck" there are two narrators, Rick (Jack Charles), an Aborigine male prison inmate, and Shelley (Diana Davidson), an elderly white middle-class woman. Though these narrators do not really share any scenes, they are connected by the stories of the drowned American G.I. and Rick's traumatic childhood.

Moffatt interweaves their strange stories to construct a critique of the dislocation and disenfranchisement of indigenous peoples and communities.

> SHOT: *Medium angle on middle-class bric-a-brac including an Aboriginal art object. The camera pans along the shelf to reveal some old black-and-white photographs. One of the photos features a young white woman flanked by American soldiers ("Yanks"). Shelley's voice-over says,* "The swamp business is the only true tragedy we've had." *The camera comes to a pause on Shelley's face, now in close angle.* "During the second World War the island was full of American soldiers. Yanks, Yanks, Yanks everywhere. They were stationed here."

Though Shelley claims the drowning of the G.I. was the only true tragedy they had experienced as a community, she later contradicts herself when she describes Rick's traumatic childhood at the hands of an abusive uncle, who appears in terrifying distorted shadows. In contrast to Shelley's story, adult Rick tells a strange tale about the drowned G.I., depicting him as a kind of swamp-thing figure who attempts to pull him under. Rick recounts the story from his prison cell. The swamp is the site where the child, Rick, plays with his little sisters and will later be transformed into a housing development for middle-class white settlers.

> SHOT: *Medium shot of Rick, an adult, secured behind prison glass. He laughs almost hysterically and says casually to the camera,* "The ghost swamp, yeah, that was me."
> CUT TO: *Wide angle of Rick, as a child, being dragged into the swamp.*
> SHOT: *Cut back to medium shot of adult Rick behind prison glass. He reminisces:* "I was seven at the time. I was okay. They fished me out." *Rick starts laughing again. He presses his hand up against the prison glass, bringing attention to it, evoking the camera lens.*
> CUT TO: *Close angle on the bubbling, muddy swamp. Adult Rick's eerie laughter bridges over the image of the creepy swamp.*
> SHOT: *Cut back to adult Rick in prison behind the glass. The camera performs a quick zoom, going in for a closer angle. Rick stops laugh-*

ing. He gazes intensely off-camera to some invisible interviewer. His
tone turns dark and menacing. "But I hated that place! That . . .
island!"
    Later, Rick speaks of the dead G.I.
SHOT: *Medium-close high angle on Rick, as a child, gazing at the G.I.*
    helmet off-screen. Adult Rick's voice-over ponders, "And I was
    thinking . . ."
SHOT: *Close angle on adult Rick in prison. Rick continues speaking.* ". . .
    of that dumb G.I. bastard down below."

The dead G.I. is of course a hybrid-monster of the swamp thing,
evoking *Creature from the Black Lagoon* (1954) and the Australian
Aboriginal folkloric bunyip monster. Barbara Creed's analysis of
Hollywood horror B movies is apt here. Creed argued that the concept of the border "is central to the construction of the monstrous in
the horror film; that which crosses or threatens to cross the 'border'
is abject. In some horror films the monstrous is produced at the border
of human and inhuman, man and beast, like the creature who lurks
at the bottom of the black lagoon."[113] The bunyip is a mythical creature from indigenous folklore that inhabits swamps, billabongs,
creeks, riverbeds, and waterholes. Bunyips are known to jump out
from under the water to attack their prey, either animals or humans.
Robert Holden explains:

The bunyip, a lurking presence in the depths of the billabong, is one
of the most enduring and terrifying of Australian-Aboriginal beliefs.
Oral tradition, pictographs and ground-carvings testify to an age-
old belief in a large amphibious man-eating creature; and ever since
colonization reports have emanated from equally terrified settlers
telling of encounters with this Australian nightmare. Early nineteenth century scientific interest in the bunyip was frustrated by
the readiness of some Aboriginal people to identify all manner of
strange skeletons, unearthly sounds from the swamp and frightening encounters as proof of the bunyip's existence. This diverse range
of "evidence" for the bunyip only became more confusing when
Europeans realized that the Aboriginal people held it in such dread
that were "unable to take note of its characteristics."[114]

Shelley and Rick use the "swamp business" as a way to transfer trauma into a scary story. The shot of Rick in his cramped jail cell crudely applying a prison tattoo to his arm contrasts harshly with Shelley in her comfortable middle-class bungalow. Moffatt seems to make the point that their scary stories serve as points of disconnection rather than connection. These are stories that do not bridge cultural divides. Shelley knew Rick was being brutalized but did nothing to help him. In Moffatt's world it is Rick's childhood that is the true tragedy, not the drowning of the soldier; it is the real scary story.

The second segment is titled "Choo, Choo, Choo, Choo" and is told through three different narrators: a Chinese man; Mickey, an alcoholic white working-class man; and Ruby, an elderly Aborigine woman. Moffatt connects these three different narrators across the "Choo, Choo, Choo, Choo" segment through strange happenings and spooky stories about unexplained ghost sightings and UFOs. The Chinese man functions as a tour guide, telling the story of the ghost of a little white blind girl as if he were speaking to a tourist. Breaking the fourth wall, he addresses the camera, positioning the viewer as a tourist. The story told by Mickey, the drunken white man, who was the conductor on the train that killed the little white blind girl, is marked by haziness, confusion, and incoherence.

SHOT: *Medium-long shot on Mickey, standing in a shabby kitchen. Behind him a sign reads Beware of Trains. The tap drips. Mickey says, "I . . ." There is a long pause. "I have a friend." Another long pause. "She visits me at night." Pause. "She's a ghost, but I call it a spirit." Pause. "Who is she?! I don't want to tell who it is. But it's not the little girl." The man turns to face the camera. Spooky music plays in the background.*

SHOT: *Close angle on a sheet of braille.* "The little . . ."

SHOT: *Medium angle on Mickey, who taps his hands against his eyes. He pulls his hands away and looks outward at the wall.* "These spirits . . . perhaps they do try to tell us something. I try to work it out. I believe in these things. I also believe in the hovercrafts. I mean . . . the UFOs. They've been in our family for years." *Mickey hiccups and then turns to the camera.*

Moffatt cuts to an earlier time period (possibly the 1960s). The setting is a homestead in a highly stylized Australian outback landscape. Two Aborigine boys spot starlike objects in the purple sky. They try to alert the adults, but only the children manage to see the lights. Ruby narrates:

> When we lived out here strange things would happen. Sometimes we'd see these things in the sky. Our old people would call them "min" lights. Those old Murray people, they never knew what they were. And neither did we. They just used to come.

In figure 1.3, the elderly Ruby breaks the fourth wall.

The third segment, "Lovin' the Spin I'm In," is narrated by three storytellers, Dimitri, a Greek-Australian businessman; Voula, Dimitri's wife; and a doomed couple, Beba and Minnie, who perform their story through a silent ghost-dance. Beba and Minnie, star-crossed lovers, are dead, having perished in a fire in Dimitri's warehouse. These storytellers have different motives for telling their story. The point Moffatt makes with the deployment of these disparate and disconnected voices across gender, race, and ethnicity is that they tell stories differently. But difference is not enough here. Moffatt intercuts these voices not in an attempt to create a coherent story but to depict the idea of a shared past (a haunted history) that is complexly

FIGURE 1.3 Ruby, *Bedevil.*

layered with differing experiences that have little in common with one another.

Through methods of distanciation and a dissonant multivoiced narration, the content of the ghost story becomes irrelevant, disrupting the whole point of horror in the first place, which is to create a believable imaginary world where monsters prey upon innocent victims. Though Moffatt does create frightening and unnerving worlds with strange and creepy ghosts, the most disturbing moments are the ones in which indigenous peoples, their cultures, and their place in the world are placed under threat. The drowned G.I., the little white blind girl, and the dead lovers serve as horrific colonial tropes, which Moffatt's disparate and alienated storytellers deploy to narrate and reconstruct the past. These ghosts are highly representational of the feelings and experiences of indigenous people, who have been subject to violence, land dispossession, and the fracturing of communities and homes, as well as loss of language and culture, as a result of capitalist postcolonial projects such as tourism and urban land development.

THE REVISIONIST COUNTER-FRONTIER NARRATIVES

My Brilliant Career, My American Cousin, Thousand Pieces of Gold, The Piano, and *The Ballad of Little Jo* work in the classical narrative tradition to tell revisionist stories of female agency and resistance within the confines of patriarchy. These films evoke Anglo-American feminist recuperative and revisionist projects that aimed to excavate and render visible forgotten or marginalized female-authored texts and voices from the past. A key theme that is common throughout these revisionist feminist films is the suppression and silencing of the heroines' voices by patriarchal structures. Across all these films, the heroines experience issues with communicating or being heard, both literally and figuratively. Though these films feature female silence and communication issues, the filmmakers foregrounded the suppression of the female voice in the soundtracks of their films, echoing the work of Kaja Silverman. Central to Silver-man's arguments is that the female voice is always embodied, which means it has little or no discursive authority. According to Silverman, it is the disembodied voice that has the most authority. Silverman deployed Irigaray's (*This Sex Which Is Not One* and *Speculum*) theories of feminine language in her analysis of Hollywood sound regimes.

> The female subject, on the other hand, is excluded from positions of discursive power both inside and outside the classic filmic diegesis; she is confined not only to the safe place *of* the story, but to the safe places *within* the story (to positions, that is, which come within the eventual range of male vision and audition). Both constituents of the surveillance system—visual and auditory—must be in effect for it to be really successful. To permit a female character to be seen without being heard would be to activate the hermeneutic and cultural codes which define woman as "enigma," inaccessible to definitive male interpretation. To allow her to be heard without being seen would be even more dangerous, since it would disrupt the specular regime upon which dominant cinema relies; it would put her beyond the reach of the male gaze (which stands in her for the cultural "camera") and release her voice from the signifying obligations which that gaze enforces.[115]

One important method the filmmakers use throughout these revisionist frontier films is the disembodied female voice, primarily through the devices of voice-over narration and the voice-off, which is a diegetic voice belonging to a character who is heard but not seen in the frame. These devices establish the heroines not only as the leading protagonists in the narrative but also as authorial voices. Throughout these films the male voice is rendered ineffectual or silent and is often relegated to interior spaces. This is particularly true of powerful patriarchs. Another key way these filmmakers foreground the female voice is by rendering visible female silence.

THE PIANO

I am a big admirer of the novelists of the nineteenth century,
from George Eliot to Charlotte Brontë. And especially Emily
Brontë, who inspired me for this film.[116]

—Jane Campion

It is a weird lullaby and so it is; it is mine.

—Ada from *The Piano*

Jane Campion sets *The Piano* in the mid-nineteenth century on a New
Zealand/Aotearoa frontier. The narrative revolves around a young
mute woman, Ada (Holly Hunter), whose father has shipped her and
her daughter, Flora (Anna Paquin), to the New World to marry a man
she "has not yet met." The film's conflicts are set in motion when Ada's
husband, Alisdair Stewart (Sam Neill), trades Ada's beloved piano to
George Baines (Harvey Keitel) in exchange for land. Stewart is land
hungry. As part of the deal, Stewart offers up Ada as Baines's private
piano teacher; the lessons are to be conducted at Baines's rustic homestead, where he lives alone. Ada is enraged by her husband's callous
actions and initially refuses to teach the "ignorant" Baines, who has
seemingly "gone Native." However, Stewart forces Ada to obey him,
which in turn renders Ada into an unaffectionate, angry wife. Intrigued
by and attracted to Stewart's new, silent, inscrutable wife, Baines offers
Ada a counteroffer so she can earn back her piano. Baines offers her
one black key for every visit in which she will permit him to "do things
to her." Despondent and desperate without her piano, Ada reluctantly
agrees, entering into a dangerous exchange with Baines. In figure 1.4,
Ada meets both her husband, Stewart, and her soon-to-be lover, Baines,
for the first time. A Maori man stands in the background of the shot.

The Piano is working primarily within the Gothic and maternal
melodrama, although it engages with tropes of the Western to weave
a "strange lullaby" about a white-settler family in an untamed wilderness. The dramatic conflicts in *The Piano* are all focalized around

FIGURE 1.4 Ada and Maori man, *The Piano*.

domestic turmoil—female sexual transgression, mother-daughter conflicts, domestic abuse, and a loveless marriage—rather than frontier territory wars. Though Ada's husband has land disputes with the local Maori, these serve only as a device to render Stewart a villain; he treats the local indigenous people as he treats his wife, callously. Campion subverts the rugged lone white male frontier hero of the Western through Baines, who is more primal and brooding than rugged; he frequently appears in the nude, evoking the beast in the boudoir figure, although Baines is not really a serious threat. It is Campion's deployment of the European fairy tale, specifically "Bluebeard" by French writer Charles Perrault (1628–1703), that serves as template for the structure of the story. Perrault also wrote "Cinderella," "Sleeping Beauty," and "Little Red Riding Hood."

The story of "Bluebeard" focuses on an innocent new bride who has married the murderous Bluebeard, a wealthy aristocrat whose wives keep disappearing in the confines of his castle.[117] More horror than fairy tale, "Bluebeard" is a cautionary tale about domestic violence and rape.[118] Feminist literary critic Kari E. Lokke argued, "This tale of the wealthy, seemingly chivalrous aristocrat who murders seven young brides and inters them in his cellar brings together violence and love, perversion and innocence, death and marriage in an unsettling combination."[119] Campion, however, does more than just imply the "Bluebeard" fairy tale; she staged it as a play within a play. Though the larger white-settler community has minimal screen time in *The Piano*, they appear in the mounting of an amateur production of the gruesome narrative. Onstage the murdered wives are performed by local settler women, and Ada's daughter, Flora, is cast as an angel. Campion never shows us the ending of the settler production because it is interrupted by Maori audience members, who, unlike the passive white-settler spectators, attempt to rescue Bluebeard's wife, right off the stage. On the surface the rescue scene is played for comedy, although it also works as a subversion of the colonial script in which white men save brown women from brown men, evoking Spivak's work on subaltern women. Here we have Maori men (brown men) saving white women from white men. However, Campion deploys the Maori characters as racialized comedic devices, rendering them childlike and simplistic, not unlike the racist depiction of indigenous peoples in countless Westerns. Ada, Stewart, and Baines do not participate in the production; they will act out their own kind of "Bluebeard" drama later on.

Like Bluebeard, Stewart, driven by jealousy and lust, attacks Ada with an axe, chopping off one of her fingers, clipping her wings, as he rationalizes it. Stewart is driven to violence after his stepdaughter, Flora, shows him her mother's love note to Baines, which has been burned into the side of a dismembered piano key ("Dear George, you have my heart"). As in the Bluebeard story, it is a key that proves Ada's undoing. No one, however, not even Baines, can save Ada from Stewart's brutality; only Ada can save herself. Though Ada is victimized by Stewart, she does manage to escape her oppressive marriage in the end.

A number of scholars have analyzed Campion's usage of the "Bluebeard" story. Feona Attwood examined how Campion uses fairytale figures to disturb traditional patriarchal narratives.[120] Jaime Bihlmeyer explored Campion's use of Bluebeard "as an agent of a multiplex and extra-lingual dialogism linked to femininity and the female gaze."[121] Mirroring Ada's situation with that of Bluebeard's wife, Campion destabilizes the trope of the white-settler family, calling into question their status as civilized, their actions rooted in sexual transgression and violence.

Through Campion's explicit reference to Bluebeard, the film eludes thwarting female desire in subservience to an oedipal script. By going back to the premodern folktale, the source of all melodrama, Campion bypasses the Hollywood woman's film, a form focalized around female sacrifice, rendering Ada a powerful force to be reckoned with.

Campion constructs Ada's point of view and voice through her gaze and, ironically, her voice, despite the fact that she is mute. Ada, however, manages to speak through her daughter, Flora, who serves as her mother's sign-language interpreter. Because of Ada's muteness, Stewart and the larger white-settler community see her as infantile and even "touched." Campion, however, assigns authority to Ada's voice in the film's sound regime by opening and closing the film with Ada's voice-over narration; it is the only time we hear Ada's actual speaking voice, although it is a disembodied voice.

SHOT: *Extreme close angle on Ada's eyes peering through her fingers. She gazes into the camera lens. Ada's voice-over:* "The voice you hear is not my speaking voice, but my mind's voice."

SHOT: *Close angle on distorted subjective point of view shot through Ada's fingers.*

SHOT: *Cut back to previous shot. Ada's voice-over:* "I have not spoken since I was six years old."

SHOT: *Wide angle on Ada's daughter, Flora, riding her pony. Flora's grandfather holds the reins. Ada's voice-over:* "No one knows why. Not even me."

SHOT: *Medium-long-angle crane shot on Ada crouching under a tree. She stands and the camera trucks upward, Ada falling out of frame. Ada reenters the frame, now a high-angle and bird's-eye-view vantage point. The camera follows Ada as she walks along the grass. Ada's voice-over:* "My father says it is a dark talent. And the day I take it into my head to stop breathing will be my last."

Though Ada's narration may be strange, it has dramatic agency. The next lines she speaks are, "Today he has married me to a man I have not yet met. Soon my daughter and I will join him in his own country. My husband said my muteness does not bother him." What will torment Stewart, however, is Ada's will, her "dark talent," which is so powerful that he will not be able to suppress it despite his best and cruelest efforts. Ada's will possesses so much power that it eventually speaks to Stewart.

SHOT: *Medium-close angle on a distraught Stewart leaning over Baines, lying in bed. Stewart has a gun aimed at Baines's head. Stewart asks,* "Has Ada ever spoken to you?"

SHOT: *Medium-long angle on Baines, who replies apprehensively,* "You mean in signs?"

SHOT: *Medium-close angle on Stewart.* "No, words. Have you ever heard words?"

SHOT: *Medium-long angle on Baines.* "No, not words." *Stewart's off-screen voice replies,* "You never thought you heard words?" *Baines shakes his head no, unsure of Stewart's next move.*

SHOT: *Medium-close angle on Stewart. He taps his head.* "I heard it here. I heard her voice here in my head. I watched her lips. They didn't make the words, but the harder I listened, the clearer I heard her." *Baines, off-screen, says, "You punished her wrongly."*

SHOT: *Medium-close angle on Baines.* "It was me—my fault."

SHOT: *Medium-close angle on Stewart, who continues,* "She said, 'I'm afraid of my will, of what it might do. It is so strange and strong.' She said, 'I have to go. Let me go.'"

SHOT: *Medium-close angle on Baines. Stewart's off-screen voice, impersonating Ada, says,* "Let Baines take me away. Let him try and save me."

Though Baines does take Ada and Flora away, essentially rescuing her from a stifling and loveless marriage, it is Ada's voice (in Stewart's head), her dark talent, that actually saves Ada, her daughter, and even Baines (from despair and a life of loneliness). Ada's voice is so powerful that it transcends conventional speech and discourse.

Some feminist critics have taken issue with Campion's feminist revision.[122] On the one hand, the film does seem to conclude with a happy-ever-after ending, typical of the fairy tale, in which Ada, Baines, and Flora settle in a nice middle-class house in Nelson, New Zealand. However, Campion actually ends the film with a gloomy, haunting underwater image of a lifeless Ada floating above her piano, what the Maori warriors refer to as a coffin.

SHOT: *Medium two-shot on Ada and Baines on a white porch, lace curtain wafting in a soft breeze. Ada dons a translucent black veil over her head, which covers her face; it is some kind of trick she is using to develop her speaking voice. Baines manhandles Ada playfully, and seductively places her up against the porch wall. He kisses Ada somewhat savagely through the black veil. Lifting the veil, Baines continues his romantic assault. The camera pulls out. Ada's voice-over:* "At night . . ."

SHOT: *Canted close angle on the piano sitting at the bottom of the ocean. Ada's voice-over:* "I think of my piano in its ocean grave." *The camera pulls out to reveal a rope floating upward. Ada's voice-over:* "And sometimes of myself . . . floating above it." *The camera continues pulling out to reveal a lifeless Ada floating above the piano, held in place by the rope, which is attached to her foot, a kind of reverse hanging. Ada's voice-over:* "Down there, everything is so still and silent . . ." *The camera continues to pull out. The shot becomes increasingly murky. Ada's voice-over:* ". . . that it lulls me to sleep. It is a weird lullaby. And so, it is. It is mine." *The camera continues to drift away from Ada and her piano. Ada's voice-over:* "There is a silence. Where hath been no sound. There is a silence where no sound may be. In the cold grave under the deep, deep sea."

Though this final shot could be interpreted as a dream or nightmare, it might also be seen as an alternative ending to Campion's romance. The death of the transgressive heroine was common to Hollywood woman's films, particularly those in which the heroine was afflicted with an illness or had committed a subversive act (e.g., adultery). However, in contrast to the classic Hollywood woman's film, Campion does not disavow Ada's desire and voice. Ada's voice and will have the power to resist oppression. She is a kind of enigmatic feminine spirit from tales of old. Indeed, earlier on, Ada does push her piano overboard after she has chosen Baines over Stewart. She even attempts to go down with it, placing her foot in the rope. At the last minute, however, Ada chooses to save herself ("my will has chosen life"), although the piano itself cannot be saved.

Though Campion destabilizes the white-settler family construct, she did so at the expense of Maori people. Commenting on *The Piano*, Merata Mita said, "I thought that the Māori characters were very flawed. . . . They were sort of draped around the shrubbery and stuff, like some kind of spectacle, you know—hovering. And I thought to myself, my gosh, the Māori are a hovering kind of people."[123] Leonie Pihama argued, "*The Piano* provides a series of constructions of Māori that are located firmly in a colonial gaze."[124] Reshela DuPuis argued, "The film's sexual symbolism relies heavily on profoundly racist depictions of the indigenous Māori people of New Zealand, and on culturally coded, deeply racialized representations of their land."[125] Maori filmmaker Barry Barclay claimed that *The Piano* was "one of the most obnoxious films I know of from the point of view of white supremacism."[126] Other critics made the case that Campion has deployed the Maori respectfully as "a Greek chorus" or as "ironic commentators and sharp critical observers of Pākehā settlers."[127]

THE BALLAD OF LITTLE JO

When I stumbled upon information about the real Little Jo I saw that her story was a classic Western story about a rugged individualist who carves out a place for herself in the American West. American history is full of women who did exactly that. Women came from all over the world to make lives for themselves, the same as men did.[128]

—Maggie Greenwald

Set in the late nineteenth century, *The Ballad of Little Jo* recuperates and reconstructs the life of Josephine Monaghan (Suzi Amis), a real pioneer woman of the American West. At the beginning of the film, Josephine, a society girl, is banished into exile by her father for having a child out of wedlock. Forced to give up her son, Josephine is punished harshly for her transgression and is rendered a fallen woman. Cast onto the streets with no (male) protector, Josephine immediately falls victim to predators. Narrowly escaping gang rape, Josephine decides to mutilate her beautiful face and dress in male clothing, an illegal offense at the time, to safeguard herself against sexual violence and exploitation. (See figure 1.5 for Josephine's dramatic transformation into a man, including the facial scar.) Assuming the male identity of Little Jo, Josephine finds work as a shepherd, a miner, and later a home-

FIGURE 1.5 Josephine/Little Jo, *The Ballad of Little Jo.*

steader. Little Jo settles near Ruby City, a somewhat women-less milieu, and receives mentoring from two crusty older miners, Percy
Corcoran (Ian McKellen) and Frank Badger (Bo Hopkins). Though
Percy and Frank are initially suspicious of Little Jo's peculiar ways,
they take her under their wing in a fatherly fashion. To ward off speculation and the revelation of her secret, Little Jo keeps to herself, never
marrying. Little Jo is content with this self-imposed seclusion until
she comes to the rescue of Tien Me Wong, "Tinman" (David Chung),
an ailing Chinese immigrant, who is being lynched by a mob of angry
white men, which includes Frank. The mob agrees to cut Tinman down
on the condition that Little Jo give him a job. Little Jo agrees to hire
Tinman as her live-in cook, risking discovery of her secret. It is not
long until Tinman figures out that Little Jo is actually a woman, and
the two outcasts become romantically involved. This romance, however, is shrouded in the dread of revelation. Little Jo says, "Do you
know what would happen if they knew about us? They'd kill us."

The Ballad of Little Jo is explicitly working within and against
the conventions of the Western and melodrama, particularly romance. Greenwald subverts the figure of the Western hero through
the cross-dressing Little Jo, whose taciturn and rugged frontiersman
act conceals loneliness, maternal yearnings, and illicit female desire.

Though the film is set on the American frontier, Greenwald structures the narrative conflicts and dramatic tension around Little Jo's male masquerade and her interracial and illegal romance with Tinman. Greenwald builds much of the film's dramatic suspense around Little Jo's fear of discovery by constructing moments in which she unintentionally and unconsciously forgets her male masquerade, revealing female/feminine desires. Through her romance with Tinman, Little Jo is able to rediscover her humanity, and feminine sexuality, which she has had to suppress in her role as a "lone rugged male." On Greenwald's frontier, white masculinity is toxic and dehumanizing. Tinman can be seen as a romantic catalyst of sorts, offering Little Jo reprieve from this toxic masculine space, albeit temporarily, fleetingly. Despite the fact that Little Jo and Tinman find some semblance of happiness with each other, outside their bedroom looms the threat of violence and even death. In contrast to the Western, Greenwald renders the larger white-settler community as threatening and monstrous, more uncivilized than civilized.

With regard to the construction of voice, Greenwald foregrounds voice production in the film's sound regime. Voice is in fact central to Josephine's construction of Little Jo, a key element in her deception and disguise. Josephine not only must look like a man, albeit a peculiar one, she must sound like one too. Little Jo develops a male/masculine voice that is gruff, clipped, commanding, and unemotional. This is exemplified in the following scene.

> SHOT: *Two-shot long angle on Little Jo and Tinman. Tinman places a fork and knife in front of Little Jo. Little Jo sits stiffly, like a "rough-around-the-edges" man would.* "Thought the meal was supposed to be ready when I got home." *Tinman replies,* "I did not know what time. Tomorrow it will be ready." *Tinman rushes around in the background and then presents a plate of food to Little Jo. Little Jo takes a bite.* "Needs pepper."

Little Jo's voice is never polite, never hesitant, and never apologetic, and, to her discovery, it also has power and authority. When Frank Badger and his racist pack of friends attempt to lynch Tinman, Little Jo commands, "Cut him down, Frank!" Frank and his gang comply;

Little Jo is also wielding a pistol at them. Though Little Jo's male voice helps her to hide and to assert power, it also makes her more socially visible. As an educated, propertied white man, Little Jo is expected take on a leadership role in the community, something she is extremely reluctant to do. This hypervisibility is of course dangerous for Little Jo, as it is for Tinman. Greenwald also never completely silences Josephine's real voice, her feminine/female voice. We hear this voice sporadically, a reminder that Little Jo's masquerade is a tenuous, fragile construct. The key way Greenwald weaves in Little Jo's female voice is through voice-over narration via the letter-writing device.

Though Josephine has been banished from her home and civilized society, she maintains correspondence with her sister, Helen (Jenny Lynch), who is raising Little Jo's son as her own. The letters between the sisters offer Little Jo a connection to her former life as a society girl and her role as a mother, which she has been denied. The letter-writing device was a common trope of the Hollywood woman's film. Mary Ann Doane argued that devices such as letter writing in melodramas construct a presence-in-absence effect, which involves the heroine being separated from her object of desire.[129] The primary object of desire for Little Jo is her son, who represents her former feminine self. The letters also work as a device to build dramatic suspense, as their contents reveal the truth about Little Jo; their discovery is a danger. Doane argued that the woman's film "activates an entire apparatus of waiting, near misses, separations and accidental meetings."[130] Indeed, when her friend Percy accidentally reads one of Little Jo's letters to her sister, he turns against her, deeming Little Jo a whore, and then attempts to rape her. Little Jo's real female voice is rendered treacherous on Greenwald's frontier.

THOUSAND PIECES OF GOLD

Set on a nineteenth-century American frontier, *Thousand Pieces of Gold* is an adaptation of Ruthanne Lum McCunn's biography of Lalu/Polly Nathoy (Rosalind Chao), a real Chinese pioneer woman of the West who endured a difficult journey from slave girl to independent businesswoman. Overall, Kelly's film is working in the revisionist tradition and deploys the conventions of the Western and the melodrama. In Lalu, Kelly constructs a strong female figure of resistance and agency. Lalu's story begins in rural China, where her father, a starving farmer, sells her into slavery, though Lalu naively believes she is to be someone's wife in the new world. In figure 1.6, Lalu waits for her phantom husband while donning a bridal veil. In actuality, Lalu has been purchased as a saloon girl/prostitute by the callous Hong King (Michael Paul Chan), and finds herself in an Idaho mining town inhabited primarily by men, both Chinese and white. The only women in town appear to be prostitutes, although none are Chinese. The film's narrative conflicts and dramatic suspense are focalized around Lalu's victimization at the hands of Hong King. When Lalu discovers that she is to be "one hundred men's wife!" she resists and threatens suicide. Hong King doesn't want to lose his investment, so he reluctantly allows Lalu to work as his personal slave girl and concubine rather than a saloon whore. Along her journey to emancipation, Lalu becomes romantically involved with two different men, Jim (Dennis Dun), a Chinese immigrant who works for Hong King, and Charlie Beamus (Chris Cooper), a white Civil War veteran. With the help of Charlie, Lalu finally manages to escape Hong King after Charlie wins her in a card game. However, despite Charlie's seemingly chivalrous act, Lalu refuses the damsel-in-distress role and rejects Charlie's sexual and romantic advances. Lalu will not trade one master for another, even if Charlie is nicer. Lalu hence saves herself, on her own terms. Lalu will

FIGURE 1.6 Lalu, *Thousand Pieces of Gold.*

develop feelings for Charlie but only after she has established successful laundry and boarding house businesses and Charlie has stopped drinking. In the end, Lalu will end up saving Charlie after he is shot by anti-Chinese protestors. Hence, Kelly's film resists falling into a colonial discourse of "white men saving brown women from brown men."[131]

Kelly foregrounds the silencing and suppression of the female voice throughout the film. As a Chinese woman in the English-speaking American West, Lalu discovers that learning the white man's language is essential to her survival, especially with regard to resisting sexual exploitation and gaining financial independence. In fact, it is not until Lalu learns to speak like the white demons that she finds the tools for resistance and agency. Lalu's lovers, Jim and Charlie, are the first to teach her English words. The two words Lalu will use as her mantra throughout her enslavement to Hong King are *no whore*. Here Kelly seems to be espousing the "No means no" slogan of the antirape campaign of the women's movement. These words have power. When Lalu speaks Chinese it is misunderstood and rendered useless. Even the letters Lalu writes to her family in China are never answered, signaling a kind of communication breakdown and a severing of her former life and identity. After Lalu learns the white demons' language, she establishes a successful laundry business and secures a job as manager and cook of a boarding house.

Kelly structures the drama through Lalu's female desiring gaze. In stark contrast to the oppressive and predatory Hong King, Lalu's male lovers, Jim and Charlie, are depicted as more passive males who do not assert their dominance over Lalu; they in fact often acquiesce to Hong King, even when they disagree with him. Though both men want to buy Lalu from Hong King (Charlie manages to win her), Kelly manages to subvert their gaze and render them as passive. As a poor Chinese immigrant, Jim is a powerless subaltern male who has a subservient position to Hong King. Without citizenship papers Jim is a vulnerable male, one with no permanent home. That vulnerability is dramatized near the end of the film in the sequence in which a gang of white male settlers drive all the Chinese people out of town. As a propertied white man, Charlie is not powerless, but he is depicted as weak or afflicted because he is an alcoholic Civil War vet, haunted by his traumatic experiences as a prisoner of war at the notorious Andersonville Prison.

Charlie's problems plague him so much that he has handed over the management of his saloon to Hong King. Afflicted males and alcoholism are common to the melodrama. Susan Hayward argued:

> Through a portrayal of masculinity in crisis, melodrama exposes masculinity's contradictions. The male either suffers from the inadequacies of his father (*Rebel Without a Cause*), or is in danger of extinction from his murderous or castrating father, or finally, he fails in his duty to reproduce (the family), or simply fails his family.[132]

Thomas Elsaesser identified the deployment of alcoholism as a key trope for masochism in the 1950s melodrama. Elsaesser argued:

> This typical masochism of melodrama, with its incessant acts of inner violation, its mechanisms of frustration and over-compensation, is perhaps brought most into the open through characters who have a drink problem (*Written on the Wind*, *Hilda Crane*, *Days of Wine and Roses*).[133]

Some scholars critiqued Kelly for erasing the issue of race in her film. Laura Hyun-Yi Kang argued that the film "allows a revisioning of U.S. history that not only incorporates but relies upon the dark, female body to redeem the American myth of manifest destiny and its white male actors."[134] Though Kang conceded that Kelly's film does not reproduce stereotypes of Asian women as either sexually licentious or dragon ladies, rooted in Orientalism, he did argue that a white male heterosexist gaze constructs the film's point of view and resolution. Kang saw Hong King as rooted in the racist stereotype of Chinese men as villainous traders of female bodies. I would concur with Kang here. Hong King is very one-dimensional and seems to be deployed as a convenient device, a foil for the heroine, typical of melodramatic plots. Kang took issue with the film for deploying the Asian female body as a way for men to assert power and territorial rights and critiqued Lalu's choice to stay with a white man, Charlie, over fleeing with the exiled Chinese at the end; Kang argued that this is a resolution rooted in white supremacy. I would concur that despite the fact Lalu is a disenfranchised subaltern woman, Kelly does not deploy an antiracist

and decolonizing lens. I do not entirely agree that a male gaze structures the film's point of view, however. Though Kelly seems ambivalent with regard to the role of race in the sexual objectification and
exploitation of a Chinese woman, she does not fall into the melodramatic trap of disavowing Lalu's desire, and she ensures that the white
men are not the film's heroes. Like Julie Dash's *Daughters of the Dust*,
Kelly's film was financed through the Public Broadcasting Service's
American Playhouse series, which emphasized the telling of distinctly
American stories from the margins. Kelly's re-visioning of the Western
renders Chinese people and culture visible in the frame. In many ways,
the Chinese community stands in as a substitute for indigenous people,
who are conspicuously absent on Kelly's frontier.

MY BRILLIANT CAREER

*This was a love story where a heroine turned the guy down. And
it seems quite strange now, but truly twenty-five years ago that
was like a completely radical thing to do—for the happy couple
not to end up together and for the woman to be the one who
actually made the decision. I remember Greater Union, they were
one of the investors, and who distributed the film in Australia,
and David Williams was the head of Greater Union, and in every
way was passionate about the film, but he was very nervous
when we were making it. I did have some meetings where he said
he wasn't sure about that ending. He felt it might make audiences
angry, and especially might make women angry. I said, David I
really believe in the end. People will understand Sybylla's point
of view when she says "not now." If you're a real romantic you
can believe, okay, well maybe she'll run into Harry in ten years'
time walking down a street in Paris, and there he'll be.*[135]

—Gillian Armstrong

Based on Miles Franklin's proto-feminist coming-of-age novel, *My
Brilliant Career* is structured around Sybylla Melvin's (Judy Davis)

journey from girlhood to womanhood, taking place over the course of a few years. While Sybylla dreams of having a brilliant career on the stage or in the world of literature and art, what her father calls dreams of grandeur, her impoverished family has other plans in store for her. As a result of circumstances beyond her control, Sybylla finds herself shipped from one place to another, garnering difficult life lessons along the way. The starting point for Sybylla's journey is Possum Gully, her family's drought-ridden farm. Sybylla is the eldest daughter in a large and ever-expanding family that can no longer afford to keep her; her despondent mother has arranged for Sybylla to go into "service." Fortunately, Sybylla is rescued from servitude when her wealthy maternal grandmother, Grandma Bossier (Aileen Britton), invites her to stay at Caddagat, a large estate and prosperous sheep station. Naively, Sybylla accepts the invitation, unaware that she is to be made ready for the marriage market. Despite her plain looks, her unconventional behavior, and her disinterest in marriage, the spirited Sybylla catches the attention of two eligible bachelors, Frank Hawdon (Robert Grubb), a stuffy Englishman, and Harry Beecham (Sam Neill), a dashing, wealthy sheep farmer. Sybylla and Harry are immediately attracted to each other. Because of Harry's attentions, Sybylla is invited to stay at Five-Bob Downs, a grand estate belonging to Harry's Aunt Gussie (Patricia Kennedy). It is here that Harry and Sybylla fall in love, although Sybylla's feelings are not enough for her to accept Harry's marriage proposal. Though Sybylla desires Harry, she needs time "to find out what's wrong with the world and me, who I am, everything." Meanwhile, Sybylla's father has dug himself further into debt, forcing Sybylla to leave the elegant and sophisticated world of Caddagat and Five-Bob Downs to work as a governess for the large McSwat family. Surrounded by pigs, muck, and screaming children, the uneducated McSwats are part of the Australian squattocracy, living roughly. Like Grandma Bossier, however, the McSwats deem Sybylla too much trouble, and they send her back to her family home, Possum Gully. Still in love, Harry tracks Sybylla down and proposes marriage again, and again Sybylla refuses, explaining that she would destroy him if they were to marry. Sybylla instead finishes her book. In figure 1.7, Sybylla reads aloud from her work in progress at Possum Gully.

FIGURE 1.7 Sybylla, *My Brilliant Career.*

Though under pressure from her distributors to deliver a happy-ever-after ending, Armstrong and her producer, Margaret Fink, were adamant that the ending of the film reflect the book. They believed that to do otherwise would have altered Franklin's feminist message. In doing this, Armstrong resisted the conventions of tragic romance and, hence, melodrama. Though Sybylla likes Harry, and possibly loves him (though she never declares that), her true desire is to find herself first; that is the driver of the film. All along Sybylla has been insisting that she doesn't want to be a wife and a mother, and when she refuses Harry for the final time, we realize that she means every word. Sybylla says to Harry in earnest:

> Maybe I'm ambitious, selfish. But I can't lose myself in somebody else's life when I haven't lived my own yet. I want to be a writer. At least I'm going to try. But I've got to do it now. And I've got to do it alone.

Sybylla's desire for independence is similar to the lone (male) hero trailblazing across uncharted territory. Armstrong frequently depicts Sybylla driving a horse-drawn carriage, perhaps symbolizing Sybylla's oft-stated desire to live her own life. For Sybylla, trailblazing is to be accomplished not by fighting wars or staking out a land claim but by finding her voice as a writer.

With regard to the construction of the female voice, Armstrong opens and concludes *My Brilliant Career* with Sybylla writing and reading from her autobiographical novel, which, she asserts unapologetically, is "all about *me*." Sybylla has to discover who *me* is as she takes on various personas throughout the film: bush farmer's daughter, debutante, lover, governess, and eventually writer. Through this discovery journey, Sybylla takes on various types of female voices across the class divide, discovering that none of them have much power. Sybylla realizes that to truly be a *me*, to become a full subject, she must never speak in any of these female voices. She finds herself by writing "all about me." The film is an indictment of the power of words and voice. Sybylla writes:

> So, now I've written it all down. Why? To try and make sense of it. It may come out sounding like a couple of nails in a rusty tin pot. My ineffectual life may be trod in the same round of toil. But I want to tell everyone about my own people. How I love them and pity them, pity us all.

In regard to the male voice, though, Armstrong exposes the gender inequity in a patriarchal system; male voices are accorded little power onscreen or offscreen. Sybylla's father never speaks in the film, though he has enormous power in her life. When he does appear in the frame, it is as a small figure in wide-angle landscape shots or on the periphery of the interior shots, sitting in a chair, looking haggard and exhausted. Armstrong renders Frank Hawdon a complete fool throughout the film; he speaks in a clipped upper-class British accent. Harry Beecham's voice is the only strong male voice in the film, although it never has the power of persuasion. When Harry does make his very earnest and emotional marriage proposal, Sybylla does not bend to his will. Even when he promises anything she wants, Sybylla can only reply with "I'd destroy you." Even Sybylla's Uncle Julius (Peter Whitford) is told to hold his tongue by his mother, the grand matriarch Grandma Bossier, with whom he still lives. Armstrong assigns authority to the female voices in the sound regimes of the film.

MY AMERICAN COUSIN

I think it's women who have the stories that come from the heart, and it's the women who are very committed and won't be stopped. I think women have a terrific sense of humour and we've always told stories among ourselves. Maybe we haven't had quite as much self-confidence as we'd like to have in telling our stories to a wider audience, but I think that's changing.[136]

—Sandy Wilson

Sandy Wilson's semi-autobiographical *My American Cousin* is set on a majestic mountainous Canadian landscape in 1959 British Columbia. Wilson's film is working in the revisionist tradition and is the only comedic film in this study. Wilson's coming-of-age story is told through the eyes of twelve-year-old Sandy Wilcox (Margaret Langrick), the eldest daughter in a large farming family struggling to make ends meet. Though the film is a fiction, it is based on Wilson's life growing up in British Columbia on Paradise Ranch, a working cherry farm (the film was shot on the actual property where Wilson lived with her family in the 1950s). The narrative revolves around Sandy's infatuation with Butch (John Wildman), her handsome American cousin, who has paid an unexpected visit, arriving in the middle of the night in a flashy red Cadillac convertible. Major Wilcox (Richard Donat), Sandy's father, is less than pleased about the sudden appearance of Butch and puts him to work in his cherry orchard in order to keep him out of trouble. Doing his best James Dean impersonation, the dreamy Butch immediately attracts the attention of all the young females in the area, including his younger cousin, Sandy. It doesn't take long for Butch to disrupt life at Paradise Ranch, bringing excitement and romance to a place where "nothing ever happens!"

In figure 1.8, Sandy meets the sexy Butch, and his red Cadillac, for the very first time at Paradise Ranch.

Wilson deploys the conventions of the Western, the maternal melodrama, and the teen romance, albeit through a comic lens. Though scenes are played out on the open roads amid a virginal, empty land,

FIGURE 1.8 Sandy and Butch, *My American Cousin.*

Wilson constructs the film's conflicts in the familial. Wilson in fact deploys frontier stereotypes as comedic devices. On one level, Sandy is a typical farmer's daughter to be kept virginal at all costs. However, Wilson depicts Sandy as a sexually curious teen who doggedly pursues her uninterested cousin. On the surface, Butch is a virile white American male who drifts into town, but beyond the facade he is actually a spoiled runaway teen who is dodging the consequences of having impregnated a girl back home; the Cadillac, in fact, belongs to his mother. Constructed through Sandy's gaze, Butch is rendered an object of near hysterical teenage female desire, not unlike the Hollywood stars Sandy moons over. Standing in for the local town patriarch is Sandy's father, Major Wilcox, a man who exudes defeat and tries in vain to protect his daughter from "cherry pickers" and keep order at Paradise Ranch, with middling results. Kitty Wilcox (Jane Mortifee), Sandy's mother, the seemingly maternal settler wife, spends most of her time absconding from household duties to rehearse her leading role in an amateur production of Ibsen's *Hedda Gabler*. Tensions arise between mother and daughter partially because of Kitty's hobby and her growing dependence on the rebellious Sandy to help out with the household and mind her younger siblings. Sandy, like her mother, spends most of the film escaping the confines of the home and all the responsibilities that come with it. This is a key conflict in the film.

Wilson foregrounds the female voice through various devices. The film is bookended with Sandy's voice-over narration, excerpts from her top-secret diary, which express her teenage thoughts and desires. However, the film is not exclusively constructed through a teenage vision. In fact, the film opens with a layering of different diegetic and nondiegetic female voices.

> SHOT: *Wide-angle bird's-eye-view shot on the isolated Wilcox home-stead at night, situated at the edge of a lake amid an epic British Columbia landscape. A woman's voice sings "Some Enchanted Evening." Camera zooms in to a closer view of the house. The sounds of children are heard. Sound bridge of Sandy's voice-over:* "Dear diary . . ."
>
> SHOT: *Close angle on a page from Sandy's diary. Sandy continues, "NOTHING EVER HAPPENS!" The words are printed out in big letters across the page. The camera zooms out to reveal Sandy sitting on her bed. The song "Some Enchanted Evening" continues playing off-screen. There is a sound bridge: Sandy's mother's voice says in an overly dramatic manner,* "From now on you have a hold over me!"
>
> SHOT: *Long take. Interior shot of Kitty, Sandy's mother, in her bathrobe turning down the lights and tidying up the living room area. She carries a script from Ibsen's* Hedda Gabler *in her hand. She walks determinedly toward the camera. The camera follows her as she approaches her husband, who is hunched over a calculator. Kitty says,* "John, you're always adding up numbers and we still never have any money." *John replies,* "Well, if it hadn't been so cold this winter we would have come out ahead this year." *Kitty yells at the kids to settle down. She turns her attention back to her husband and offers him a look of exasperation, perhaps meant for both the kids and him. Kitty walks away, leaving John to his calculator. Here the patriarch, "the Major," is framed sitting dejectedly in a chair hunched over his adding machine.*

The ironic use of the romantic song about love and enchantment subverts the idea of domestic bliss. Though Major Wilcox has a significant presence in the film, his voice is also attributed little power in the sound regimes of the film. He is apologetic, his voice lacking authority or confidence.

RE-VISIONING THE MYTH OF THE FRONTIER
THROUGH A DECOLONIZING LENS:
WHITE COMPLICITY

Loyalties and *The Wake* differ from both the revisionist and decolonizing deconstructive frontier women's films. Both tell hard-hitting
contemporary stories of colonial oppression of and violence against
indigenous peoples. As in the decolonizing deconstructive films of
Merata Mita, Julie Dash, and Tracey Moffatt, subaltern female points
of view and desire structure both of the films' looking relations and
voice construction, destabilizing a colonizing white masculinist gaze.
Like the revisionist films, both *Loyalties* and *The Wake* follow the rules
of classical narrative storytelling and adhere more strictly to genre
conventions. The major theme in both of these films is white complicity in the colonial oppression of indigenous peoples, and both feature
white-settler characters in major roles. Both Anne Wheeler and Norma
Bailey are white-settler filmmakers, and both had previously made
documentary films for the National Film Board of Canada about
the Métis community in Northern Canada. Similarly to Mita's *Mauri*,
the films are working in the social realist mode. Antithetical to the
Hollywood cinema, the social realist aesthetic privileges the everyday
in the frame. Like Mita, Wheeler and Bailey cast nonprofessionals
alongside professional actors and collaborated with indigenous communities. Bailey and Wheeler embrace Trinh T. Minh-ha's method
that speaks nearby, rather than for, subaltern women.

> A speaking that does not objectify, does not point to an object as if
> it is distant from the speaking subject or absent from the speaking
> place. A speaking that reflects on itself and can come very close to a
> subject without, however, seizing or claiming it. A speaking, in brief,
> whose closures are only moments of transition—these are forms of
> indirectness well understood by anyone in tune with poetic lan-
> guage. Every element constructed in a film refers to the world around
> it, while having at the same time a life of its own.[137]

Observing the conventions of Gothic melodrama, Wheeler and Bailey
structure the dramatic conflicts and suspense around a villain who
preys upon the vulnerable. Both films were penned by Sharon Riis and

follow a similar pattern, in which the villain takes the form of a white male figure of authority who is driven by dark and racist desires. In *Loyalties* the villain is a pedophile-rapist doctor, and in *The Wake* it is a racist Mountie. Both men wield their power not only over women and children but also over less powerful indigenous men. As in the Western, these white figures of authority exercise their power across frontier spaces, and they do so through acts of violence. Complicit white characters are privy to the amoral and criminal actions of these white villains, with whom they often have close bonds, and are consequently placed within a moral dilemma in which they must choose between loyalty to their own and doing the right thing.

LOYALTIES

I wanted to make some sort of statement on the history of women in the west, on the interdependence of women living in remote areas. I am not into films for the sake of making films. And I feel very strongly that if you are going to make a two-and-half-million dollar film, that you should be saying something.[138]

—Anne Wheeler

Wheeler sets *Loyalties* in the remote community of Lac La Biche in Northern Alberta, Canada. The narrative revolves around two women, Lily Sutton (Susan Wooldridge), a privileged British housewife, and Roseanne Ladouceur (Tantoo Cardinal), a Métis single mother struggling to make ends meet. We soon discover that Lily is trapped in an unhappy marriage. Though her husband, Dr. Sutton (Kenneth Welsh), oozes charm, he is emotionally distant toward his children and sexually uninterested in his beautiful wife. Overwhelmed with settling into a new house, an elegant cabin-style mansion, and the demands of motherhood, Lily begs her diffident husband to find her help. He reluctantly agrees and hires Roseanne, whom he has treated for injuries incurred from a beating at the hands of her drunken Métis boyfriend, Eddy (Tom Jackson). Divided by race and class, the two women initially do not get along. However, Lily soon comes to depend on the tough-as-nails Roseanne, a self-proclaimed bigmouth. Isolated and depressed, Lily turns to Roseanne for advice, and the two women become chummy. Their friendship, however, is tenuous because Lily harbors a shameful secret about her emotionally distant husband—the very reason the Suttons have fled England for the backwoods of Canada.

Loyalties is primarily working in the melodrama and Gothic thriller traditions to destabilize tropes of the frontier myth-narrative, particularly with regard to indigenous peoples. The story revolves around two troubled families, the Suttons, an upper-middle-class British family, and the Ladouceurs, a Métis family. As is typical of melodrama, both families are under duress. The Suttons are experiencing marital problems, although these are rooted in criminality and sexual deviance. Roseanne and her boyfriend, Eddy, father of two of her children, have split up because of Eddy's alcoholism and violence, rooted in his disenfranchisement as an indigenous man. Wheeler and Riis parallel both families explicitly, and we are positioned to see the Ladouceurs as the more normal family of the two, although she avoids romanticizing them. When Lily visits Roseanne in her small, rustic home, which she shares with her mother, Beatrice (Vera Martin), Lily remarks about the simple surroundings, "Oh, it's so nice here." Roseanne cuts Lily's sentiment with a wisecrack: "You gonna make a speech about the happy poor next?"

The two families have mirror trajectories but in reverse of each other. As Roseanne and Eddy resolve their issues, the Suttons draw further apart, the horrible truth driving a wedge between them, culminating in a horrific climax in which Dr. Sutton rapes Roseanne's thirteen-year-old daughter, Leona (Diane Debassige). Wheeler positions the white-settler family as not only dysfunctional but also dangerous to indigenous women. In contrast, Roseanne and Eddy's relationship is normalized despite their difficulties and their casual living arrangement. This is depicted in the scene in which Roseanne and Eddy make future plans together, in between their lovemaking. The love scene is shot in one long take; Wheeler resists the typical shot-reverse-shot technique used in love scenes. The long take is often used as a democratic shooting device, resisting the privileging of one gaze over the other. It is a filming technique common to documentary realist aesthetics.[139]

SHOT: *Medium-close angle on two photographs attached to a bedroom mirror; one is of Eddy. The camera pan-tilts down along the wall. Roseanne's voice is heard off-screen.* "The only difference between her and me is money. But, what a hell of a difference. Maybe I should go back to school too." *Eddy laughs off-screen.* "And take what? How to keep your mouth shut 101." *Eddy laughs again. The camera pauses on Roseanne and Eddy in bed together. She wears his shirt; he is bare chested. Roseanne playfully punches him.* "Shut up about my mouth!" *Eddy laughs again. He leans in for a kiss.* "I love your mouth." *They kiss. Roseanne gazes at him.* "Are you going to stop asking me, Eddy?" *Eddy replies,* "What's the matter now?" *She says,* "The problem between you and me." *Eddy seductively leans over Roseanne.* "I don't see no problem." *Roseanne says,* "I'm going to go talk to Mavis at the bar. And if she'll give me my job back, I'm going to take it." *Eddy stops his lovemaking and flops back onto the pillow. He takes a drag on his cigarette.* "Why? I make enough money." *Roseanne explains,* "Because I want to. I like it. In all these years we've been together, Eddy, I've never fooled around on you once. So, what's the big deal?" *Eddy thinks about it. Roseanne sits up. Eddy turns to her.* "I'll give it a try, Rose. But you've got to stop putting me down all the time. You gotta stop telling me and everyone else what a loser I am." *Roseanne thinks about it.* "I'll give it a try, Edward." *They embrace and return to their lovemaking.*

Wheeler depicts Eddy sympathetically as a displaced and marginalized masculine subaltern figure. As an undereducated and unemployed Métis man, Eddy copes through alcohol and violence. Like the male indigenous characters in *Mauri* and *Bedevil*, Eddy has been rendered as a criminalized other who has no legitimate identity, even as a father and a provider. In truth, Eddy has no self-worth, and why should he? He's been reduced to just another drunk Indian in the eyes of society and even in the eyes of Roseanne, who has been brutalized by his violence. Despite his violent past, Roseanne does not fear Eddy; he's not the real threat to her. Dr. Sutton is the figure to be feared.

With regard to Gothic thriller tropes, Wheeler opens her film with a distorted dark hand-held shot of a house, the Sutton home in England. Rain pelts down on Robert, Lily's son (Christopher Barrington-Leigh), who approaches the house tentatively. Robert doesn't enter but sneaks up to the window to peer inside, where he sees his father and a female in the midst of physical struggle. It is not clear what is happening, but it is evident from the crashing and the voices that an act of violence is taking place (we will learn later that Robert witnessed a rape). Wheeler and Riis depict Dr. Sutton as a Bluebeard or vampire figure who preys upon innocent virgins; this explains why he has no sexual interest in his wife. Wheeler constructs Dr. Sutton's sexually predatory gaze as a deviant, although powerful, one. Wheeler emphasizes the vampire parallel by opening the film's final rape sequence with a movie clip from *Dracula*, starring Bela Lugosi, which Leona is watching on television at the Sutton home, where she is babysitting. Though Lily Sutton seems the typical settler wife and mother, representing civilization and culture (this is emphasized by her upper-class English accent), Wheeler and Riis render her into a Bluebeard's helpmate, enabling her husband's sexually deviant and criminal behavior by her silence. Wheeler stages Lily's disturbing acceptance of her helpmate role in the following scene.

> SHOT: *Medium angle on a full-length bedroom mirror. Lily enters the frame with her hair in pigtails, wearing a silk nightgown. Lily contemplates her reflection. She kneels down and adjusts her childlike hairstyle. She leans in closer to examine her face and is startled by the sound of a door opening. She turns self-consciously. When she turns back to her reflection, she is suddenly disgusted with herself. Afraid of being seen, she hastily pulls out the pigtails and shakes her hair out. She then scampers away from the mirror as if afraid to look at herself any longer. Thunder strikes ominously.*

Wheeler deploys Lily's disturbing silent gesture as the unspeakable truth about her marriage to Dr. Sutton and, more shockingly, that she *knows*. Lily not only tries to see herself through her husband's perverted male gaze; she passively resigns herself to remaining invisible and silent. In this moment Wheeler positions Lily not as a downtrodden wife but as an enabler who is too weak and frightened to do anything about it. With Lily depicted as complicit, our identification and empathy shift to Roseanne.

Wheeler and Riis position Roseanne, an indigenous woman, as the moral center of the narrative and construct Roseanne's voice and gaze as the normal one, empowering her in the visual and sound regimes of the film. Though Roseanne and her family are victimized by colonial oppression and violence, they are not victims. In stark contrast to Lily, Roseanne has a strong voice and an intimidating gaze, a gaze that stares down Dr. Sutton's lecherous ogling despite her second-class status as an Indian. Throughout the film, characters, including Roseanne herself, refer to her big mouth and tendency to boss everyone around. Roseanne is always good for a wisecrack, a sarcastic comment, and the hard truth. When Lily accuses Roseanne of flirting with her husband, Roseanne exclaims in disgust, "I wouldn't touch that creep with a crowbar!" At this point in the film we realize there is something strange about Dr. Sutton. Wheeler and Riis position Roseanne's big mouth as the voice of authority, one that can express a number of hard truths for us and for Lily. In contrast, Lily is unable to speak any truths, even when her despondent son brings up the forbidden topic and displays outward hatred toward his father. In the aftermath of Sutton's brutal rape of Leona, Roseanne turns to Lily and screams, "What kind of woman are you?! Bitch!" Moments later, a traumatized Roseanne will attempt to seek vengeance on Lily's husband (see figure 1.9). Fortunately, Lily stops Roseanne from committing murder, although it is not initially clear who she is protecting.

FIGURE 1.9 Roseanne, *Loyalties.*

Here Roseanne articulates the question we are all asking in that sickening and horrifying moment. How could Lily have remained silent about Sutton's sexual violence for so long? Here Roseanne's voice damns Lily for her complicity, forcing Lily to wake up. And it will be Roseanne's big mouth that is given authority by the justice system (two white cops) at the end of the film, albeit with the aid of Lily.

SHOT: *Police officers' point of view on the front door of Beatrice's home. Roseanne opens the door and walks proudly onto the front porch. The police officer's voice-off:* "Roseanne . . . Ladouceur?" *Roseanne looks at the policeman sardonically.* "Think I changed my name, Marvin?"

SHOT: *Over-the-shoulder shot from Roseanne's point of view. The two police officers look at each other awkwardly.* "We had a complaint . . . uh . . . Mrs. Sutton . . ."

SHOT: *Medium two-shot on Roseanne, with Beatrice in the background. The policeman continues talking.* ". . . Lily Sutton?" *Roseanne replies with a shaky voice,* "Yeah." *He continues:* "Well, she says that . . . the complaint is that . . . her husband . . . that is Dr. David Sutton . . . sexually assaulted your daughter last night." *Roseanne and Beatrice stand there dumbfounded. The policeman continues,* "Now as you may be aware . . ." *Roseanne closes her eyes.* "A spouse is not entitled under the law to press charges against a marriage partner when . . . uh, the incident involves a third party. In other words, Mrs. Sutton cannot lay charges against Dr. Sutton, but she suggested that you . . ." *Roseanne nods her head, tears coursing down her tired, distraught face.* ". . . might be willing to lay charges?" *Roseanne nods her head. She says, simply,* "Yeah." *The policeman asks,* "Yes? Yes?" *Roseanne nods her head.*

SHOT: *Wide angle on Beatrice's property. Roseanne's voice-off:* "Yes."

It is in this moment that Roseanne's voice, her words, have the power to defeat Dr. Sutton, to fell the monster. Lily is vindicated for us because she has finally done the right thing, shifting her allegiance from her depraved husband to Roseanne. Lily's female gaze and voice shift from a colonizing masculine logic to a decolonizing one. Wheeler and Riis turn the "white men saving brown women from brown men" colonial script[140] on its ear.

THE WAKE

[For the Daughters of the Country *series of films about Métis women] I developed the ideas from reading the history. . . . I said, OK, I'll make these fictitious people and this is what they're going to do.[141]*

—Norma Bailey

The Wake is one of four television dramas that made up the *Daughters of the Country* series (1987), financed and distributed by the National Film Board of Canada, intended to "re-open the history books to document the evolution of the Métis people."[142] A white-settler filmmaker, Norma Bailey produced the entire series and also directed *The Wake.* Set in Northern Alberta in 1985, the narrative revolves around two Métis women, Joan Laboucane (Victoria Snow), a hardworking single mother, and Donna (Diane Debassige), Joan's troubled teenage cousin. The key conflict in the film is structured around Joan's controversial romance with Jim (Timothy Webber), a white Royal Canadian Mounted Police (RCMP) officer.

Joan meets Jim on the night Donna purposely locks herself and her younger siblings inside their house after their mother, Cora, is taken to a hospital for diabetic shock and alcoholism; Cora also makes ends meet as a sex worker. Donna's act of rebellion is really a desperate last resort to foil social services and keep her sisters and brothers together. In order to get Donna to open the door, Joan is sent for by the RCMP, who have aggressively surrounded Donna's small, ramshackle house. Before Joan has a chance to talk to Donna, however, one of the RCMP officers, Crawford (Frank Adamson), belligerently kicks down the door, knocking the frightened Donna to the ground. Despite Donna's efforts, her siblings are placed in foster care, and she is sent to live with Joan, who has agreed to act as her guardian until Cora is better. In figure 1.10, a frantic Donna comforts her younger sibling while she

FIGURE 1.10 Donna (center), her younger sibling, and Joan, *The Wake*.

and Joan negotiate with a white social worker (out of frame). The next day, Jim, a rookie Mountie, feeling guilty about Crawford's brutal actions, formally apologizes to Joan, who is taken aback. "I've never gotten an apology from a cop before." Joan is charmed by Jim's chivalry and good, albeit naive, intentions "to do some good around here" and enters into a relationship with him. Donna, however, mistrusts Jim and feels betrayed by Joan for her choice in men. In fact, no one in the extended family is very happy about "Joanie's Mountie." Despite familial criticisms, Joan continues her relationship with Jim, prompting Donna to move in with her great-grandmother, Kookum, who lives off the land. Jim's stress at work intensifies, and though he feels uneasy about Crawford's blatant racism ("They're not like you and me"), he is unable to stand up against it. Jim's loyalties to Joan will be put to the test when he becomes complicit in the tragic deaths of four Métis teens.

Bailey and Riis deploy the conventions of the Western, melodrama, and romance genres to render visible white complicity in the colonial oppression of indigenous peoples. Bailey constructs white complicity in the figure of Jim, the RCMP officer. In many ways, Jim functions as the contemporary version of the lone Western hero, a cop substituting for a cowboy. Jim's partner, Officer Crawford, a racist bully, is the bad guy who obsessively patrols the roads, seemingly looking for opportunities to harass and beat up on Indians. Bailey and Riis are evoking the sympathetic or pro-Indian Western in which the viewer empathizes with indigenous peoples. The difference here is that there will be no white male hero riding to the rescue, as epitomized in Kevin Costner's *Dances with Wolves* (1990). Most Western narratives are driven by the good guy/bad guy dichotomy, but Bailey dismantles such binaries. Though Jim is positioned as the good cop to Crawford's bad cop, he is part of the problem, representing colonial oppressive power as an RCMP officer. As in Mita's *Mauri* and Moffatt's *Bedevil*, indigenous peoples have a deep distrust for and aversion to the police; the RCMP and indigenous peoples have a troubled relationship, going back to unhonored land treaties. The problematic history of the RCMP and indigenous peoples haunts the film and the relationship between Joan and her Mountie. Jim is the male version of Lily in *Loyalties*, passively bearing witness to acts of violence against more vulnerable people and not doing anything about it. On Bailey and Riis's contemporary frontier there is no space for good (white) guys. Jim wants to protect his job more than he wants to protect Joan, her children, or Donna and her friends. Like Wheeler, Bailey and Riis never represent the Métis characters as voiceless victims, and they resist the stereotypes of the noble savage, Indian princess, and squaw.

Bailey foregrounds the Métis (subaltern) voice and gaze in the film's visual and sound regimes. Similarly to Roseanne's role in *Loyalties*, Joan and Donna are positioned as morally superior to their white counterparts and adversaries, the Mounties, Jim and Crawford. When Joan learns that Jim is implicated in the tragic deaths of four Métis teens, Donna's close friends, she gives him advice on how he should do the right thing. Though Joan seems to be slipping into the Indian princess (Pocahontas) role, in which she comes to the aid of a white male figure of authority, Bailey and Riis do not fall into the romantic plot trap; Jim will not get off that easily.

JOAN: "You've got to make out a report. God, it's going to be hell to pay from both sides. But you can do it. I'll help you."

JIM: "Joannie, I . . . I can't do that. I can't. I can't make some kind of public statement. That would be the end of me, and Crawford . . . Look, it was a terrible, terrible thing that happened, but me making some kind of public statement isn't going to bring those kids back!" *Joan pulls away from Jim.* "All that'll happen is that I'll lose my job. It's everything I ever wanted."

JOAN: *Shocked, she turns and glares at Jim with disbelief and disgust. She spits at his feet and walks out the door.*

Here Bailey frames Joan as the empowered one, with a condemning female voice and gaze. When Jim refuses to step up and do the right thing, Joan walks away from him—for herself, her children, and her community. Jim is left alone, cowering like a child on his living room floor, overcome with shame and white guilt. On Bailey's frontier there will be no forgiveness given to white oppressors. Bailey cuts to the wake for the four dead teens Crawford has essentially murdered. Though the scene is heartbreaking, Joan and her family have not been defeated. In the final scene of the film, Joan's grandmother, Kookum, imparts her wisdom about surviving as an indigenous person, spoken in her mother tongue.

SHOT: *Three-shot of Joan, Donna, and Kookum weeping together. The women have wrapped their arms around one another. Donna's mother, Cora, hovers at the very edge of the frame, only partially in the shot.* Kookum says, "Don't take it so hard. These things have happened before. That's why we all have to be brave and love one another while we're together on this earth." *(This dialogue is captioned.)*

Kookum's are the last spoken words of the film, giving the female indigenous voice authority.

CONCLUSION

Chapter 1 asked, What constitutes a feminist text, and what is its method of production? Though all these films were working within the narrative feature format and deployed the codes and conventions of the Western and the melodrama, the filmmakers constructed their feminist stories of female emancipation and resistance against oppressive forces of power in differing ways. Two different narrative models were deployed across this corpus of films, revisionism and deconstruction. Working within and across these narrative models, the films evoked many of the key second-wave feminist debates about the role of women's storytelling in political mobilization. In many ways, these films were ahead of their time, modeling innovative methods of production in women's cinema and even cinema as a whole.

The deconstruction films—*Daughters of the Dust, Mauri,* and *Bedevil*—told harrowing and traumatic stories of indigenous and black women struggling against colonial and gender oppression. Their deconstructive practices included nonlinear narrative structures and distanciation, espoused by many feminist film theorists of the 1970s, mainly Laura Mulvey and Teresa de Lauretis, who turned to the avant-garde film as *the* model for feminist cinema. And yet, though these films evoked the work of those theorists, they were also answering another call, one voiced by antiracist and anticolonial feminist theorists. By integrating culturally specific and ancient storytelling practices and rituals (e.g., African griot in *Daughters, waitia* in *Mauri*) with cinematic language, these films constructed an oppositional gaze[143] and spoke to a female subaltern spectator[144] through a multivoiced narrative.[145] Through these methods, the films deployed the conventions of the female melodrama and Gothic melodrama to tell authentic stories of subaltern families battling colonial exploitation and violence, evoking the work of earlier African American filmmakers such as Oscar Micheaux. These films modeled Peter Brooks's idea that melodrama as a form could speak covertly about the unspeakable through expressive visual signs (cinematic language). Through these methods, the filmmakers rendered visible indigenous and black women's voices, countering dominant frontier myth-histories, particularly the Western. Faye Ginsburg identified this practice as screening out trauma. Ginsburg argued:

> Obviously, I didn't invent this phrase made famous by Sigmund Freud, to talk about the way people screen out trauma with other

memories that replace or cover over an experience that's unbearable for them to actually recollect. Instead, in Indigenous communities in which people have experienced enormous historical trauma, disruption, dislocation, genocidal practices and more, the trauma is two-fold. It's in the initial event of colonial contact that has been so violent and degrading, but then it's in the denial of that trauma. What you see again and again is that one of the first things that people want to do is recuperate those histories, to tell those stories, to make sure those stories are told, to honour their dead, to honour what has happened to them. Literacy may not be widespread in these communities, but oral performance is a kind of idiom that people know well.[146]

Being the first narrative feature films to be directed by black and indigenous women, the films also modeled a new kind of women's cinema, a decolonizing women's cinema in a first world context, predating Barry Barclay's idea of a fourth cinema.

The revisionist films—*The Piano*, *My American Cousin*, *My Brilliant Career*, *Thousand Pieces of Gold*, and *The Ballad of Little Jo*—answered Claire Johnston's 1973 call for feminists to embrace the entertainment film. Aimed at a more commercial market, these films adhered more strictly to storytelling traditions of the classical narrative cinema with an emphasis on one central heroic protagonist, a three-act structure, dramatic arcs, and happy endings. In spite of these constraints, these films managed to foreground female voices through an active desiring female subject. They would have passed the Bechdel test.[147] One could argue that these five films picked up where female directors of the woman's film of the 1930s and 1940s, such as Dorothy Arzner, left off, but without the burdens of working within a masculinist Hollywood studio environment or under the heterosexist rigidity of the dreaded Hays Code. Though none of these women's films explicitly constructed a lesbian gaze, it could be argued that they queered the straight male gaze. These films evoked Gayle Rubin, Adrienne Rich, Monique Wittig, and Luce Irigaray, who advocated for intense bonds between women, especially mothers and daughters, and for female desire outside the confines of "a male sexual purlieu."[148] This female desire was foregrounded in the film's sound regimes, in which female voices were privileged and male voices were silenced. All of the films deployed voice-over narration as a storytelling device, evoking the work of Kaja Silverman on the female voice in cinema, disrupting "the specular regime upon which dominant cinema relies; it would put her beyond the reach of the male gaze (which stands in here for the cultural 'camera') and release her voice from the signifying obligations which that gaze enforces."[149]

These films, however, were delimited in their re-visioning of white-settler frontier myth-histories, either because they ignored race and colonial structures of power or because they followed racist scripts. Though *Thousand Pieces* featured a Chinese woman, the film did not comprehensively deploy an oppositional or decolonizing gaze. In a number of these films, indigenous peoples were deployed as devices or were conspicuously absent from the frame, falling into the trap of the vanishing Indian myth-history.

Loyalties and *The Wake* straddled deconstruction and revisionism. As revisionist narratives, they followed a linear structure and were focalized around a central protagonist, although *Loyalties* featured two female protagonists. Bailey and Wheeler deploy a decolonizing lens in their depictions of the struggles of subaltern women and communities, focalizing their narratives around indigenous trauma. Wheeler deployed the codes of Gothic melodrama to depict Dr. Sutton as a white rapist (beast in the boudoir) who preys on indigenous girls. *The Wake* destabilized iconic frontier tropes of the Western, particularly the heroic Mountie figure, a rugged lone white male, who committed heinous acts of violence against indigenous children and youth. Their decolonizing gaze was rooted in a social realist tradition, which rejects romanticism and glamorization, what Mulvey would have called spectacle and visual pleasure, embracing a key tenet of the counter-cinema.

2

DEBUNKING THE CULT OF TRUE WOMANHOOD/MOTHERHOOD ON THE FRONTIER

I think a lot of women's major creative energies have gone into bringing up children. I personally believe that it is a huge commitment to bring a life onto the earth, and that's probably one of the reasons why in a business as taxing as the film business there are so few women directors.[1]

—Gillian Armstrong

Nineteenth-century colonial discourses which drew distinctions between primitive/barbarous societies and civilized/Christian ones allocated a special place to white women as bearers of culture, morality and order.[2]

—Marilyn Lake

Nanny knows that being treated as "mules uh de world" lies at the heart of Black women's oppression. As dehumanized objects, mules are living machines and can be treated as part of the scenery. Fully human women are less easily exploited.[3]

—Patricia Hill Collins

ONE OF THE key strategies these ten filmmakers deploy for reimagining and reconstructing feminist frontiers is to destabilize or decolonize the cult of true (white) womanhood/motherhood on the frontier, a key trope of dominant frontier myth-history narratives. As mentioned in chapter 1, though the frontier in the Western has been a historically masculine space, it is a genre that has depended heavily on particular tropes of femininity. Jane Tompkins argues that the Western depicted the (American) frontier as a "womanless milieu" rooted in an aversion to "women's discourse and the feminine."[4] In the 1960s, historian Barbara Welter argued that the cult of true womanhood was a Christian discursive construct rooted in four traits: piety, purity, submissiveness, and domesticity, personified in the angel in the house. "Put them all together and they spelled mother, daughter, sister, wife-woman. Without them, no matter whether there was fame, achievement, or wealth, all was ashes. With them she was promised happiness and power."[5] According to Welter, "Purity was as essential as piety to a young woman, its absence as unnatural and unfeminine. Without it she was, in fact, no woman at all, but a member of some lower order. A 'fallen woman' was a 'fallen angel,' unworthy of the celestial company of her sex."[6] In 1942, British writer and feminist Virginia Woolf urged women everywhere to kill this "intensely sympathetic" and "utterly unselfish" angel in the house figure.[7]

Many second-wave feminists, such as Betty Freidan, Shulamith Firestone, Gayle Rubin, Dorothy Dinnerstein, Adrienne Rich, Jane Lazarre, and Nancy Chodorow, argued that the angel in the house figure was a patriarchal construct masked as biological and natural in order to keep women powerless and exploitable for their productive and reproductive labor.[8] They advocated for society to dispense with gender stereotypes, particularly around motherhood, which divided men and women into rigid boxes. However, these gender boxes were not easily eradicated because the economies of modern industrialized capitalist nations were highly dependent on a private/public dichotomy.

Marxist feminists argued that women's work, unpaid domestic labor, was necessary not only for the survival of the nuclear family unit but also for the survival of the economy as a whole. Male workers could be fully exploitable only if they had dependents they were expected to provide for. Hence, the patriarchal family was a construct that was not natural but was beneficial to male members of the ruling class, rendering men dependent on a paycheck and women dependent on a man. In turn, women's work such as housework, child care, and food production was rendered naturally feminine and in the process was rendered completely invisible. In *More Than a Labour of Love*, historian Meg Luxton argued that because women's work has always been performed out of love for their families, it was often deemed natural to being a woman. Luxton argued that housework was not quantitatively considered work and hence not measurable as productive labor, rendering it invisible. This invisibility and naturalness rendered women's work endless and hence more exploitable within the economy.[9] This is why "women who perform both wage labour and domestic labour have been described as 'working wives' or 'working mothers,' as if to deny that what they do in the home is also work."[10] Economist Marilyn Waring argued that the exploitation of women's unpaid reproductive labor has been enabled by a sexist system of national accounting based on the private/public binary, rendering invisible not only the domestic labor of women but also women as subjects. "The people who are visible to you as contributors to the economy are the people who will be visible when you make policy."[11] Waring advocated for a new qualitative economic model rather than a quantitative one in order to render visible women's work; it is only through visibility that women can ever hope to attain full equity in society.[12]

In dominant frontier myth-history narratives, the angel in the house figure appears in the form of the settler wife and mother or (virginal) daughter, representing civilization, domesticity, Christianity (Protestantism), and white frontier femininity. Examining the eighteenth-century Canadian writings of the Strickland sisters, British émigrés, Elizabeth Thompson identified the figure of the pioneer woman archetype, who was both a lady and a hard worker willing to rough it in order to help make her husband's or father's farm a success. According to Thompson, through a ladylike code and a labor of love, the good pioneer woman was deployed by colonial forces of power to civilize masculinist frontier spaces plagued by marauding males prone to drinking, gambling, and violence, not to mention miscegenation.[13] The good pioneer woman figure appears in popular settler narratives such as Laura Ingalls Wilder's autobiographical Little House on the Prairie book series and the subsequent television series (1974–1982).[14] If there was ever an angel figure on the American frontier, it was the long-suffering, industrious, and lovely settler mother Ma Ingalls. Laura Ingalls (Wilder), the plucky daughter (and author), embodied a more modern version of white frontier girlhood and womanhood, one with desires and ambitions that operated outside of domesticity, although not exclusively.

The figure of the good pioneer woman was also rooted in the Madonna/whore dichotomy, which divided women into two groups: good girls, who had sex only for procreative purposes, and bad girls, who engaged in sex outside of marriage or in sex work. In response to this rigid patriarchal construct, second-wave feminists addressed the role of sex for pleasure in female emancipation, although this proved to be a divisive issue, and the "sex wars" ensued. Anglo-American feminists were generally divided into two groups, the antipornography feminists and the pro-sex feminists. Though all feminists saw the necessity of dismantling and re-visioning traditional codes and rules of sexuality rooted in heterosexist patriarchy, they did not see eye to eye on how sexual desire, pleasure, and identity should operate within gender relations. These feminists were generally divided on the issues of censorship and sexuality laws.

The antipornography feminists focused their arguments on sexual exploitation of and violence against women and sought to change laws. These feminists argued that patriarchy was rooted in men's predatory sexual behavior and was a key source of women's oppression, and gender equity was impossible when women were placed in submissive, passive, or servile positions in the sex act. This aspect of patriarchy was epitomized in, and in fact dependent upon, the institutions of pornography and prostitution, which sexually objectified women and girls. As feminist activist and political theorist Robin Morgan famously said, "Pornography is the theory, rape is the practice."[15] Andrea Dworkin referred to pornography as "a kind of nerve center of abuse." Spearheading the antipornography movement with *Pornography: Men Possessing Women*, Dworkin argued that porn and prostitution normalized heterosexual male desire as predatory and violent, which encouraged and incited rape.[16] Dworkin, along with Catharine MacKinnon,[17] sought to outlaw pornography because it violated women's civil and human rights.[18] This resulted in harsh fines and constraints to all producers of content featuring sexually explicit material, including lesbian-produced erotica and porn, consumed by women, leaning dangerously close to a right-wing conservative agenda.

The antipornography feminists were accused of essentializing hetero-sexual male desire as predatory and violent. And the correlation be-tween porn consumption and sexual violence against women has never been proven conclusively.

In contrast, the pro-sex feminists did not aim to change laws or moral rules about sex. They argued that sexual desire and pleasure were a fundamental aspect of women's subjectivity, and they rejected placing restrictions on sexual acts or rigidly defining correct pleasure. Referred to as the "anything goes" feminists, they supported sado-masochism, commercial sex between adults, porn, and intergenera-tional consensual adult sex, arguing that these sexual practices were not inherently negative for, or oppressive to, women. Female submis-sion and passivity in the sex act did not necessarily lead to women's victimization and exploitation, and they were a potential source of sexual pleasure and fulfillment. Deploying the seminal work of phi-losopher and social theorist Michel Foucault, namely *The History of Sexuality* (1976), Gayle Rubin identified these regulatory laws as rooted in sex negativity, which permeated all modern Western Christian culture and was the foundation for a sexual value system in which human sexuality had been compartmentalized into good and natural sex versus bad and abnormal sex.[19]

> Western cultures generally consider sex to be a dangerous, destruc-tive, negative force. . . . Most Christian traditions, following Paul, hold that sex is inherently sinful. It may be redeemed if performed within marriage for procreative purposes and if the pleasurable aspects are not enjoyed too much. In turn, this idea rests on the assumption that the genitalia are an intrinsically inferior part of the body, much lower and less holy than the mind, the "soul," the heart, or even the upper part of the digestive system (the status of the excre-tory organs is close to that of the genitalia). Such notions have by now acquired a life of their own and no longer depend solely on reli-gion for their perseverance.[20]

In conjunction with the pro-sex feminists, the French feminists exam-ined how women and the feminine had been othered within a West-ern patriarchal phallocentric language. They advocated for women to embrace the female body, understood and experienced outside of masculine parameters. Irigaray argued that "woman has sex organs just about everywhere. She experiences pleasure almost everywhere."[21] Generally speaking, however, the French feminists, such as Julia Kristeva and Hélène Cixous, advocated for a maternal female body rather than a sexual one.

Antiracist feminists argued that the sex wars for subaltern women were much more complex. In colonial white-settler societies, the Madonna/whore dichotomy was deployed by colonial forces of power to oppress subaltern women, who could never be angels on the frontier. The good pioneer woman was a figure steeped in not only sexual purity but also whiteness, and she has also served as a key trope to render subaltern women economically and sexually exploitable. Vron Ware argued that the presence of white women in colonial contexts was intrinsic to the construction of white-settler societies, which were dependent upon the exploitation of subaltern women. Ware asserted:

> Gender played a crucial role in organizing ideas of "race" and "civilization", and women were involved in many different ways in the expansion and maintenance of the Empire. The presence of white women, for example, demanded that relations between the "races" be highly regulated. The increasing number of white women who travelled out to join their husbands and families in the colonies, or to work in their own right as missionaries, nurses and teachers, often had far-reaching effects on the social lives of male settlers, and consequently on the status and sexual exploitation of black women.[22]

Anticolonial scholar Enakshi Dua argued that national discourses about white British femininity are possible only through the casting of subaltern women as imagined dark others and low-paid workers.[23] The public/private split was not a reality for subaltern women because frontier economies were highly dependent on their labor. Unlike the farmwife's and farm daughter's unpaid, invisible labor of love in the patriarchal settler family unit, subaltern women's labor was frequently practiced outside the domestic sphere and was strongly associated with slavery, low-paid servile employment, and sex work. Unlike white women, black women's reproductive duties were never tied to their natural role as women but rather to their place as exploitable commodity objects for their white masters' profit and sexual pleasure. Patricia Hill Collins argued that "African-American women's experiences as mothers have been shaped by the dominant group's efforts to harness Black women's sexuality and fertility to a system of capitalist exploitation."[24] As property, slave women were routinely forced to part with their children, and so there was no economic benefit for slave owners to allow their female slaves to form maternal bonds with their biological children. The representation of black women as primitive and highly sexual was economically advantageous to slave owners who deployed slave women's reproductive bodies in breeding programs.[25]

Antiracist feminists argued that the subaltern woman (indigenous woman, slave woman) has been frequently deployed by colonial forces of power as the marker for savagery, primitivism, and sexual licentiousness and hence denied the status of lady or even mother. In *Ain't I a Woman?*, titled after Sojourner Truth's famous 1851 speech,[26] bell hooks argued:

> The shift away from the image of white woman as sinful and sexual to that of white woman as virtuous lady occurred at the same time as mass sexual exploitation of enslaved black women—just as the rigid sexual morality of Victorian England created a society in which the extolling of women as mother and helpmate occurred at the same time as the formation of a mass underworld of prostitution. As American white men idealized white womanhood, they sexually assaulted and brutalized black women.[27]

Hooks argued that the rape of black women was socially and culturally sanctioned because the slavery system was ideologically and economically dependent upon it. It was the construction of black women as sexual savages that gave white men and even black men the permission to rape black women. "An animal cannot be raped."[28] Evelynn M. Hammonds argued that white women were expected to be passive, virginlike, de-sexed Madonnas who performed the sexual act only for procreative purposes in their reproductive duty as good frontier wives. "White women were characterized as pure, passionless, and de-sexed, while black women were the epitome of immorality, pathology, impurity, and sex itself."[29]

One of the crucial ways black women resisted being constructed as "whores of the nation" was through the "politics of respectability." Evelyn Brooks Higginbotham argued:

> Especially in the roles of missionary or teacher, black church women were conveyers of culture and vital contributors to the fostering of middle-class ideals and aspirations in the black community. Duty bound to teach the value of religion, education, and hard work, the women of the black Baptist church adhered to politics of respectability that equated public behavior with self respect and the advancement of African-American people as a group. They felt certain that "respectable" behavior in public would earn their people a measure of esteem from white America, and hence they strove to win the black lower classes' allegiance to temperance, industriousness, thrift, refined manners, and Victorian sexual morals.[30]

A key figure that emerged from the black women's church movement was the supermoral black woman, strongly rooted in the cult of true womanhood. Like the angel in the house or the good pioneer woman, the supermoral black woman was chaste, passionless, and de-sexed. Black women reformers saw this figure as a way to be seen in the public eye as respectable, countering the negative and dangerous representation of the black Jezebel. The construct of the supermoral black woman, however, was oppressive and helped breed a culture of repression. Michele Wallace argued that the black superwoman figure has been largely constructed by white society as a reason to ignore or neglect black women's reproductive and socioeconomic issues.[31]

A central issue for antiracist and anticolonial feminists has been the code of silence about subaltern women's sexual exploitation and rape. Patricia Hill Collins referred to this as a politics of silence. Collins identified three reasons why there has been such institutionalized and internalized silence about black women's sexuality. First, there has been the suppression of black women's voices by dominant groups who control the schools, news media, churches, and government. Second, there was a taboo against discussing sexual abuse and violence that implicates black men and hence "violates norms of racial solidarity." Third, black women have seen the benefits of remaining silent about their sexuality. Collins argued that "this secrecy was especially important within a U.S. culture that routinely accused black women of being sexually immoral, promiscuous jezebels."[32] Hence, subaltern women have had to combat two issues surrounding their sexuality, hypervisibility and the politics of silence.

Another political strategy deployed by black and subaltern women was to embrace the identity of motherhood. Long denied the experience of forming maternal bonds, African American women have seen motherhood as a privilege rather than a prison and domesticity as a haven from white supremacy and sexual violence. However, as hooks argued, this did not necessarily lead to fewer negative stereotypes of black womanhood, Aunt Jemima being a crude example. "In more recent years the labeling of black matriarchs emerged as yet another attempt by the white male power structure to cast the positive contributions of black women in a negative light."[33]

Like African American women, indigenous women were valued only as exploitable objects. Anticolonial feminists argued that indigenous women were also constructed as whores and as sexually licentious. In her seminal article "The Pocahontas Perplex," Rayna Green argued that the Mother Earth figure was deployed to objectify North American indigenous women in colonial discourse.

> The Indian woman, along with her male counterparts, continued to stand for the New World and for rude native nobility, but the image of the savage remained as well. The dark side of the Mother-Queen figure is the savage Squaw, and even Pocahontas, as John Barth suggests in *The Sotweed Factor*, is motivated by lust. Both her nobility as a Princess and her savagery as a Squaw are defined in terms of her relationships with male figures.[34]

Anticolonial scholars argued that the Mother-Queen and dirty squaw tropes were deployed as discursive tools in the colonial genocide of indigenous communities and nations. In the attempt to "Kill the Indian, save the man,"[35] North American indigenous families and communities were torn apart by state-funded assimilation projects such as Canada's Indian Residential Schools, in which children as young as six were forcibly removed from their parents and homes and forbidden to speak their mother tongue.[36] Indigenous homes and mothers were often deemed unfit by colonial forces of power, though indigenous children suffered terrible abuses at the hands of their Christian caretakers.[37] In Australia, black Australian children often suffered a similar fate to their Canadian counterparts; known as the Stolen Generations, Aborigine children were taken from their mothers to be placed in white foster homes.[38] Most of the children who were torn from their indigenous mothers and communities were trained to be domestic servants or low-paid manual laborers intended for a white-settler economy. The disruption and destruction of indigenous families was rooted in and justified by racist and colonial tropes of subaltern womanhood and motherhood. Australian and indigenous feminist scholar Aileen Moreton-Robinson argued that "the rape and sexual abuse of Indigenous women by white men is tolerated in society because the imagined sexual promiscuity of indigenous women is perceived as biologically driven."[39]

Across these ten films, the cult of true womanhood/motherhood is debunked through a female lens that is maternal. Most of the films feature central characters who are mothers or who foreground the importance of the mother-daughter relationship, or both. Through the role of motherhood and maternal bonds, the female protagonists and characters resist patriarchal and colonial oppression and find empowerment. The filmmakers evoke the work of the French poststructuralist feminists who advocated for reclaiming and reconstructing womanhood and motherhood outside of patriarchy, which has disavowed and marginalized maternal embodied knowledge. Philosopher and literary critic Hélène Cixous advocated for "white ink," a revolutionary writing that was rooted in the maternal body. Cixous argued:

> It is necessary and sufficient that the best of herself be given to woman by another woman for her to be able to love herself and return in love the body that was "born" to her. . . . In women there is always more or less of the mother who makes everything all right, who nourishes, and who stands up against separation; a force that will not be cut off but will knock the wind out of the codes.[40]

Expanding on and challenging the pioneering work of French psycho-analyst Jacques Lacan, Julia Kristeva argued that female subjectivity was possible only by rejecting the law of the father embedded in an oppressive paternal tongue. To resist patriarchal oppression, Kristeva advocated for a language that is "pre-lingual" before the infant child enters the mirror stage (Lacan) or the oedipal complex (Sigmund Freud). Kristeva called this stage the semiotic, a pre-paternal language akin to motherhood and pregnancy "which seems to be impelled also by a non-symbolic, non-paternal causality."[41]

In feminist film scholarship of the 1970s and 1980s, the representation of the maternal and motherhood was central, particularly in the analyses of the maternal melodrama of the 1940s and 1950s, as well as in early cinema. Scholars focalized much of their writings on maternal melodramas, particularly *Mildred Pierce* (1945)[42] and *Stella Dallas*[43] (1937). Lucy Fischer argued, "There arose a virtual cottage industry dedicated to criticizing *Mildred Pierce*."[44] Two recurring themes emerged across feminist film scholarship: the thwarting of maternal desire and the deployment of the good mother/bad mother paradigm. In the early 1970s, Molly Haskell identified Hollywood's representation of womanhood as rooted in motherhood and sacrifice, a woman's "ultimate *raison d'etre*, her only worth-confirming 'career.'"[45] Analyzing *Stella Dallas*, Linda Williams argued:

> The device of devaluing and debasing of the actual figure of the mother while sanctifying the institution of motherhood is typical of the "woman's film" in general and the sub-genre of the maternal melodrama in particular. In these films it is quite remarkable how frequently the self-sacrificing mother must make her sacrifice that of connection to her children—either for her or their own good.[46]

Mary Ann Doane, analyzing the maternal melodrama, argued:

> All of these texts bring into play the contradictory position of the mother within patriarchal society—a position formulated by the injunction that she focus desire on the child and the subsequent demand to give up the child to the social order. Motherhood is

conceived as the always uneasy conjunction of an absolute closeness and a forced distance. The scenario of "watching the child from afar" thus constitutes itself as a privileged tableau of the genre, and it is clear why *Stella Dallas* has become its exemplary film.[47]

Across this scholarship, feminists saw the necessity of challenging the place of the mother in society as well as the deployment of the maternal in discourse, though there has been much criticism of their biological determinism and their white middle-class angle of vision. The other tendency was that most of these feminists saw motherhood and the maternal as oppressive and an obstacle to gender equality. E. Ann Kaplan described this attitude toward motherhood within the second-wave women's movement as negative.

> At that time feminism was very much a movement of daughters. The very attractiveness of feminism was that it provided an arena for separation from oppressive closeness with the Mother; feminism was in part a reaction against our mothers who had tried to articulate the patriarchal "feminine" in us, much to our anger. This made it difficult to for us to identify with Mothering and to look from the position of the Mother.[48]

In regard to women filmmakers, there also seemed to be a tendency to focalize stories and themes around motherhood and the maternal. Early prefeminist Hollywood women directors such as Dorothy Arzner and Ida Lupino often featured mothers as central heroines and tackled maternal issues including unwanted pregnancies, adoption (Ida Lupino's *Not Wanted*, 1949), and mother-child relations (Arzner's *Sarah and Son*, 1930). Sandy Flitterman-Lewis argued that French filmmaker Marie Epstein deployed the maternal to "say something different" from her French male contemporaries, the same directors who saw themselves as countering the dominant cinema but who were driven by nationalist sentiment rooted in the patriarchal. Flitterman-Lewis claimed that Epstein's *La Maternelle* followed a pre-oedipal structure foregrounding a child's point of view and reworked the fantasy of the primal scene through female desire for the mother (maternal object).[49] Flitterman-Lewis argued:

Marie Epstein shifts the focus of her narratives from the traditional masculine trajectory of Oedipal desire to desiring relations of the feminine (relations between mothers and daughters in particular) and in doing so, realigns point-of-view structures to emphasize both the *child's* vision in the primal scene and the unconscious structure of fantasy.[50]

Interestingly, Alice Guy-Blaché, whose *La fée aux choux/The Cabbage Fairy* (1896) is now credited with being the first fiction narrative film, preceding Georges Méliès's *A Trip to the Moon*, deployed the trope of the maternal outside masculinist visual and sound regimes. In *La fée aux choux*, Guy-Blaché depicts a modern fertility figure garbed as a corseted Cabbage Fairy who plucks wiggling newborn babies out of cabbages, metaphorically giving birth to all of them single-handedly. Although Guy-Blaché's Cabbage Fairy may not initially seem like a feminist icon, she can be read as an autonomous and powerful maternal figure. Guy-Blaché not only situates her fertility figure in a nondomestic setting, a vegetable patch with no paternal figure in sight; she also ensures that her fairy returns the cinematic gaze. Guy-Blaché and her Cabbage Fairy mirror each other's conflated desire to (re)produce and peer through the lens. Guy-Blaché's lens not only depicted women's procreative powers as positive and creative forces but literally gave birth to cinema as a medium. Guy-Blaché is now known as the first woman filmmaker to work in the motion picture film industry, and so it can be concluded that the first gaze in the narrative cinema was not only a female gaze but also a maternal one. *La fée aux choux* represents a dramatic contrast to the silent cinema trick films of Guy-Blaché's male contemporaries, such as Georges Méliès, a magician, and Émile Cohl, who was often falsely credited with having directed a number of Guy-Blaché's films.[51] Feminist film scholar Lucy Fischer argued that trick films reflected an antifeminine film culture rooted in patriarchal womb envy, in which filmmakers could assert their procreative powers and simultaneously contain the female body. When women were not disappeared in the tricks, they were either dismembered or killed in a cinematic chamber of horrors.[52] The trick films that did not render women invisible or depict violence toward them featured magic that had strong procreative and reproductive connotations, such as the pulling of rabbits from hats or flowers from cones.[53]

In the early part of her career, Guy-Blaché gained considerable influence and power, eventually owning various film companies in France and America. Guy-Blaché has been credited with directing more than four hundred one-reel films[54] in France between 1896 and 1907 and more than three hundred one-reel films in the United States between 1910 and late 1913. Unfortunately, Guy-Blaché was put out of business by the restructuring of the American film industry in 1917. She directed her last film, *Tarnished Reputations*, in 1920.[55] Despite a prolific film career, Guy-Blaché's contribution to world cinema would soon be forgotten, her films disappearing from the archives for decades, including the historically important *La fée aux choux*. However, Guy-Blaché was rediscovered after she published her memoir in 1976 titled *Autobiographie d'une pionnière du cinéma, 1873–1968*.[56] This publication appeared around the same time as women were just beginning to enter film schools and receive financing for their first films. Guy-Blaché in many ways can be seen as the great-grandmother icon for women's filmmaking. Her disappearance from world cinema is representative of the absence of women filmmakers in general. It would be another fifty years until women filmmakers would return to the narrative cinema in any significant way. Interestingly, taking up where Guy-Blaché left off, many of these new women filmmakers would construct narratives through the lens of motherhood and the maternal.

In many ways, the films in this study seemed to answer a call to action to reimagine womanhood through a feminist lens. Evoking some of the key feminist debates about motherhood, women's labor, the public/private sphere dichotomy, and female sexuality, the films reconstruct frontier spaces that allow for a new kind of womanhood. All of these filmmakers aimed to debunk the cult of true (white) womanhood and follow Virginia Woolf's example to "kill the angel in the house."[57] Deploying the trope of true womanhood, the rest of this chapter examines how the films fall into two distinct feminist narratives. The subaltern womanhood/motherhood narrative evokes and is perhaps animated by the antiracist and anticolonial feminist debates about subaltern resistance and agency in the face of colonial oppression. At the center of these narratives is an empowered sub-altern maternal figure. The angel on the frontier counternarrative evokes feminist debates about the role of patriarchy and domesticity in the subjugation of women. At the center of these films is a rebellious daughter, although maternal desire is foregrounded in the films' visual and sound regimes.

THE SUBALTERN WOMANHOOD/ MOTHERHOOD NARRATIVE

Daughters of the Dust, Mauri, Bedevil, The Wake, and *Loyalties* feature subaltern women as the central characters who find empowerment in motherhood or maternal roles, reproductive labor, and matrifocal family structures. The family and the domestic arena are depicted as a site of refuge from colonial oppression and exploitation. The film-makers depict subaltern domestic spaces as places where characters find temporary relief from oppressive conditions on the frontier, where they are rendered more vulnerable to colonial surveillance, violence, and entrapment. This is not to say domestic spaces are conflict-free zones. However, the core conflicts are rooted in mecha-nisms of colonialism and racism rather than in patriarchy. Subaltern domesticity is not structured around oppressive gender roles in which women are subjected to patriarchal dominance and control. In the subaltern narrative, domestic spaces are sites of female empower-ment, rooted primarily in female and maternal desire. This empow-erment is enabled through the preservation of culture and language, as well as in the thwarting of the white angel in the house trope, his-torically deployed by colonial forces of power to render subaltern women more suited to hard labor or sexual exploitation and rape. The empowerment of subaltern language and culture is constructed through reproductive labor, women's work, and female rituals. The filmmakers suggest that through women's work, isolated and eco-nomically impoverished subaltern communities can thrive and be nourished, as well as remain connected to their own cultures. This women's work often involves a careful balancing or fusion of subaltern cultural practices and modern technologies. These films privilege images of women's work such as food and handicraft production in the films' mise-en-scènes.

The subaltern maternal figure practices resistance through her role as a mother in her family and extended family, as well as in the community, offering comfort and solace, imparting wisdom, and teaching survival skills and strategies to her daughters. Three subaltern maternal figures recur across these five films: the great-grandmother subaltern figure, the young subaltern mother figure, and the community other-mother figure. The great-grandmother is an elder wisewoman figure whom the family and community turn to for guidance, healing, and even protection from colonial violence and oppression, as well as preserving family history as a storyteller, as discussed in chapter 1. Though the great-grandmother figure is strong and empowered, she is also a survivor of traumatic colonial exploitation and violence; she is hence a figure of great suffering. The young subaltern mother is a working mother. Not part of a patriarchal family, she works outside the home, primarily in low-paid and low-skilled jobs. These heroines are not career-oriented or goal-driven women with lofty aspirations to succeed in the (white) male professions; they *must* work. Nor do they harbor yearnings for artistic expression suppressed by a masculinist culture. Instead, these heroines are struggling to survive in a hostile frontier environment in which male sexual and racist violence threatens them at every turn. The role of decent work is a key theme across these films. Working in a decent occupation (i.e., not sex work) affords these women some respectability in a sexist and racist frontier culture, which has historically constructed, colonized, and marginalized women, including unwed mothers, as sexually available and licentious, as fallen dark angels. In this sense, the films engage with a politics of respectability. The community other-mother figure is borrowed from Patricia Hill Collins's work on African American motherhood. Collins argued:

Community othermothers have made important contributions in building a different type of community in often hostile political and economic surroundings. Community othermothers' actions demonstrate a clear rejection of separateness and individual interest as the basis of either community organization or individual actualization.

Instead, the connectedness with others and common interest expressed by community othermothers models a very different value system, one whereby Afrocentric feminist ethics of caring and personal accountability move communities forward.[58]

The community other-mother appears in various forms across these films.

As far as this place is concerned we never enjoyed our womanhood . . . Deep inside, we believed that they ruined our mothers, and their mothers before them. And we live our lives always expecting the worst because we feel we don't deserve no better. Deep inside we believe that even God can't heal the wounds of our past or protect us from the world that put shackles on our feet. Even though you're going up North, you all think about being ruined too. You think you can cross over to the mainland and run away from it?

—Eula in *Daughters of the Dust*

Eula makes her impassioned speech on the beach to her large extended Peazant family, a family that also comprises her Sea Islands Gullah community. Eula, who has been victimized by rape, speaks a truth that most of the women have buried—so deeply that when it is spoken it serves to break the shackles of silence that now enslave them as ruined black others. Speaking this truth is essential to black and indigenous women transcending and healing from hundreds of years of colonial sexual exploitation and violence. In *Daughters of the Dust*, there is a marked absence of a desiring white male gaze to render black women into whores of the nation. And yet, its felt absence functions as a ghost haunting the margins of the frame. Julie Dash also renders the rape act absent in the frame, even though it is a central theme in the film. The absence of a white male desiring gaze and the act of rape does not mean Dash de-emphasizes their historical significance in African American women's history. The rape of Eula is a major story line, the source of Eli and Eula's problem. Rather than featuring the rape act as a spectacle and vilifying the white rapist, Dash foregrounds the internal anguish, shame, and oppressive silence around rape and the sexual exploitation of black women. One key conflict is between Yellow Mary, a fallen woman, and many of the Peazant women, who judge Yellow Mary for her shameful lifestyle back on the mainland. These women function as supermoral black women who have chosen silence and denial about sexuality and desire as a means of survival. Dash depicts the place of shame and silence around black women's sexual exploitation in the African American community in the following scene.

SHOT: *Extreme wide-angle shot on the beach of Peazant men, women, and children. A woman's voice screams joyfully, "Viola! Viola!" One of the elderly Peazant mothers runs across the frame screaming Viola's name repeatedly. The other Peazants stop what they are doing and turn their attention to Viola's sobbing and ecstatic mother. Viola enters the frame and embraces her mother. Mr. Snead, the photographer, stands a few paces back. The Peazant family gathers around the emotional mother-daughter reunion.*

SHOT: *Extreme wide-angle shot on Yellow Mary and Trula approaching the beach area from a different direction to that of Viola and Mr. Snead. Haagar's daughter Iona and a girl named Myown accompany the two women.*

SHOT: *Wide-angle shot on the Peazants. The camera trucks in as they turn their gazes to the approaching Yellow Mary and her entourage. Haagar is center frame. She gestures to another Peazant woman, who turns to stare at the approaching party. She says,* "That Gussie's daughter, ain't it?"

SHOT: *Wide angle on Yellow Mary, Trula, Iona, and Myown walking happily together.*

SHOT: *Medium-close shot on the Peazant women.* "Old man Peazant's granddaughter done come home."

SHOT: *Wide-angle shot on one of the Peazant women.* "Oh, she got ruined. Yellow Mary gone off and get ruined."

SHOT: *Medium-close shot on Peazant woman, who continues to stare at Yellow Mary.* "What that she got with her?"

SHOT: *Medium-close shot on Haagar, who yells angrily,* "Iona!"

SHOT: *Point-of-view long shot on Yellow Mary, Trula, Iona, and Myown. Haagar screams, "Iona!" Iona runs out of the frame toward her mother.*

SHOT: *American shot on Haagar, who is flanked by Viola and other members of the Peazant family. She glares at Yellow Mary with contempt. Iona enters the frame and obediently comes to her mother. Haagar says,* "You go warn Nana Peazant. It'll likely kill her to see this heifer has returned." *Iona says,* "But, Ma, I don't think . . ." *Haagar ignores her daughter and stalks toward Yellow Mary, exiting the frame. The other Peazants follow after Haagar. Viola, who has separated herself from the prodigal Yellow Mary, holds a Bible firmly across her chest. Everyone gazes at Yellow Mary with disapproval and curiosity.*

SHOT: *Close shot on Viola gazing at Yellow Mary.* "All that yellow wasted."

SHOT: *Long shot on Yellow Mary and Trula approaching the group. Yellow Mary smiles when she comes closer. She pauses in front of the group. She looks around and spots someone she knows. She flashes a big smile and says,* "Is this the same little girl I used to rock in Gussie's yard?" *Eula moves through the group to greet Yellow Mary.*

SHOT: *Medium-long shot on Yellow Mary, who embraces Eula warmly and joyfully.*

SHOT: *Low-angle American shot on Haagar and other Peazant women glaring at Yellow Mary. The same Peazant woman who spoke earlier says,* "That shameless hussy."

Clearly there is a marked difference between the ways Viola and Yellow Mary are greeted by their families. Within the Peazant family Viola, the Christian missionary, is accepted and warmly received by her relatives, whereas Yellow Mary, a prostitute, is met with much disapproval and even rejection, except from the younger females such as Iona and Eula. Women such as Haagar and Viola see Yellow Mary through a damning gaze that constructs her as a sexual object, a shameless hussy, rather than the traumatized and lonely person she is. These family women distance themselves from "scary" and "new kinds" of women such as Yellow Mary and Trula because they represent what all African Americans on the frontier fear, the overexposure of the black female body as a sexualized object—the Jezebel of Ibo

Landing. Later, Eula challenges this construction of Yellow Mary, a construction that in reality could be applied to all of them. Even the rigid Christian missionary Viola is vulnerable to such racist stereotyping because the denigration of the black female body is the way white oppressors inscribe their dominance over the whole group. As Eula says in her impassioned speech on the beach, "We're all good women. We're the daughters of those old dusty things Nana carries in her tin can." In figure 2.1, Yellow Mary embraces Eula and Trula, "daughters of those dusty things."

Nana Peazant, a former slave and a great-great-grandmother, is a wise-woman figure, a powerful matriarch who her family turns to for guidance and her magical healing powers. Dash constructs a number of dramatic conflicts around Nana's maternal desire, her plan to prepare her many daughters for what awaits them when they migrate north to the mainland. It is Nana Peazant who holds the key to keeping the family together, even though many of them will never see her again because Nana refuses to leave Ibo Landing with her large family. Nana's refusal to leave is met with resistance by her family who see crossing over to the mainland as their only hope for a future and their survival as a community. Nana takes it upon herself to ensure that their stories, rituals, language, and cultural traditions, rooted in their

FIGURE 2.1 Eula (left), Yellow Mary, and Trula, *Daughters of the Dust.*

African homeland, are never to be forgotten. Nana's desire to give the Peazants a connection to their ancestors is met with resistance and even anger. Nana's daughter-in-law, Haagar, who rejects Nana's "salt-water African" ways, exclaims, "I don't want my daughters to know anything about that mess!" For Nana, this forgetting is akin to losing one's identity, and this can only mean a kind of spiritual death of the self and the community. Haagar believes that moving forward is about forgetting Ibo Landing. Haagar says, "Where we're going, Nana, there'll be no need for an old woman's magic." Yet that is exactly what Haagar will need the most. Nana's wisdom is, in fact, the Peazants' foundation for a future, their only hope for survival.

Dash is careful not to represent Nana as a kind of black super-woman, however. Despite her queenly status as Mother Peazant, Nana is not all-powerful. Though Nana sits on her throne of sticks, she is also an aging former slave who has suffered greatly. This seems forgotten by some of the younger Peazants, who look to her not only for answers but for miracles. This is depicted in her grandson Eli's des-perate plea, "Why didn't you protect us, Nana?" Though Nana puts much faith in her roots and glass bottles, she cannot save Eli's wife, Eula, from rape or Yellow Mary from ruin or Jake from prison or even prevent the splintering of her family. Nana's role as cultural preserver, historian, griot, blood-mother, and other-mother has taken its toll physically and emotionally. Dash depicts Nana's suffering in the scene in which Nana breaks down on the beach while she reflects upon her "scraps of memories" from her old tin box. With her many daughters gathered around her, Nana cries, "We came here in chains and we must survive. We must survive! There's salt-water in our blood." Nana may not be able to work miracles, but she can pass on the memories and stories of the ancestors.

Dash constructs the young subaltern mother as a highly revered figure, one with great moral authority and wisdom. Despite being a victim of rape, mother-to-be Eula embraces her reproductive body not as a sign of shame or burden but as one of empowerment. It is Eli, her husband, who feels shame and anger at the sight of Eula. He says, "When I look at her, I feel I don't want her no more." In a key moment in the film, Eula is framed in a long shot. In the frame, she is dressed all in white and flanked by old-growth trees, and she stretches her body into a dance pose, accentuating her pregnant belly. In that moment, the spirit of her unborn child runs into her body. Eula smiles and wraps her arms around her belly, cradling the unborn child. Eula's maternal love is so powerful that it can overcome the shame and horror of the rape, a form of colonial domination. Eula is also the one who tries to bring a stop to all the family quarreling. In an impassioned speech to her family, Eula begs them to accept Yellow Mary.

> If you love yourselves, then love Yellow Mary because she's a part of you. Just like we're a part of our mothers. A lot of us are going through things we feel we can't handle all alone. There's going to be all kinds of roads to take in life. Let's not be afraid to take 'em. We deserve them 'cause we're all good women. Do ya . . . do ya understand . . . who you are?! And what we have become? We're the daughters of those old dusty things Nana carries in her tin can. We carry too many scars from the past. Our past owns us. We wear our scars like armor for protection. Thick hard ugly scars that no one can pass through or ever hurt us again. Let's live our lives without living in the folds of old wounds.

The community other-mother is Viola, an unmarried Christian missionary who brings Bible lessons from the mainland. Viola imparts the words and teachings of Jesus Christ, a white god that the Peazant children know little about. Viola sees Christianity as a strategy to help young African American women and girls avert sexual exploitation and crime. This is depicted in the following scene set on the beach.

> SHOT: *Wide-angle shot on Viola surrounded by children of various ages. She has just finished reading from the Bible. She says,* "You know, when I left this island . . ."
>
> SHOT: *Medium-long shot on Viola as speaks to the children.* ". . . I was a sinner and I didn't even know it. But I left this island, touched that mainland, and . . ."
>
> SHOT: *Cut to wide-angle shot on Yellow Mary standing on the shoreline and gazing out toward the sea. Viola's voice-off:* "And fell into the arms of the Lord." *The camera tracks out to a wider frame. A child asks,* "What they got out there anyway, Viola?"

SHOT: *Medium-long shot on Viola with the children.* "Life, child. The beginning of a new life."

SHOT: *Medium shot on a teenage girl with a parasol.* "Who they, out there?"

SHOT: *Medium-long shot on Viola with the children.* "Jesus Christ, baby. The son of God." *Viola looks out toward the same sea as Yellow Mary.*

There is another scene in which Viola gives "lady lessons" to the Peazant girls on the beach. Dash deploys this scene as a commentary on how young black women are expected to perform respectable femininity. Through these lessons, Viola teaches the young women how to sit, stand, and walk properly. Yellow Mary stands as an example of what happens to young African American women if they do not act like proper ladies. They get raped and "ruint." Viola's teachings stand in contrast to Nana's teachings, which are rooted in embracing the old souls. Nana teaches traditions to maintain one's identity and cope with the trauma of the painful past, one marred by slavery and racist violence. Viola's teachings are about the future, the modern white world. Viola says, "Nana was never educated; all she knows are simple things, things that people told her a long time ago." Nana does not want to stop her family from migrating to the mainland, but she doesn't believe they should forget about African ways of healing, dreaming, speaking, and being. Later, Nana's and Viola's disparate teachings will merge, represented in the hoodoo scene.[59]

SHOT: *Extreme wide-angle (bird's-eye-view) shot on the Peazant family gathered around Nana. Nana walks toward Viola and takes her Bible away from her. Nana says to everyone,* "We done took old Gods and given 'em new names. They saw it all here that day, those Ibo."

SHOT: *Close angle on Nana's hand tying a hoodoo charm (in the form of a hand) tightly onto Viola's Bible.*

SHOT: *Extreme wide angle. Nana holds Viola's Bible with the hoodoo charm up to everyone.* "This hand, it's from me, from them, from us. Same soul as you all."

SHOT: *Extreme close angle on Nana's hands holding the Bible and hoodoo charm. She says,* "Come, children, kiss this hand full of me."

Though Viola is initially upset by Nana's "heathen" gesture, she does eventually kneel down and kiss Nana's hoodoo charm and the Bible, a hybrid symbol of African Americanness. Everyone except Haagar kisses the hand. Nana not only blesses her children before they leave Ibo Landing forever but also teaches them how to integrate the two seemingly disparate worldviews of the colonizer and the colonized in the New World. Anthropologist Katrina Hazzard-Donald explains hoodoo as the "embodied historical memory linking" African Americans back through time to previous generations and ultimately to their African past. It is also a paradigm for approaching both the world and all areas of social life."[60]

In Merata Mita's *Mauri*, being a mother is deemed not only an important role and experience as a woman but also essential to the survival of the community as a whole. Reproductive power is emphasized throughout Mita's film, which opens with a birthing scene, depicted in a highly ritualistic and reverent way. In the Maori community, the figure of the mother is held in high esteem. In stark contrast to the angel in the house figure, mothers are not part of a nuclear patriarchal family unit; they are part of a community, and they may or may not be formally married.

The young subaltern mother appears as Remari, a woman who conceives a child out of wedlock. Instead of depicting Remari as a fallen angel, Mita represents her as powerful and beautiful, a kind of contemporary Maori fertility figure. Indeed, Remari's reproductive body brings empowerment to her Maori community because the love child she conceives with Paki/Rewi will inherit the lands Pakeha settlers stole after Remari marries Steve Semmens. Though Paki/Rewi has told Remari that he can never be with her, she still pursues him. As the wise elder Kara says, Remari has the hots for him. Remari is not coy or ashamed of her desire for Paki/Rewi; it is part of who she is. Mita represents Remari's sexual agency in a decolonizing way. This is exemplified in the campfire lovemaking scene.

SHOT: *Close angle on Remari as she gazes at Paki/Rewi.* "What's eating you, then?"

SHOT: *Close angle on Paki/Rewi looking into the fire.* "None of your business."

SHOT: *Close angle on Remari, who is ticked off.* "So, it's none of my business? Well, what are ya, queer or something?"

SHOT: *Close angle on Paki/Rewi. He turns abruptly and then starts to laugh.*

SHOT: *Close angle on Remari, who is not amused. She stands up.*

SHOT: *Paki/Rewi watches her. Remari, off-screen, says,* "Well, prove it, then." *Paki/Rewi looks up at Remari.* "Don't be stupid."

SHOT: *Close angle on Remari gazing down at Paki/Rewi.* "Come on. Come on, let's see if you're man enough to get it up." *Paki/Rewi says, off-screen,* "It's not that." *Remari challenges him.* "Isn't it? Do you know what it's like to be horny?"

SHOT: *Close angle on Paki/Rewi. He thinks about it.* "All right."

SHOT: *Long shot on Paki/Rewi standing up, meeting Remari's challenge. He takes her hand and kisses her fingers.* "Have it your way." *He roughly places her hand on his crotch.*

SHOT: *Medium-close angle on Remari, over the shoulder of Paki/Rewi, who laughs mockingly. Remari gazes at him with astonishment.*

SHOT: *Medium-close angle on Paki/Rewi, who says with anger,* "What's the matter? You wanted to know if I had any, didn't you?"

SHOT: *Medium-close angle over the shoulder on Paki/Rewi and Remari, who remains silent. Paki/Rewi says,* "Look, just let things be." *Remari says softly,* "What do I have to do to get through to you?" *There is a moment of silence between them. Remari takes off her jacket.* "Look at me! I'm here now. I'm real."

SHOT: *Medium-close angle on Paki/Rewi, who replies,* "Look, it's got nothing to do with you, with sex. It's something else. I'm not free."

SHOT: *Medium-close angle over the shoulder on Paki/Rewi looking at Remari.* "You're married?" *Paki/Rewi shakes his head no. Remari asks,* "Well, then what?" *Paki/Rewi turns to her.* "I'll only hurt you." *Remari says desperately,* "I'm hurt now. You couldn't hurt me any more than you're hurting me now." *Paki/Rewi says,* "I'm sorry." *Remari sighs.* "You're always bloody sorry." *Paki/Rewi says with anguish,* "I'm not the man you think I am."

SHOT: *Close angle on Paki/Rewi.* "I'm just not good enough. I can't . . ." *Remari's hands come into the frame, touching Rewi's shoulder. She says,* "Don't." *Remari's hands cup Paki/Rewi's face.* "It's all right."

SHOT: *Close-angle two-shot on Remari and Paki/Rewi, their faces close together. She says,* "It's all right." *Paki/Rewi cries,* "God, I'm burning up. I need to tell someone." *Remari says quietly,* "You're not ready." *They embrace gently. Remari strokes his neck. Paki/Rewi breathes heavily. He says,* "Remari."

SHOT: *Close angle on Rewi over Remari's shoulder. Still embraced Paki/Rewi says passionately,* "Remari. Just don't let me go." *They kiss.*

SHOT: *Long angle on Paki/Rewi and Remari passionately kissing. Smoke rises from the campfire. They tumble to the ground together, and the campfire's flames fill the foreground.*

In this scene, Mita constructs Remari's desiring gaze as neither primitive nor animalistic, even though Mita frames her amid nature and fire. Remari refuses to be either an eroticized Indian princess or a dirty squaw. Mita makes this explicit when Remari declares, "I'm real!" Conversely, Paki/Rewi also refuses to be some desired object. It is only when Paki/Rewi renders himself vulnerable with his fears and emotional needs that the couple can make love and realize their desire and love for each other. This is a desire rooted in subjectivity, not oppressive gender or race relations. This scene stands in stark contrast to the scene in which old Mr. Semmens talks about Remari to his son, Steve.

MR. SEMMENS: "Agh! I've told you a thousand times you're not marrying that dirty black whore!!"

STEVE: "I'll knock your bloody teeth in!"

MR. SEMMENS: "They put her up to this. It's a trick. We'll lose everything! Look, Son, you can root her on the side. You don't have to marry her. I mean, why buy a cow when you can milk one through the fence?"

STEVE: "Sometimes I feel like killing you."

MR. SEMMENS: "What about the farm? The land? Everything? They'll take the lot!"

STEVE: "It was never ours. You and the council jacked up the sale of that land from under their feet!"

Mita is also very careful in her construction of Steve Semmens, the local white man who desires Remari. In order to destabilize a white male colonizing gaze, Mita renders Steve as passive. Steve is a white man who doesn't want to oppress or sexually exploit Maori women, although he is constantly encouraged to do just that by his unstable father. Steve refuses to be a colonizer. In fact, Steve commits a radical act by asking for Remari's hand in marriage. Hence, Steve does not gaze at Remari as some "dirty black whore" he can "root on the side," historically a common practice among white-settler men.

Remari, like Kara, also serves as a moral and political watchdog, guiding men, such as her two lovers, Steve and Paki/Rewi, to do the right thing. She has no qualms about reprimanding Steve or Paki/Rewi, and she has little fear of colonial authorities, epitomized in her encounter with the local police. In the following night scene, Remari stands up to a local police officer, also a Maori man, who is chasing after the fugitive Paki/Rewi.

SHOT: *Wide angle on a dark forested area with a police car in the foreground. Remari emerges from the dark interior of the trees. She carries a lantern and thermos. In the foreground of the shot the policeman opens the door of his patrol jeep. Remari and the cop approach each other.*

SHOT: *Medium angle on an older white policeman asleep on the job.*

SHOT: *Full shot on Remari and the cop. Remari, smiling, says,* "Want a cup of tea?"

SHOT: *Over the shoulder (Remari) medium-angle two-shot. The young cop says,* "What's this?"

SHOT: *Reverse angle. Remari gestures toward her thermos.* "An offer of a cup of tea." *She keeps her frozen smile in place.*

SHOT: *Back to angle on the young cop. He looks down at Remari's thermos, then off-screen, and then up Remari's body.* "That all you offering, love?"

SHOT: *Back to angle on Remari.* "Mrs. Semmens to you . . ."

SHOT: *Back to cop. Sound bridge: Remari continues.* "PIG." *The cop drops his grin. Suddenly, the cop's attention is caught by something off-screen.* "Out of the way!"

SHOT: *Wide angle on a house. Paki/Rewi gallops away on horseback.*
SHOT: *Two-shot on cop and Remari. The cop leaps out of the frame.*
   "You BITCH!" *Remari calls out,* "Go, Rewi! He's seen you!"
SHOT: *Wide angle on Rewi galloping out of the frame.*
SHOT: *Two-shot on the cops in the police car. The young cop starts up the engine and drives off in pursuit of Rewi. As the car drives away, the frame shifts to reveal Remari watching from the side of the road.*

Here the police officer, though a Maori, attempts to sexually objectify Remari, reducing her to a dark fallen angel. Mita seems to make the point that despite the police officer's race, his allegiance is with the colonial oppressor, and hence he can see Remari only through a colonizing male gaze.

The great-grandmother figure appears as Kara, *Mauri*'s pivotal character, the one who holds the resolutions to the other characters' problems. Kara is also an other-mother for the Rapana family and her North Island Maori settlement. Mita depicts Kara as a mentor, primarily to her great-granddaughter, Awatea, whom she is raising in her small, rustic home, teaching her how to survive as a Maori female in a masculinist, racist white-settler society. Kara teaches Awatea how to harvest locally grown flax leaves and then how to weave a *kete* from them.[61] When Awatea finishes her kete, it is an important moment for her. Kara exclaims excitedly, "Your first kete!" When Awatea asks her granny what a tar baby is, Kara responds, "The opposite to white maggot." Kara teaches Awatea to never back down from one's oppressor.

Mita represents Kara's other-mothering in simple gestures such as cups of tea and nourishing rustic meals cooked over an open fire. At the kitchen table, Kara's great-nephew, Rewi, embraces her and says, "You know, being here with you is the only time I can believe in something that is better than what I've known in the past." On his prodigal return back to his childhood Maori home, Willie also takes in the pleasure of Kara's kitchen. While savoring a cup of tea she has made him, Willie says, "Just the way I like it." In figure 2.2, Kara watches from her kitchen window for Willie's return home. For a tough Maori gang leader, the comment is poignant. Mita also represents Kara's other-mother role in more profound spiritual gestures, particularly in

FIGURE 2.2 Kara, *Mauri*.

the scene in which she presents Willie with a special Maori pendant. This scene is the last time Kara will see Willie alive.

> SHOT: *Medium angle on Kara putting a Maori pendant around Willie's neck. Willie gazes at his reflection in the mirror. The camera tracks around them. The clock ticks (time is running out).*
>
> SHOT: *Close angle on Willie smiling proudly.*
>
> SHOT: *Close angle on Kara observing Willie's expression in the mirror.*
>
> SHOT: *Medium angle on Willie as he turns and embraces his aunt warmly.*
>
> SHOT: *Medium-close angle on Hemi, who is outside Kara's home, awaiting Willie, the designated leader of his gang. He gazes enviously at Willie and Kara through the window.*
>
> SHOT: *Hemi's point of view. Medium long shot on Kara and Willie embracing. They pull apart and walk toward the doorway together.*

Through this quiet scene Mita represents a profound moment in Willie's life, one in which Kara acknowledges him as a complete Maori man despite his criminal lifestyle. Mita ensures that it is the subaltern great-grandmother who performs this ritual of honor, offering Willie some inner peace and resolution about his Maori identity.

Mita depicts Kara's power as a community other-mother in relation to Paki/Rewi. On the run from the law, Paki visits Kara on her death-bed. Desperate and lost, Paki begs Kara, "Tell me what I must do?" At this point Paki has confessed his sin of stealing Kara's nephew Rewi's identity, including Rewi's sacred Maori pendants, meant to protect one even in death. Despite Paki's spiritual crimes against one of his own, Kara, even in her weakened state, does not turn him away. To Kara, the haunted and desperate man at her bedside is just another Maori son in trouble. Kara's acceptance of Paki in that moment is not about forgiveness—only the dead can do that—but about her other-mother role in her Maori community.

Earlier in the film, Kara epitomizes maternal strength and resis-tance when she stands up to a visiting Pakeha government official who has come to her settlement to make another bad deal with the Maori community. Kara insists on calling a meeting of the community's own. In an act of rebellious defiance, Kara refuses to address the Pak-eha official directly and speaks only in her Maori language, chanting a *waitia* to a group of Maori female elders. Through waitia, Kara sends a strong message to her community: never back down. Kara's desire to protect her people and the land from further encroachment and exploitation is depicted in the following sequence.

SHOT: *Long shot on Maori elder women dressed in black as they rise up from beneath a hill. The soundtrack features a female voice singing a waitia.*

SHOT: *Long shot on five Maori women, including Kara, who are seated on a platform in a meeting area. Kara stands as she sees the other Maori women approaching the meeting area. Kara begins to chant a speech. The other women stand. The camera tracks out to a wider frame, revealing Maori men standing.*

SHOT: *Reverse-angle wide shot on Maori women approaching. Majestic mountains are featured in the background. The women chant a response to Kara.*

SHOT: *Medium three-shot on Kara with the Maori women. She continues to chant.*

SHOT: *Wide high angle on the elder Maori women approaching the meeting. Maori men walk in behind them. As they all approach the meeting area, a Maori man pushes his way through the women, knocking them aside, in order to make a path for the Pakeha government official, a white man. One of the elder Maori women nudges the official with her walking stick. The camera follows the government official, who is now flanked by two Maori men dressed in suits. They come to a pause and offer a quick bow to Kara.*

SHOT: *Medium three-shot on Kara, who continues to chant.*

SHOT: *Wide angle on the government official, his two Maori attendants, and the group of Maori elder women and men seating themselves on benches. The ocean is featured in the background.*

Here Mita depicts solidarity among subaltern women as community other-mothers and community resistance against colonial oppression through maternal desire and collectivity. At the end of this scene, the Pakeha government official leaves, unmoved by the Maori's request for the government to back down. In reality, the meeting has been a public relations stunt staged by government officials to appear as if they have consulted with the Maori elders. Despite this defeat, however, the Maori community other-mothers have shown leadership and strength as a network of mothers and women against colonial domination.

So, it's about this English woman, and her loyalties toward her husband who she knows has sexually abused children in the past and she has covered for him. She makes a friendship with this woman whose child he rapes and the English woman has to decide whether she's going to stand beside her husband or with her new friend, her very unlikely friend, the Métis woman. [62]

—Anne Wheeler on *Loyalties*

In *Loyalties*, two young mother figures are the film's major characters Roseanne Ladouceur, a Métis single mother, and Lily Sutton, a British upper-middle-class housewife. Wheeler and screenwriter

Sharon Riis construct these two mothers as oppositional characters, initially at odds with each other because of their differences in social class and race. Roseanne is the young subaltern mother figure, who must work to support her three children and her mother, Beatrice, with whom she lives. Lily is seemingly the angel on the frontier, struggling to adjust to her life in the New World. Wheeler, however, resists depicting Lily as a damsel in distress in need of rescuing or a marker of proper femininity and civilization. Complicit in her husband's sexual criminal past, Lily is more Bluebeard's helper than victim; it is Roseanne and her daughter, Leona, who are most under threat. Despite the facade of a beautiful family and a luxury home adorned with all the latest modern conveniences, Lily is unable to cope with motherhood, primarily because of her husband's "problem" and the fact that she spent most of her childhood at boarding school; motherhood was never properly modeled for Lily. Despite her privilege and education, Lily is not depicted as a very knowledgeable mother. Lily may be educated, but she isn't very wise.

In contrast, Wheeler depicts Roseanne as a wise and empowered subaltern mother, a woman who knows how to survive on a racist and sexist contemporary Canadian frontier, destabilizing the Indian princess/squaw trope. Though as an impoverished unmarried mother Roseanne is treated like a whore of the nation, she will become Lily's role model for motherhood, as both a blood-mother and an other-mother outside the confines of patriarchy. In figure 2.3, a defeated Lily leans against other-mother Roseanne.

A key way in which Wheeler constructs Roseanne as empowered is through her defiance, particularly toward Dr. Sutton's sexually predatory behavior. Roseanne has been resisting men like Sutton her whole life. Hence, through Roseanne, Wheeler reverses the colonizing male gaze. This is exemplified in the following laundry room scene. Roseanne has used her employer's washing machine and dryer to wash her family's clothing because she cannot afford modern appliances.

SHOT: *American shot on Leona in the laundry room folding clothes. She hears someone approach and looks up, startled.*

SHOT: *Medium angle on Dr. Sutton smiling. He says,* "Sorry, I didn't mean to startle you." *He walks toward Leona.*

FIGURE 2.3 Roseanne and Lily, *Loyalties.*

SHOT: *Medium-close angle on Leona smiling self-consciously. She looks down.*

SHOT: *Medium angle on Dr. Sutton's hands as he picks up a pair of women's underwear. He slowly begins to fold it. The camera tilts up to his face.* "So, today is washing day, is it?"

SHOT: *Medium-close angle on Leona. She nods but is unable to speak. She gazes down from embarrassment. Dr. Sutton's voice, off-screen, says,* "Where's Lily? Do you know?" *Leona shrugs her shoulders.*

SHOT: *American shot on Leona and Dr. Sutton standing in close proximity to each other. Roseanne's voice, off-screen, says,* "Shopping," *in answer to Dr. Sutton's question. Roseanne enters the frame. She positions herself between her daughter and her employer and picks up the folded laundry, including the underwear Dr. Sutton fondled. She gives Leona a disapproving look. Dr. Sutton moves away from the laundry machines, giving Roseanne the space to organize her clothes. The camera follows as Dr. Sutton moves to the door frame leading into the rest of his home. Roseanne says,* "Just don't stand there, Leona. Get the other stuff out of the dryer." *Leona is framed out of the shot. Roseanne grabs her garbage bags filled with clean clothes and makes her way to the doorway where Dr. Sutton stands. She tries to move past him, but he blocks her from exiting.* "I thought perhaps I could give you a ride home." *Roseanne says,* "That's okay, I've got my truck." *Dr. Sutton abruptly brings his hands up to Roseanne's neck and face.* "Let me see that." *He wants to "examine" the injury she received the night Eddy beat her up.*

SHOT: *Medium-angle over the shoulder on Roseanne, who flinches at Dr. Sutton's touch. She glares at him with disdain. He says,* "It's coming along very nicely."

SHOT: *American shot on Roseanne and Dr. Sutton, still blocking the doorway with his arm. Roseanne ducks under his arm and quickly exits the laundry room. Leona enters the frame, carrying the garbage bags of laundry. As she follows after her mother, Dr. Sutton intercepts. Putting on his best gentleman act, he says,* "I'll take that. It's too heavy for you." *He carries the bags for Leona.*

Wheeler constructs Roseanne's use of direct eye contact and protective gestures as her only form of resistance against Dr. Sutton and, in fact, all predatory white men. Roseanne sees through Dr. Sutton's gentlemanly charm, and so he must resort to more explicit forms of sexual aggression such as unwanted touching and blocking doorways. Through these territorial gestures, Dr. Sutton sends a clear message to Roseanne—I own you. There is no doubt that Dr. Sutton's behavior goes far beyond harmless flirting; he is a real threat. Though Roseanne knows Dr. Sutton holds power over her as her employer and a privileged, respected member of the white-settler community, she does not allow him to claim physical or sexual access to her or her daughter. Unfortunately, Leona is very naive. In contrast to her mother, Leona is rendered completely passive by Dr. Sutton's privilege and his authoritative gaze and voice. Leona cannot return his gaze and is rendered silent throughout the entire scene. This is a much different Leona from the one who talks back to her mother in her own home. As in the rest of the film, Roseanne's critical, empowered maternal gaze is also a judging gaze, a gaze that condemns Dr. Sutton for what he is—a sexual predator who preys on powerless subaltern females. As Lily says of Roseanne, "I feel like she's always judging me." In this sense, Roseanne serves as a lone Greek chorus in the film, passing commentary on the actions of the characters around her. However, as previously discussed and demonstrated, Roseanne is not merely a device. She is a fully drawn character with dramatic agency, her primary purpose being to protect her family; Leona is safe only when her mother is there to shield her from harm.

Roseanne's mother, Beatrice, practices other-mothering as a means of keeping her family together in the face of economic disparity and systemic racism in late-1980s Canada. Though Beatrice has a small role in *Loyalties*, Wheeler positions her as an important subaltern maternal figure who speaks key words of wisdom and warning about indigenous womanhood on a postcolonial frontier. Beatrice provides a loving and stable home for Roseanne and her children when Roseanne breaks up with the troubled Eddy. Beatrice is also raising her grandson, whose parents are absent. In one heart-wrenching scene, Beatrice's daughter Marlene returns home with some men, demanding custody of her son. It is evident from Marlene's erratic behavior and the company that she keeps that the boy is better off staying with Beatrice. Though Beatrice and Roseanne cannot prevent Marlene from taking her son with her, they can offer words of wisdom to him. Beatrice reminds the unhappy boy, "Remember, no matter what happens, it's not your fault. It's got nothing to do with you." Roseanne steps in and hands her nephew some cash. "Put this in your sock. Don't give it to her, no matter what. If it gets bad, you get on a bus and get back, okay?" Without these indigenous other-mothers, Marlene's son would most likely end up in the foster care system or worse.

Wheeler avoids depicting Roseanne and Beatrice as supermothers or Earth Mother figures, however. Though Roseanne is strong, she is not perfect, partly because of her desire for her abusive boyfriend, Eddy. And though Roseanne is a strong mother, she is unable to protect her daughter from rape. In fact, Dr. Sutton rapes Leona when Roseanne is out at the local drinking hole celebrating Lily's birthday. Leona has been left in charge of the younger children while Roseanne and Lily take the night off from motherhood. Wheeler resists representing Roseanne and Lily's night out as parental negligence, however. Both women believe that Dr. Sutton is far away on a fishing trip with friends. Unbeknownst to the two mothers, Dr. Sutton has decided to come home early. The women discover Dr. Sutton raping Leona, but they are too late. The damage has been done. The rage, guilt, and pain Roseanne feels, and will most likely feel for the rest of her life, is an example of the kind of cost subaltern mothers pay in a racist and sexist frontier society.

In Norma Bailey's *The Wake*, maternal figures play a key role. The central character, Joan, a single mother, not only looks after her own young children but also takes in her teenage cousin, Donna, after Donna's mother, Cora, is hospitalized for alcoholism and diabetes. In order to support herself and her children, Joan works as a grocery store clerk. Though Bailey sets her film in contemporary times, Joan must still contend with the stereotype of the squaw, especially as a single mother. Throughout *The Wake*, Bailey privileges a desiring empowered female Métis gaze. However, when Joan desires a white man, a Royal Canadian Mounted Police (RCMP) officer, Jim, her desire is depicted as misdirected and even wrong. Joan's family and community deem her relationship with Jim both dangerous and disloyal.

> JOAN'S MOTHER: "You never listen to me. Look, you got a decent job, you got the kids, you got me to look after them. You got a nice place there."
>
> JOAN'S UNCLE: "Yeah, Joanie. You take up with this white man, you're gonna lose that place."
>
> JOAN: "For Christ's sake, I'm not going to marry him!"

The history of white men in positions of power sexually exploiting indigenous women in Canada haunts the film's frame. Bailey represents this history primarily through the character of Cora, Joan's cousin, who is a sex worker. Despite the risks and rifts Joan's desire for a white man creates, Joan doesn't let anyone dictate who she should and should not desire.

> SHOT: *Extreme wide-angle shot on Joan and Jim on her front stoop. She is in her dressing gown and slippers. They embrace.*
>
> SHOT: *Medium-close angle on Joan and Jim embracing and kissing. Smitten, they giggle in between kisses. Jim manages to pull himself away and say good-bye. The camera now over her shoulder, Joan watches Jim walk away. Jim turns around to gaze at Joan. He turns around and walks to his truck.*
>
> SHOT: *Long shot on Joan happily watching Jim depart. After a few moments Joan turns and goes back inside her house, out of the wintry cold air.*

SHOT: *Medium shot on Joan as she enters her kitchen from the outside. She smiles to herself. Becoming self-conscious, she ties the belt around her robe. She walks over to the counter to pour herself a cup of coffee. Her cousin Donna is at the stove cooking eggs. Joan is about to talk to her, but Donna gives her the cold shoulder. Joan notices the rebuff and sighs.*

SHOT: *Donna places the plate of eggs in front of Joan's son. Donna helps herself to some toast, all the while ignoring Joan.*

SHOT: *Medium-long angle. Joan eyes Donna. She walks over to the fridge to check the time. Joan's romantic escapade has officially ended. Feeling awkward, she joins Donna at the table. Donna keeps her eyes downcast. Joan smiles at her son.*

Bailey manages to normalize Joan's desire for Jim, even if it is dangerous. Bailey carefully avoids depicting Joan as either the dirty squaw or a Pocahontas figure, the Indian princess who aids white men.

Cora, Donna's mother, is the other young subaltern mother. Struggling with substance abuse and illness, Cora works as a prostitute to feed her three children. In the eyes of white society, however, Cora is a bad mother, just another dirty squaw who lives off the system. Bailey resists judging Cora as a bad mother, however, and renders her a sympathetic figure. Bailey has us see Cora through the eyes of Joan, who has empathy for her cousin. Joan saves her condemnation for white men, the guys who buy Cora's sexual services. Bailey depicts Cora and Donna's grim life in one of the film's most disturbing and tragic scenes. On returning home from school, Donna passes a white man exiting her house—one of her mother's johns.

SHOT: *Medium angle on Donna, who walks into the hallway of her house. She stops when her attention is caught by something. She gazes off-screen.*

SHOT: *Full shot on Cora lying unconscious on a disheveled bed. Her bedroom is a mess. She wears a simple cotton nightgown. Donna walks into the frame. Her younger brothers and sisters watch television in the living room.*

SHOT: *Medium shot. Donna gazes down at her mother's body on the bed. She approaches her with caution, not knowing what to expect. Donna*

turns her gaze out the window and says with contempt, "You bastard."
Donna turns her gaze back to her mother. "Mom?"
SHOT: *Full shot on Donna leaning over Cora, who is still unconscious.*
Donna pulls down her nightdress and then covers her with some
blankets. "Mom?"
SHOT: *Close angle, Donna's point of view on Cora. Donna leans into the*
shot. "Jesus." Donna's hands pull the blankets up to her mother's
neck. "Mom?"
SHOT: *Medium angle on Donna still trying to cover up her mother's*
unconscious body, a body Cora has just sold to a white man. Panicked,
Donna yells to her friend, "Marlene!"
SHOT: *Full shot on Donna, who turns her attention back to her mother.*
"Get the ambulance."

In this scene Bailey renders the white john as what he is, a bastard.
Donna is given the voice to judge and condemn the nameless and face-
less white man. She blames him for her mother's current state, which
is probably not directly his fault. Donna blames white men in general
for what her mother has become, an alcoholic whore who turns tricks
in the home while her kids watch television. Throughout the scene,
Bailey has Donna repeat "Mom," as if to assert Cora's identity first as
a mother rather than a prostitute. Though Cora does sell her body and
is an alcoholic, Donna honors her with the label *Mom*. In this scene,
the white male desiring gaze is rendered invisible, although it remains
a powerful and dangerous presence in the lives of Donna, Cora, and
Cora's other children. After this episode, Cora is admitted to the hospital and her children are placed in foster care, except for Donna, who
stays with Joan. Later in the film, Cora will get her life back on track,
thanks to Joan's support. After Cora is released from the hospital, she
gets new medication for her diabetes and finds decent work at a local
laundromat. Cora's new job, albeit low-paid, means a steady income
and also means getting her kids back, not to mention some dignity.
For a person who has been degraded and exploited so badly, it is a
wonder Cora has any hope left at all.

Joan also serves as an other-mother to Donna, exemplified in the
scene in which Joan helps her teenage cousin prepare for the Mardi
Gras beauty pageant. While cutting down Donna's pink bridesmaid

gown, which she wore at the beginning of the film, Joan imparts important coping and survival skills to her.

> SHOT: *Medium-close angle on Donna's muddied pink satin bridesmaid shoes. Joan's hands pin up the hem of the pink bridesmaid gown. Joan asks,* "Where do you want the hem? Above the knee or below the knee?"
> SHOT: *Medium angle on Joan looking up at Donna, who stands high up on a chair. Donna's hands hold up the bottom part of the dress. Donna replies,* "Below." *Joan nods her head. The camera follows Joan's arm as she places pins in the fabric of the dress. Donna is featured in the frame, but Joan is not in the shot. Donna says worriedly,* "I don't know if I want to do this, Joan. I don't know if I want to go through with all this stuff right now." *Joan stands up to face her unhappy cousin and says encouragingly,* "Hey, come on. You don't have to take the whole weight of the world on your shoulders. Gotta have a little fun too. And don't forget, the time Mardi Gras comes around, Cora . . . she'll be out of the hospital, and you'll be all together again." *Donna replies hesitantly,* "Yeah, but . . ." *Joan interjects,* "No BUT! Come on, take a look." *The camera follows Joan as she guides Donna to a full-length mirror. Donna can't bring herself to look at her own reflection. Joan says admiringly,* "You're a real pretty girl. Everybody's hustling tickets for you like crazy." *Donna looks down self-consciously and says quietly,* "I need shoes." *Joan replies matter-of-factly,* "Well, you go to welfare. You get a voucher for winter boots and trade them in for shoes. It's easy."

In Bailey's simple staging, Joan teaches Donna that life isn't all duty and disappointment. In the face of despair, one finds ways to feel good about oneself. Joan wants Donna to compete, not only for Donna but also for her Métis community, which is rallying behind her. By competing in the Mardi Gras Beauty Queen Contest and wearing a below-the-knee dress, Donna resists the role of the whore/squaw. During the pageant sequence, Bailey emphasizes Donna as a figure of resistance in the shot of her standing alongside privileged white girls also vying for the crown. For Donna it's more than just a high school contest, however; it's about standing up to racism and bringing dignity to her family and community. In one shot, Bailey debunks the colonial dichotomy of angel on the frontier and dirty squaw. Even though Donna loses the contest to a rich white girl, she has come out a winner to her friends; she will never be anyone's whore of the nation.

The subaltern great-grandmother figure appears as Joan and Donna's grandmother, Kookum, who tries to live as her ancestors did—off the land and without state handouts. Kookum offers her troubled and unhappy great-granddaughter, Donna, a place to stay, emotional comfort, and some important survival lessons. Donna is upset and feeling lost because of the placement of her younger siblings in foster care and her mother's bad reputation in town.

SHOT: *Long shot on Donna as Kookum tucks her into bed on the couch. As Donna quietly weeps, Kookum says,* "When you feel bad, my girl . . ."

SHOT: *Close shot on Donna sobbing. Kookum continues speaking,* ". . . don't turn it inside. Turn it out!"

SHOT: *Close shot on Kookum, who says,* "Get real mad! Of all my grandchildren . . ."

SHOT: *Close shot on Donna. Kookum says,* ". . . all those years . . ."

SHOT: *Close shot on Kookum as she says,* "There's none like you."

SHOT: *Close shot on Donna. She has stopped crying and is smiling.*

In figure 2.4, Donna helps her kookum in trapping rabbits, which they will later cook in an exterior fire pit.

In addition to Kookum, Joan's mother is another important wise great-grandmother figure. Joan's mother comes to her aid by helping her with child care. And Joan's mother seems to be eternally in the kitchen, whether it is a family meeting, a wedding reception, or a wake, making tea and preparing sandwiches for anyone who walks through her door. Though Joan's mother doesn't have a large role, Bailey establishes her important place in Joan's life and the Métis community. Without her mother, Joan wouldn't be able to go out to work. Through her mother's help, Joan is enabled to provide for herself and her children with a decent job and a nice place to live.

Community other-mothering is a recurring trope in *The Wake*. The community other-mother appears at weddings, wakes, and other

FIGURE 2.4 Donna and Kookum, *The Wake.*

family gatherings, feeding and emotionally supporting members of the community. Bailey sets these gatherings in people's modest homes and community centers on the reservation. In Bailey's frame, these women are more than just background players handing out plates of food; they are figures of resistance providing support and a sense of belonging to their community. Joan also plays a community other-mothering role as a member of an indigenous scholarship committee. Joan meets with mothers from her community to discuss and plan special scholarships for accomplished Métis high school students. These community other-mothers see their role as leaders initiating their own programs in the face of government handouts.

In *Bedevil*, Tracey Moffatt deploys indigenous motherhood and mothering practices as a device to dismantle the codes of horror and ethnographic films. In regard to the horror genre, Moffatt seems to take up Barbara Creed's article, "Horror and the Monstrous-Feminine: An Imaginary Abjection." Using Julia Kristeva's *Powers of Horror*, Creed examined the monstrous-feminine in the horror film in relation to the maternal figure and what Kristeva termed *abjection*, that which does not "respect the borders, positions, rules," that which "disturbs identity, system, order."[63] In regard to ethnographic film, with its Eurocentric history of othering subaltern women in "primitive" societies, it is the gaze and voice of the subaltern mother that is rendered knowledgeable. Moffatt privileges a subaltern maternal voice and gaze.

In the "Choo, Choo, Choo, Choo" segment, the subaltern great-grandmother figure appears as the loud and exuberant all-female netball team, who have come together to picnic in the bush. As they race along in the back of a truck, the women sing along to a pop song while wearing funky sunglasses and cheeky T-shirts. Moffatt shoots these scenes with ironic humor. Deploying the style of an ethnographic documentarian, Moffatt has the elder Ruby address the camera directly, and at one point she wipes the camera lens with a cloth as if to cleanse it. Through Ruby's gesture, Moffatt foregrounds the construction of the gaze, one that has to be wiped clean first by an indigenous great-grandmother. Ruby also appears as a young subaltern mother who lives with her husband, her sister-in-law, two boys, and a baby. The sister-in-law works, along with Ruby's husband, on the railway tracks, and so it is possible that Ruby is caring for some of her children. Both women look after the children in what seems to be a happy extended family. Simple pots of tea, the delivery of household supplies via the train, and Ruby's husband returning home from a hunt all represent a safe and peaceful domestic space. However, the peaceful space is disturbed by the invasion of the ghost of the little white blind girl, who was tragically killed on the railway tracks near Ruby's home. The little white blind girl haunts Ruby as she calmly goes about her everyday domestic chores, clearing dishes and hanging laundry. In this horror story, a nonreproductive white female child is the monster, not the mother. In figure 2.5, Ruby and her husband embrace near the haunted tracks where the ghost of the little blind girl lurks.

The elaborate and hybrid cooking lesson sequence is an example of how Moffatt constructs an anticolonial aesthetic through the subaltern great-grandmother figure. In the bush-cuisine cooking sequence, subaltern great-grandmothers collectively prepare their hybrid bush meal near the elder Ruby's dilapidated former home, once haunted by the little white blind girl. Though Moffatt films the

FIGURE 2.5 Young Ruby and husband Stompie, *Bedevil.*

cooking scenes in a positive and fun way, she sets the action at the site of Ruby's haunting, where the little white blind girl used to drive her crazy, and hence the nightmares of the past are ever present. Foregrounding the subaltern grandmother's voice, the elder Ruby shouts out, with an undercurrent of disdain, that it's a "bloody Queen Victoria bush-cuisine!" Earlier, Ruby had yelled to one of her teammates, "And don't forget about the wok! The wok!" Wearing funky sunglasses, the women sauté local foods in Chardonnay. They bury fresh meat they have killed in underground barbecues they have dug themselves. The elder Ruby and her fellow maternal teammates are figures of resilience and survival who refuse to be victims of colonization or primitive objects of an ethnographic gaze. Navigating a complex multicultural postcolonial landscape, these subaltern maternal figures deftly fuse the ways of the colonized and the colonizer (Victorian Britain) to emerge as full subjects and figures of resistance.

In the "Lovin' the Spin I'm In" segment, Imelda is the great-grandmother figure, who is forced to relocate by greedy land developers. Moffatt constructs Imelda as a somewhat silent character, but her vigils for her lost son represent the act of remembering as a form of anticolonial resistance. As a Torres Strait Islander woman, Imelda is perceived by the settler characters, particularly the Chinese and Greek businessmen, as an other. When Dimitri, a Greek immigrant shopkeeper and landlord, tries to evict Imelda from the building where he wants to put in a dance club and casino, Imelda proves a worthy opponent. Imelda is unwilling to relocate from the place where her son, Beba, died mysteriously. The characters who do sympathize with Imelda are the transgender "Frida Kahlo," who lives in the same building complex, and Dimitri's young wife, Voula, and their teenage son. These characters are disenfranchised, all under the control of Dimitri, who is driven by capitalist desire. They understand Imelda's candle vigils for her dead son as a sign of resistance and reject Dimitri. Dimitri vaguely tolerates these strange rituals. Though Imelda's maternal love is a force Dimitri must deal with, it is not enough to stop Dimitri's plans to tear down Imelda's home. When Imelda is forcibly removed from her home, she does not have the power, physically or emotionally, to fight off her oppressors—they are in fact her relatives.

THE ANGEL ON THE FRONTIER COUNTER-NARRATIVE

The angel on the frontier counter-narratives include *My American Cousin*, *My Brilliant Career*, *The Ballad of Little Jo*, *Thousand Pieces of Gold*, and *The Piano*. Across these narratives, frontier domesticity and motherhood are depicted as *the* site of (white) women's oppression, evoking second-wave (white) feminism of the 1960s and 1970s. In these films, agency and resistance are represented in the figure of a rebellious (virginal) daughter figure whose transgressions challenge and destabilize the cult of true womanhood. The dramatic conflicts are constructed around the daughter's desire to break free from patriarchal oppression as a means of finding her voice and subjectivity. A key strategy the daughter heroines deploy in order to resist patriarchy is to reject the role of wife and mother.

Despite this seemingly negative portrayal of motherhood as an oppressive or delimiting role for women, Campion, Wilson, Armstrong, Kelly, and Greenwald structure their narratives through a maternal logic, echoing the theories of the French poststructuralist feminists who turned their lenses to the prelingual features of the maternal body, as well as Adrienne Rich. Rich argued for the "pre-patriarchal" features of motherhood, stating that women's desire, knowledge, and power is rooted in a female maternal body.[64] Maternal desire often drives the films' plots and structures the films' gazes and acoustic regimes. Because these films are working in the popular cinema mode and are constrained by a masculinist logic inherent in classical narrative conventions (their funding would have been dependent on it), this maternal logic often functions outside the films' plots. The maternal functions somewhat covertly and is expressed as excess in the mise-en-scène and soundtrack, similarly to the Hollywood melodramas of the 1940s and 1950s. Maternal sacrifice is a key theme here, but not in service of the patriarchal household or heterosexual romance. In regard to female and gender stereotypes, the filmmakers' portrayals of mothers are never one-dimensional and never fall into what E. Ann Kaplan identified as the three main mother paradigms in Western Christian culture: the all-sacrificing angel in the house; the overindulgent mother, satisfying her own needs; and the evil, possessive, and destructive all-devouring one.[65] At the level of the plot, many of the mother figures are enabled with dramatic agency in the heroine's/ daughter's journey toward subjectivity. Hence, across these films maternal desire is privileged as the driving force.

Three kinds of mother figures appear across the angel on the frontier narrative: the oppressed white-settler mother figure, the wise subaltern maternal figure, and the Mother of the Empire figure. I borrow the term *Mother of the Empire* from feminist historian Julia Bush, who examined the construction of maternal imperialism in the colonies.

> Queen Victoria, of course, represented the ultimate maternal icon, the "Great White Queen," and "Mother of the Empire" whose loving care for her colonized subjects was deeply imbued with superiority and controlling power as it was with a sense of Christian duty. For Victoria embodied maternal imperialism at its most authoritative, and through her royal status resolved the paradoxes implied by strong female rule accompanied by a conservative outlook on gender roles.[66]

The white-settler mother is an unhappy, oppressed figure who is either overburdened with reproductive and farm labor or dominated by a powerful patriarch. Though she is generally a sympathetic character, she is often at odds with her rebellious daughter. However, despite the white-settler mother's inferior social status, the filmmakers empower her in the narrative as a dramatic agent. The Mother of the Empire figure is generally an unsympathetic character, primarily motivated by maintaining the status quo. Her power is rooted in her associations and relations with (white) colonial patriarchs and her privileged status in society as a British female authority figure. Her feminine identity is rooted in the Old World, in this case Britain and Queen Victoria, and she sees herself as an instructor in the art of proper (British) white femininity. She is generally at odds with the films' heroines, who balk at her old-fashioned and stuffy ideas or reject traditional female roles in the patriarchal family. The Mother of the Empire's agency is constructed through her desire to assert her influence over the heroine. Strangely, even though this controlling figure aims to maintain the law of the father, her actions often inadvertently lead to the rebellious daughter figure realizing her desires. The elder or subaltern wisewoman figure is different from the Mother of the Empire figure. In contrast, she is generally a sympathetic figure and functions as a helper to the heroine by offering support, advice, and key knowledge. Though she seemingly has minimal purpose in the films' plots, she is vital to the heroine's journey. This figure is similar to the subaltern great-grandmother figure in the antiracist and colonial narratives but has a far less prominent role and is not represented through an antiracist or anticolonial lens.

Throughout *My Brilliant Career*, Gillian Armstrong subverts the role of the good pioneer woman primarily through the rebellious figure of Sybylla, whose professional and artistic aspirations are repeatedly thwarted by the demands of her large farming family burdened by drought and financial woes. As the eldest daughter, Sybylla is expected to help care for her younger siblings and carry her weight on the farm, not dally on the piano or write novels. Sybylla's mother, Mrs. Melvyn, a disgruntled farmwife overburdened by childbearing and domestic duties, deems Sybylla's artistic ambitions to be unrealistic and selfish. This is a source of much tension between mother and daughter. This tension is depicted in the scene in which Mrs. Melvyn informs Sybylla that the family cannot afford to keep her anymore.

SHOT: *Close angle on Sybylla as she plays the family's piano, which is in dire need of tuning. Sybylla hums along as her disgruntled mother enters the frame. Mrs. Melvyn parks herself beside the piano, folding her hands in front of her with purpose. Sybylla blatantly ignores her.*

SHOT: *Medium-close angle on Mrs. Melvyn, looking displeased and concerned.* "Sybylla, I want to have a talk with you."

SHOT: *Close angle on Sybylla, still hammering away on the piano, while Mrs. Melvyn looms in background of the shot. Sybylla says flippantly,* "Talk away." *The camera follows Mrs. Melvyn as she places her hand over Sybylla's hands, putting a stop to her playing. Mrs. Melvyn pulls her hand away, and Sybylla slams the piano shut.*

SHOT: *Long shot on Sybylla sitting at the piano, arms crossed in frustration. Mrs. Melvyn stands erect beside her. Mrs. Melvyn pauses for a moment and then moves away from her angry daughter. Wringing her hands, she says,* "You're a young woman now, and . . ." *Distraught, Mrs. Melvyn raises her hand to her mouth.* "I have been thinking about this a great deal." *With a pained expression, Mrs. Melvyn says,* "We can't afford to keep you any longer. Do you think you could earn your own living?" *Sybylla keeps her back to her mother and replies,* "Of course!" *Mrs. Melvyn asks tentatively,* "And how would you do that?" *Sybylla turns defiantly and declares,* "I'd like to be a pianist." *Mrs. Melvyn sighs with exasperation.* "Oh, Sybylla! That takes years of practice and you know we can't afford it." *Sybylla replies with indignation,* "You've thought of something already, haven't you?" *Mrs. Melvyn nods gravely.*

Mrs. Melvyn goes on to explain that she has arranged a domestic servant's position for Sybylla, which is of course unacceptable. Sybylla directs her anger at her mother despite the fact that the family's financial problems are due to drought and the father's mismanagement of the farm. As an impoverished woman with too many mouths to feed, Mrs. Melvyn is placed in an impossible position as a mother. Despite her seeming coldness toward her daughter, Mrs. Melvyn acts out of maternal desire when she writes to her own mother, the wealthy cattle station matron Grandma Bossier, for help. This action leads to an invitation from Grandma Bossier for Sybylla to stay with her at Caddagat, to be offered up on the middle-class marriage market.

With the fortitude of a military commandant, Grandma Bossier oversees and orchestrates Sybylla's transformation from a wild, unkempt bush-farmer's daughter to a poised and proper young lady in the hope she will attract the attentions of a wealthy man. Armstrong constructs a makeover sequence that depicts Grandma Bossier's and Aunt Helen's methods as bordering on the cruel and the absurd. Sybylla treats the whole beauty regime process with disdain and mockery, exemplified in figure 2.6.

Grandma Bossier's work is in vain, however, because Sybylla doesn't want to get married; she wants to have a career. Sybylla soon learns that Grandma Bossier's world of elegance and culture is as confining and delimiting as the domestic drudgery her poor mother endures on the family farm, "having a baby every year." Though Sybylla is initially encouraged by the fact that her artistic talents seemingly prove more valuable in the privileged and refined realm of Caddagat, it becomes apparent that in Grandma Bossier's world, young ladies display their artistic talents only as a means to catch a husband or entertain dinner guests in the parlor, no more. Uninterested in Grandma Bossier's plans for her future, Sybylla is a difficult and rebellious pupil.

One of the ways Sybylla rebels is by taking on the persona of an Irish servant girl, one strongly associated with ethnic femininity, fallen women, and lowbrow entertainment, the very opposite of the lady persona Aunt Helen and Grandma Bossier have gone to great pains and expense to construct. As the Irish servant girl, Sybylla is at more liberty to flirt openly with men and show disdain for confining,

FIGURE 2.6 Sybylla at Caddagat, *My Brilliant Career.*

ladylike decorum. This is exemplified in the dinner party scene in which Sybylla plays ribald pub songs on her grandmother's parlor piano, much to the amusement of the male guests, particularly her fun-loving uncle and the besotted Harry Beacham. As Sybylla dances with one of her suitors, Frank Hawdon, she bellows out a pub song about young women drinking and losing their virginity. Though Sybylla knows how to play more refined classical pieces, such as Robert Schumann's "From Foreign Lands and People" (1838), which recurs throughout the film, Sybylla defiantly chooses to play only popular pub songs in Grandma Bossier's parlor. Though all of Sybylla's male admirers are enchanted with her unusual "hidden talents," Grandma Bossier and Aunt Helen are not. When they learn of her "bacchanalian debauch," Sybylla is reprimanded. Even when it is suggested by her uncle that Sybylla is talented enough to "go on the stage," Grandma Bossier is enraged. "I would rather have you go about on the streets like a common prostitute than go on the stage!"

The whipping incident in Harry's den is another example of how Armstrong constructs Sybylla's unladylike rebelliousness. After Sybylla deserts Aunt Gussie's boring and uptight ball in favor of the servants' barn dance, Harry comes in search of Sybylla, only to find her dancing with a ruggedly handsome male farmhand. Harry is jealous and shocked by Sybylla's reckless behavior while simultaneously aroused by her passionate and impulsive nature. Harry decides to take charge of Sybylla and the situation, dragging her away from the barn dance and into his private hunting den. Sybylla is not so easily controlled, however.

SHOT: *Medium-long shot as Harry bangs open the door to a hunting den, shoving Sybylla roughly inside. It is a very masculine space, filled with guns and hunting paraphernalia. Harry glares at her with lust and anger. He turns and closes the door calmly but firmly. Sybylla, off-screen, says,* "Didn't you like me dancing with the peasants? *Harry replies,* "I'm not going to make a big thing of this." *He stalks toward her. Sybylla, off-screen, says teasingly,* "I disgraced you, didn't I?" *The camera follows Harry's movements, bringing Sybylla into the frame. He says calmly,* "I have to go away for a few days."

SHOT: *Sybylla replies casually,* "Oh? More shearing somewhere else?" *Sybylla picks up a riding crop. She's fuming mad. Harry, off-screen, says loudly,* "I must be told if it's yes or no?!" *Sybylla plays with the riding crop.* "What's the question?"

SHOT: *Medium angle two-shot. Infuriated, Harry yells,* "Bloody woman!" *He prowls toward Sybylla. Framed with Sybylla in a medium-close angle, Harry says firmly,* "I thought . . . I thought we should get married!" *Sybylla looks a little dumbfounded. She says with indignation,* "Well, what a handsome proposal!" *She storms away from him and says,* "How could anyone say no?" *Harry replies with disdain,* "How dare you?" *He moves menacingly toward her, but Sybylla stands her ground. Seizing her by the waist, he pulls Sybylla's body against his. As he attempts to kiss her, Sybylla raises the riding crop and impulsively strikes him across the face. Harry rises from the blow, clasping his injury.*

SHOT: *Medium-close angle on Harry staring down at his hand, where there is blood. He gazes at Sybylla with utter disbelief. He forcefully snatches the riding crop away from her, hurting her hand in the process. Sybylla winces in pain. Bringing her hand to her mouth, she gazes at Harry with fear and regret. Harry backs away from her, leaving the frame. Sybylla drops down onto a bench in defeat.*

SHOT: *Medium angle on Harry, who wipes blood from the side of his face. He turns his gaze to Sybylla.*

SHOT: *Medium-high angle on Sybylla with her hands held tight at her chest, her head bowed down in regret and shame. She says quietly,* "Harry, I . . ." *She squeezes her eyes shut and shakes her head.* "I'm sorry." *Harry, off-screen, says gently,* "It's my fault. It was stupid of me."

SHOT: *Medium-low angle on Harry, who gazes at Sybylla with empathy and concern, not to mention a little amusement.* "I should really get back to my guests."

Armstrong infuses the whipping scene with sexual frustration on a number of levels. First, Sybylla refuses to submit to Harry as either a sexual object or a wifely figure because she is afraid of losing herself. Both characters are constrained by the mores of the times and are expected to behave according to strictly defined roles assigned to their class and gender. Harry is especially cognizant of these roles and knows they cannot consummate their relationship until they are married. Though Sybylla would never make Harry a very good society wife, given her rebellious nature and her upbringing, he wants her. Second, though the scene has echoes of a romance novel, Armstrong turns it into a statement about feminist resistance and agency. By locating the scene in such a masculine space, surrounded by guns and whips, Armstrong seems to set up Sybylla and Harry as worthy opponents rather than lovers, battling each other for control. Sybylla will never submit.

Women such as Grandma Bossier, Aunt Gussie, and Aunt Helen function as Mother of the Empire figures and are all trapped in their own gilded cages of sorts, symbolized by Aunt Gussie's enormous exotic bird cage and bird-feather paintings. In Grandma Bossier's world, beauty regimes, poise, and female cultural refinement are essential to finding a wealthy husband—such as Frank Hawdon—and survival. When Grandma Bossier tires of Sybylla's games, she speaks frankly with her, outlining her options as a plain-looking young woman with no breeding and no connections.

GRANDMA BOSSIER: "Now listen to me, Sybylla. In a few years he'll [Frank Hawdon] come into quite a large fortune in England. He comes of a very good family, and he'll make someone an excellent husband."

SYBYLLA: "Well, it won't be me."

GRANDMA BOSSIER: "Do be realistic, child."

SYBYLLA: "Well—I am. To begin with, I don't love him."

GRANDMA BOSSIER: "That is not the point."

SYBYLLA: "It is to me."

GRANDMA BOSSIER: "Sybylla, do you want to be a burden on your family forever? With no status in decent society or a home of your own?"

SYBYLLA: "I will not be married off to someone I detest, by YOU or anybody!"

GRANDMA BOSSIER: "At times I fear for you, my girl. You are rude to your elders and betters and often lack all gentility." *(Pause.)* "Very well. You may not be prepared to apologize to Frank, but I expect you to apologize to ME—when you have regained your . . . humor. And your manners!"

Needless to say, Sybylla and her grandmother clash, a classic Old World versus New World conflict. Both characters realize they stand for very different values and ideas about womanhood. Grandma Bossier tires of Sybylla's notions about female independence and finally sends her back. Though Grandma Bossier's exile of Sybylla initially seems harsh, her actions inadvertently lead Sybylla to the McSwats' farm, which in turn will lead Sybylla back to Possum Gully, her family home, where she will realize her dream to write a book. Grandma Bossier's actions ironically help Sybylla, aiding in her tumultuous journey toward selfhood.

Mrs. McSwat is a minor character in *My Brilliant Career*, though she plays a key role in Sybylla's journey. Though a white-settler mother, Mrs. McSwat is a more positive version than Mrs. Melvyn's depressed, downtrodden figure, although she certainly is not a role model for Sybylla. After Sybylla fails to play by Grandma Bossier's rules, rejecting not one but two marriage proposals from Frank and Harry, she is sent away from Caddagat to work as a governess at the McSwats' prosperous, albeit muddy, bush-farm. Sybylla's father is in debt to the McSwats, and so Sybylla's labor is offered as payment. Mrs. McSwat is an almost hypermaternal figure, seemingly less burdened by motherhood despite her large brood. When Mrs. McSwat misinterprets Sybylla's feelings for her eldest son as romantic, she sends her back home because the son has been promised to another farmer's daughter, a wealthy one. Sybylla, as an impoverished Melvyn, can offer no valuable family connections. The McSwats take pity on Sybylla, however, and wipe the Melvyn debt clean. Without the McSwat debt, Sybylla doesn't have to go into domestic service or even get married. Hence, Sybylla is free to reject Harry's second marriage proposal, despite her attraction to him, and stay with her family at Possum Gully to write her novel.

My American Cousin is told through the eyes of the mischievous twelve-year-old Sandy Wilcox. Sandy's desiring gaze is directed toward her older, glamorous cousin Butch, who exudes, and performs, masculine sexuality in the vein of James Dean and Elvis Presley. Sandy's active desiring female gaze provides the basis for much of the film's comedy and is the key way Sandy Wilson debunks the trope of the virginal angel on the frontier. Much to the dismay of her parents, Sandy rejects the role of dutiful daughter and finds all sorts of ways to rebel against their ideas of proper feminine conduct, a source of major conflict between Sandy and her parents.

As the eldest daughter in a large farming family, Sandy is expected to help her mother, Kitty Wilcox, manage the children and aid in the family's cherry orchard business. With the arrival of her American cousin, Sandy's hormones kick in, and she spends most of the film chasing after him like a lovesick puppy. Though Sandy's mother is irritated by her daughter's fascination with Butch, Sandy's father, Major Wilcox, is driven to the edge of reason about it. The sexy and wild Butch represents everything that Major Wilcox is not. He is older but not an authority figure. He is fun and rebellious and completely unconnected to domesticity. Wilson explicitly foregrounds Major Wilcox's somewhat uptight (and Victorian) attitude toward gender relations and heterosexuality in his extremely awkward talk to Sandy about the birds and the bees.

> SHOT: *Wide angle on the Paradise Ranch truck driving along the road, surrounded by majestic forest. Major Wilcox's voice-over:* "I think the time has come for me to talk to you about, um . . . males and females . . . together. I'm afraid it's a very complicated business." *The truck pauses and then turns a corner. Sandy's voice-over:* "Yeah, I know. Me, Thelma, Sue, and Lizzy talk about it all the time." *Major Wilcox replies uncomfortably,* "Ah." *He clears his throat and brings the truck to a stop beside a mailbox. Sandy leaps out of the truck to grab the family's mail.*
>
> SHOT: *Medium-close angle on Sandy as she climbs back in the truck with the mail. She casually rifles through it.*
>
> SHOT: *Medium-close angle on Major Wilcox, who clears his throat again. He looks disconcerted. Resuming the difficult topic, he says,* "As I was saying to you . . ."
>
> SHOT: *Medium-close angle on Sandy flipping through the pages of a* National Geographic *magazine. He continues.* "The attraction between the male and female is natural and necessary to the continuation of the species." *Sandy offers her father a sideways glance and then rolls her eyes. The sound of a bee buzzing is foregrounded in the soundtrack. Sandy stifles a giggle.*

SHOT: *Medium-close angle on Major Wilcox, who gazes stoically out the windshield of the truck, too embarrassed to return his daughter's gaze. He continues.* "The female excites the male. And once it's excited the man is overcome with . . . uh . . ." *The Major searches desperately for the right words.* ". . . Uncontrollable urges."

SHOT: *Medium-close shot on Sandy, who turns to her father, mortified. She exclaims,* "Uncontrollable urges?!"

SHOT: *Medium-close shot on the Major, who is growing more discomfited by the second. He replies,* "Yes, they're rather difficult to explain." *Shakily, he puts his aviator sunglasses on and starts up the engine of the truck. He clears his throat yet again.*

SHOT: *Wide-angle bird's-eye-view shot on the truck driving along the rural road surrounded by forest and lake. The Major continues.* "You can see it when a bull knows there's a cow nearby. That bull will break through fence, wire, a door, walls, anything that stands between him and that cow." *The camera pans the path of the truck as it drives off in the distance. Sandy's voice chimes in.* "You mean you were like that with Mom?" *The Major replies,* "No, of course not! Well . . . not exactly." *Sandy says calmly,* "Sounds complicated, Dad." *The Major sighs.* "Yes, it is. Well, it's good to have the chance to talk with you like this."

The Major's sex talk is rooted in patriarchal notions of female sexuality. Sex is about procreative duty, not pleasure, and only men have uncontrollable sexual urges. The woman is there to receive male sexual advances passively, and it is her duty as a reproductive body to do so. The Major is of course depicted as a comic figure; his words of wisdom are represented as old-fashioned, bordering on the ridiculous. For Wilson, it is the female characters, such as Sandy and her girlfriends, who have the uncontrollable urges.

On Wilson's 1950s frontier, women and girls pursue male objects of desire despite the risks. Sandy and her girlfriends cannot seem to contain their hysteria in the presence of Butch, who manages to send all the females around him into fits of arousal. Even the cool and collected Shirley Darling, Sandy's teenage nemesis, ditches her loyal and boring boyfriend, Lenny, to have a secret tryst with Butch at the Dominion Day dance. Major Wilcox himself is reduced to an object of female sexual desire by the middle-aged, and married, Gladys Rutherford, who can't seem to contain her lust while on the dance floor with him, despite the Major's disinterest and discomfort. The rendering of the male characters as objects of female desire is a key way Wilson debunks the fallen angel trope. This is exemplified in the scene at the lake in which Butch performs a striptease for Sandy and her girlfriends on the beach.

SHOT: *Medium-long angle on Butch submerged in the lake water. He waves his wet jeans in the air, having deftly removed them underwater. He shouts to the girls who sit gazing at him on the beach,* "Hey, come back in!" *He laughs tauntingly.*

SHOT: *Long-angle shot on Sandy and her three friends, dressed in their modest bathing suits. They giggle nervously. Sandy says,* "What if he gets an uncontrollable urge?" *Thelma says knowingly,* "Yeah, we'd get in trouble." *The other friend exclaims nervously,* "Oh my gosh!"

SHOT: *Over-the-shoulder full shot on Sandy and her friends gazing out at Butch, still submerged in the water. Butch teasingly says,* "Hey girls, don't ya want to have some fun?" [See figure 2.7.] *Lizzie answers seductively,* "Yeah." *Sandy turns to her.* "Lizzie, don't you dare!" *Butch warns,* "I'm coming to get you!" *He surges out of the water, scaring the girls, who shriek excitedly. Butch laughs. He has managed to put his pants back on underwater. He struts out of the lake in front of his young female admirers in tight wet jeans.*

FIGURE 2.7 Butch (in water), Sandy, and friends at the lake, *My American Cousin.*

Though the film is family oriented and comedic, Wilson constructs a feminist commentary about female sexuality and desire that exists outside strict Victorian moral codes about sex. In contrast to Major Wilcox's ideology that sex is procreative, here sexual desire, constructed through a female (heterosexual) gaze, exists outside masculine parameters, marriage, and even heteronormative romantic love, echoing the sex-positive feminists of the 1970s. Sex is presented as potentially fun, not a duty. Though Butch gets some perverse pleasure out of scaring the girls for a moment, he is not depicted as a sexually aggressive male. Rather, Butch is a kind of peacock, shamelessly displaying his body in front of the girls, who collectively enjoy the show. Female characters do not face any real punishment for acting on or pursuing their sexual desires but rather assert a level of control over the males in their lives.

As a white-settler mother, Sandy's mother, Kitty Wilcox, on the surface is similar to Mrs. Melvyn in *My Brilliant Career*. A dissatisfied farmwife, Kitty seems oppressed by her labor of love, which also includes the unpaid work of canning cherries for the family's business. Through Kitty, however, Wilson turns the good pioneer woman trope on its head. Despite the demands of motherhood and domesticity, Kitty makes time to perform the lead role in an amateur theater production of Henrik Ibsen's *Hedda Gabler*. Wilson's deployment of *Hedda Gabler* is apt here because the play is structured through the point of view of a repressed, bored, and angry privileged housewife who tries to manipulate the various men in her life, albeit with devastating consequences. Wilson sets the comical running-lines scene in the Wilcox kitchen, the primary site of unpaid domestic labor. Here Wilson makes mockery of the good pioneer woman figure.

SHOT: *Medium-long two-shot on Sandy and her mother, Kitty. Sandy reads aloud from her mother's script,* "From now on you have a hold over me." *Kitty repeats the lines,* "From now on you have a hold over me." *As she practices her lines, Kitty wipes down the kitchen counter. Sandy plays "Mr. Brack" and reads in a deep male voice.* "My dearest Hedda, I shall not abuse my position."

SHOT: *Close shot on Kitty, who recites undramatically,* "In your power all the same, at the mercy of your will and demands. And so, a slave, a slave! No. That I cannot tolerate. Never!" *Kitty pauses and then makes a few mental notes. She takes off her apron and walks over to her red purse. The camera follows her into a medium-long angle. She continues reciting.* "I can hear perfectly well what you are saying. But, how am I going to get through the evenings out here?" *Kitty fishes for something in her purse. She pulls out a red lipstick and takes the cap off.*

SHOT: *Close shot on Kitty, who gazes into the kitchen mirror. She resumes her role as Sandy's mother and turns to her daughter.* "Now, Sandra, please make sure that Ruth and Pixie get to bed on time." *Kitty turns back to the mirror and applies her red lipstick.*

SHOT: *Close shot on Sandy, who watches her mother. Kitty's voice is heard off-screen.* "And I don't want you hanging around those pickers."

SHOT: *Close shot on Sandy giving her mother a look of exasperation. She replies,* "Ok . . . ay." *Sandy turns her attention back to the script. As* "Mr. Brack," *she reads,* "We shall have a very pleasant time together here, you and I." *Kitty's voice-off:* "That is what you're looking forward to, isn't it, Mr. Brack? You as the only cock in the yard." *Sandy looks pointedly up at her mother.*

SHOT: *Close shot on Kitty, who returns her gaze to the mirror. Raising two fingers to her temple, she takes aim and shoots, making gunfire sounds for effect. (Hedda has just committed suicide.)*

SHOT: *American shot on Kitty and Sandy. After her mock suicide, Kitty quickly turns away from the mirror and reaches for her red purse. Sandy reads aloud,* "Shot herself . . . shot herself in the temple! Think of it! By merciful God, one doesn't do that sort of thing!" *Kitty continues to ready herself to leave the house.* "Bye, Sandra. Don't forget to put away the laundry. Tell your father I'm gone. I'll be back around ten." *No longer* "Mr. Brack," *Sandy replies lightheartedly,* "Bye, Mom! Break a leg, knock 'em dead." *Kitty exits the house. Once her mother is out of sight, Sandy picks up her mother's lipstick and applies it to her own lips while standing on her tiptoes at the kitchen mirror, the same place where her mother as Hedda committed her mock suicide.*

On the surface, Wilson's deployment of Ibsen's *Hedda Gabler* is played for comic effect. The play, a tragedy, is a scathing critique of bourgeois values and patriarchy and is one of the first texts to feature a feminist heroine. Literary critic Joan Templeton made a connection between Hedda Gabler and Hjørdis from *The Vikings at Helgeland*, since the arms-bearing, horse-riding Hedda, married to a passive man she despises, indeed resembles the "eagle in a cage" that Hjørdis terms herself.[67] It is through her role as Hedda that Kitty (and Wilson) voice discontent about the role of the bourgeois middle-class housewife within patriarchy, echoing and underscoring Sandy's rebellion against the dutiful daughter role. Even if the viewer is not familiar with Ibsen, the lines Kitty recites are so melodramatic that they serve as a humorous contrast to her boring life as a settler wife and mother.

Sandy's grandmother, Granny Wilcox, is a Mother of the Empire figure. She has a similar bearing to that of Grandma Bossier, although she does not have the same level of wealth and social status. She also has a much smaller role in the narrative, appearing in only one scene. The purpose of Granny Wilcox seems to be more as a comic device than anything. However, despite this minor role, Wilson deploys Granny Wilcox as a way to construct a brief feminist commentary about Old World Victorian womanhood and femininity. Wilson depicts this in the garden tea scene, in which Sandy and her father pay Granny Wilcox a visit.

SHOT: *Medium shot on Granny Wilcox, who offers someone off-screen a plate of biscuits.* "Another bikkie?" *Off-screen, Major Wilcox replies politely,* "Oh, no thank you."

SHOT: *Medium-close shot on Major Wilcox as he sips from a delicate china teacup. Granny Wilcox, off-screen, says,* "Tea, Sandra?" *Sandy, off-screen, replies,* "Oh, no thanks, Granny . . ."

SHOT: *Full shot on three characters sitting in Granny's garden. Sandy stands in the foreground with her back to the lens. Granny and Major Wilcox sit at a tea table. In the background is a majestic lake and mountains. Sandy continues,* "I think I'll just have a glass of water." *Sandy slouches as she speaks. Granny Wilcox replies with indignation,* "WADER? What on God's great earth is WADER?"

SHOT: *Medium-close shot on Sandy. Confused and irritated, she replies,* "Water. In the tap, in the lake, falls from the sky . . ."

SHOT: *Medium-close shot on Major Wilcox, who looks at his mother with resigned confusion. Granny Wilcox replies with feigned understanding.* "Wa-TER!"

SHOT: *Medium-close shot on Granny Wilcox. She sets down her cup of tea with purpose and turns to the impatient Sandy.* "Now, please let me hear you say "wa-TER," as it was meant to be spoken."

SHOT: *Medium shot on Sandy looking bored and irritated. She exclaims in a dramatic manner,* "WATER!!" *Sandy glares at her grandmother and then turns theatrically toward the house. She marches into the house, almost colliding with her aunt. Granny Wilcox, off-screen, says,* "Very good. That wasn't so difficult, now, was it? What these young children do with the Queen's language . . ." *At this point Sandy has disappeared into the house.*

Speaking in the "Queen's language," Granny Wilcox holds court in her backyard garden, criticizing her granddaughter, *Sandra*, for her improper pronunciations and manners while doling out tea in elegant English china teacups. This scene is set against the majestic and un-civilized British Columbia landscape—hardly an English garden. By framing Granny Wilcox's British-style tea party against a rugged wilderness, Wilson constructs a humorous and ironic contrast that highlights the absurdity of Granny Wilcox's stifling Old World values. Granny Wilcox's old-fashioned ways hold little meaning or interest for Sandy. Although Wilson does not critique Granny's British imperialism, there is the implication that Granny Wilcox's world is on its way out, mainly as a result of the influence and growing seductiveness of American youth culture such as rock and roll, Hollywood, and fast cars, represented by Sandy's cousin Butch. Unlike Sybylla's nineteenth-century grandmother, Grandma Bossier, Granny Wilcox has little power or authority in a mid-twentieth-century North American society. Granny Wilcox may think she is superior to everyone else because of her Britishness, but Wilson represents her as irrelevant and out of step, not only with her granddaughter but with the New World. Immediately after Sandy's exchange with Granny Wilcox, Sandy calls one of her girlfriends to gush about the handsome Butch and his amazing, cool car.

In *The Piano*, Campion debunks the white angel on the frontier trope through Ada and her seven-year-old daughter, Flora. On the surface, Ada appears to be the white-settler mother; however, Ada's actions are driven not by maternal desire but rather by her fetishistic desire for her lost piano and, later, her sexual desire for George Baines. Though Ada could be construed as a bad mother, selfishly concerned with her own desires and pleasures, Campion resists this monolithic representation. Instead, Campion constructs Ada as a rebellious daughter who subverts the rules of the patriarchal family. Indeed, Ada has the same legal status and rights as that of her daughter. Sold into marriage by her father against her will, Ada immediately rejects Stewart, the man her father has chosen for her. Like the rebellious heroines in Armstrong's *My Brilliant Career* and Wilson's *My American Cousin*, Ada subverts her role as the dutiful daughter. Ada's rejection of Stewart is conflated with her rebellion against her father, a rejection of her role as white-settler wife and mother in the patriarchal household.

As a settler wife and mother, Ada is useful to her husband, Stewart, for her iconographic value as a beacon of Victorian femininity and Christian morality. Ada and Flora have been brought to Stewart's New Zealand/Aotearoa homestead to civilize a homosocial masculine frontier space. However, Ada subverts her civilizing role by prostituting herself in exchange for her beloved piano, which her husband has callously traded to Baines in exchange for land. Hurt and enraged that her husband has no regard for her wants and desires, Ada enters into a deal with Baines in which she can earn her piano back, one black key for every visit. Ada's transgression can be seen as an act of resistance against her unfeeling husband and her father as both men use her as an exchange commodity. Visually and thematically, Campion's characters seem to be drawn from the archetypes of a typical Western. Like the saloon girl, Ada is paid for entertaining (playing for) and sexually servicing transient lonely white men (cowboys and outlaws) such as Baines. This is exemplified in the proposition scene, set in Baines's bachelor homestead, a dark and unkempt masculine space.

SHOT: *Establishing shot on Baines's bachelor homestead. Flora waits on the porch, playing with a wild-looking dog.*

SHOT: *Medium-close shot on Baines, who prowls around as Ada plays the piano, lost in her music. Baines comes to a pause and stares longingly at Ada.*

SHOT: *Baines's point of view of Ada's exposed neck. The subjective camera tracks into Ada's neck, almost predatorially. Baines sets his roughened hand on Ada's small, white neck. He bows his head to kiss her there.*

SHOT: *Close-angle reverse shot on Baines kissing Ada's neck.*

SHOT: *Medium angle on Ada, who gasps at Baines's intimacy. She rises from her piano, bringing her hand to her mouth in shock. The camera follows her as she backs away from Baines. Though she is surprised by Baines's actions, she does not leave.*

SHOT: *Medium-close angle on Baines, who says carefully,* "There's a way you can have your piano back. You want it back?"

SHOT: *Medium-close shot on Ada, who returns Baines's gaze. She waits.*

SHOT: *Medium-close shot on Baines. He says matter-of-factly,* "I'd like us to make a deal."

SHOT: *Medium-close angle on Ada listening. Baines continues,* "There's things I'd like to do while you play."

SHOT: *Medium-close angle on Ada, who turns away, disgusted by Baines's sexual suggestion. She begins to leave.*

SHOT: *Medium-close handheld camera on Baines, who offers in desperation,* "If you let me, you can earn it back."

SHOT: *Medium angle on Ada, who starts to collect her jacket and sheet music.*

SHOT: *Medium-close angle on Baines. He continues with his "deal."* "One visit for every key."

Baines and Ada continue to barter. Ada will make her own demands, insisting on one visit for every *black* key, which is, as Baines remarks, impressed, "considerably less." Baines agrees to Ada's price. Ada is hardly the good pioneer woman.

Campion constructs Ada as neither a faithful wife nor a very maternal mother. Though Ada loves her daughter, Flora, dearly, their relationship is not a typical mother-daughter one; like Ada herself, it is enigmatic. In some sense, Campion (dis)places the maternal role onto Flora, constructing a role reversal between mother and daughter.

Throughout the film, Ada's daughterlike features are emphasized. One of the first things Stewart says to and about Ada is "You're small. I didn't think you'd be small." This smallness can be linked to Ada's inferior or childlike status in the Stewart household. In many ways, Ada and Flora are two sides of the same coin of womanhood. Campion depicts the role reversal between Ada and Flora in the wedding portrait scene.

> SHOT: *Medium-long two-shot on Flora and Ada. Wearing a mock-bridal gown (it's only half a gown attached by ties at the back) and headpiece, Ada gazes at her reflection in the mirror. Flora stands beside the mirror, facing her mother with a scowl on her face. She demands unhappily, "I want to be in the photograph!" Ada doesn't reply.*

In figure 2.8a, Ada offers her daughter (off-screen) a puzzled look, while flanked by Nessie and Aunt Morag who have orchestrated the wedding photograph ritual. In figure 2.8b, Flora glares back at her mother, angry and confused that she cannot be in the matrimonial portrait. This shot/reverse-shot sequence exemplifies Flora's jealousy over her mother's new role as Baines' wife and typifies the mother-daughter role-reversal in the film.

Later, after the wedding portrait session is over, Ada literally rips off her wedding gown, which is held at the back by ties, like a paper-doll dress or a child's dress-up costume. Like a costume, the dress serves one purpose, to aid in a performance or masquerade of marriage. With this somewhat violent gesture, Ada rejects the role of Stewart's bride. Instead, Ada can think only of her beloved and abandoned piano. As soon as she has ripped off the gown, to the shock of Aunt Morag and Nessie, Ada rushes to the nearest window and gazes out forlornly. Campion cuts to the abandoned piano on the beach as it lies in wait for its lost mistress. In contrast to her mother, Flora longs to be a part of the wedding portrait, a visual representation of the traditional nuclear heteronormative white-settler family.

Flora wants her mother to play by the rules of patriarchy and accept her role as a white-settler wife. With an unruly mother acting like a rebellious daughter, Flora takes on maternal or wifely qualities. Driven by her (maternal) desire to save the patriarchal family, Flora

FIGURE 2.8A Ada (center), Nessie, and Aunt Morag, *The Piano.*

FIGURE 2.8B Flora, *The Piano.*

shifts from aiding her mother to trying to control her, especially in regard to her mother's affair with Baines. When Ada is with Baines, Flora is not needed for her communication skills (her ability to speak and sign) or her companionship and hence is banned from Baines's home, where Ada conducts her "music lessons." This creates conflict between mother and daughter, disrupting a seemingly happy relationship. As her mother and Baines become more attached, Flora attaches herself more closely to Stewart, her stepfather, whom she had previously refused to call *Father*. Driven by her desire to save the family from ruin, Flora betrays her mother's trust to Stewart, not once but twice.

The first time Flora betrays her mother is in the "tree cleansing" scene. Stewart is punishing Flora for kissing and rubbing herself up against tree trunks (a kind of sexual practicing she learned from the Maori children). While scrubbing down the tree trunks, Flora explains to Stewart why Baines still doesn't know how to play the piano, despite all those lessons. "She never gives him a turn. She just plays what she pleases. And sometimes she doesn't play at all." Stewart asks suspiciously, "When's the next lesson?" Flora tells him, "Tomorrow." Stewart spies on Baines and Ada, confirming his suspicion that they are having an affair. This leads Stewart to imprison Ada in their house, boarding up all the windows and barring the door from the outside. (This is quite perplexing to Aunt Morag, who can't imagine how that will keep the Maori out.) While Stewart is boarding up the windows, it is Flora who instructs him on where to place the boards. Pointing to the window, Flora yells, "Here, Papa!" Ada tries to ignore what is being done to her, but Flora decides to give Ada a lecture, as a mother would to a child. As Stewart hammers away at Ada's prison, Flora admonishes her mother, "You shouldn't have gone up there, should you? I don't like it, and nor does Papa."

The second time Flora seemingly betrays her mother is after Ada promises Stewart not to see Baines again. Stewart permits Ada some limited freedom and has removed the barriers to the doors and windows. However, Ada can't forget about Baines and breaks her promise to Stewart and Flora. Campion represents Ada's resistance to Stewart's stifling and oppressive control through the following piano key scene.

> SHOT: *Close angle on the side of a piano key Ada has dislodged from her piano. She has burned in the message* "Dear George, you have my heart. Ada McGrath." *(Her maiden name.) Ada wraps the key in a handkerchief.*
>
> SHOT: *Long shot on Ada silhouetted behind hanging sheets. Flora's angel wings hover at the bottom of the frame. These are the same wings she wore in the production of Bluebeard performed earlier in the film. She is playing with her dolls. She says in a no-nonsense, motherly voice,* "And be quiet!"
>
> SHOT: *Medium angle on a washtub. Flora's hands scrub her dolls' clothes. She continues speaking in her mother's voice,* "You just have to be naked until I finish washing and drying your clothes."

SHOT: *Ada emerges from behind the sheet, carrying the piano key behind her back. She approaches Flora. Ada bends down and hands Flora the piano key. In sign language, Ada asks Flora to take the key to Baines. Flora shakes her head defiantly.* "No, we're not supposed to visit him." *Desperate, Ada pleads with Flora. Flora turns stern on her mother and places the piano key down, refusing to obey her wishes. Ignoring her mother, Flora returns to hanging up her dolls' clothes. Angered, Ada firmly places the piano key into Flora's hands. She grabs her forcefully and instructs Flora,* "Go." *Flora submits and marches off, seemingly following her mother's orders.*

The scene reflects a power struggle between mother and daughter, with Ada trying to assert her power as the real mother in the relationship. However, Flora knows her mother's relationship with Baines threatens the survival of the patriarchal household, so instead of delivering the piano key to Baines, she delivers it to Stewart, "Papa." Upon seeing the piano key and its romantic message, Stewart becomes enraged. Driven by jealousy and possessiveness, Stewart exacts violent revenge on Ada.

Though Flora's actions initially seem like betrayals rooted in her desire for a "normal family" in the patriarchal sense, Campion renders Flora's actions as subversive. In the end, Flora's actions inadvertently lead to her mother's salvation. Like Sybylla and Sandy, Ada is a lost daughter saved by a maternal figure. Flora's actions lead Stewart and Baines to confront the reality that Ada will never allow her will to be possessed—by anyone. These actions include not only Flora's diverted delivery of her mother's engraved piano key to Stewart but also the horrific delivery of her mother's bloody severed finger to Baines courtesy of Stewart. Used as a go-between by her parents, Flora is driven to a hysterical breakdown, which she experiences on delivering her mother's finger to a distraught Baines. For the first time, Flora regresses into a child, unable to form any words. Realizing she has been traumatized by the crazed and depraved Stewart, Baines and his Maori housekeeper/confidante, Hira, take the frightened Flora under their protection and care. As Hira reminds Baines, Flora is just a little girl. This is a fact that everyone in the film seems to have forgotten. Flora's transformation back into a little girl culminates in her mother's successful rejection of the good pioneer woman role, though Ada has been brutalized and severely punished for her transgression. Despite having lost her finger, Ada does not lose herself. After this act of violence enacted against her mother, Flora never speaks in the film again. At the very end of the film, Flora, Ada, and Baines form a new kind of family, one that has, in Hira's words, "gone beyond the veil." In this new family structure, Ada learns how to speak words again—like an adult. Baines and Ada continue their passionate relationship. And Flora embraces her role as daughter. Campion represents this in the last image of Flora, which captures her in a moment of carefree abandon. Shot in slow motion, Flora performs cartwheels in a garden, donning angel wings like a sprite or fairy. Campion's final image of Flora mirrors the earlier scene on the beach in which Baines has escorted Ada and Flora to visit the abandoned piano; this is the scene in which Baines falls in love with Ada. Ada plays her beloved piano on the beach against an oceanic landscape as Flora frolics happily barefoot in her white petticoats, cartwheeling across the sand, while Baines stands silently aside, transfixed by Ada. It is the only other moment in the film in which Campion permits Flora to be a child.

With regard to the Mother of the Empire figure, Campion has her appear as Aunt Morag. Perhaps because of her wild and primitive surroundings, Aunt Morag seems intent on maintaining her imperial British ways—and authority. Like Granny Wilcox (*My American Cousin*) and Grandma Bossier (*My Brilliant Career*), Aunt Morag is a relic from the past, steeped in Old World Victorianism. Aunt Morag sees it as her duty to bring and maintain British Victorian culture to the wilderness of the New Zealand bush. One of the key ways Aunt Morag attempts to accomplish her goals is to control Ada, and in this way Aunt Morag serves as a kind of Bluebeard's helper. As previously discussed, Campion's film has been analyzed as a feminist revisioning of fairy tales, particularly "Bluebeard." Rose Lovell-Smith identifies the female helper in "Bluebeard" as neither evil nor good but as an ambiguous figure who, despite her strangeness and grotesqueness, ends up helping the heroine find her way.[68] Throughout the film, Campion depicts Aunt Morag as a gossipy old crone who successfully raises doubts and suspicions in Stewart's mind about Ada's mental health and ability to perform her wifely duties. She even criticizes Ada's piano playing as dark and unnatural. In comparison with Ada's non-traditional and shocking behavior, Aunt Morag's staunch Victorian British values seem stale and, given the setting, absurd. Tellingly, partway through the film Aunt Morag simply fades from the story.

Hira is an elderly Maori woman who functions as a subaltern maternal figure. In some sense, she mirrors Aunt Morag as an elderly maternal figure of authority. Although a minor character in the film, Hira does have a few key dramatic moments through her involvement and affiliation with Baines. Although the nature of their relationship is never made clear, Hira is Baines's confidant and adviser and also cooks for him at times. Given that Baines seems to associate mainly with the Maori and is adorned with *Tā moko* (face tattoos), he seems to have been adopted into the Maori community, and Hira has taken him under her wing. Though Baines has a wife back in England, Hira seems to occupy a caretaker place in Baines's lonely, isolated existence, though there is no sexual connotation to their relationship. Campion depicts Hira and Baines's relationship in the following scene.

> SHOT: *Camera pans along a Maori canoe where naked Maori children frolic. The setting is bucolic. The camera pauses on Hira, who is seated on a large branch of a tree extending out onto the water. She is positioned above everyone else in the frame. A naked child is seated beside her. Baines, positioned below Hira, scrubs his laundry at the edge of the river. Hira says,* "You need a wife. It's no good having it sulk between your legs for the rest of your life."
>
> SHOT: *Medium angle on a laughing Maori woman holding a giggling child.*
>
> SHOT: *Medium-close angle on Baines. He smiles but does not reply.*

When Baines reveals that he already has a wife living back in England, Hira tells him, "You need another wife. Such a treasure should not sleep on your stomach at night." Within the fairy-tale context, Campion seems to construct Hira as a woodland fairy figure, in stark contrast to Aunt Morag's Bluebeard's helper role. Hira's association with nature and the erotic could also be seen as part of the film's repeated referencing to the fairy tale, a form in which preternatural woodland mythical creatures play a key dramatic role in the destinies of the hero and heroine.[69] Fairies, particularly fairies like Queen Mab, wielded great power and influence in the lives of others, often through maternal or fertility powers. Queen Mab can be traced back to Hera, the Greek goddess of marriage and the life of women.[70] Like a fairy godmother, Hira (Hera) is instrumental in bringing the two lovers, Ada and Baines, together and keeping the villain (Stewart) at bay. As if following on Hira's words, Baines does seem to see Ada beyond the arrangement that has made him wretched and made her a whore. Baines wants Ada as his lover *and* wife. Later, when Stewart attempts to confront Baines about his affair with Ada, Hira physically bars Stewart from entering Baines's house, functioning as a protectress. Hira also comes to the aid and protection of a traumatized Flora.

SHOT: *The framing is tight on Baines and Flora. Baines shakes Flora, who screams hysterically,* "He chopped it off!!" *Baines becomes desperate. He asks frantically,* "What did she tell him? What did she tell him!" *Hira intercepts Baines and gently pulls Flora away from him. Hira says to Baines pointedly, in Maori,* "She's just a little girl." *Flora begins to weep uncontrollably. Hira cradles Flora and speaks soothingly to her in Maori. Baines is framed out of the shot.*

SHOT: *Medium angle on Baines, who is seething with anger. Enraged, he says,* "I'm going to crush his skull!"

SHOT: *Medium-close angle on Hira and Flora, who screams,* "NO!!!" *Hira gazes at Baines with disapproval. She continues to soothe Flora, rocking her in her arms. Flora warns Baines,* "He'll chop it off!!!"

SHOT: *Medium angle on Baines, who out of desperation drives his fist into a nearby tree.*

Baines does not seek revenge on Stewart but remains with Hira and Flora at his homestead. Campion later foregrounds Hira's subaltern maternal voice as a kind of sendoff to Ada, Baines, and Flora as the new family departs the island, moving far away from Stewart. As the Maori war canoe carries them and the piano out to sea, Hira sings a lament (waitia) against the roaring of the waves. It is Hira's last form of counsel for Baines. Hira sings:

> You are like seaweed drifting in the sea, Baines. Drift far away, drift far beyond the horizon. A canoe glides hither, a canoe glides thither, but you, though, will journey on and eventually be beyond the veil.[71]

Campion's representation of Hira could be construed as a racist Native Earth Mother figure, and that would be a fair assessment. Though Hira can be interpreted as fairylike figure that has stepped out of a fairy tale, without considering the racist connotations associated with particular kinds of imagery, Campion falls into a colonial trap. Campion has been heavily criticized for racist representation of the Maori, as discussed in chapter 1. Though Campion gives Hira a few interesting moments, her portrayal feels incomplete and underdeveloped. In many ways Campion misses an opportunity with Hira, who could have been developed into a much richer and more complex figure. Campion renders Hira into a visual device, not unlike what countless Westerns have done to indigenous women in general.

In *Thousand Pieces of Gold*, Nancy Kelly debunks the angel on the frontier myth through the figure of Lalu as an oppressed fallen angel. Like Ada in *The Piano*, Lalu is traded among men, first in China, between her father and Chinese slave traders, and later in the American West, among Hong King, Jim (her Chinese lover), and Charlie Beamus, a white man. In many ways Lalu is a rebellious daughter figure who resists oppression and sexual exploitation by male figures of authority, primarily Hong King, who illegally purchases Lalu as a sex slave for his saloon (slavery has been abolished at this point in history). To mark his celestial angel as his property, Hong King renames Lalu China Polly, an Oriental sex object intended to service his male saloon patrons. In so doing, Hong King renders Lalu an exotic commodity for white male desire. When Lalu discovers that she is to be "one hundred men's wife," she fiercely resists, threatening suicide. Hong King backs down after Charlie talks him out of using Lalu as a prostitute. Charlie says, "You keep her for yourself, King. Anyone can see she'd make a lousy whore." Charlie also points out to Hong King in a heated moment, "You don't own her! Now, you can't own a person. It's against the law—those days are gone. You break the law, you'll never get your citizenship papers." Throughout the film Lalu asserts that she will never be a China Polly for anyone. Hence, rather than rejecting the role of settler wife and mother, as Sybylla, Ada, and Sandy do, Lalu rejects the role of the dark fallen angel, seen in figure 2.9. In Kelly's frame, there are no white-settler wives and mothers; the only white women in the film are prostitutes (fallen angels). Though Berthe, a local German prostitute whom Lalu befriends, tries to convince her that selling her body to the local men is not a bad way to make a living, Lalu refuses. Indeed, Lalu's mantra throughout the first half of the film is "No whore," some of the first English words she learns from Charlie.

Lalu resists the dark fallen angel role through hard, decent work, such as starting a laundry business and managing a boarding house for itinerant gold miners. In this way, Lalu is similar to Roseanne in

FIGURE 2.9 Lalu (as China Polly),
Thousand Pieces of Gold.

Loyalties and Joan in *The Wake*, subaltern women who destabilize an oppressive male gaze through the politics of respectability and decent work. This is exemplified in the scene in which Charlie takes Lalu back to his home after he has won her in a card game from Hong King. Kelly does not let Charlie play the white knight in shining armor, however. Despite being rescued by Charlie, Lalu does not consider herself indebted to him and refuses to play the typical damsel in distress.

> SHOT: *Medium angle on Lalu. Charlie enters the frame, carrying a drink. He offers it to Lalu.* "Say you, say you like a drink, huh?" *Lalu turns her face away from him. Charlie drinks from the glass. He returns his gaze to her and tries to coax her into drinking with him.* "Come on, just a little one, huh?" *He pushes the glass toward her face. Lalu knocks the glass out of his hand and turns away from him. Charlie grabs her around the waist and attempts to kiss her, roughly. Lalu struggles against his drunken advances. He groans out of desire. She flinches. Charlie tries to restrain Lalu as she struggles against him. Frustrated, he says,* "I'm no Hong King. You got nothing to be afraid of." *Lalu continues to resist, trying to break free of his hold. Lalu says, disgusted,* "You just like them." *Losing his patience, Charlie says accusingly,* "Look, I staked everything I own on you! I'd like a little appreciation." *Lalu manages to escape his strong grip, exiting the frame. Charlie gazes at her, bewildered by her rejection and distress.*
>
> SHOT: *Medium angle on Lalu, who glares at Charlie with fear and trepidation. She is breathless from their struggle.*
>
> SHOT: *American angle on Charlie, who picks up bags of money, his winnings from his poker game with Hong King.* "You want money for it? Is that what you want?" *He throws the money down on the table in anger.*
>
> SHOT: *Medium angle on Lalu, who declares,* "I am not a whore!"
>
> SHOT: *Medium angle on Charlie, enraged.* "I ruined a man for you! I thought you'd be happy!" *He stalks around her.*
>
> SHOT: *Medium angle on Lalu, who backs away cautiously from him. Charlie reaches out and seizes her by the arms. While gripping her forcefully, he shakes her. He exclaims,* "Look, if I hadn't won, there'd

be a hundred men!" *Lalu pulls out of his grip.* "Then I'd die and leave this place!" *Charlie yells,* "Polly, you're with me now!" *Lalu responds with* "You win me from Hong King! Then you gamble me away to someone else, like cow, like sheep." *Charlie pleads, trying to caress her.* "No, no, you don't know what you're saying." *Lalu shoves his groping hands away.* "You want Chinese slave girl? That what you want?" *This seems to sober Charlie up. He says quietly,* "No. I don't want a Chinese slave girl." *He staggers away from her, defeated.*

Unlike the subaltern heroines in Dash, Moffatt, Wheeler, Bailey, and Mita, Lalu's subaltern identity is relegated to the background or periphery of the narrative and the frame. Instead of identifying with her Chinese culture and building connections in the Chinese community on Golden Mountain, Lalu transforms herself into an independent woman, an identity that leans toward the good pioneer woman figure. In some sense, Lalu transforms from a fallen dark angel into an angel on the frontier. As Charlie says to Lalu, "Some of us, we just need an angel like you to save us from ourselves." As Lalu becomes more successful, she slowly adopts a more Western way of being, donning expensive Victorian ladies' fashions and becoming more fluent in English. Though she can eventually afford to live independently, she does not move to Chinatown. Instead, Lalu forms friendships among the white characters in the town, particularly Charlie, who is desperately in love with her, and the prostitute Berthe, who teaches her how to make apple pie. Lalu realizes that appealing to Euro-American cultural tastes means economic independence and respect from the whites. When Lalu cooks for the white miners at the boarding house she serves them pancakes, albeit while donning a large knife for protection. Though the white miners could overpower her physically, they come to respect Lalu and cease to objectify her as a "pearl of the Orient." The Chinese characters, on the other hand, either rape and imprison Lalu (Hong King), abandon her (Lalu's father; Jim) or stand by and do nothing to help her (Chinese miners and Li Ping). It is through the figure of Charlie, a white man, that Lalu finds the most support and strength, even though he initially lies to her and tries to rape her.

Though Lalu doesn't forget that she is Chinese—she still celebrates Chinese New Year—her success is rooted in her ability to adapt to the white man's ways. Even at the end of the film, when the Chinese are being driven out by racist whites (not Charlie), rather than joining them on their forced exodus or returning to China, which has been her stated desire throughout the film, Lalu settles in the River of No Return with Charlie. Interestingly, it is Li Ping, the elderly owner of the Golden Flower general store, who convinces Lalu to stay in America and "to drink the soup of forgetfulness." This echoes Charlie's earlier advice when he tells Lalu that "sometimes you just can't go back to the way you were." This forgetfulness is in direct contrast to the message spoken throughout the subaltern narratives by elderly maternal figures such as Nana Peazant in *Daughters of the Dust* and Kara in *Mauri*, who urge the younger generation to never forget who they are and where they came from. Lalu refuses to be a "dead ghost" and decides to make a new life on her own terms as neither a China Polly nor a Chinese daughter (thousand pieces of gold). Though Lalu may not transcend marginalization as a Chinese woman, she is empowered to reinvent herself, to cross the river, as a frontier woman. Through Kelly's lens the Chinese community retreats into the distance of Lalu's individualistic female story of surviving in the West. Lalu is more like Sybylla in *My Brilliant Career*, an ambitious young woman determined to carve out a life on the frontier as a free, independent agent, on her own. Interestingly, Kelly never shows Lalu accepting Charlie's proposal to live with him at his new homestead. The final shot, in which Lalu appears alone, attests to the story of independence.

In our culture the same thing has been done to Asian men that's been done to women. In Westerns, they're extras, they're in the background, or they're in the kitchen. They're asexual, and they're slaves who work their whole lives taking care of white men.[72]

—Maggie Greenwald

The cult of true womanhood is destabilized in Maggie Greenwald's *The Ballad of Little Jo* through the central heroine, who transforms herself, both physically and emotionally, from Josephine, a bourgeois society girl, into Little Jo, a frontiersman on a late-nineteenth-century-America Western frontier. There are a few white-settler mother figures, but they are very peripheral characters, not unlike in a typical Western. And yet, Greenwald's film is far from typical. Her deployment of female frontier tropes is strategic in her debunking of the angel on the frontier mythology. Though Josephine is biologically a mother, she is rendered a fallen angel when she is banished from her home and society for having her child out of wedlock. As a proper young woman who has willingly engaged in sexual relations outside of marriage, Josephine has, in the eyes of society and the father, committed the worst kind of sin and transgression for a respectable woman. As punishment, Josephine's father ruthlessly banishes her and her "bastard" to the streets, where she is at the mercy of strangers, mainly marauding predatory white males. Like Ada in *The Piano*, Josephine is a rebellious daughter who resists patriarchal oppression through transgressive acts. Despite being sent into exile, which is a kind of death for Josephine, she survives, but not as a fallen angel. Josephine refuses to be rendered into a lowly sexual object, debunking the Madonna/whore dichotomy by assuming the identity of a man.

Greenwald foregrounds the construction of gender binaries through the romance between Little Jo and Tinman. In the bathing scene, Greenwald deploys the classic shot/reverse shot of the Hollywood romance to construct Little Jo's sexual attraction to Tinman while also destabilizing the heterosexual male gaze. In this sense, Greenwald queers the gaze.

SHOT: *Long shot on Jo as she opens the corral and leads her horse out. She pauses when something catches her attention. The camera trucks into a close-up on her face, emphasizing her gaze.*

SHOT: *American shot on Tinman's reflection in the water while he bathes in the lake. The camera tilts up to reveal Tinman, bare chested, washing himself, his long hair flowing down his back. The camera lingers on his sleek, muscular body, which bears a number of scars.*

SHOT: *Medium angle on Jo, who drags her gaze away from the half-naked Tinman. She knows she shouldn't be staring at him in that way. She turns to mount her horse.*

SHOT: *American shot on Tinman, still washing himself. His eyes are closed, and he seems lost in the sensations of his rustic bath.*

SHOT: *Medium angle on Jo astride her horse. She continues to stare at Tinman with unbridled desire.*

SHOT: *Long shot on Jo. The camera follows as her horse trots toward Tinman.*

SHOT: *Long shot, high angle, Jo's point of view on Tinman bathing. The camera's movement suggests Jo's movement. Tinman gazes up at her.*

SHOT: *Medium low-angle shot on Jo as she gazes down at Tinman. She continues to ride slowly as she gazes at him but now through guarded, hardened eyes, masking her desire. She says sternly in her best male voice,* "I left you some mending."

SHOT: *Long shot on Tinman, who continues to wash his body. He returns Jo's gaze and nods. He says, almost tauntingly,* "Yes, Mr. Jo."

SHOT: *Medium-close shot on Jo, who continues to hold her gaze of authority on Tinman. She rides out of the frame.*

SHOT: *American shot on Tinman, who gazes after Jo, perplexed. He returns his attention to his bathing, but then, after a moment, he looks up to watch Jo ride away.*

In many ways Tinman and Little Jo are mirror characters. Both characters bear bodily scars, evidence of sexist and racist/colonial oppression and exploitation (Tinman was almost worked to death

FIGURE 2.10 Jo and Tinman, *The Ballad of Little Jo.*

on the railways), and both are victimized by white male figures of authority. They both harbor secrets, and both play gendered or racialized roles in order to survive. Tien Me Wong must play the role of Tinman, a subservient other who has been feminized or demonized (a ravisher of women) by white society. Little Jo plays the part of frontiersman in a constant masculine masquerade that requires her to act not only tough but also mean. When the two characters become lovers, Little Jo is finally able to let down her guard and expose herself, though that self is no longer the society girl she once was. Figure 2.10 depicts her freedom, albeit forbidden, to realize her sexual desires outside the marriage bed or patriarchal constructs. Though she engages in this forbidden bad-girl and even illegal sex at great risk, it is worth the companionship and joy it brings her.

SHOT: *Medium-close angle on Jo lying with Tinman in bed. Jo's hand rests on his long black hair along his scarred chest. The camera tilts up to reveal Tinman's face. Jo asks gently,* "Who are you, Tinman?" *He replies playfully,* "You are the mystery one, Mr. Jo." *Jo gazes up at Tinman.*

SHOT: *Medium angle on Jo and Tinman gazing at each other with admiration and desire.*

SHOT: *Medium-close-angle two-shot. Jo notices a wound on Tinman's ribs. Concerned, she asks,* "Who did this to you?" *Tinman replies,* "Hoodlums in San Francisco." *He then points to another scar.* "White men in mining town." *He leans forward to show her his back, marred with scars.* "Railroad boss." *Jo lovingly caresses his scars.*

SHOT: *Close shot on Jo. Tinman crosses the frame as he leans back onto the pillow. He brings his hand to the scar along her face, but she flinches. He asks,* "And this?" *Jo doesn't answer. She takes his hand and guides it away from her scarred face. She reaches over him.*

SHOT: *Medium shot. Jo reaches across Tinman to open her bedside table drawer. She retrieves a keepsake box and places it on his lap. She opens the lid and pulls something out.*

SHOT: *Close shot on Jo's hand retrieving a small portrait of her former self as the lovely Josephine, the one taken by the photographer who fathered her child. She hands the portrait to Tinman. Off-screen, Tinman asks, "Who is this society girl?" Off-screen, Jo laughs sardonically.*

SHOT: *Medium-close two-shot on Jo and Tinman. Jo says, smiling, "It's me. Can you imagine?" Tinman shakes his head in disbelief while studying the portrait. He says, "I like you much better as you are." Jo turns to him and asks, surprised, "Why?" He replies honestly, "This white girl would never do this to me." Jo laughs.*

SHOT: *Close shot on Jo's portrait. Tinman glides his thumb across its surface.*

Little Jo's gender identity transformation is rooted in her desire not only to survive on a harsh frontier as an independent agent but also to provide for her son, whom she leaves in the care of her sister Helen. Though Little Jo spends most of the film as a man and childless, maternal desire looms over this film. Greenwald never lets us forget that Little Jo is a mother, harboring painful maternal longing for her lost child, expressed in the letters she writes to her sister. Greenwald deploys these letters as a device to construct maternal desire through the film's soundtrack. Though these letters seem somewhat inconsequential, they are instrumental in Little Jo's connection with the past and her identity as a woman and a mother.

> Dear Jo, it's been so long since we heard from you. Laddie gets bigger every day. He's already such a handsome little man. You'd be so proud of him. Jo, he's asked for you so much, and longed for you so terribly, that I finally told him you had died.

The death of Laddie's mother is in fact the death of "Josephine Monaghan." Soon afterward, Little Jo will experience her full transformation into a true man of the West by committing an act of gun violence. When the Western Cattle Company sends hired guns to murder Little Jo and her neighbors, she and Frank Badger fight back. Despite this rite of passage into manhood, Little Jo cannot control her emotions and breaks down in tears, having killed a man. And despite Little Jo's act of violence, Greenwald ensures that maternal desire remains a driving force in the film. Over the film's credits a woman sings a lament about a mother's loss of her child. The opening lyrics are "My sweet son, the blue of night has fallen. I can't be by your side."

The other white-settler mothers who appear in the film seem to represent a role Little Jo might have played if she had not been branded a fallen angel. Ruth Badger is the tough-as-nails middle-aged wife of Frank Badger. Though Ruth is a white-settler farmwife and mother, she functions as a maternal wise-woman figure rather than a Mother of the Empire figure. This is primarily because the film is set in the late nineteenth-century American West and the United States is no longer a colony. Though Ruth has a small role, appearing only once in the film, Greenwald gives her dramatic agency. Ruth Badger seems to be one of those real women of the West that feminist historians had been trying to foreground in frontier historiography. Ruth provides support to the central heroine, Little Jo, through her healing skills and her influence over her hotheaded and racist husband. The first time Ruth helps Little Jo is when she comes to the rescue of Tinman, Little Jo's lover, who suffers from weak lungs. Through her healing knowledge, Ruth is able to help Tinman fight off a bad lung attack, literally saving his life. Here Greenwald privileges Ruth's maternal knowledge and power. In a montage sequence, Greenwald depicts Ruth's homespun medicinal methods in elaborate detail.

SHOT: *Medium-close shot of Ruth's hands ripping white muslin into narrow strips.*

SHOT: *Medium-close shot as Ruth gazes at Tinman with concern.*

SHOT: *Close shot on Ruth's hands applying black tar onto the muslin strips with a knife.*

SHOT: *Close shot on Ruth's hand cutting an onion into thick slices.*

SHOT: *Medium-close shot on the soles of Tinman's feet. Ruth has tied the onion slices to the soles of his feet with the muslin strips. The camera tracks up his body. Ruth finishes tying the muslin strips with tar onto his chest. The camera pauses on a close shot of Tinman as he lies unconscious, struggling to breathe.*

SHOT: *Close shot on Ruth's hand mixing herbs with a mortar and pestle.*

SHOT: *Medium shot on Ruth's hand spoon-feeding Tinman one of her homemade medicines. She has to practically force it down his throat. The camera tilts up to Ruth's face. She says soothingly, as if she were speaking to one of her own children,* "Come on, there, little fella. Come on back."

When Little Jo and Frank bring Ruth the pine branch she has requested, Frank asks quietly (rare for Frank) if Tinman is going to make it. This is the same person who attempted to lynch Tinman earlier on in the film. Ruth replies, "He's got one foot on the other side." Ruth's knowledge as a healer is privileged in the frame.

Greenwald's film explicitly contrasts Ruth's homespun maternal knowledge with capitalist and masculinist power by associating the Tinman healing sequence with two key turning-point scenes. While Ruth continues to heal Tinman, Frank gives Little Jo a letter from her sister, Helen. In the letter, Helen informs Jo that she has finally told Jo's son, Laddie, that his mother is dead, solidifying Jo's final relinquishing of her maternal and hence feminine identity. The arrival of Mr. Gray, the owner of the Western Cattle Company, and his family follow this scene. In this scene, Jo reveals that she is selling up. Frank is enraged and pulls his usual Western tough-guy tactics, all involving gun violence. He slams his fist into Little Jo and pulls his gun on the rigid and coldhearted Mr. Gray.

SHOT: *Medium-angle over-the-shoulder two-shot. Aiming his gun at Little Jo, Frank scolds her like a wayward son.* "You're the one I oughta shoot, you puny bastard, helping them squeeze me."

SHOT: *Reverse angle. Jo gazes defiantly at Frank.*

SHOT: *Reverse angle. Frank says with disappointment,* "My God, boy, I thought you'd amount to somethin'." *Ruth appears in the doorway of Little Jo's house, having tended to Tinman.*

SHOT: *Reverse angle. Little Jo looks down in shame.*

SHOT: *Long shot, over-the-shoulder shot of Mrs. Gray, an elegantly dressed society woman. She gazes at Little Jo, Frank, and Ruth with curiosity and trepidation. Frank bellows,* "Ruth!" *Ruth replies* "Yep" *in a resigned manner, as if she has been bellowed at her whole life.*

There's no denying she's as tough as Frank, tougher even. Still hold-
ing his gun, Frank swaggers over to the Gray family.

SHOT: *Medium two-shot of a nervous Mrs. Gray and her young son.*
Frank approaches the carriage.

SHOT: *Medium shot on Frank, who takes off his hat, perhaps as a gesture*
of courtesy to Mrs. Gray. Frank threatens, "When you come to my
house, Mr. Gray, either give your wife and kid guns or leave 'em
home." *Frank walks away in disgust. He's not about to start some-*
thing with women and children around.

SHOT: *Medium two-shot on Mrs. Gray with tears in her eyes. Her son*
gazes at Frank.

SHOT: *American shot as Frank passes and Ruth closes Little Jo's front*
door, carrying her medicine bag in her arms. She gazes at Little Jo,
who enters the frame. Pull focus on Little Jo as she turns to face the
Gray family.

SHOT: *Medium two-shot on Mrs. Gray and her son. Mrs. Gray returns*
Little Jo's gaze and then looks down in shame and defeat. She knows
what it's like to get bullied. Mr. Gray enters the frame, readying the
horses' reins.

SHOT: *Medium two-shot, Little Jo in the foreground, Ruth in the back-*
ground. Ruth says pointedly to Little Jo, "Seems a shame." *Ruth's*
words turn Little Jo's head. Ruth shakes her head in disappointment
at Little Jo and exits the frame.

Shortly afterward, when it is revealed that Ruth's healing remedies
have helped Tinman fight off his deathly attack, Little Jo concludes
that she will not sell her property to Mr. Gray after all; she will stay
and fight with Frank. Ruth's words have had impact. In these scenes
Ruth's maternal knowledge is privileged, and her actions have dramatic agency, leading to Jo's decision to fight the Western Cattle
Company with everything she has. Here Ruth helps Jo realize her desire to build and keep her home with Tinman.

The other white-settler mother is a Russian immigrant mother who
has traveled with her large family to America to build their homestead. Unfortunately, the land the Russian family has claimed is
desired by the ruthless and corrupt Mr. Gray. Though Little Jo is a

loner and keeps her distance from the other (male) miners and farm-ers, she does form a bond with the Russian family, especially after she learns that they are to be her closest neighbors. Little Jo is in fact the person who helps the family find their homestead—a vacant lot in the middle of nowhere. A very maternal figure, the Russian mother has what Little Jo will never have, a close bond with her son. Here Greenwald deploys the Russian mother as a device to emphasize Little Jo's yearning for her own child, someone she will never know or teach things to. However, Little Jo and the Russian mother share something—they are both others in the eyes of society. As an impover-ished Slavic, non-Anglo immigrant woman, the Russian mother would have been deemed foreign and most likely feared and even despised by farmers like Frank Badger. Indeed, later the Russian mother will be tragically slaughtered, along with her children, by the Western Cattle Company's hired guns.

CONCLUSION

Chapter 2 examined how these films re-visioned or deconstructed womanhood and motherhood in their stories of female emancipation and resistance in white-settler frontier contexts. Across the films, the key feminist debates about the place of domesticity, women's work, and motherhood in the oppression of women were reflected. All of the films focalized their re-visionings and deconstructions around the trope of the good pioneer (white) woman, rooted in the cult of true womanhood, though she does not actually appear in all the films. The films' representations and deployments of this trope differed greatly, particularly across the axes of race and class. Through close textual scene analysis, this chapter examined how the ten films deployed this trope in order to render visible their different narratives and feminist discourses about womanhood and motherhood.

The subaltern womanhood and motherhood narratives—*Daughters of the Dust, Mauri, Bedevil, Loyalties,* and *The Wake*—either ignore the good pioneer white woman trope or foreground her complicity in the oppression of subaltern women. Across these counter-narratives, she is a shadow figure who haunts the frame with her proper white femininity, a ghost deployed by capitalist colonial forces of power to render subaltern women into the "mules uh de world" and whores of the nation. Evoking antiracist and anticolonial feminist theories about the role of subaltern mothering in female empowerment and resistance, these filmmakers debunk damaging racist stereotypes of subaltern women. The filmmakers counter these stereotypes by constructing their own maternal tropes: the great-grandmother subaltern figure, the young subaltern mother figure, and the community other-mother figure. Dash celebrates black motherhood and reproductive bodies, countering dominant racist representations of black women such as the asexual savage, promiscuous Jezebel, super-moral de-sexed black woman, or black superwoman in white-settler narratives. Mita, Moffatt, Wheeler, and Bailey all counter the racist trope of the indigenous woman as primitive sexual object, Mother Earth, or dirty squaw. By voicing the experiences of subaltern women, these films refute a politics of silence around black and indigenous women's sexuality.

In these narratives, all the central protagonists and characters are mothers, often desiring single mothers, who not only nurture and protect their families but also have desires outside their role as mothers, normalizing subaltern female sexuality. Central to the films' iconography is the subaltern household. Though these households are mired in poverty and under constant threat of white male intrusion, they are also sites of temporary refuge from colonial sexual violence and danger. Children and babies are central figures across all these films, as seen in figure 2.11, which depicts a caring indigenous mother (Moffatt) and father attempting to comfort a child in distress in *Bedevil*. Though these children and babies signify vulnerability, innocence, and hope, they are also attributed a special kind of vision, such as the omniscient Unborn Child in *Daughters*, the old-soul Awatea in *Mauri*, and the street-smart Donna in *The Wake*. Many of the children in these films experience trauma and suffer horrible violent abuse, such as Rick in *Bedevil* and Leona in *Loyalties*.

The depiction of the family in indigenous cinema is, as Joanna Hearne argued, a political act.

FIGURE 2.11 Young Ruby, Stompie, and baby, *Bedevil*.

Envisioning Native families in the cinema is always a political act, and representations of youth in particular stake claims about the future of Indigenous nations as legitimate, and legitimating, heirs to the land. Controlling the signs of Indigeneity in visual representations engages issues of identity and the ongoing presence of Native tribes as distinct peoples with claims to their homelands and, in the United States, to the sovereignty acknowledged in nation-to-nation treaties.[73]

The Piano, *The Ballad of Little Jo*, *Thousand Pieces of Gold*, *My Brilliant Career*, and *My American Cousin* work in the angel on the frontier counter-narrative, destabilizing the good pioneer woman trope by rendering visible gender relations and women's work within patriarchal structures of power. The films depict domesticity as the site of patriarchal oppression, where men exploit women's reproductive and productive labors. Countering the notion that women's work was ever a labor of love, the films depict good pioneer women as domestic drudges or caged birds. In stark contrast to the subaltern womanhood and motherhood narrative, these films seem ambivalent and even negative toward motherhood and the maternal, as expressed in three maternal figures that recur across these films: the oppressed white-settler mother figure, the wise subaltern maternal figure, and the Mother of the Empire figure. Empowerment and emancipation are represented in the figure of the rebellious young daughter whose journey toward selfhood is realized by rejecting and resisting mother-hood and the domestic. These daughter figures find fulfillment either by carving out an identity in the historically male terrain (*Ballad, Thousand Pieces, My Brilliant Career*) or by pursuing forbidden desires outside the home (*The Piano, My American Cousin*). However, despite this seeming reluctance to embrace the role of motherhood as a site of empowerment, the films foreground maternal desire in the film's visual and sound regimes, with the exception of *Thousand Pieces*. This deployment of maternal desire evokes the work of early female cin-ema directors (Guy-Blaché) and maternal melodramas, especially those directed by women (Dorothy Arzner, Marie Epstein, Ida Lupino). It could also be argued that these films' expression of the maternal evokes Kristeva's concept of a pre-lingual language, although it is more anxiety ridden than celebratory. This is not dissimilar to read-ings of maternal melodramas by Mary Ann Doane, Linda Williams, and E. Ann Kaplan. However, they also lay bare the contradictory po-sition motherhood holds within patriarchy itself, echoing the work of Epstein. Like Epstein's films, these films shift the focus of their narratives "from the traditional masculine trajectory of Oedipal de-sire to desiring relations of the feminine (relations between mothers and daughters in particular) and in doing so, realign point-of-view structures to emphasize both the child's vision in the primal scene and the unconscious structure of fantasy."[74]

The key way the angel on the frontier counter-narrative's re-visionings of womanhood are delimited is through their failure to either interrogate the good pioneer white woman trope or to acknowl-edge its power. Though all the films render visible the exploitation of motherhood and women's work under patriarchy, they do not address how white (British) femininity was possible only through the relega-tion of subaltern women to imagined dark others and low-paid work-ers or how gender played a crucial role in organizing ideas of race and civilization, and how women were involved in the expansion and maintenance of the Empire. Though *Thousand Pieces* features a sub-altern woman as the central protagonist, it does not deploy an inter-sectional lens to Lalu's sexual exploitation and enslavement. The only other women in the film are prostitutes, all of them white, who are also subjected to the same oppressions as Lalu. If anything, the film mimics racist scripts of Chinese men as villainous traders of female bodies and colonial narratives about subaltern men. That said, though these films do not address race or the intersectional relationship between race and gender, not to mention class, they resist the dominant myth-history narrative that the frontier was a womenless milieu.

3

FEMINIST SYMBOLIC FRONTIER LANDSCAPES

The very act of making a film like Ballad *is so subversive that it becomes a critique. I wanted to make a Western and I knew I wanted to make a Western that had a woman as the main character. But the story does change when a woman is put at the center. And I would be a liar if I said there was not a tremendous amount of me in it. As a filmmaker, I'm working on male terrain and my subject matter is also "male terrain."[1]*

—Maggie Greenwald

Since indigenous people are not supposed to be there—for the lands are "empty"—they are symbolically displaced onto what I call anachronistic space, a trope that gathered full administrative authority as a technology of surveillance in the late Victorian era. According to this trope, colonized people— like women and working class in the metropolis—do not inhabit history proper but exist in a permanently anterior time within the geographic space of the modern empire as anachronistic humans, atavistic, irrational, bereft of human agency.[2]

—Anne McClintock

IN DOMINANT FRONTIER myth-history narratives, wide-open, uncharted rugged territory, free for the taking, has been a central visual motif across the four white-settler nations featured in this study. As discussed in the introduction, frontier iconography has been "creatively" deployed by white-settler colonial societies "to promote nationalism, and to legitimize the process of colonization and the subjugation of Indigenous peoples."[3] This creative invention is what Raymond Williams called a "selective tradition" in which "certain meanings and practices are selected for emphasis" in the interest of "the dominance of a specific class. It is a version of the past which is intended to connect with and ratify the present."[4] In large part because of U.S. imperialist domination of world cinema and television screens in the latter part of the twentieth century, the iconography of the American West has become the most visually iconic and symbolic of frontiers. As noted in chapter 1, a frontier myth exists in different forms in diverse national imaginaries, but the American version has been the most powerfully articulated and internationally influential. The big-sky landscapes featured in the paintings of Frederic Remington (1861–1909) and in classic Hollywood Western films have become embedded in our collective imagination as *the* frontier.[5] Hence, the power of the Western has not been in its historical accuracy or even Americanness but in its value as a myth system in which familiar iconography serves as a generic motif that legitimizes and privileges a white-settler worldview. Douglas Pye argued that "the Western is founded, then, on a tremendously rich confluence of romantic narrative and archetypal imagery modified and localized by recent American experience."[6] Pye's seminal work on the Western is relevant to this study because he saw it outside of the American context, rooted in "much older ideas and myth."

> So, the images of the garden connect with much earlier images—the Garden of Hesperides and other earthly paradises to be found in the direction of the sunset—and the opposition of garden and desert can easily take up the biblical images of the Promised Land and the wilderness. Similarly, views of the Indian are at least partially formed from earlier images of the noble savage—the potential sources of a number of conflicting but interrelated streams of thought and imagery.[7]

In his pioneering text *Horizons West*, film historian Jim Kitses also argued that Western themes are organized under the central dichotomy of wilderness and civilization.[8] The dichotomous form of the Western is also rooted in Frederick Jackson Turner's frontier thesis, a historical model in which frontier landscapes were marked by an ever-changing "fall line" that pushed westward. Turner argued that these fall lines were symbolic markers of the figurative movement away from the Old World; namely, Europe. Turner concluded that the frontier had all but closed by 1890, but this closing had created a kind of American identity crisis.

> In these successive frontiers we find natural boundary lines which have served to mark and to affect the characteristics of frontiers, namely: the "fall line"; the Alleghany Mountains; the Mississippi; the Missouri where its direction approximates north and south; the line of the arid lands approximately the ninety-ninth meridian; and the Rocky Mountains. The fall line marked the frontier of the seventeenth century; the Alleghenies that of the eighteenth; the Mississippi that of the first quarter of the nineteenth; the Missouri that of the middle of this century (omitting the California movement); and the belt of the Rocky Mountains and the arid tract, the present frontier. Each was won by a series of Indian wars.[9]

Tellingly, most Westerns take place about thirty years before the closing of the American frontier. J. Hoberman identified the time period of the Western genre as "a twenty-five-year long mop-up operation between Lee's surrender at Appomattox and the defeat of the Sioux at Wounded Knee."[10] The Western's obsessive focus on such a specific time period seems to echo Turner's identification of a national identity crisis and exemplifies Williams's theory of the selective tradition. Turner's frontier thesis is relevant to this study because of its importance as a model for frontier historiography. Rooted in a visual dichotomy of civilized and uncivilized spatial iconography, Turner's fall lines were significant for the symbolic meanings that were attributed to them rather than for their spatial and temporal specificity. Richard Slotkin described Turner's frontier thesis as "the basis of the dominant school of American historical interpretation [which] would provide the rationale for the ideologies of both Republican progressives and Democratic liberals for much of the ensuing century."[11] Australian historian Nathan Wolski identified Turner's work as a highly influential model, along with the records and sketches of

Australian Aborigines by William Thomas (1793–1867), who was an assistant Protector of Aboriginals in the mid-nineteenth century.[12] Wolski critiqued these nineteenth-century works for their rigid and delimiting definitions of frontiers and the central tenet that frontiers close when indigenous active physical resistance ends. Wolski advocated for a deconstruction of linear subaltern resistance and the frontier as a specific space. Deploying the theories of Edward Said and pioneering cultural theorist Homi K. Bhabha, Wolski argued that resistance can be intransitive, meaning not explicitly acted out in a physical way.[13] Wolski argued:

> The necessity for broadening our ideas on what constitutes resistance and for whom, but also the subsequent need to develop a newer model of the frontier—a model which moves away from the idea of frontiers as temporally and spatially circumscribed, to one which accounts for the invisibilities, misrecognitions and fractured/ambivalent intentions which characterize the contact period in Australia.[14]

Judith Kleinfeld's examination of the "frontier romance" is particularly apt here. Kleinfeld traced the meaning of the word *frontier* in different cultures, where it has had a variety of different interpretations. Kleinfeld argued:

> The original meaning of *frontier* was a border or a boundary, the very opposite of its Americanized meaning of inviting possibility. *Frontier* in the European sense means a *boundary*, not an open space, a *limit*, not a beckoning place. In French, for example, the word *frontiére* means simply the border and figuratively implies a boundary. In Mandarin Chinese, the most common dictionary term for *frontier* is "bian jie," meaning "boundary." In Cantonese, the word for *frontier* is "huang die," which carries negative connotations. In the Chinese cultural cosmos, one does not set out for the frontier, one is sent to the frontier, a place of punishment and exile, a wilderness as wasteland. During the American expansion west, the meaning of the word *frontier* was turned on its head, its dominant definition changing

from its European meaning of "border" and "boundary" to its American meaning of "openness" and "possibility." The *Australian National Dictionary* and the *Western Canadian Dictionary and Phrasebook*, for example, explicitly label this positive meaning of the word *frontier* an "Americanism."[15]

Across these ten films, the filmmakers reimagined and reconstructed the meaning of *frontier* outside traditional historiography and narrative models. Predating Wolski, these women filmmakers constructed frontier spaces that fall outside geographical (spatial) and even temporal fall lines marked by a series of Indian wars.[16] In many ways, the filmmakers re-imagined and reconstructed frontier landscapes as both boundaries or wastelands that women and subaltern people are sent to as punishment and as places of possibility for resistance and agency.

Women and subaltern people in Westerns have primarily served the frame as visual devices, in a similar vein to the landscape as a symbolic space, to be protected, owned, coveted, tamed, and violated, all in the name of civilization and expansionist projects. However, in these films, female and subaltern characters were rendered visible as active agents who deployed frontier landscapes for their own uses and desires, and often at great risk. With regard to genre, the films debunked the interior/exterior binary in which women and the feminine are relegated to domestic spaces, interior locations such as homesteads or saloons. Cinematically, the filmmakers deployed space as a key storytelling device that provided insight into the characters as well as the filmmakers' feminist agendas. By rendering visible women and femininity in frontier spaces through a female lens, the filmmakers constructed new symbolic feminist landscapes, asserting that the frontier was never what Jane Thompkins called a "women-less milieu." Thompkins argues,

Given the pervasiveness of and the power of women's discourse in the nineteenth century, I think it is no accident that men gravitated in imagination toward a women-less milieu, a set of rituals featuring physical combat and physical endurance, and a social setting that branded most features of civilized existence as feminine and corrupt, banishing them in favor of the three main targets of women's reform: whiskey, gambling and prostitution.[17]

In these films the landscape itself becomes the emblem for female transgression and desires, although the outcome is often punishment or imprisonment. Violence here takes on a different purpose and is depicted differently from the typical Western violence. The violent acts that are committed in these films are of a personal, domestic, or sexual nature. However, the female and subaltern characters are never rendered into victim figures. Rather, the female protagonists fit into the convention of the feisty heroine, a mainstay of the Victorian melodrama (ingénue), the Western (cowgirl), and the horror film (the final girl). Throughout these films, the heroines are visually associated with exterior locations and the land and frequently cross and obscure boundaries that separate civilized and uncivilized spaces. As in the Western, these frontier spaces are often hostile or dangerous, posing physical threats to the heroines, primarily in the form of (white) patriarchal or colonial figures of authority. Two kinds of feminist landscapes emerge across this work, informed by differing political, cultural, and aesthetic ideas and conventions: the decolonizing symbolic frontier landscape and the female transgressive symbolic frontier landscape.

THE DECOLONIZING SYMBOLIC FRONTIER LANDSCAPE

The decolonizing symbolic frontier landscape is featured in *Mauri*, *Daughters of the Dust*, *Bedevil*, *Loyalties*, and *The Wake*. The filmmakers structured their frontier through a decolonizing lens, which renders visible subaltern peoples' agency and resistance to colonial oppression, such as economic exploitation, land dispossession, forced migration, and enslavement. These filmmakers represented their frontier spaces as "a boundary, not an open space, a limit, not a beckoning place."[18] Economic deprivation through geographic isolation and captivity threatens to destroy these subaltern communities' way of life, which was once dependent on their free access to, and movement across, the land. Hence, the frontier featured in these films is no longer a place of possibility.

The key visual motifs that recur across these films are racial segregation, the hypervisibility of subaltern women, the criminalization and imprisonment of subaltern men by colonial forces of power, the feminization of subaltern communities, and racialized and sexual violence. Many of the subaltern heroines are forced to work in or navigate across frontier spaces in order to access labor and economic opportunities. Unlike white-settler farm wives, these women are, ironically, more visible on the frontier and are afforded more freedom of movement, though they suffer sexual exploitation, abuse, and even rape through this imposed hypervisibility. In contrast, subaltern men's movement across the frontier is criminalized and delimited. As in the horror film and the Gothic melodrama, various kinds of ghosts and monsters haunt the films' landscapes, serving as metaphors for the horrors and violence of colonization. Though these filmmakers foregrounded the victimization of subaltern people in frontier spaces, covert strategies of resistance were made central in the films' frontier iconography. The key way the filmmakers created subaltern resistance was by constructing a frontier through a decolonizing lens that visually expresses unspeakable subaltern female desire. This subaltern female desire is expressed through culturally specific iconography, myths, and rituals.

In *Daughters of the Dust*, the Peazants, descendants of African captives, are literally cut off from the mainland, rendered dependent on their backbreaking work as sharecroppers. Their only hope for survival is to leave.

At the turn of the century, Sea Island Gullahs, descendants of African Captives, remained isolated from the mainland of South Carolina and Georgia. As a result of their isolation, the Gullah created and maintained a distinct, imaginative and original African American culture.

—Title card at the opening of *Daughters of the Dust*

Julie Dash constructs an idyllic African American frontier land-scape set in the South Carolina and Georgia Sea Islands and marked by Gullah[19] and West African culture, constructed through a black fe-male desiring gaze. Like Nana Peazant, who carries scraps of memo-ries in an old tin box, Dash tells her story of African diaspora, chattel slavery, and black resistance through objects, food, hand gestures, games, and religious symbols. Like Nana's glass bottle trees, these objects stand as reminders of "who was here and who's gone on." The film's domestic spaces are rich with Gullah culture in the form of handmade baskets and homemade patchwork quilts, artifacts now found in American heritage museums. Domestic spaces feature brightly colored rooms filled with dried flowers and herbs. One of the recurring metaphors throughout the film, though not histori-cally accurate, is the indigo dye on the hands of the elders. Dash created the indigo-dyed hands as a "new kind of iconography around slavery in contrast to the visual associations of whips and chains."[20] Garbed in starched whites, characters languish among old-growth trees, emerge fully clothed out of rivers, and dance along epic sea-swept sandy beaches. Set to an inspired African musical score, the opening sequence of *Daughters of the Dust* demonstrates Dash's frontier aesthetic.

SHOT: *Close angle on dust running through an African American woman's hands.*

SHOT: *Long shot on Nana Peazant bathing, fully dressed, in a river.*

SHOT: *Wide angle on riverboat.*

SHOT: *Long shot on Yellow Mary standing in a boat. She wears a white gown and veil. Three African American men row and steer.*

SHOT: *Close angle on Yellow Mary's hand fingering her Saint Christopher pendant.*

TITLE CARD: *Daughters of the Dust*

SHOT: *Wide-angle aerial shot on the Sea Islands. Title card over picture:* Ibo Landing, The Sea Islands of the South, 1902

VOICE-OFF: *Male voice chanting an Islamic prayer.*

SHOT: *An African American man, Belial, prays to the sea.*

SHOT: *Close angle on Belial.*

SOUND BRIDGE: *Belial's voice chanting.*

SHOT: *Wide angle on Sea Island topography.*
SHOT: *Close angle on Islamic prayer book; pages flutter in the breeze.*

This opening montage establishes that the Sea Islands are a world unto themselves, somewhat remote. On Dash's symbolic frontier, there are no white people. Instead, characters tell stories about whites, all of which are horrific. Despite the beauty of the Sea Islands landscape, which Dash lovingly depicts as idyllic (with cinematographer Arthur Jafa), it is not a safe space. Danger always looms. White slave owners, white rapists, and the lynch mob are deployed similarly to the way that the horror story deploys the monster, as fearsome (male) forces that lie in wait in the bushes for their next victim. Both Eula and Yellow Mary are victims of rape. Eula knows that identifying her rapist will not lead to justice because, as Yellow Mary says, "the raping of colored women is as common as the fish in the sea" and will only lead to more suffering and death. In figure 3.1, Yellow Mary, Eula, and Trula (partially hidden) wander together on the beach.

The other ghosts that haunt Dash's landscape are the Peazants' Ibo ancestors. Ibo Landing, which was a slave-trading post, is thought to be a sacred and mythical place where an act of legendary slave resistance occurred. Eula tells the story while standing at Ibo Landing.

When those Ibo got through sizing up the place real good and seeing what was to come, my grandmother said they turned, all of them,

FIGURE 3.1 Yellow Mary, Eula, and Trula,
Daughters of the Dust.

and walked back in the water. Every last man, woman, and child. Now you wouldn't think they'd get very far seeing as it was water they were walking on. They had all that iron upon them. But chains didn't stop those Ibo. They just kept walking like the water was solid ground. And when they got to where the ship was, they didn't so much as give it a look. They just walked right past it, because they were going home.

Eula's impassioned retelling of the Ibo Landing myth is juxtaposed with a more realistic account told by old Bilal, who "came with the Ibo." Remembering that traumatic day, Bilal says, "When they went down in that water, they never came up. Ain't nobody can walk on water." The reality is, in fact, more horrific than the myth. This real history haunts all the Peazants, but Dash never explicitly shows violence in the frame; all of the violence has occurred off-screen and is recounted through oral storytelling or depicted through religious and cultural symbols. An example of Dash's stylized approach to representing history can be seen in figure 3.2, in which a life-size wood carving of a ghostly human form drifts along the river's shoreline, a totem to Ibo Landing's tragic past. Bodily wounds and scars are

FIGURE 3.2 African sculpture, *Daughters of the Dust*.

verbally referred to throughout, and Dash offers us no cinematic re-
alizations. This is in stark contrast to the typical Western or horror
film genres, in which blood and wounded or dead bodies abound.
Eula says:

> We carry too many scars from the past. Our past owns us. We wear
> our scars like armor . . . for protection. Our mother's scars, our
> sister's scars, our daughter's scars . . . thick, hard, ugly scars that no
> one can pass through to ever hurt us again.

Despite the horrors of the past and the ongoing looming threat of
colonial violence, Dash's frame is also one of possibility, which she
represents through the motif of romantic love, a trope often deployed
in the Western. There are a number of lovers in the film, such as the
newlyweds, as well as Eula and Eli, although their relationship is
deeply troubled. It is Iona and her indigenous lover, St. Julien Lastchild, who offer hope and the promise of a new tomorrow, though we
know they will face a difficult path together. At the film's conclusion,
Iona is forced to choose between St. Julien and her family in a romantic, albeit heart-wrenching, scene.

SHOT: *Long angle on St. Julien Lastchild on his horse, galloping through
fields.*

SHOT: *Medium-long angle on Nana Peazant. She turns as if she senses
something. The wind picks up. Dramatic, inspiring music plays. The
camera trucks into Nana as she gazes intently into the distance.*

SHOT: *Long angle on St. Julien riding.*

SHOT: *Extreme wide-angle on the Peazant family at Ibo Landing as they
board a vessel bound for the mainland. St. Julien enters the frame
astride his horse.*

SHOT: *Long angle on the Peazant family aboard a barge. Iona catches
sight of St. Julien. She turns to kiss her sister and then leaps out of
the barge.*

SHOT: *Medium-angle slow-motion shot of Iona's feet running toward
St. Julien.*

SHOT: *Wide angle on the Peazant family in the barge as Iona races
toward St. Julien off-screen.*

SHOT: *Medium-long angle on Iona's mother, Haagar, who suddenly notices that her daughter has left the barge. Haagar rises up to bring Iona back.*

SHOT: *Wide angle on Iona approaching St. Julien astride his horse. Haagar attempts to follow her daughter.*

SHOT: *Medium angle on the Peazant family watching the scene.* Haagar (voice-off) calls out, "Iona!"

SHOT: *Long shot on Daddy Mac forcibly holding back Haagar, who continues to call out to her daughter in desperation.* "Iona!"

SHOT: *Medium-long shot on Iona and St. Julien, now both astride the horse. Iona clings to St. Julien with tears in her eyes. They ride off together, away from the Peazants.*

SHOT: *Long shot on Daddy Mac, who continues to restrain Haagar as she sobs for the loss of her daughter.*

SHOT: *Long-angle and slow-motion shot as St. Julien and Iona gallop into the frame, riding among the old-growth trees. They pass Nana Peazant, who has decided to stay on the island.*

SHOT: *Medium-long angle on Nana, who holds her indigo-stained hand to her heart as St. Julien and Iona pass her by. She turns and watches them as they ride off together.*

SHOT: *Medium-close follow shot on Iona and St. Julien galloping across the frame.*

SHOT: *Bird's-eye-view shot on St. Julien and Iona riding away.*

Some critics have found fault with Dash's representation of St. Julien Lastchild, arguing that he is erotized as an indigenous other, rendered silent in the sound regimes of the film.[21] Indeed, St. Julien is a romanticized figure, literally a handsome man who rescues Iona on a white horse. However, neither Iona's nor Dash's gaze objectifies him. Instead, Dash constructs an indigenous male as a dashing romantic figure rather than a noble savage, a dangerous threat, or a vanishing victimized Indian. There are not too many films in which an indigenous male character is depicted as desirable and heroic.

As in Dash's frame, in *Mauri*, Merata Mita's subaltern frontier landscape is embedded with a shameful and dark colonial history in which the Maori have been pushed out by Pakeha settlers. The shrinking Te Mata Settlement has been literally pushed to the edge of the sea. Mita's mise-en-scène is distinguished by wide-angle shots of bucolic New Zealand/Aotearoa landscapes, infused with Maori iconography and rituals focalized around cultural identity. Land territory disputes and land invasion are key themes throughout the film, and boundaries are a central visual motif. As discussed in chapter 1, Mita represents the history of broken promises to the Maori by the Pakeha government through the two feuding families in the film, the Rapanas and the Semmenses. This is depicted in the placenta burial scene.

SOUND BRIDGE: *Maori chanting (waiata).*

SHOT: Full shot of Maori elders, men and women, conducting a placenta burial. They perform a chant.

SHOT: *Wide-angle shot of landscape. Steve Semmens, a white man, enters the frame, astride a horse.*

SHOT: *Close angle on Steve watching with curiosity the Maori placenta burial ritual.*

SHOT: *Medium-close angle on Kara chanting.*

SHOT: *Wide angle on Maori elders surrounded by epic Oceanian landscape. Steve continues to approach on horseback.*

SHOT: *Close angle on Kara as she notices Steve's approach. She continues chanting.*

SHOT: *Full shot on the Maori group. Keeping his distance, Steve intrusively passes by the elders.*

SHOT: *Close angle on Steve, who stops at a distance to voyeuristically watch the ritual.*

SHOT: *Close angle on Kara, who continues to chant. She returns Steve's gaze.*

SHOT: *Close angle on Steve, who gazes back momentarily but then turns away and gallops off on his steed.*

SHOT: *Close angle on Kara gazing after Steve.*

SHOT: *Full shot on male elder who delivers a speech in the Maori language. The others listen.*

SOUND BRIDGE: *Male elder continues speaking.*

SHOT: *Close angle on Kara as she buries the placenta in the trunk of an old tree.*

SHOT: *Close angle on Kara's hands burying the placenta.*

SHOT: *Wide-angle moving shot of bird flying along a New Zealand/Aotearoa coastline.*

Though Mita does not represent Steve's intrusion as aggressive, but one of ignorance and indifference, she constructs Steve's Pakeha gaze as both intrusive and naive. Though Mita depicts Steve as a sympathetic character who aims to make amends for his father's racism and thievery, he is also rather simple. Steve seems somewhat oblivious to the traumatic history of Maori land dispossession and how that stands between himself and Remari, the woman he loves and wishes to marry. The following scene emphasizes the significance of boundaries in the Maori community and Steve's ignorance about his trespassing and his white male privilege.

SHOT: *Wide angle on epic oceanic landscape. Astride his horse, Steve enters from the corner of the frame while a pickup truck comes to a stop along the side of the road. Steve rides toward the truck. Rewi gets out from the driver's side.*

SHOT: *Long shot on Rewi at the truck. Remari is in the front passenger seat. Pointing his finger at Steve, Rewi yells,* "You stay away from here!"

SHOT: *Long shot on Steve astride his horse, looking concerned. He says,* "I didn't mean to offend."

SHOT: *Long shot on Rewi at the truck. Rewi says,* "You might own everything else around here, but not this place." *Remari gets out of the truck. Steve, off-screen, says,* "Sorry."

SHOT: *Long shot on Steve astride his horse. He tips his hat to Remari. He begins to dismount his horse. He says apologetically,* "I didn't realize . . ."

SHOT: *Wide angle. Steve continues to dismount. He nervously mutters,* ". . . that they were . . . uh . . . that, that . . . they were down there."

SHOT: *Long-angle two-shot on Rewi and Remari, who chastises Steve.* "You were brought up here. You should know better!" *Remari turns away in anger. The camera follows her.*

SHOT: *Long shot on Steve holding the reins of his horse. He steps toward Remari. He asks sheepishly,* "Can I see you later? It's important." *Steve moves toward the frame. Remari says,* "I don't know, we're busy."

SHOT: *Medium-long angle on Remari with Steve partially in frame. The Maori elders, including Kara, gather around the truck, along with Rewi, who all watch Remari and Steve with interest. Remari turns to Steve.* "Okay—later." *Remari turns away, still angry.*

SHOT: *Deep-focus medium-close angle on Rewi glaring at Steve. Kara and the Maori elders dominate the background. Steve says, off-screen,* "But, you haven't said when." *Kara moves toward Rewi, who looks ready to kill Steve. Kara leans into Rewi and says,* "If you don't like it, why don't you do something about it?" *Rewi replies,* "Like what?" *Kara replies,* "Like marry her." *Rewi shakes his head despondently.* "No. I can't." *Kara says,* "You keep pushing her away. It's cruel to watch."

SHOT: *Long shot on Steve, who presses Remari.* "But you haven't said when."

SHOT: *Long angle on Remari as she helps the elders onto the back of the truck. Exasperated, she says,* "I did. I said, LATER."

SHOT: *Medium angle on Steve, who seems forlorn and frustrated. Realizing he won't get the answer he's looking for, he mounts his horse.*

Mita resists using shot-reverse-shot between Remari and Steve. She destabilizes Steve's gaze by showing other members of Remari's Maori family and community continually interrupting their exchange, including Steve's male rival for her attention, Rewi. Steve will have to go through Remari's family before he can actually get to her.

Willie Rapana gives Steve permission to pursue his cousin Remari only because he knows that is how the Rapana family will get their land back. Uncle Willie and his gang members have cultivated intimidating street-gang personas by wearing leather jackets and carrying guns, but they also maintain their cultural identity with Maori tattoos. Through these bodily acts of resistance, these characters see themselves as protectors and defenders of their land and Maori women. They use their gangster personas to intimidate Steve, sending a strong message that his intentions with regard to Remari had better be honorable. Mita shoots the following scene, in which Steve must prove his worth to Willie, at night around a firepit. The scene is played for tension and humor.

SHOT: *Wide-angle shot. Steve places a case of beer in front of Willie, who is flanked by two gang members and Remari at the firepit. Steve removes his hat and positions himself between Willie and Remari. The other gang members stand guard, looming over Steve.*

SHOT: *Close angle on Remari as she smiles at Steve. Willie, off-screen, says,* "Rumor has it, you might be part of the family one day."

SHOT: *Tight low angle on Steve and Willie, while two gang members, including Hemi, hover over them in a dominating position. A large bald guy opens beer bottles with an axe. Willie says,* "If you play your cards right, that is." *Steve nervously glances at the gang members opening his beer with an axe. He turns to Willie.* "What do you mean? I love her." *Willie leans in and says,* "It's not enough." *Steve turns his gaze toward Remari.*

SHOT: *Close angle on Remari, who returns Steve's gaze. Steve, off-screen, says,* "I'll do anything for her." *Willie, off-screen, says,* "That's beginning to sound more like it." *Steve replies,* "My father's always on at me about her, but he won't stop me."

SHOT: *Tight low-angle shot on Steve and Willie while Hemi and the large bald guy continue to loom over them. Steve says,* "I want to marry her." *Willie looks toward the fire reflectively.* "Pity about your old man. A bullet through the head would have been cleaner. Then again, he would have suffered for his sins, if you get my drift?" *The gang members continue snapping the caps off beer bottles with an ax, directly over Steve's head.*

SHOT: *Medium-close angle on Willie with Steve partially in frame.* "In more practical terms, mate, what are you willing to give her? YOU!" *Steve turns toward Remari.*

SHOT: *Medium-close angle on Remari staring into the fire.*

SHOT: *Medium-close angle on Steve with Willie partially in the frame. Steve replies firmly,* "Everything." *Willie says tauntingly,* "Everything?" *Steve returns Willie's gaze and repeats with confidence,* "EVERYTHING."

SHOT: *Reverse angle on Willie, who turns to one of his men.* "Give him a drink, bro."

SHOT: *Medium angle on Hemi. The large bald guy looms in the background. Hemi takes a long swig of his beer.*

SHOT: *Medium angle on Steve, who waits politely to be offered a drink.*

SHOT: *Medium angle on Hemi, who continues glugging his beer. When he finishes drinking, he passes his bottle to Steve.*

SHOT: *Extreme low-angle medium-long angle on Steve as he accepts Hemi's beer. He almost wipes the lip of the bottle with his hat but reconsiders his actions.*

SHOT: *Medium-close angle on Hemi glaring at Steve.*

SHOT: *Medium-close angle on Steve, who returns Hemi's gaze. Willie observes the exchange in the background. Steve takes up Hemi's challenge and takes a swig of the beer.*

SHOT: *Medium angle on Hemi, who lunges at Steve, but Willie intercepts him from doing violence.*

SHOT: *Medium-close angle on Steve as he turns to Remari.* "Walk you home, Remari."

Mita also depicts her frontier as a place of possibility through reproduction and the marriage of Remari and Steve. In many ways, the Rapanas have their day of justice through Remari's marrying a Pakeha; Remari is actually pregnant with Rewi's child, and hence the child will have only Maori blood. The wedding scene is a significant visual expression of hope for the Maori community.

SHOT: *Long shot of Remari dressed in a white bridal gown. Steve is dressed in a formal suit and top hat. They stand in front of a small white church. A barbed wire fence is in the foreground. They smile and wave. Off-camera, the wedding guests celebrate. Confetti rains down upon them.*

SHOT: *Close angle on a Maori boy chanting. He is dressed in Maori regalia.*

SHOT: *Medium-close angle on Maori girls chanting and gesturing, also dressed in Maori regalia.*

SHOT: *Medium shot on a Maori girl chanting and gesturing. The camera pans to reveal more Maori children participating in the celebratory ritual.*

SHOT: *Wide angle on the wedding party walking arm in arm in procession toward the camera, with the oceanic landscape in the background.*

The bridesmaids wear long pink dresses and carry pink bouquets. The groomsmen wear formal black suits and gray top hats.

SHOT: *Long shot of wedding guests awaiting the arrival of the wedding party in the open air. The Maori children's chanting continues over the soundtrack.*

SHOT: *Wide angle on the wedding party walking arm in arm toward the camera.*

SHOT: *Moving medium angle on the Maori children chanting. They continue to perform a dancelike ritual with hand gestures.*

SHOT: *Close angle on an elderly Maori woman.*

SHOT: *Close angle on a blond white child dressed in Maori regalia.*

SHOT: *Medium-close angle on Remari and Steve walking in procession toward their guests. Remari smiles.*

SHOT: *Wide angle on the entire Maori wedding group clustered in front of a Maori meetinghouse. Children continue to perform. The wedding guests wait as the wedding party approaches the* marae *(a communal and scared meetinghouse).*

Remari and Steve's wedding ceremony is a pivotal scene in which Maori and Pakeha come together at the tribal marae shown in figure 3.3. Rather than Maori spaces being represented as anachronistic and stuck in anterior time, Mita depicts them as places that resist white imperial surveillance and intrusion. This is a form of restitution for the Rapana family.

FIGURE 3.3 Remari and Steve's wedding at the marae, *Mauri.*

The rape scene in Loyalties *we kept until the last day of the*
shooting. And of course everybody was terrified of it. I was
dreading it because I knew very clearly in my mind what I
wanted, and the scene wasn't nice. Everybody had anticipated
it for five weeks. What is it going to turn out like. We knew that
this was the soul of the film.[22]

—Anne Wheeler

Anne Wheeler's *Loyalties* is set on a contemporary western Canadian frontier in which indigenous peoples live below the poverty
line and non-indigenous settlers, especially whites, live in nice
middle-class suburbs with manicured lawns. In the Northern Alberta
community of Lac La Biche, indigenous peoples (First Nations and
Métis) are segregated not only by race, but also by class, via the Canadian Indian reservation system. Wheeler represents this racial
and class divide through two families, the Suttons and the Ladouceurs. Both families live on the outskirts of town, surrounded by
pristine lakes and ancient forest. Interestingly, for the privileged
Suttons, Lac La Biche is hardly a place of possibility but rather a
kind of wasteland to which they have been banished, what Lily describes as "so far away from everything." However, we soon understand that the Suttons are running from something and are hiding
out "on the lip of civilization." For the Ladouceurs, the land represents a boundary where they are now deemed squatters by the colonial authorities. Despite the fact that it is 1985, Roseanne and her
people are treated like trespassers on their own lands. Tellingly, the
Sutton home is situated on land that once belonged to Roseanne's
people; Beatrice makes a point of passing on this truth to the current
owner, Dr. Sutton.

The scene in which Lily Sutton and her three children travel to Lac
La Biche follows the prologue scene, a flashback to Dr. Sutton committing rape, which his son witnesses through a window. This second opening sequence juxtaposes the untamed western Canadian
landscape with a forlorn Lily, who has been forced to relocate from
England with her three children. Wheeler depicts Lily's situation

through imagery of the vast landscape (wasteland) and the airplane cabin (imprisonment).

SHOT: *Wide angle of an airplane flying low across a forested Albertan landscape.*

SHOT: *Medium shot of Lily, close to tears, gazing sadly out the window.*

SHOT: *Traveling bird's-eye-view landscape shot of forest and river.*

SHOT: Medium two-shot, from behind, of the pilot and Lily, who sits in the copilot seat. We do not see their faces until Lily turns around.

SHOT: *Tight shot on Lily's sleeping children strapped into their seats.*

SHOT: *Close angle on Lily's baby.*

SHOT: *Medium two-shot of Lily and the pilot.*

SHOT: *Extreme wide shot of the airplane flying against a big sky and a setting sun.*

SHOT: *Tight shot on pilot, who says,* "You up here on some kind of holiday?"

SHOT: *Reverse shot on Lily, who snaps her head to face the pilot. She replies nervously,* "Oh, no, we're joining my husband."

SHOT: *Reverse shot back to the pilot, who smiles and says,* "English, eh?"

SHOT: *Reverse shot on Lily, who replies with polite disdain,* "Yes." *The pilot continues off-screen,* "So, uh, how come . . . Lac La Biche?"

SHOT: *Reverse shot on the pilot, who says,* "You really don't seem like the type."

SHOT: *Back to Lily, who turns to gaze out the window again. The pilot says, off-screen,* "Oh, uh, sorry, none of my business."

Wheeler ends this sequence with another wide angle on the descending airplane. Instead of depicting Lily's new home as a place of possibility, Wheeler emphasizes her sadness and containment. Lily and her children seem trapped in the small aircraft, which hovers over an empty and remote, albeit grand, frontier. The Sutton home is tellingly perched on a lookout point high above everything, but like the plane it is also very confining and removed. In many ways, Lily is a prisoner in her own home. As discussed in chapter 2, Lily is the classic oppressed angel on the frontier, although one who is complicit in her husband's criminality. In the opening, Wheeler also sets Lily up as a displaced person, one who belongs nowhere. Lily's salvation is possible only when she literally abandons her luxury home/castle. Significantly, Wheeler and Riis set the rape scene outside that castle in the woods.

In the final shot of the film, set amid the untamed Northern Alberta landscape, Lily arrives at Beatrice and Roseanne's house with all four of her children packed in the car. The normally pristine Lily is a mess. Roseanne sees her pain and shame and instructs Lily's children to go into the house. "Go with Kookum. She'll take care of you." Lily says to Roseanne, "I couldn't stay. He's still there." Roseanne embraces Lily as a sister, one mother to another. Roseanne says, "Don't worry about it. We got plenty of room, eh." The two mothers are framed in a medium two-shot while they embrace. Wheeler has the women exit the frame together. Wheeler cuts to an extreme bird's-eye-view wide angle of Beatrice's dilapidated wood-frame house. Roseanne and Lily walk into the house together, arm in arm. Wheeler constructs the film's resolution in the mothers' solidarity, which has managed to cross the lines of race and class. This resolution becomes possible only when Lily refuses to be complicit in patriarchy and colonization.

Norma Bailey sets *The Wake* on a contemporary wintry Northern Alberta frontier. Bailey's mise-en-scène is marked by powerful iconic images of subaltern resistance and empowerment in the face of systemic police brutality and racist violence. Bailey shot *The Wake* at the Brokenhead Ojibway Nation Reserve and cast First Nations and Métis people to play the indigenous characters, although it should be noted that the actor Victoria Snow, who played the central protagonist, Joan, is not indigenous (the film was criticized for this casting choice).[23] Though Bailey and Wheeler both worked with writer Sharon Riis, their frontiers are constructed through a slightly different lens. On Bailey's frontier there is a stronger sense of a Métis community and collective subaltern resistance. Though Joan and Donna are the central figures in the film, they are often framed surrounded by their families and community. This is quite different from Wheeler's depiction of the indigenous characters in *Loyalties*. Though Roseanne in *Loyalties* has her immediate family, who often appear in the frame with her, signifying support, there is very little sense of Roseanne belonging to a larger Métis community. Bailey's frontier mise-en-scène works in a similar fashion to that of Dash and Mita. Bailey's film is bookended by two large Métis community gatherings, the wedding/ wake at the beginning of the film and the wake for the four dead teenagers at the film's end.

A key motif throughout Bailey's film is the open road. The road is deployed in a number of ways by the characters in the film. In some ways, the road represents freedom of movement and interconnectivity among the Métis community within a remote and difficult landscape. The road also affords access to economic opportunity; it is how Joan travels to work so she can support her children. However, the road is also depicted as a dangerous space, where police brutality most often happens, and indeed it will be on the road where four teenagers are literally driven to their deaths by Officer Crawford.

The road is also a highly visible space where indigenous women are often rendered vulnerable by white men. It is how Cora's johns seek out her prostitution services. The road is a boundary symbolizing indigenous containment within colonial structures; it is not a space of possibility. Indigenous peoples travel the open road at great risk. Bailey opens *The Wake* on a wintry country road setting.

> SHOT: *Extreme wide-angle shot on a country road. The film's title,* The Wake, *is superimposed over the frame. A female country singer's voice is heard. A red truck approaches. The camera pans as it passes by the frame. A small-town diner comes into view. In front of the diner is a car covered in plastic pink carnations. Two indigenous men struggle to push a car out of an icy, muddy rut.*
>
> SHOT: *Close-angle shot on a young indigenous man pushing the car. He is dressed in a winter coat, but a pink ruffled dress shirt and a pink boutonniere can be seen peering out. The female country singer continues on the nondiegetic soundtrack.*
>
> SHOT: *Close-angle shot on the car wheel spinning in the mud; a string of plastic pink carnations dangles down the side of the car.*
>
> SHOT: *Full shot on the two young indigenous men pushing the car.*
>
> SHOT: *Close-angle shot on an indigenous man in a cowboy hat with a cigarette hanging out of the side of his mouth. He is also wearing a pink ruffled dress shirt and a pink boutonniere.*

SHOT: *Close-angle shot on an indigenous man who has stopped pushing the car to brush snow and dirt from his clothing. He returns to pushing the car.*

SHOT: *Full shot on the groom, who gets out of the car. The camera follows him as he joins the other two men who have been pushing. The man in the cowboy hat starts digging around the wheel with a shovel. All three men try to get the car out together.*

Later we cut to Joan kneeling in the snow, attaching a chain from the stuck car to a Ford pickup as shown in figure 3.4. Joan is dressed in a pink lace bridesmaid dress, cowboy boots, and a practical winter coat. Though she has clearly gussied herself up for a wedding, she doesn't think twice about getting her hands dirty to help out the guys. Even the bride has joined in, now driving the car while the three men, including the groom, push with all their might. As Joan drives the truck, the car is freed from the mud and snow, saving the wedding day (and the wake). This scene is about indigenous collectivity. Though Joan is instrumental in getting the car out, she doesn't do it alone. It is the group working together that makes it happen, that solves the problem, that allows for things to move forward. Though the road is

FIGURE 3.4 Joan, *The Wake.*

a place where bad things can happen, indigenous people can find ways to survive, but as a community. Bailey's frame privileges the collective over individualism.

Another key feature of Bailey's landscape is the decolonization of the white male gaze. In the very opening of the film, Bailey ensures that the white male gaze is not one we should trust. While the car is being hauled out of the snow and mud outside, the bride and Donna, Joan's teenage cousin, wait inside the diner.

SHOT: *Two-shot on the bride and Donna, who wears a pink bridesmaid dress, sitting at the diner's counter. The arm of a middle-aged white man looms in the foreground holding a coffee pot, hovering at the edge of the frame. The bride jumps out of her seat when her fiancé calls her to help out with the truck.* "Hey, you just stay here and keep warm. Finish your coffee." *Donna nods her head and looks downward.*

SHOT: *Close-angle shot on Donna's pink satin shoes, covered in mud. Her hand comes into the frame and she attempts to clean off the mud with a tissue.*

SHOT: *Medium-angle shot on Donna as she finishes wiping off her shoes. The white man's arms come into the frame and pours coffee into her cup. She glances up at him with trepidation and then quickly casts her gaze downward.*

CUT TO: *Medium-close angle shot on the white man ogling Donna. He turns away and the camera follows him, revealing a young Asian woman holding a baby, standing behind the serving counter. She has a black eye. The white man passes her by with indifference. It is implied that they are a married couple.*

SHOT: *Medium-angle shot on Donna, who looks at the woman and her baby. Donna turns to glance at the white man, who is now serving the other costumers in the diner. Donna turns back to the mother and baby.*

SHOT: *Close-angle shot on the woman, holding her baby close to her. She gazes back at Donna and smiles.*

SHOT: *Close angle shot on Donna as she smiles back at the woman and baby.*

The representation of the only white character in the opening scene as a wife abuser and sexual predator establishes that this frontier will not center its story and identification on white settlers. Most of the white characters in the film, including the seemingly sweet-natured Jim, are racist or sexually predatorial or both. In contrast to *Loyalties*, villainy does not take the form of one perverse beast or monster but is embedded in the white community as a whole. Racism is so entrenched on Bailey's frontier that it is ordinary; it shapes the frontier. This is exemplified in the high school fight scene.

SHOT: *Full shot on Donna walking with her Métis friends, a girl and two boys, in the snowy parking lot of their high school. In the background of the frame, white teens mingle with one another. One of the Métis boys remarks to Donna,* "Hey, Donna, there's your competition." *He is referring to the Mardi Gras Pageant that Donna is competing in. Donna and her friends look off-screen at the competition.*

SHOT: *Medium moving shot on a white teenage girl flanked by white male teenagers. They loiter in the school parking lot.*

SHOT: *Medium-close angle on Donna. She turns her gaze away from the white girl and looks downward. Her male friend says, off-screen,* "I hear her old man is going to buy her a car if she wins."

SHOT: *Full shot on the white girl and other white teens who stand together in a circle, smoking. Donna's girlfriend says, off-screen,* "He's a dentist." *One of the white male teens turns his gaze off-screen. He takes a drag of his cigarette and yells,* "Hey Donna! You wanna?" *His friends laugh at the sexual taunt.*

SHOT: *Medium shot on Donna striding away from the white kids. She turns her gaze briefly toward the taunting white teens but remains silent.*

SHOT: *Full shot on the white male teen, who continues to harass Donna.* "Hey, you wanna go, eh? You wanna go?"

SHOT: *Medium moving shot on Donna. She turns sharply toward them.* "Fuck off, asshole!"

SHOT: *Medium-close shot on the white male teen.* "Oh, come on, Donna, the old lady must have taught you a couple of tricks, eh?" *The white male teen makes a sexually lewd gesture with his tongue.*

SHOT: *Full shot on Donna's two male friends charging through the gang of white teens toward Donna's offender. A fistfight ensues.*

SHOT: *Donna and her girlfriend dash into a pickup truck.*

After roughing up the white boys, Donna's protectors manage to get away in the pickup truck, Donna's girlfriend at the wheel. Even supported by her friends and male protectors, Donna is rendered what Rayna Green identified as the savage squaw.[24] By publicly marking Donna a whore, the whites assert their racial dominance over the Métis at the school and within the community as a whole. Indeed, Bailey implies a parallel with the white male teens and Donna's mother's white male johns. When the Métis boys retaliate in Donna's defense, they are standing up against white male sexual exploitation of all their indigenous women. Bailey sets up the scene so that the viewer cheers for the good guys (the indigenous kids), not the white racist bullies and their complicit white female cheerleaders. It is somewhat simplistic, but Bailey does destabilize the white male gaze.

Throughout *The Wake*, Bailey's frontier features indigenous male strength and protection, even though there are few indigenous men with speaking roles. This is perhaps best exemplified in the final scene of the film, in which a guilt-ridden Jim, Joan's Mountie, drives up to the community center to attend the wake for the deceased Métis teens. As Jim approaches the center, he is met by a wall of large Métis men, including Joan's brothers, who block his way into the building. Joan is inside mourning with her children and her cousin Donna, who is the lone survivor of the traffic "accident," which Jim could have prevented. In a collective act of resistance and solidarity, the men refuse Jim the privilege of relieving his white guilt or expressing grief on their territory. Dejected and defeated, Jim is denied access to Joan, her children, and the Métis community as a whole. This scene echoes the fight scene between Donna's friends and the white bullies or the previous wake, at the beginning of the film, in which Joan's ex refuses to "let into" her because she has "five or six brothers" inside. Bailey concludes her film with a wide-angle shot of those same "brothers" protecting their people and their territory.

In *Bedevil*, Tracey Moffatt's Australian postcolonial frontier is structured through a highly stylized lens in which landscapes appear like paintings or theatrical sets. Moffatt is perhaps better known internationally as an art photographer who subverts white colonial tropes of the Australian outback by foregrounding Aboriginal and Torres Strait Islander peoples in dramatic tableaux photos. Rather than using wide-angle shots and emphasizing the expansiveness of the Australian frontier, as depicted in countless Australian and Hollywood Westerns, Moffatt depicts frontier landscapes as shallow spaces, claustrophobic and eerie, keeping more in the horror tradition. In the "Choo, Choo, Choo, Choo" segment, an Aborigine family lives along a railway track, seemingly stranded in the middle of nowhere, cut off from the larger white-settler community and the modern world. In "Lovin' the Spin I'm In," Imelda, an elderly Torres Strait Islander, is physically forced from her home to make way for a new development project. In "Mr. Chuck," Rick, an Aborigine man, spins strange tales of his childhood from his cramped prison cell.

Similarly to *Daughters* and *Loyalties*, Moffatt opens *Bedevil* with wide landscape shots of an Australian desert landscape. Moffatt's Australian frontier, however, is a hyperreal space underscored by an ironic use of eerie music. Moffatt constructs her film's opening through a narrow-angle aesthetic, framed through a subjective lurking camera,[25] used here to emphasize crowding and confinement.[26]

SHOT: *Close-angle overhead shot tracks through desert plants and weeds toward a murky, bubbling swamp. A subjective camera tracks around the swamp. Eerie music and atmospheric sound effects construct a creepy soundscape.*

SHOT: *Medium-long shot on three Aborigine children wedging themselves between trees and weeds as they walk toward something.*

SHOT: *Long shot as camera tracks around a murky, bubbling swamp.*

SHOT: *Medium-long shot on the children walking.*

SHOT: *Long shot on swamp.*

SHOT: *Long shot on children approaching the swamp. They pause at its edge and then sit down. They begin to divvy up candy from a plastic bag.*

SHOT: *Close angle on the swamp's bubbling surface. Distorted sounds of predatory animals dominate the soundtrack.*

SHOT: *Long shot on children as they continue to parcel out their candy. Camera tilts down to the bubbling surface of the water. The children's images are reflected in the surface of the swamp water. Ominous music plays.*

SHOT: *Close angle follow-shot on a child's feet walking along a fallen tree trunk that serves as a makeshift bridge across the swamp.*

SHOT: *Close-angle overhead shot on the swamp's bubbling surface.*

SHOT: *Long shot on all three children as they walk across the swamp. The children come to a stop halfway along and sit down on the rickety bridge. Rick dangles his legs into the murky water and then starts tossing his candy into the swamp, as if he were feeding something.*

SHOT: *Medium shot on Rick continuing to throw his candy into swamp.*

SHOT: *Close angle on Rick's candy dropping into the swamp, the distorted animal noises dominating the soundtrack.*

SHOT: *Extreme long shot on children suspended over the bubbling swamp. Rick continues to drop candy into the swamp. He then leans over to reach out for something.*

SHOT: *Close angle on Rick's arm reaching into the swamp. Steam rises from the water's surface.*

SHOT: *Close angle on a girl gazing at Rick struggling.*

SHOT: *Close angle on Rick's arm reaching into swamp. Rick struggles as something from below seems to have taken hold of him.*

SHOT: *Overhead shot on Rick as he is yanked into the swamp.*

SHOT: *Close angle on the girl as muddy water splatters all over her.*

SHOT: *Medium long shot on the swamp. The camera whip-tilts up to the treetops. Though Rick is now out of the frame, we hear him struggling. Dramatic, suspenseful music plays.*

These are not wide-open spaces full of possibility but prisonlike boundaries that delimit movement and opportunity for indigenous peoples. Using the codes of horror and Gothic fairy-tale, Moffatt subverts the way indigenous people have been, and continue to be, constructed as monstrous others in frontier discourse and popular art. In horror, the other is always the monster, a distorted manifestation of society's fears and anxieties. In this scene, the monstrous other is actually the ghost of a white American G.I. lurking below the surface of the swamp, ready to do violence at any time. Deploying the visual tropes of fairy tale, such as the haunted swamp (forest), candy, and the gobbling up of children by monsters, Moffatt evokes suppressed truths (and horrors) about postcolonial violence committed against indigenous children (i.e., the Stolen Generations). Indeed, Moffatt herself was taken away from her indigenous mother and placed into foster care with a white family. Moffatt's mise-en-scène seems also to echo film theorist Bill Nichols's work on ethnography, which he equated with pornography. Nichols equated the two forms because both depend on a controlling gaze that silences and objectifies the primary "actors." Nichols argued:

> Both pornography and ethnography promise something they cannot deliver: the ultimate pleasure of knowing the Other. On this promise of sexual or cultural knowledge they depend, but they are also condemned to do nothing more than make it available for representation.[27]

Moffatt reverses the gaze here. The American G.I. as the other is someone or something we never get to know. The G.I. apparently drove his jeep into the swamp one night while he was drunk, a shameful way for a soldier to die. He is a pure horror device representing *the* threat. He is something out of a Gothic fairy tale or bad horror B-movie. The indigenous children cease to be the objects of our gaze; instead they are rendered into vulnerable figures of resistance, not unlike the children in *Hansel and Gretel*. Through a fusion of tropes from ethnography, horror, and Gothic fairy tale, Moffatt constructs the Australian frontier as a haunted and threatening space. Moffatt's fusion of Gothic fairy-tale, horror, and ethnography is depicted in figure 3.5, which features Rick as a child, innocently playing with his sisters around the haunted swamp.

Like the ghost of the little blind white girl in "Choo, Choo, Choo, Choo," the American G.I. ghost does not speak, and he rarely opens his dead eyes, layered in swamp muck. In the scene in which Shelley tells about the American G.I., there is a blocking of the white male gaze.

SHOT: *Blurry blue image as if looking through an unfocused kaleidoscope. Shelley's voice-over is laid over the image. "Then one night a poor G.I. . . . ." Very briefly a close angle of the G.I. ghost, covered in*

FIGURE 3.5 Young Rick with sisters, *Bedevil.*

swamp muck, is superimposed over the blurry blue background. It fades in and out quickly.

SHOT: *Close angle on Shelley in her home. She continues to tell her story.* ". . . whom I knew drove his tank straight into the quicksand swamp . . . sank . . . without a trace and was never found."

SHOT: *Close angle on black-and-white photograph of Shelley as a young woman flanked by numerous G.I.s. One of them holds her hand. A black G.I. smiles and waves at the camera. They appear to be at a party or in a bar. The camera zooms in closer to Shelley in the photograph. She is smiling brightly at the camera. Shelley's voice off-screen continues,* "The children in the area have always told tales about him . . ."

SHOT: *Close angle on G.I. in the photograph, framed in profile. His eyes are somewhat obscured. He has been caught midaction of spitting water at someone. He is framed at the periphery of the photograph. The camera swish-pans to reveal that he is spitting at Shelley. Shelley's voice, off-screen, says,* "The ghost of the G.I. . . ."

SHOT: *Close angle on Shelley in her home. She continues speaking.* ". . . pulling them in." *She raises an eyebrow and smiles as if she doesn't believe such tales.*

SHOT: *Close angle on the G.I. in the photograph, his spitting frozen in time. An image of his ghost, covered in swamp muck, is very briefly superimposed over the photograph. Again his eyes are obscured.*

SHOT: *Medium angle on Shelley standing and gazing out a window.*

The swamp is also the site where a new suburban housing project is underway, a project that employs working-class white men. White children visit their fathers on-site, donning matching clothes and play tool belts. White working-class wives bring their husbands lunch. Rick and his sisters stand by and watch while the white community builds over wild frontier space and the haunted swamp. The following scene features a group of white housebuilders, a white woman, two white children, Rick, and his little sisters, who have gathered around the dead G.I.'s helmet and ammunition belt, which someone has fished out of the swamp.

SHOT: *Close angle on murky swamp water under wood planks of a newly built platform. Steam rises from the black water. Animalistic monster sounds emerge over the image.*

SHOT: *Close angle on adult Rick in prison. He laughs demonically.*

SHOT: *Rotating shot of the G.I.'s helmet and ammunition belt. They have been cleaned and displayed as if they were in a museum.*

SHOT: *Medium-close high angle on Rick as a child sitting with a group around the muddy G.I. helmet and ammunition belt. Rick gazes up.*

SHOT: *Medium-close low angle of a white man staring down at Rick in a menacing and sexually predatory manner. He is blond, well-dressed, and clean-cut. The soundtrack features animalistic monster growls and horror-style music. The blond man turns his gaze away from Rick.*

SHOT: *Medium close angle on Rick, who continues to gaze up at the blond man with a blank expression on his face.*

SHOT: *Close angle on the blurry silhouette of the blond man. He turns his head in profile.*

SHOT: *Medium-close angle on Rick, who continues to gaze up at the blond man.*

SHOT: *Close angle on the blurry silhouette of the blond man. He sticks out his tongue in an animalistic and sexual way.*

The real monster here is colonial expansionism, which has been a literal horror story for Aborigine and Torres Strait Islander people and communities. This is exemplified in the segment "Lovin' the Spin I'm In," through the characters Minnie and Beba, the tragic mixed-race couple, and the transgender woman who assumes the identity of Frida Kahlo. As ghosts, Minnie and Beba haunt the warehouse where Imelda, Beba's mother, and the transgendered Frida live on borrowed time. The landlord, Dimitri, a Greek immigrant businessman, aims to convert the warehouse into a casino, a potentially more profitable venture. However, Dimitri's plans are threatened by the memory of the Minnie and Beba tragedy, a story that Imelda keeps alive with newspaper clippings and an ever-burning candle vigil by the warehouse's red loading door. Though we never entirely get the whole story from either Dimitri, his wife, Voula, or Imelda, it is understood that Minnie and Beba were cursed lovers because they broke cultural sexual taboos by marrying outside of their communities and cultures. As Dimitri says, "It was about marriage, the whole clan were down on them. They had to get the hell out." Because Minnie and Beba chose to break these laws, they were outcasts and ended up working for Dimitri and living in the warehouse, where they died under mysterious circumstances. Moffatt depicts the power of Beba and Minnie's desire in the following deal-making scene.

SHOT: *Wide-angle shot on a parking lot crammed between Dimitri's sandwich shop and the warehouse. Dimitri stands with two businessmen, one Greek and the other Chinese. The Chinese businessman is on his mobile phone yelling at someone. "Frida Kahlo" enters from the opposite end of the frame. She walks purposefully toward the warehouse. Frida catches the attention of the Chinese businessman, who pauses from his phone conversation to stare at her, who in turn ignores the men. Frida opens a side door.*

SHOT: *Medium-angle shot on Frida opening the door. She turns to gaze at the businessmen.*

SHOT: *American shot on Frida in the background, who gazes at the three businessmen. Dmitri and the Greek businessman continue arguing about zoning laws. The Chinese businessman looks stunned. Frida enters the warehouse. The Chinese businessman turns to the other men and says in reference to Frida,* "What was THAT?" *Dimitri tries an avoidance technique.* "That's a nice phone. Is that the latest model?" *The Chinese businessman turns away from Dimitri in frustration and returns to his call. He says into his phone,* "Call you back." *He hangs up.*

SHOT: *Medium-close angle shot on the Chinese businessman. He turns to Dimitri.* "I asked you if you still had anyone living there, DIMITRI."

SHOT: *American shot on the three men. Dimitri tries to laugh off the question.* "I . . . I can see that you would . . ." *While Dimitri tries to fumble through an answer, the Greek businessman turns his attention to a news clipping about the "mysterious deaths" of the "doomed couple," Minnie and Beba, that has been pasted onto the outside of the warehouse's red loading door. He moves toward it.* "What's this, Dimitri?"

SHOT: *Close-angle shot on Dimitri, who turns his gaze sharply in the direction of the news clipping.*

SHOT: *Medium-angle shot on the Greek businessman, who rips the clipping off the door.*

SHOT: *Medium-angle shot on Dimitri, who is beginning to panic. He says to the Chinese businessman,* "Twenty-four hours and they're out of here! Yeah, twenty-four hours tops!"

SHOT: *Medium-angle shot on the Greek businessman holding the news clipping in his hands.* "You had trouble here a while back."

SHOT: *Medium-close angle shot on Dimitri glaring at the Greek businessman, who says, off-screen,* "Yeah! I remember!"

SHOT: *Medium-angle shot on the Greek businessman, who hands the clipping to the Chinese businessman.* "It was in the paper. See, look!"

SHOT: *Medium-close angle shot on the Chinese businessman, who gazes down at the clipping.*

SHOT: *Medium-close angle shot on Dimitri glaring at the Chinese businessman, who says,* "What . . ."

SHOT: *Medium-close angle shot on the Chinese businessman, who backs up a bit.* "What trouble?"

SHOT: *Medium-close angle shot on Dimitri.* "Guys, I can explain the whole situation." *The Greek businessman says, off-screen,* "That's shit, Dimitri. Let's go." *He crosses the frame.*

Through the characters of Frida and the doomed lovers, Minnie and Beba, Moffatt foregrounds the sexual hierarchy within white-settler communities, one divided not only by gender and sexuality but also by class, race, and ethnicity. Though Dimitri, Voula, and the Chinese businessman are themselves people of color, they have power through their patriarchal heterosexuality and class privilege. They position themselves as not only dominant but also morally right. They are disgusted by and fearful of the transgendered Frida and spooked by Minnie and Beba's story. In fact, their expansionist and capitalist dreams are threatened by Frida, Beba, and Minnie because they represent everything that goes against heterosexist colonialism. Frida and the lovers are constructed as other by Voula and the businessmen, primarily because of their sexuality and desire. However, unlike popular depictions of subaltern and marginalized (and illegal) desire, these characters are represented as the persecuted, the shunned, and the exiled. Moffatt does not construct identification or empathy with Dimitri, Voula, or the businessmen. Rather, we are positioned to identify with their teenage son, who is sympathetic, intrigued, and drawn to the Minnie, Beba, and Imelda story. When Voula and Dimitri's son joins Minnie and Beba in a ghost dance, he crosses over to the other side, rejecting his father's way (the law of the father).

Maintaining an indigenous way of life is used as a means of resistance against capitalist and colonial expansionism in *Bedevil*. In the "Choo, Choo, Choo, Choo" segment, Ruby's husband is a stoic and imposing indigenous man who still manages to hunt, although his hyperrealistic hunting grounds are now haunted by the ghost of a little white blind girl, not to mention wire fences and the railroad delimiting the movement of wild animals. In "Mr. Chuck," young Rick acts out his rage against white society by stealing from Shelley's store and ripping apart the chairs in a movie theater that now sits over the swamp where he played with his sisters. Later, when he is an adult in prison, Rick gets caught up in a prison fight and applies homemade tattoos to his body, a potentially deadly practice. The self-tattooing shot is framed with a shaky handheld camera, as used in documentary or ethnographic films. Ironically, the ethnographic image teaches us about postcolonial indigenous male prison culture, rather than the popular subject of primitive culture.

THE FEMALE TRANSGRESSIVE
SYMBOLIC LANDSCAPE

The female transgressive symbolic landscape is featured in *My Brilliant Career, My American Cousin, Thousand Pieces of Gold, The Ballad of Little Jo*, and *The Piano*. Across these films the frontier space functions as a wasteland where bad females are banished and also as a place of possibility, offering the female heroines escape from patriarchal oppression and domestic confinement. With the exception of *The Piano*, none of these films feature indigenous peoples.

In *My Brilliant Career*, Sybylla is shipped around the Australian frontier by her parents in hope that she will find a place or at least earn her keep. Gillian Armstrong's frontier space is a vast and empty landscape. It is the wide-open landscape that offers Sybylla escape from the middle-class marriage market. Like the Western hero, Sybylla seems to prefer the outdoors to the domestic sphere, which Armstrong depicts as either confining and dull (Caddagat and Five-Bob Downs) or the site of rural domestic drudgery (Possum Gully and Barney's Gap). Despite Sybylla's desire to be a part of "the world of art literature, and music," Armstrong depicts Sybylla as most alive while climbing trees, taking long walks, and dancing in the rain. Armstrong visually aligns Sybylla's feminist spirit with her relationship with the wide-open landscape, which does not try to contain or delimit her.

Throughout *My Brilliant Career*, Armstrong deploys space as a key storytelling device in Sybylla's journey to selfhood across an Australian frontier at the turn of the twentieth century. Though Armstrong stays faithful to the novel's plot, particularly the unconventional unromantic ending, she manages to express 1970s second-wave feminist ideas about female desire visually, departing from the Victorian morals of Miles Franklin's 1902 proto-feminist text. Armstrong provides a kind of feminist visual commentary about Sybylla's journey from bush-farm daughter to writer through the depiction of landscapes. There are three different settings Sybylla visits in the narrative, bookended by Sybylla's family farm, Possum Gully. Initially, Possum Gully is a dreary place, plagued by drought, where Sybylla sees herself as overburdened by farm and domestic labor. By the end of the film, however, Possum Gully will be the place where Sybylla realizes her dream of writing a book, signifying Virginia Woolf's idea of a "room of one's own."[28] The places in between are Caddagat, Five-Bob Downs, and the McSwat farm, all representing a different phase of Sybylla's transformation.

At Caddagat, Sybylla discovers romance and passion in the handsome and wealthy Harry Beacham. Armstrong foregrounds Sybylla's desiring female gaze in the film's mise-en-scène, particularly through the use of bucolic rural landscape shots. Armstrong stages Sybylla and Harry's first meeting in a blossoming apple tree.

SHOT: *Wide angle on landscape. Sybylla sits high up in an apple tree, picking blossoms while singing a folk song. Harry approaches on horseback, drawn to Sybylla's singing. Harry dismounts his horse.*

SHOT: *Low angle on Sybylla in the tree from Harry's point of view. Sybylla continues singing. Harry enters the frame; only his legs are in the shot. He bends down and looks up at Sybylla precariously balanced on a tree branch. Sybylla finally notices him and stops singing. She pushes her skirts down, accidentally knocking the ladder away. Now stranded on the tree branch, she tries to regain composure.*

SHOT: *Medium-close angle on Sybylla. Harry, off-screen says,* "Do you, um, need a hand?" *Sybylla returns his gaze straight on.* "No, thank you."

SHOT: *Medium-close angle on Harry. The camera follows as he rises. He smiles flirtatiously.* "You're new here, aren't you? Do you work in the kitchen?"

SHOT: *Medium-close angle on Sybylla, who glares down at him. She decides to play along. She says in a faux-Irish accent,* "I'd be obliged to ya, sir, if you'd take yourself out of the way. Unless you want me foot in your big fat face?"

SHOT: *Medium-close on Harry grinning devilishly.*

SHOT: *Medium two-shot on Sybylla climbing down from the tree while Harry attempts to "help" her. She slides down against his body, her skirts rising above her waist. Harry grips her around the waist, quite pleased with Sybylla's unladylike position. He prevents her from adjusting her skirt.*

SHOT: *Long shot on Sybylla struggling out of Harry's firm grip. Harry says,* "How about a . . . a reward?" *Sybylla replies,* "Let me go."

Harry hesitates for a moment and then pushes her away, a little roughly. He bends down and helps Sybylla pick up the blossoms she has dropped. Sybylla says, "You should be ashamed, a gentleman like yourself peepin' and pryin' on innocent girls. You'll have me sacked, you will." *Sybylla smiles coyly and then runs away from him.*

As noted in chapter 2, while playing the part of the Irish servant girl, Sybylla can be sexual with Harry, something she could never do in Grandma Bossier's parlor. Perhaps the most iconic scene in the film is the one that features Sybylla and Harry's pillow fight, which was featured on the original poster for the film's theatrical release. This scene takes place at Five-Bob Downs, the grand estate Harry will one day inherit. Here Sybylla and Harry engage in a wild, uninhibited "man chase" across the magnificent gardens and fields of the estate, a lush setting for a budding romance.

SHOT: *Extreme wide-angle on Sybylla and Harry swiping at each other with their bed pillows.*

SHOT: *Medium-long angle on Sybylla chasing Harry.*

SHOT: *High-angle long shot as Sybylla pursues Harry. She breathes heavily. Harry slows down and lets Sybylla take another swipe at him. He grabs holds of her pillow. He begins to twirl her around as if dancing, while he repeatedly swipes at her. Sybylla falls to the ground, having lost her footing. She lies face down, exhausted from their roughhousing. Harry picks up her discarded pillow, circles about and then throws it at her on the ground. He comes to his knees, also exhausted, and then flops to his back beside her. He still clutches at his pillow. The two lie together in the tall grass, exhausted.*

SHOT: *Medium-long angle as Sybylla gets up, grabbing her pillow, and takes one big swing at Harry, who proceeds to grasp hold of the other end. He pulls her down beside him. Laughing, she rolls on her back. Harry tucks the pillow under his head and relaxes.*

SHOT: *Close-angle shot on Sybylla gazing at Harry while lying in the grass.*

SHOT: *Close-angle shot on Harry gazing back at Sybylla, smiling broadly.*

SHOT: *Close-angle shot on Sybylla, who continues to gaze at Harry, but her expression has become more serious. She turns away.*

The sexual overtones in the scene are obvious. Armstrong sets a number of Sybylla and Harry's scenes in exterior locations, which she deploys to express their passion for each other, a passion rooted in raw human connection rather than parlor games and the middle-class marriage market.

In contrast to the exterior settings, Armstrong represents female confinement through her depiction of interior and domestic spaces. During her stay at Aunt Gussie's Five-Bob Downs, Sybylla tries out the feel and fit of the cage/mansion but realizes nothing is worth giving up one's freedom for, even the handsome Harry Beecham. Though Harry is the classic Prince Charming, Armstrong deliberately counters his appeal with a mise-en-scène that depicts domestic spaces, even opulent ones, as prisons, foregrounding frames with bars and harsh verticals as seen in figure 3.6. When Aunt Gussie asks Sybylla if she would "fancy living" in a house like Five-Bob Downs, Sybylla says, "No, I'd get lost." A cage is what Harry has to offer Sybylla, but as she knows, she would lose herself if she accepted him.

Despite her intense attraction to Harry, however, Sybylla is not prepared to give up her dream of becoming a writer. Knowing they cannot consummate their passion outside the confines of marriage, Sybylla, in the end, refuses Harry. Their second breakup scene is set

FIGURE 3.6 Harry, Aunt Gussie (center), and Sybylla, *My Brilliant Career*.

at Possum Gully, Sybylla's family bush farm, and is framed in a harsh, drought-ridden landscape as seen in figure 3.7. Again, Sybylla is positioned near a tree, but this one is dead, symbolizing not only the death of their passion but also of Sybylla's sexual adventures on an early twentieth-century Australian frontier. Sybylla and Harry are a doomed couple.

Here Armstrong seems to evoke the second-wave feminists of the Anglo-American movement, which espoused the idea that women must walk away from heterosexual desire and marriage to have a voice and identity, to have a brilliant career. Armstrong concludes her film with a breathtaking wide-angle sunset shot, reminiscent of the Western.

Sandy in *My American Cousin* is the only heroine who is not banished or sent away for transgressions or economic need. However, Sandy is a contained figure who sees the majestic wilderness about her as a kind of prison where she is trapped under her parents' gaze. Sandy Wilson sets her coming-of-age story on a 1950s Canadian frontier in British Columbia. A key trope throughout the film is the open road. Like Sybylla in *My Brilliant Career* and Ada in *The Piano*, Sandy feels confined and delimited by domestic chores and societal expectations and finds freedom on the open roads, particularly in her American cousin's (stolen) red Cadillac, much to the dismay of her anxious

FIGURE 3.7 Sybylla and Harry, *My Brilliant Career.*

parents. It is on the frontier roads that Sandy seems most happy, driving around with her teenybopper friends and finding new ways to rebel. The road is also where Sandy commits various risky acts, such as breaking curfew, stealing car keys, and running away from home, most of which are motivated by her teenage hormones and her crush on Butch. Most of this road activity takes place in Butch's red Cadillac. His arrival in the Cadillac promises not only glamor, but also escape from domestic drudgery and isolation, from a place where "nothing ever happens!" Through the deployment of the color red, Wilson and her production designer add an erotic dimension to the film's mise-en-scène and to Sandy's frontier landscape. In many ways, the car itself represents freedom and escape, excitement and adventure. Wilson sets a number of key scenes in and around cars and trucks. In contrast, the home is depicted as a confining space, isolated from community and culture. Though the Wilcox home and cherry farm are set amid majestic mountains and postcard-worthy lakeshores, both Sandy and her mother, Kitty, take every opportunity to hit the road when they can. Wilson foregrounds and contrasts the female confinement with the male characters' labor, which occurs outdoors. Sandy's yearning to be outdoors is depicted in the following sequence.

> SHOT: *Full shot on Sandy and her family (five siblings) posing for a photograph in front of Butch's red Cadillac, parked amid epic mountains, forest, and lake. Sandy makes "bunny ears" behind the head of one of her brothers. Butch is off-screen as the photographer. He says,* "Got it."
>
> SHOT: *Medium angle on Butch with the camera. Sandy enters the frame and Butch hands her the camera. Sandy's father, off-screen, says,* "Danny and Eddie, come along now. Butch, it's time to get up to the orchard."
>
> SHOT: *Wide angle. Major Wilcox exits the frame, followed by two of his able-bodied sons (one of his sons is wheelchair bound) and Butch. Kitty puts on her apron, which she had taken off for the photograph.* "Sandra, we've got lots of cherries to can this morning." *Despondent, Sandy replies,* "Come on Mom, can't I stay out a little while longer?"

SHOT: *Medium angle on Butch, who has returned to his car to get his transistor radio. He finds a song that he likes. Kitty, off-screen, says,* "No, I need you in the kitchen. Come." *Butch exits the frame.*

SHOT: *Wide angle on Sandy as she pushes her brother in his wheelchair toward the house.*

The red Cadillac also signifies danger in the form of sexual threat. Sandy and her girlfriends are as impressed by Butch's car as they are with Butch himself. They do everything they can to score rides from him, even when he is unaware. Butch and the car are closely aligned as objects of female desire because together they form a kind of sign for sex and freedom. In figure 3.8, Sandy and her boy-crazy friends take a joy ride in Butch's Cadillac.

It is by riding around in Butch's car that Sandy discovers her own desiring gaze. This is exemplified in the scene in which Sandy sneaks into the back seat of Butch's red Cadillac in an attempt to evade her frantic father, Major Wilcox, after she has escaped the house to attend the Canadian Dominion Day dance. Sandy ends up riding alone with Butch in the middle of the night. Though Butch does not act as a sexual predator toward Sandy (he has made it clear he's not interested in her), he is a reckless and sexually active teenage boy, which gives the scene a slight sense of excitement.

FIGURE 3.8 Sandy (right) and friends, *My American Cousin.*

SHOT: *Full shot (through the windshield) as Butch drives along a dark highway. He tries to find a radio station, but he can't get any reception (because of the fact that he's in the "boonies"). Suddenly Sandy pops her head up from the back seat. She says,* "Can I ride in the front seat now?" *Butch is startled.* "Where did you come from?!" *Butch pulls to a stop. He turns to Sandy and shakes his head, although he's clearly amused by her impish behavior. Butch starts to comb his hair.* "Boy, are we gonna get it." *Sandy replies,* "Yeah, I know. Let's run away from home." *Butch continues to comb his hair.* "You and me?" *Sandy implores,* "I'm serious!"

SHOT: *Medium-angle two-shot on Butch and Sandy. Butch turns to his cousin.* "Got any money?"

Wilson filmed the scene for laughs. She also aligns Sandy's (white) virginity with the land; both are seemingly under threat from young males and Americans. Throughout the film, Sandy's parents worry about the young male cherry pickers. "And stay away from those pickers!" Butch, in fact, refers to Sandy and her mother, Kitty, as cherries. "One's too ripe and the other's too green."

Wilson also deploys the car and the open road as symbols for maternal desire and longing. It is the car that enables the two mothers in the film, Kitty Wilcox and Butch's mother, Dolly Walker, to move across frontier landscapes and the narrative, rendering them dramatic agents rather than mere devices. Both mothers reclaim their lost children using the car. Butch's mother uses the car to reclaim her lost son and her lost red Cadillac, revealed at the end of the film to be "Mommy's car." This revelation of maternal ownership renders Butch a boy rather than the man he pretends to be. Interestingly, after Dolly's arrival at Paradise Ranch, Butch seems to lose his sexy James Dean swagger. Under his mother's gaze, Butch is rendered into a scared kid who has screwed up—stealing a car and getting a girl pregnant. Dolly also sabotages Sandy's plans to run away with Butch in the red Cadillac when she drives away with him in the father's car. Dolly is at the wheel while Butch looks on helplessly at Sandy, who has been left alone at the side of the road, their plans to run away together foiled. It is Butch's father who now drives the red Cadillac, a kind of foretelling of what the future Butch will become, a dominating American patriarch. This shot represents the (American) patriarch's power, a power that usurps the mother's ownership of material possessions, although not that of her child. Kitty also reclaims her lost child by car. In the final scene of the film, after a dejected Sandy has been abandoned at the side of the road by Butch, Kitty enters the frame, driving in her ordinary station wagon. Trying to comfort her lovesick daughter, Kitty says of men and boys, "They're just buses, there's always another one coming along." Wilson frames mother and daughter driving off together (into the sunset) but, tellingly, not back home to Paradise Ranch. Instead, mother and daughter drive to Kitty's dress rehearsal for *Hedda Gabler*. In this way, Sandy's mother replaces Butch, Sandy's so-called rescuer and romantic interest. Kitty's desire to have Sandy with her is fulfilled at the end of the film, a maternal desire that has been resisted by Sandy throughout. Sandy is exactly where she should be at her age, with her mother, not in the domestic sphere but in a car on the wide-open roads.

In *Thousand Pieces of Gold*, Lalu is shipped to America after her impoverished father sells her into slavery. Nancy Kelly's film is set on an American frontier landscape in the late nineteenth century. Though the story is working within the same time frame and setting of a typical Hollywood Western, Kelly renders visible Chinese American people and history on her frontier. Most of the action in the film takes place in the town, Golden Mountain, which is more of a mining camp and primarily occupied by itinerant gold miners. Devoid of white-settler families, Golden Mountain is composed of makeshift tents, wooden planks, a saloon, and a Chinatown. As previously mentioned, there are no indigenous peoples on Kelly's frontier, with the Chinese serving as a close substitute. At the center of Chinatown is the Golden Flower of Prosperity General Store and Post-Office, operated by the elderly Li Ping, a wise old man figure. Li Ping helps Lalu remain connected to her Chinese history and culture (language, clothing, food, medicine) and helps her send letters and money back to her family in China. Most of the spaces depicted in the film are interior male homosocial environments and, hence, not domestic. Surrounding the town is the epic and unforgiving mountainous Idaho landscape, depicted in figure 3.9, in which Jim leads a tentative Lalu toward the town of Golden Mountain. This landscape holds promise in its

FIGURE 3.9 Lalu and Jim, *Thousand Pieces of Gold*.

beauty and vastness, but it is also unforgiving, the mountains functioning like a hard border or what Turner identified as a "fall line,"[29] literally impeding any hope of escape from Hong King's enslavement.

Kelly depicts three main interior spaces that represent Lalu's journey from slavery to independence. In the saloon, Lalu ("China Polly") is Hong King's sexual slave. At Charlie's homestead, Lalu (Polly) is a free woman, working hard to earn her keep, but is neither lover nor wife to Charlie. At the boarding house, Lalu (Miss Polly) is an independent, successful businesswoman. Hence, in her journey to freedom and independence Lalu must navigate and negotiate predominantly male spaces, cut off from female and Chinese communities; even the local Chinese men have disdain for her because she is a "Northerner." Kelly depicts Lalu's relationship with this male homosocial frontier in the arrival scene.

SHOT: *Wide angle on the center of the mining camp, Golden Mountain. Chinese and white men assemble at various buildings, talking and mingling. There are no women in sight.*

SHOT: *Full shot on Lalu and Jim (Li Po) approaching the center of town on horseback. Lalu gazes at her new surroundings with trepidation. Behind them are Jim's donkeys, loaded with goods he is delivering to Hong King. Lalu is one of his deliverables.*

SHOT: *Long shot on a group of men, Chinese and white, gazing at Jim and Lalu as they approach on horseback.*

SHOT: *Long shot on men languishing with two saloon girls; one is only partially dressed. Some of the men turn their gaze toward the direction of Lalu and Jim. One of the men remarks to the women,* "Looks like you've got competition."

SHOT: *Full shot on Lalu and Jim approaching the center of town. A woman's voice off-screen says,* "China Polly."

SHOT: *Long shot on men with the saloon girls on the porch. One of the women says,* "Yeah, I heard he was bringing one in."

SHOT: *American shot on the group of white men. A young man gazes toward Lalu and says,* "Hey look, there's Hong King's Chinese girl." *Two other men turn their heads, enthralled by the new arrival. The camera follows as one of the men stalks toward Lalu and Jim.* "Well, well . . ."

Though Lalu has journeyed across wide-open spaces and gazed up at magnificent star-filled skies, when she arrives at Golden Mountain the setting turns claustrophobic and hostile. As Lalu approaches Hong King's saloon, where predatory men close in around her, we soon realize that her new frontier home is a prison. In this sense, the frontier in *Thousand Pieces* is depicted as a wasteland to which Lalu has been banished (by her father), although Lalu is not being punished for any transgression. Such punishment will come later, when Lalu resists her sexual enslavement.

Much of the conflict and violent action in the film occurs in interior spaces or Chinatown. Violence across Kelly's frontier is either sexual or racist, though never both, which is fairly atypical of the Western. On Kelly's frontier, the saloon is primarily the site of sexual violence rather than gun violence. It is in the saloon where Hong King repeatedly rapes Lalu and where he offers her up as his "Pearl of the Orient" for "pokes," a form of organized gang-rape. With regard to racist violence, an anti-Chinese ("Chinks Go Home") movement, organized by The League, is gaining ground in the area. It reaches a crescendo at the Chinese New Year Festival, which features the only gun violence in the film. During the fireworks display, angry racists violently attack the revelers, and Charlie is struck down by a bullet, perhaps because he is deemed "China lovin' Yankee scum" for loving and helping Lalu. The racial hatred recreated here is rooted in actual historical events, telling an untold dark piece of frontier history, exemplifying what Richard Slotkin has called a "mythology of violence."[30] Later, the Chinese will be driven out of town. In the Chinese banishment sequence, at the end of the film, Kelly constructs new and shameful frontier landscape images expanding on the Western, but through a racialized lens. The sequence emphasizes banishment and exile.

> SHOT: *Medium angle. As Lalu rides away from the town, she pauses to speak with Li Ping, the owner of the Golden Flower of Prosperity store.* "At home we often went away, but we always came back."
> SHOT: *Medium angle on Li Ping, who sits in a wagon. He says wearily,* "Lalu, have they answered your letters or replied to the gold you sent?"
> SHOT: *Medium angle on Lalu as her silence answers Li Ping's question—her family has never answered her letters.*
> SHOT: *Medium angle on Li Ping, who says,* "Sometimes it is better to drink the soup of forgetfulness, to cross the river to be born on the other side." *Li Ping gestures to his driver to drive on. Li Ping departs with the banished Chinese. Lalu watches after him.*

Li Ping's words of wisdom inform Lalu's decision to turn around and settle with Charlie at the River of No Return, what she now calls home. The last frame of the film is an extreme wide-angle image of Lalu standing alone near her homestead at the edge of the river, countering classic Western iconography in which the American frontier was a white-settler and masculine space. In this final mise-en-scène featuring majestic mountains, Kelly suggests that her new Chinese American female frontier is one of possibility.

In *The Ballad of Little Jo*, Josephine Monaghan is banished to the streets by her father when she commits the ultimate transgression by bearing a child out of wedlock. Like *Thousand Pieces of Gold*, Maggie

Greenwald's film is set in the late nineteenth-century American West. Greenwald represents Josephine's journey from damsel in distress to autonomous "frontiersman" visually through her trajectory across and within frontier spaces. Like Lalu, Josephine is sent into exile by her father and must navigate hostile male homosocial landscapes. Greenwald represents Little Jo's exile into hostile territory in the film's opening title sequence.

> SHOT: *High-angle medium shot on a parasol. A dirt road surface is visible. A woman's skirts come into view. The title,* The Ballad of Little Jo, *is superimposed across the screen.*
>
> SHOT: *Wide-angle back view on Josephine Monaghan, a well-dressed Victorian lady, as she walks (away from camera) alone along a rough rural road carrying a travel bag and parasol. Trees and bush surround the road. A man on horseback rides toward her. As he passes her, he slows down and turns his head to gaze at her. She does not acknowledge him. He rides out of the frame. Another rider crosses the frame. An elderly man driving a horse-drawn wagon comes up behind Josephine. Two soldiers on horseback approach from the opposite direction. The wagon driver does a double take when he passes Josephine. The riders approach Josephine and bring their horses to a halt. They openly gawk at her. One of the riders says,* "What do we have here?" *They begin to circle her with their horses. The other rider says,* "Woo-wee! What's a pretty little filly like you doing traveling all alone?" *Josephine ignores them.* "So long, little lady." *As they gallop off, they give a few backward glances. She continues to walk along the road. More horse-drawn wagons enter the frame, stirring up road dust.*

While on the road, Josephine is picked up by the seemingly friendly elderly traveling salesman, who offers her his protection. Unbeknownst to Josephine, the salesman will attempt to sell her as a whore to the two soldiers she met earlier on. Afforded little safety from rape and sexual exploitation as an unprotected vagrant female on the frontier, Josephine finds safety and independence by masquerading as a man, Little Jo. Greenwald's frontier functions as a kind of wasteland for women.

Most of the action takes place in and around Ruby City, where Little Jo settles. Ruby City is similar to Golden Mountain in *Thousand Pieces*, more of a mining camp than a town. Though there are some white-settler families around, they are not foregrounded in Greenwald's mise-en-scène. Little Jo's friend Frank Badger has a wife and children, but we rarely see them; Frank spends most of his time drinking in the saloon. There are the Addies, who run the saloon, but they are atypical of the white-settler family because they are associated with alcohol, gambling, and prostitution. Most of the residents are white itinerant gold miners or lonely homesteaders like Little Jo. In order to ward off suspicion about her male masquerade and find some semblance of safety, Little Jo finds work in isolated spaces, such as sheepherding, gold mining, and, later, homesteading, all solitary, albeit backbreaking, jobs. Like Lalu, Little Jo wards off sexual exploitation through hard labor, working just as hard as any man. Greenwald emphasizes Little Jo's trials and tribulations while acquiring the skills and physical strength required to survive on a hostile frontier—as a man.

SHOT: *Close angle on a rock. A pickax enters the frame, slamming down on the rock.*

SHOT: *The camera tilts up from the rock to Little Jo wielding the pickax, which is much too heavy for her. Grimacing, she struggles against the weight of the pickax as she heaves it up and slams it down again.*

SHOT: *Medium angle on the pickax getting stuck in the ground. Camera tilts up to Jo, straining with her labor.*

SHOT: *Full angle on a cart being pushed across rough and craggy terrain. The front wheel gets stuck.*

SHOT: *Long shot on Jo toiling with the cart in the pouring rain. As she pushes against the cart, she slips into the mud.*

Though Little Jo's frontier existence is difficult and an eternity away from her life as a society girl, it is safe from sexual violence, although not all kinds of violence.

As in *Thousand Pieces*, violence in *Ballad* is depicted differently from that in the typical Western. Greenwald's frontier is in fact very violent, and much of that violence is directed toward women, children, and subaltern peoples, particularly the Chinese. As previously discussed, Little Jo's lover, Tinman, will be nearly lynched by a mob of racists in the center of town, led by a drunken Frank Badger. Little Jo will save Tinman from that fate. Perhaps the most disturbing act of violence in the film is committed by Percy, Little Jo's friend and mentor, who violently attacks a prostitute with a knife, permanently scarring her face. Percy turns on the young woman because she "wouldn't put it in her mouth." Later, Percy will attempt to rape Little Jo when he discovers that Jo is a woman and therefore "a whore." As we saw in chapter 2, another key act of violence in the film is the massacre of the Russian family by hired guns who work for the Western Cattle Company. The company will stop at nothing to remove any barriers to their acquisition of land. Greenwald emphasizes the Russian mother's death through extensive shot coverage of the murder scene, depicted in figure 3.10, in which gunmen encircle their doomed victim like wolves.

SHOT: *Close angle on Little Jo's hand holding a bunch of wildflowers. The camera tilts up to Little Jo's face as she stares dumbstruck at the sight before her. The camera pans over to reveal the bloodied body of the Russian father, dead on the ground. The camera roams across the Russian homestead to reveal the bloodied bodies of dead children. The camera cranes upward over the thatched roof of the house. Surrounded by three hired guns, the Russian mother frantically attempts*

FIGURE 3.10 Murder of the Russian mother,
The Ballad of Little Jo.

to escape. Rather than killing her at first, however, then men toy with her, laughing diabolically.

SHOT: *Slow-motion medium shot on Russian mother's skirts as she tries to flee the hired guns.*

SHOT: *Slow-motion medium shot on a horse's galloping legs as a hired gun pursues the Russian mother. The Russian mother's anxious breathing is foregrounded in the soundtrack.*

SHOT: *Slow-motion medium shot on the Russian mother's skirts as she continues to run for her life.*

SHOT: *Slow-motion medium shot on the horse's galloping legs.*

SHOT: *Slow-motion medium shot on the Russian mother's skirts. She exits the frame.*

SHOT: *Slow-motion medium shot on the horse's galloping legs. The camera tilts up to the hired gun. He wears a hooded mask. He raises his rifle, takes aim, and fires a shot.*

SHOT: *Slow-motion long shot on the Russian mother falling to the ground.*

SHOT: *Slow-motion medium-long shot on the Russian mother as she falls to the ground. A gunshot wound in her chest is visible.*

SHOT: *Slow-motion long shot on the Russian mother falling.*

SHOT: *Medium shot on Jo, who has just witnessed the brutal murder while concealed behind hanging laundry. A handmade quilt and bedsheet frame Jo's face as she gasps in shock and horror. Jo ducks to hide from the hired guns.*

SHOT: *Long shot on the lifeless body of the Russian mother. One of the hired guns circles her body, examining his kill. One of the men yells, "Let's go!" The Russian mother's killer exits the frame.*

SHOT: *Extreme wide angle on the hired guns galloping off together. The chimney smoke from the Russian family's house enters the foreground of the shot.*

Greenwald suggests that in the wide-open spaces of the frontier, violence and danger lie in wait, not in the form of angry "Injuns" but rather in the form of big business. Later, Little Jo will face down the Western Cattle Company as she fights to save her homestead, ironically with Frank Badger at her side.

Through these graphic scenes of violence, Greenwald suggests that Turner's frontier thesis was a myth. Turner explained the American frontier as a space marked by stages of advancement in which "primitive society" evolves to a "civilized" state of "settled farm communities" and eventually to the "factory system." This evolution of the frontier was deemed natural and necessary to the American Manifest Destiny.[31] On Turner's frontier there is no cold and calculated slaughtering of white-settler mothers by corporate thugs. On Greenwald's frontier, no women or children will be protected from capitalist greed and expansionism. Greenwald depicts the frontier as a boundary with set limits, particularly for a woman or a person of color. Though the land is beautiful, it is also violent and delimited. Little Jo is never free to reveal her true identity, even after her beloved Tien Mein Wong dies. It is only in death that Little Jo is free from her masquerade and from the cruel and unforgiving gaze of her fellow settlers.

In *The Piano*, single mother Ada, together with her daughter, Flora, are sent away (exiled) by Ada's father to what seems the edge of the world in order to gain respectability and a proper place in society. Throughout *The Piano*, Campion features wide-angle shots of the mid-nineteenth-century New Zealand/Aotearoa landscape, deploying the wild and epic oceanic environment as an expression of the characters' desires and fears. Campion's expressive mise-en-scène functions similarly to Moffatt's and Dash's, foregrounding the landscape as a highly symbolic space rather than a historical one. Like the moors in Emily Brontë's *Wuthering Heights* or the dark forests in a fairy tale, the landscape in *The Piano* functions as a mythical place where strange and horrific things happen.

There is not a very full sense of a white-settler community in *The Piano*, although white settlers are encountered during the *Bluebeard* production. With no obvious town life, the white settlers appear disconnected from one another, seemingly isolated in their own individual homesteads. Maori characters populate the frame throughout, but it is unclear where and how they live. They seem to just appear out of nowhere, mainly in the bush. Though land disputes between the white settlers and the Maori are hinted at, there are no displays of violent conflict between the two disparate communities. The film is set during the time frame of the Maori Wars (1845–1872), but Campion makes no reference to them, as if they had never occurred.[32] A number of scholars have criticized Campion for what Estella Tincknell calls an "ahistorical construction of self and identity," which obliterates history.[33] Though Campion's frontier features violence, all of this is domestic violence, including rape. Like Lalu, Ada will experience a transformation of self while navigating and negotiating strange frontier spaces. However, for Ada the frontier is not a space she wishes to settle in or belong to but rather a space that will allow for a sexual awakening, albeit one fraught with great personal risk. This is perhaps why Ada chooses to leave the island at the end of the film. Ada, like any heroine in a fairy tale, cannot stay in the forbidden forest forever.

Across Campion's mise-en-scène, Ada and her piano are depicted as foreign, out-of-place objects exported to the New World for civilizing purposes. Ada's and the piano's strangeness are emphasized throughout Campion's frame and are often juxtaposed with the rough and wild environments they have been transported to. In figure 3.11, Ada and Flora wait for Stewart on a desolate beach, surrounded by all their worldly possessions, including Ada's beloved piano, still protected in its crate (on the left edge of the frame). Like Lalu, Ada and Flora have been exiled to the New World and are each deemed to be out of place, in the eyes of both Ada's new husband, Stewart, and his Maori neighbors. Ada is like a lost soul who ended up in the wrong place, swept ashore by the raging sea. Perhaps this is the reason Ada

FIGURE 3.11 Ada and Flora with piano (left), *The Piano.*

never shares the frame with any Maori women, visually suggesting that Ada and Maori women cannot inhabit the same space, a white-settler space. However, Ada seems to belong to neither the wild New Zealand/Aotearoa frontier nor her husband's cramped white-settler homestead. Ada seems to belong somewhere in between, in an "elsewhere-ness," like an otherworldly creature.

Campion emphasizes Ada's function as a commodity, an object to be traded and possessed by men for her iconic and economic value. Campion represents Ada as a commodity by identifying her with her piano, the central visual motif that anchors the film. Throughout the film, Ada and the piano are identified as objects for exchange. When Ada and Flora arrive in Stewart's "own country," on a sea-swept, untamed Oceanic frontier, the sailors treat mother and daughter like cargo. Like Ada's piano and other possessions, Ada and Flora are carried to the beach on the shoulders of sailors and unceremoniously deposited with no one to greet them. Mother and daughter are forced to sleep on the beach overnight. When Stewart finally does arrive to greet his new bride, along with Baines and his Maori workers, Stewart treats Ada as a commodity. Despite the fact that Ada and Flora have traveled thousands of miles, Stewart never asks how Ada feels. Stewart is more concerned about Ada's value and what she has brought with her, immediately demanding a description of the contents of her trunks and suitcases. Campion emphasizes Ada's status as commodity in a medium-long shot of Ada and Flora standing against the choppy ocean waves, part of the piano crate looming in the foreground. Although the piano crate is only partially in the frame, the words *A. McGrath*, written in big, bold letters, are a dominant graphic element in the shot. Campion's deployment of Ada's name, her maiden name, visually identifies the piano as Ada's possession and also symbolically represents Ada McGrath as a commodity herself, one that Stewart has purchased. Despite this marker of ownership, Stewart abandons the piano on the beach, much to Ada's dismay. The piano's abandonment on the beach mirrors Ada and Flora's earlier abandonment by the sailors.

Stewart's rejection of the piano is rooted in his capitalist values, seemingly the only thing that motivates him to act. Stewart claims that the piano is too heavy. What he really means is that the piano is not worth the trouble and expense to bring up from the beach. The piano has no economic value for Stewart, and therefore he sees no use for it, despite the fact that his wife is very attached to it. Stewart doesn't need the piano for its civilizing purpose because he now has Ada, an educated white middle-class woman, albeit a mute one. For Stewart, Ada's muteness renders her like a pet, which is also "quite silent." It is only when Baines offers to swap Stewart eighty acres of land for the piano that Stewart agrees to retrieve it from the beach, where it would inevitably decay. It is not Ada's piano (with lessons) that Baines really wants, however; he wants Ada. Campion visually aligns Ada and the piano as objects of desire to be traded among men in the scene between Baines and the blind piano tuner.

SHOT: *Extreme close angle on the piano tuner's hand caressing the piano. He comments on the make:* "A Broadbent. A fine instrument." *The camera follows his hand and tilts up to his face, revealing that he is blind. He starts sniffing the instrument. The camera follows as he leans in closely to the piano's interior, still sniffing. He says,* "Scent."

SHOT: *Medium angle on Baines gazing at the piano. The piano tuner comes into the foreground of the shot, but Baines remains privileged in the frame through the technique of shallow focus. The piano tuner begins to tune the piano. Baines carefully drinks his tea.*

SHOT: *High-angle extreme close shot on the piano's interior. The camera moves across the interior of the piano's body.*

SHOT: *Overhead wide shot of Ada and Flora sitting in the forest. Ada gazes outward. Flora gazes up at the sky. Crane shot, camera moves down and trucks into Ada's contemplative face.*

Campion visually juxtaposes the piano and Ada (with her daughter) as objects of male desire. Through his caressing of the "fine instrument," the piano tuner treats the piano as if it were a sexual object. When he remarks upon the scent, he is making a direct reference to Ada, who has been the sole player of the piano. Later, Baines will also sniff Ada's clothing during one of their "lessons" together. The visual connection between Ada and the piano also echoes the earlier scene in which Ada and Flora are treated like cargo on the beach by the sailors and Stewart. Interestingly, Campion concludes the piano-tuning scene with a shot of Ada and Flora in the bush. This cut aligns Ada with the land, another commodity to be controlled and conquered by men.

The bush does not hold much interest or promise for Ada. Campion depicts the bush as an uninhabitable and forbidding place. Though Ada experiences a sexual awakening outside the marriage bed, she does so in another man's home, not in wide-open spaces. Ada finds the bush physically difficult to navigate, mired in mud and uneven terrain. Evoking Annette Kolodny's *Lay of the Land*, Campion sets the bush as the site where Stewart will attempt to rape Ada. For Stewart, Ada is his for the taking, not unlike the land he has procured unethically from the Maori. In this sense, the bush is a place of entrapment and danger, not unlike the forest in *Little Red Riding Hood*.

Campion's representation of Ada as a valuable possession to be used in economic exchanges between men is further emphasized by Stewart's entrapment and containment of her in domestic spaces. To depict Ada's imprisonment, Campion deploys the frame-within-a-frame device in her mise-en-scène, framing Ada through doorways, picture frames, mirrors, windows, and even a camera lens in the wedding portrait scene. Campion's visual device is reminiscent of the highly stylized melodramas of Douglas Sirk and Werner Fassbinder, films that often had to represent the unspeakable. Later, when Stewart learns of Ada and Baines's affair, he literally imprisons Ada in the home, nailing boards to the windows and doors.

CONCLUSION

Chapter 3 examined the filmmakers' construction of feminist symbolic settings as a key device to re-vision and deconstruct dominant frontier myth-histories. Two key questions animated this chapter: How did the filmmakers construct their symbolic settings to depict feminist agency and resistance? How did the filmmakers represent violence as a tool of gender oppression in frontier communities? The films generally embrace a different definition of *frontier*, one rooted in more European (boundary) and Chinese (wasteland) meanings, unlike the American interpretation, which is decidedly positive, a sign for possibilities. The films model (and predate) a more fluid idea of the frontier as described by Wolski, "a model which moves away from the idea of frontiers as temporally and spatially circumscribed."[34] This is particularly true of the films that depict indigenous resistance, such as *Mauri*, *Bedevil*, *The Wake*, and *Loyalties.* Generally, the films reject rigid and conventional ideas about frontier landscapes as depicted in dominant frontier myth-histories in few key ways.

First, the films challenge the dominant myth-history narrative by foregrounding femininity and female visibility in the mise-en-scène. Second, the films do not depict frontier spaces as organized around what Jim Kitses identified in *Horizons West* as the dichotomy of wilderness and civilization or rooted in what Douglas Pye identified as "biblical images of the promised Land and the wilderness."[35] Third, the films destabilize Turner's notion of the frontier as marked by linear fall lines, each won by a series of Indian wars. Instead, these films either ignore the Indian wars (*Ballad*, *Thousand Pieces*, *The Piano*) or are set in a time period in which indigenous active physical resistance had been harshly suppressed by colonial forces of power. Cinematically, as in the Western, the films' mise-en-scènes frame frontier landscapes as epic wide-open and contested spaces where there is an ever-present threat of violence. Violence in frontier myth-history narratives has historically been depicted as deadly male-on-male activity enacted in homosocial public spaces. As most of these films are working in the realm of melodrama, much of the violence is gendered and is often of a sexual nature. Across the films, the threat of rape looms large, reflecting real statistics for women and girls. Though this is less so in the family-friendly films, such as *My Brilliant Career* and *My American Cousin*, rape is still an implied threat. Throughout the films, rape is deployed as a weapon of power by patriarchal and colonial figures of authority.

Though the films embrace a more fluid representation of the frontier, there are marked differences among them. *Mauri*, *Daughters of the Dust*, *Bedevil*, *Loyalties*, and *The Wake* construct decolonizing symbolic frontier landscapes. The key visual motifs that recur are racial segregation, what Patricia Hill Collins called the "hypervisibility of black men and women's alleged sexual deviancy";[36] the criminalization and imprisonment of subaltern men by colonial forces of power;

and racialized and sexual violence. Detainment, containment, and banishment are rife throughout these films, represented in the form of Canadian Indian reservations, the child foster care system, Maori settlements, and slave plantations, where subaltern peoples are controlled and exploited for their labor. To echo McClintock, subaltern characters are "symbolically displaced onto . . . anachronistic space."[37] Subaltern men occupy frontier spaces tenuously, often forced into confining spaces such as criminal underworlds (*Mauri*) and prisons (*Mauri, Bedevil, Loyalties*); many find themselves aimless, without purpose or a strong identity. However, in some cases subaltern men are depicted as physically imposing and strong figures who deploy tough-guy personas to protect their families, their loved ones, and their land. In these films, subaltern children are physically attacked or raped, sometimes even by subaltern men but more often by white male figures of authority such as the police (*The Wake*), doctors (*Loyalties*), slave owners (*Daughters*), and landowners (*Mauri*). On the wide-open frontier, subaltern people are always vulnerable to violence, particularly socially sanctioned violence, such as the mob lynching. And yet there is still hope; there is ongoing resistance. Much of this resistance is depicted as standing up to racist and colonial mechanisms of oppression.

My Brilliant Career, My American Cousin, Thousand Pieces of Gold, The Ballad of Little Jo, and *The Piano* construct female transgressive symbolic frontier landscapes. Though there is a threat of violence throughout, this is usually at the hands of angry (white) patriarchs or random sexual predators such as the wandering soldiers in *Ballad of Little Jo*. Children are never the victims of physical violence or rape. Wide-open spaces take on a different meaning in these films. Though *The Piano, Ballad*, and *Thousand Pieces* feature characters who are banished to foreign frontier lands by a father, no less, *My Brilliant Career* and *My American Cousin* feature farmer's daughters who are looking for excitement and escape from a place where "nothing ever happens!" In all five films, the female protagonists find some freedom in frontier spaces, which offer opportunity or fun outside the domestic sphere. That said, all these characters take risks by venturing out into the wide-open landscapes, and some of them are severely punished for their transgressive actions; the most disturbing and extreme is suffered by Ada at the hands of her axe-wielding husband. The only film out of the five to feature a rape is *Thousand Pieces*, and it is tellingly the only film in which the main character was a woman of color. In the end, however, Lalu, like all these female protagonists, finds her rightful place on the frontier on her own terms. Like the classic Western hero, these heroines are triumphant, and the frontier does offer some possibility for independence.

CONCLUSION

Film has the power to destroy myths and demystify those areas of knowledge that are mystified. The knowledge extends and becomes common property. The powerfully negative aspects [sic] of film, of Hollywood in particular, is the way it spreads Western culture and ideology throughout the world. This is because of the commodity nature of film in the hands of capitalist countries, especially the USA, which leads to the insidious effect of corrupting the indigenous and ethnic values of other peoples.[1]

—Merata Mita

I've always described My Brilliant Career *as soft feminism but it probably has taken its message to a much wider audience than most of the small independent women's films. But there's always been criticism that implies that because I'm a woman filmmaker I should be fulfilling a certain criteria. I find it very annoying and just as sexist to say that as a woman I should only be making films about women and about women's themes, and that they should portray women as always showing the positive sides of sisterhood. But at the same time, obviously, I do feel a real moral obligation to the woman's movement, of which I am a total supporter, which means I would always worry about doing anything in my films that put women down in a sexist way, and I am conscious of that when I'm both writing and shooting my films.[2]*

—Gillian Armstrong

WHAT WERE THESE FILMS TRYING TO DO?

This study focused on two key questions: What differing conclusions did these films come to about the role of gender and the place of all women in white-settler frontier societies? What does this body of work tell us about the range of possibilities for expressing feminist politics within popular narrative forms such as the narrative feature film? As discussed, all of these herstories aimed to counter their nations' "selective tradition" by, as Merata Mita observed, "destroy[ing] myths and demystify[ing] those areas of knowledge that are mystified" through a feminist lens.[3] In order to tell their stories of female emancipation and political resistance, the filmmakers deployed a female gaze and subverted gendered tropes of dominant (white) masculinist frontier myth-histories, particularly those associated with the Hollywood Western. All the films debunk the myth that the frontier was ever what Jane Thompkins called a "women-less milieu."[4] Deploying many of the narrative conventions of the woman's film and the Gothic melodrama, the films construct female desire and the female voice as empowered and empowering. In this sense, these films fulfill a promise posed by pioneering women filmmakers such as Dorothy Arzner, Ida Lupino, Marie Epstein, and even Alice Guy-Blaché—many decades later! However, as we have examined, these films did not coherently and collectively construct a monolithic feminist counter-narrative of womanhood on the frontier.

The conclusions these films present about the role of gender and the place of women in white-settler frontier societies differ, particularly across the axis of race. As discussed, though the films foreground the oppression of women in masculinist frontier projects, they do not all acknowledge colonial structures of power in the oppression of subaltern peoples, delimiting their feminist vision. *The Piano* and *Ballad* skirt the white protagonist's involvement and complicity in the oppression of subaltern others, much like the filmmakers themselves. At times *Ballad* falls into the white savior narrative when Little Jo rescues Tinman from a mob lynching. Though *Thousand Pieces of Gold* features a Chinese female protagonist, the film fails to fully unpack the role of gender in racist oppression and does not hold the white male lead accountable in Lalu's sexual enslavement and exploitation. *My American Cousin* and *My Brilliant Career* do not address race at all and naively depict a bucolic empty landscape propagating the myth of the vanishing Indian. Notwithstanding these limitations, these ten films offer powerful lessons about the range of possibilities for expressing feminist politics within popular narrative forms such as the narrative feature film.

The Piano, My Brilliant Career, The Ballad of Little Jo, Thousand Pieces of Gold, and *My American Cousin* all proved that a female director and the female gaze were not antithetical to commercial success. As such, these films were aimed at a more mainstream audience and did not stray too far from the conventions of the popular cinema. These films did not answer Gayle Rubin's call to rewrite the psychoanalytic oedipal story of the family or model Julia Kristeva's concept of a pre-lingual language. All of these revisionist films seem to reject Laura Mulvey's counter-cinema aesthetics and Teresa De Lauretis's idea of a feminist de-aesthetics. They embrace the entertainment film as advocated by Claire Johnston. And yet, we cannot conclude that the delimitations of the revisionist films are rooted only in their cinematic (patriarchal) language, what Kristeva called the "paternal tongue." With their postcolonial narratives of Métis women and communities, Anne Wheeler and Norma Bailey provide a damning critique of (white) colonial forces of power in Canada, with their deployment of a maternal gaze and the Gothic. Even the sympathetic white characters in the films are held accountable for their complicity in the horrific violence enacted against indigenous women and children. As Roseanne screams at Lily while wielding a gun at the white man who raped her daughter, "What kind of woman are you?!"; she is screaming this question at us, the audience.

Daughters of the Dust, Mauri, and *Bedevil* do rewrite mainstream cinematic language, not so much in the way De Lauretis imagined but by answering the call of antiracist feminists such as bell hooks and anticolonial feminists such as Spivak. Deploying culturally specific storytelling conventions rooted in oral tradition, myth, and ritual, these films construct an oppositional feminist gaze and speak to a subaltern spectator. The films model a fusion of ancient storytelling traditions, counter-cinema aesthetics, and a female gaze to deconstruct and decolonize dominant frontier myth-history narratives. Accessing theatrical film distribution channels, the films reached a large audience beyond their own communities and nations, although they had limited commercial appeal. Mainstream film critics took issue with the films' nonlinear structures and multivoiced narration. Indeed, one (white male) Australian film critic declared *Bedevil* to be "a work of art" but not actually a film.[5] Tellingly, high-profile (white male) "master" directors such as Jean-Luc Godard and Ingmar Bergman have been celebrated precisely for their innovative and revolutionary deployment of narrative discontinuity and disruptive film aesthetics.[6] That said, all three films have recently been accepted into their national film canons as important works. In the case of *Mauri* and *Bedevil*, they are now deemed significant landmark works of indigenous cinema crossing national boundaries.

What does this body of work tell us about the range of possibilities for expressing feminist politics within popular narrative forms such as the narrative feature film? A key aim of this study was to exemplify how feature films working in the grand narrative tradition can serve as a tool for feminist mobilization. Traditionally, feminists have turned to the documentary form to express feminist politics. Perhaps this has been a result of financing opportunities, but there does seem to be a tendency to regard fiction, particularly popular fiction, as less serious or political. Certainly, within feminist film theory there has been a tradition disavowing the narrative cinema, particularly popular genre films. The cinema is a visual language and often visceral form capable of expressing feelings, experiences, and even complex ideas simply and covertly. By working in the fictional narrative tradition, these films could reach a wide audience and open the debate on a large public platform about feminism and what constitutes a feminist text. These women's films can be seen to bridge feminist theory and popular culture.

WHY DOES THIS STUDY MATTER?

Why examine films that are delimited in their feminist imaginings and re-visionings, that in some cases ignore race and colonial structures of power, that are what Gillian Armstrong called "soft feminism"? From the perspective of a feminist film historian, it is important to look back at all these films precisely because of those delimitations. I return to Elsa Barkley Brown's concept of the "polyrhythmic dialogue," in which multiple voices and lyrics are being sung at once. Following Barkley Brown's metaphor, each of these films stands as one lyric, and when brought (stitched) together, they form a complex and at times dissonant narrative about feminist storytelling. All of these filmmakers are significant because they took advantage of a moment in time when governments and industry aimed to address gender and racial barriers in the film and television industries through training and funding programs for women filmmakers. The films collectively represent a moment in time when female filmmakers answered a feminist call to action for women to embrace authorship and employ, in Claire Johnston's words, "icons in the face of and against mythology usually associated with them."[7] The filmmakers' determination to tell their herstories on the big screen can be seen as a political act in itself, even if the films, such as *The Piano*, are flawed. Indeed, *The Piano* is a divisive text and has garnered as much negative criticism as it has awards and accolades. A number of feminist scholars (Kathleen McHugh, Sue Gillett, Hilary Radner, Alistair Fox) hailed *The Piano* as a retelling of Victorian Gothic romance that placed female desire and pleasure in the foreground of the narrative.[8] Other scholars argued that *The Piano* reinforced female victimization and masochism and fell prey to the conventions of romance in which heroines find resolution in heterosexual romantic love. A few critics and scholars have accused Jane Campion of glorifying and romanticizing rape.[9] As discussed in chapter 1, a number of critics (Leonie Pihama, Reshela DuPuis, Barry Barclay) took issue with Campion's depiction of Maori culture and history, although some have defended the film's representation of race.[10] These films are important not because they are perfect but because they are bold. They are worth remembering and celebrating for these reasons.

All of these films could serve as excellent teaching tools, not only in feminist film theory classes but also in feminist and frontier colonial history curricula, not only for what they include in the frame but also for what they leave out, for what they may even get wrong. Accordingly, we can draw a parallel between this study and the second-wave feminist recuperative projects that aimed to resurrect the forgotten, lost, or dismissed work of female artists, writers, and filmmakers. In their seminal work, literary scholars Sandra Gilbert and Susan Gubar used the figure of the madwoman in the attic (from Charlotte Brontë's *Jane Eyre*) as a metaphor for the woman writer, who was to be hidden at all costs for the ways she disrupted proper femininity, a kind of monstrous other.[11] In a similar vein, this study resurrects the female author/auteur, many of whom have since disappeared from public consciousness and national film canons. The films analyzed here were all important trailblazing films that had an impact, but for all their innovative and pathbreaking status, they did not collectively change the industry landscape for women, or for themselves, in any profound way. Women's participation in the industry, particularly in the role of director, remains shockingly low, and the statistics are much worse for women of color and indigenous women.

Film theory and criticism, too, has been slow to focus on the work of female auteurs. *Herstories on Screen* built on the relatively small, but important, corpus of scholarship that focused on women directors working in the fictional narrative tradition (the theatrical feature format). Among the seminal texts that informed and inspired this particular study, and significantly contributed to my development as a feminist film historian and filmmaker, are Sandy Flitterman-Lewis's *To Desire Differently: Feminism and the French Cinema* and Judith Mayne's *The Woman at the Keyhole: Feminism and Women's Cinema*. Both examined the work of pioneering women filmmakers working across various national, aesthetic, and institutional contexts. However, Flitterman-Lewis's examination of Marie Epstein's forgotten French maternal melodramas of the 1930s and Mayne's analysis of Dorothy Arzner's Hollywood woman's films of the 1930s to 1940s were particularly important with regard to how melodrama has been deployed by women for the constructions and expression of feminist politics. Annette Blonski, Barbara Creed, and Freda Freiberg's *Don't Shoot Darling! Women's Independent Filmmaking in Australia* and Janis Cole and Holly Dale's *Calling the Shots: Profiles of Women Filmmakers* both use the interview approach to feature the voices of contemporary women directors, many of whom were also working in the popular cinema at the time. Both books highlight the challenges these women experienced navigating a male-dominated field; both feature some of the filmmakers analyzed in this study. Gwendolyn Audrey Foster's *Women Filmmakers of the African and Asian Diaspora: Decolonizing the Gaze, Locating Subjectivity* examines the films of black and Asian women filmmakers working in the United Kingdom and the United States, including Julie Dash's work. *Gendering the Nation: Canadian Women's Cinema*, edited by Kay Armatage, Kass Banning, Brenda Longfellow, and colleagues, was one of the first books that focused on Canadian women filmmakers working across a range of production contexts and aesthetic traditions, and it includes a chapter on Anne Wheeler's critically neglected work.

Since 2000, the publication of important new studies has signaled a revived scholarly interest in women directors working in the popular cinema, although the focus on art-house, avant-garde, and documentary cinema prevails. Christina Lane's *Feminist Hollywood: From* Born in Flames *to* Point Break critically examines the work of women directors such as Kathryn Bigelow and Penny Marshall. Lane's key argument is that though many Hollywood films directed by women (and there are only a handful) may not be feminist texts in the sense that Annette Kuhn, Teresa De Lauretis or Laura Mulvey meant, they can be seen as working in what Christine Gledhill called a "feminist orbit." Lane's application of the feminist orbit tenet was a guiding light for this study. Two other texts that are more inclusive of women directors working in the mainstream are Alison Butler's *Women's Cinema: The Contested Screen* and Geetha Ramanathan's *Feminist Auteurs: Reading Women's Films*. Both studies deploy a transnational lens, although the scope covers a wide range of filmmakers working in various (inter)national, aesthetic, and industrial contexts. Butler examines some of the same films in this study (*Daughters of the Dust, The Ballad of Little Jo*, and *The Piano*), but her overall focus is not on narrative feature filmmaking. Ramanathan's book spans most of the twentieth century (1920s to 1990s), including Dash's *Daughters of the Dust*, but her study is not defined by nation, time period, or narrative feature film. *Women Filmmakers: Refocusing*, edited by Jacqueline Levitin, Judith Plessis, and Valerie Raoul, is the outcome of an international women's film conference that brought together filmmakers, festival programmers, and scholars to discuss the state of women's filmmaking at the turn of the twenty-first century. Though most of the filmmakers featured here were working in documentary and experimental cinema, a few notable women working in popular genres, including Anne Wheeler, were featured on panels. More recently, there has been Patricia White's *Women's Cinema, World Cinema: Protecting Contemporary Feminisms*, which is international in scope and primarily examines art-house festival films by women. White argues that though women are underrepresented as directors in mainstream cinema, they have been able to carve out a prestigious niche as "feminist auteurs" within the film festival circuit. Sophie Mayer's *Political Animals: The New Feminist Cinema* is a transnational study that examines the work of a new generation of women filmmakers who benefited from their predecessors, many of whom appear in this study. However, Mayer does not look exclusively at films directed by women. Though Mayer does refer to Maggie Greenwald's *Ballad of Little Jo* as a significant revisionist Western, she highlights the film only as a forgotten work, lost in the shadows of other revisionist Westerns directed by male directors, such as *Unforgiven* (1993), directed by Clint Eastwood, and *Bad Girls* (1994), directed by Jonathan Kaplan. *Herstories on Screen* complements these new additions to the field of feminist film studies, offering a comparative analysis of the narrative and visual strategies deployed by female directors who crafted feature films in four different national contexts. *Herstories* puts the work of talented women auteurs at center stage.

Over the past forty years, feminist film theory has produced a rich theoretical and analytic corpus of work. In the face of a massive scholarly industry that analyzes male filmmakers, feminist, antiracist, indigenous, and queer scholars of film have challenged the field of film criticism and significantly invigorated the field. Scholarship in film studies is a huge field and continues to be dominated by analyses of male filmmakers—the literature on Alfred Hitchcock alone fills library shelves. Feminist scholars have challenged this asymmetry. Feminist scholars have also generated superb studies of women filmmakers, albeit those primarily working in the avant-garde style or in documentaries. We have much to learn, though, about the struggles and perspectives of women seeking to gain a toehold in popular and mainstream film markets. Yet despite these exciting new directions, the work of women filmmakers in popular and mainstream markets (narrative feature films) continues to receive minimal attention. *Herstories on Screen* contributes to that project by focusing on one cluster of female filmmakers who, as a result of second-wave feminists' success in gaining government and agency grants for telling "women's stories," grasped hold of the opportunity to make their grand feminist counternarratives. Studies such as this are needed to move women's films out of the bubble that marginalizes women's films and women filmmakers and to get women into the canon.

APPENDIX: THE FILMS

AUSTRALIA

MY BRILLIANT CAREER (1979)

My Brilliant Career was directed by Gillian Armstrong and produced by Margaret Fink. The screenplay, written by Elinor Whitcombe, is an adaptation of Miles Franklin's proto-feminist coming-of-age novel by the same name.[1] Set in the Australian outback in 1901, the story is told from the point of view of a young aspiring artist/writer Sybylla Melvyn (Judy Davis), the eldest daughter of impoverished white-settler bush-farmers (Alan Hopgood and Julia Blake). The drama is set in motion when Sybylla's parents send her away to stay with her wealthy Grandma Bossier (Aileen Britton) and Aunt Helen (Wendy Hughes) in order to be groomed for the middle-class marriage market. Sybylla is dead set against marriage until she falls in love with a handsome and wealthy sheep farmer (Sam Neill). The film was produced by the New South Wales Film Corporation, the Greater Union Organization, and Margaret Fink Productions.

BEDEVIL (1993)

Bedevil was written and directed by Tracey Moffatt and produced by Carol Hughes and Anthony Buckley. Set on a postcolonial Australian frontier (spanning the 1960s to 1990s), the hyperstylized film examines the impact of white settlement and colonization on Aborigine and Torres Strait Islander peoples. Moffatt deployed the tropes of horror and ethnographic documentary to construct a multivoiced and episodic narrative in which a diverse range of storytellers recount various ghost stories. The storytellers include Shelley (Diana Davidson), an elderly white woman; Rick (Jack Charles), an Aborigine prison inmate; Young Ruby (Tracey Moffatt), an Aborigine housewife; Older Ruby (Auriel Andrews); and Voula (Dina Panozzo), a young Greek mother. The film was produced by the Australian Film Institute.

NEW ZEALAND/AOTEAROA

MAURI (1988)

Mauri was written, directed, and produced by Merata Mita. Set on a postcolonial landscape in the 1950s, *Mauri* is told from the perspective of the Rapanas, a Maori family, who are in conflict with Mr. Semmens (Geoff Murphy), a white-settler patriarch who has cheated his Maori neighbors out of their land. At the center of the Rapana clan is Kara, a Maori *kuia*, or elder (Eva Rickard), who protects, nurtures, and counsels her large extended family. The drama is set in motion when Kara's two nephews, Rewi (Anzac Wallace) and Willie (Willie Raana), return back to their childhood and ancestral home; both are running from the law and their troubled pasts. Further complications involve a love triangle with Rewi, Mr. Semmens' son Steve (James Heyward), and Remari (Susan D Remari Paul), a young Maori woman. The film was produced by Awatea Films, Radio Hauraki and Hauraki Film Enterprises, and the New Zealand Film Commission.

THE PIANO (1993)

The Piano was written and directed by Jane Campion and produced by Jan Chapman. Set in the 1850s on a colonial frontier, the story is told through the eyes of Ada (Holly Hunter), a young mute Scottish woman who travels with her illegitimate daughter, Flora (Anna Paquin), to the New World to be the wife of a wealthy white settler, Alisdair Stewart (Sam Neill). When Stewart trades Ada's beloved piano and piano lessons in exchange for land with his business associate Baines (Harvey Keitel), Ada finds herself forced into a complicated and compromising arrangement with her new music student. The film was produced by CiBy2000.

CANADA

MY AMERICAN COUSIN (1985)

My American Cousin was written and directed by Sandy Wilson and produced by Peter O'Brien. Set in 1959 British Columbia, the semi-autobiographical film is a comedic coming-of-age story centered on twelve-year-old Sandy Wilcox (Margaret Langrick), the daughter of struggling white-settler cherry farmers (Richard Donat and Jane Mortifee). Sandy finds temporary excitement when her glamorous and reckless American cousin, eighteen-year-old Butch (John Wildman), shows up in the middle of the night driving a red Cadillac. The film was produced by the Canadian Broadcasting Corporation (CBC), Borderline, Okanagan Motion Picture Company, and Telefilm Canada.

LOYALTIES (1987)

Loyalties was directed and co-written by Anne Wheeler, co-written by Sharon Riis, and produced by William Johnston and Ronald Lillie. Set in contemporary times in the remote Northern Alberta community of Lac La Biche, Loyalties revolves around two women, Roseanne Ladouceur (Tantoo Cardinal), a Métis single mom, and her employer, Lily Sutton (Susan Wooldridge), an upper-middle-class Englishwoman who has recently emigrated to Canada. Divided by class and race, the two women eventually form a tenuous bond, until Lily's husband, Dr. Sutton (Kenneth Welsh), a pedophile, begins stalking Roseanne's twelve-year-old daughter, Leona (Diane Debassige). The film was produced by Lauron International, Wheeler-Hendren Enterprises, Dumbarton Films, Loyalties Film Productions, the Alberta Motion Picture

Development Corporation, the Canadian Broadcasting Corporation (CBC), and Telefilm Canada.

THE WAKE (1986)

The Wake is one of four dramatic films in the Daughters of the Country series. The groundbreaking series featured stories about Métis women from four different periods in Canada's history—*Ikwe* (1770s), *Mistress Madeleine* (late nineteenth century), *Places Not Our Own* (1930s), and *The Wake* (late twentieth century). Norma Bailey produced the entire series, directing two of the four films. *The Wake* was written by Sharon Riis and co-produced by Ches Yetman. Set on a remote and impoverished Indian reservation in Northern Alberta, the film centers on Joan Laboucane (Victoria Snow), a young Métis single mother, and her troubled teenage cousin, Donna (Diane Debassige). The conflict arises when Joan begins a romantic relationship with Jim (Timothy Webber), a white Mountie (police officer) who is seen as an enemy of indigenous peoples by Joan's family and her close-knit Métis community. The film was produced by the National Film Board of Canada.

UNITED STATES

DAUGHTERS OF THE DUST (1991)

Daughters of the Dust was written, directed, and co-produced by Julie Dash and co-produced by Lindsay Law, Arthur Jafa (who also was the film's cinematographer), and Steven Jones. Set in 1902 on the remote islands off the Georgia coast, the film is a multivoiced narrative that centers on the Peazant family, Gullah islanders, who identify as the descendants of West African slaves. At the center of this family is Great-Great-Grandmother Nana Peazant (Cora Lee Day), who is compelled to help her family cope with their traumatic past and an uncertain future as they gather for a last supper before migrating north. The film was produced by Geechee Girls Productions, WMG Film, and PBS's American Playhouse Theatrical Films.

THOUSAND PIECES OF GOLD (1991)

Thousand Pieces of Gold was directed and co-produced by Nancy Kelly. The other producers were Kenji Yamamoto, Lindsay Law, Sydney Kantor, and John Sham. The screenplay was written by Anne Makepeace, who adapted Ruth Lum McCunn's novel of the same name. Set in a nineteenth-century Idaho mining town, *Thousand Pieces of Gold* tells the true story of Lalu/Polly Nathoy (Rosalind Chao), a young Chinese woman who travels from the Old World to the American West when she is sold into sexual slavery by her impoverished father. Though a Chinese "slave girl" to the oppressive Hong King (Michael Paul Chan), Lalu finds her way to freedom and independence while also capturing the hearts of two men, Jim (Dennis Dunn) and Charlie (Chris Cooper). The film was produced by PBS's American Playhouse Theatrical Films, Film Four International, CPB, Filmcat Productions, and Maverick Picture Company.

THE BALLAD OF LITTLE JO (1993)

The Ballad of Little Jo was written and directed by Maggie Greenwald and produced by Brenda Goodman and Fred Berner. Set in the late nineteenth century, the film was inspired by the real-life Josephine Monaghan, a white society woman who dressed as a man in order to survive on a hostile frontier. The story begins when Josephine (Suzi Amis) is banished from her home for having a child out of wedlock. Forced to survive alone in the Wild West with no means of support or male protection, Josephine assumes the identity of Little Jo, a frontiersman, and finds guidance in two father-figures, Percy (Ian McKellen) and Frank (Bo Hopkins). Complications arise when Little Jo saves and subsequently hires "Tinman" (David Chung) as her domestic servant. The film was produced by Joco Productions and PolyGram Filmed Entertainment.

NOTES

INTRODUCTION

1. Claire Johnston, "Women's Cinema as Counter-Cinema" (1973), in *Feminism and Film*, ed. E. Ann Kaplan (Oxford: Oxford University Press, 2000), 22–33. See also Claire Johnston, "Dorothy Arzner: Critical Strategies" (1975), in *Feminism and Film Theory*, ed. Constance Penley (New York: Routledge, 1988), 36–45.
2. Julie Dash and Houston A. Baker Jr., "Not Without My Daughters," *Transition*, no. 57 (1992): 163.
3. *Merriam-Webster's Collegiate Dictionary*, accessed December 7, 2019, https://www.merriam-webster.com/dictionary/herstory.
4. Maja Mikula, "Narrative," in *Key Concepts in Cultural Studies* (New York: Palgrave Macmillan, 2008), 133–34; Jean-François Lyotard, *The Postmodern Condition*, trans. Geoff Bennington and Brian Massumi (Minneapolis: University of Minnesota Press, 1984).
5. Susan Hayward, *Key Concepts in Cinema Studies* (London: Routledge, 1996), 12–19.
6. Alexandre Astruc, "The Birth of a New Avant-Garde: La Camera-Stylo," accessed December 7, 2019, http://www.newwavefilm.com/about/camera-stylo-astruc .shtml. Originally published in *L'Écran française* on March 30, 1948, as an article titled "Du Stylo à la caméra et de la caméra au stylo."
7. American Film Institute, "100 Greatest American Films of All Time," accessed December 7, 2019, https://www.afi.com/afis-100-years-100-movies -10th-anniversary-edition/. The AFI's stated Mission and Vision reads, "The American Film Institute champions the moving image as an art form. We

believe in the revolutionary power of visual storytelling to share perspectives, inspire empathy and drive culture forward" (https://www.afi.com/about-afi/).

8. The spelling of the word "indigenous" is taken from *Webster's* Dictionary.

9. Reel Canada, "150 Canadian Films," 2017, accessed December 7, 2019, https://cdn.canadianfilmday.ca/wp-content/uploads/150-Canadian-Films.pdf. This project was funded by the Ministry of Canadian Heritage.

10. British Film Institute, "Analysis: The Greatest Films of All Time," *Sight and Sound*, 2012, accessed December 7, 2019, http://www.bfi.org.uk/films-tv-people/sightandsoundpoll2012/critics.

11. Janet Staiger, "The Politics of Film Canons," *Cinema Journal* 24, no. 3 (Spring 1985): 4–23.

12. Linda Nochlin, "Why Have There Been No Great Women Artists?," in *Women, Art, and Power and Other Essays* (Boulder, Colo.: Westview Press, 1988), 147–58.

13. Martha M. Lauzen, "The Celluloid Ceiling: Behind-the-Scenes Employment of Women on the Top 100, 250, and 500 Films of 2018" (San Diego, Calif.: San Diego State University, Center for the Study of Women in Television and Film, 2019), accessed December 7, 2019, https://womenintvfilm.sdsu.edu/wp-content/uploads/2019/01/2018_Celluloid_Ceiling_Report.pdf.

14. American Civil Liberties Union (ACLU) of Southern California, "Stand for Gender Equality in the Film and Television Industry," accessed December 7, 2019, https://action.aclu.org/petition/filmquality.

15. European Women's Audiovisual Network, "Where Are the Women Directors? Report on Gender Equality for Directors in the European Film Industry, 2006–2013," accessed December 7, 2019, https://www.ewawomen.com/research. "Only one in five films in the seven European countries studied is directed by a woman (21%). This means four out five films are NOT directed by a woman."

16. Jill Golick and Amber-Sekowan Daniels, "On Screen Report," Women in View, May 2019, http://womeninview.ca/reports/.

17. Screen Australia, "Women Working in Key Creative Roles," accessed December 7, 2019, https://www.screenaustralia.gov.au/fact-finders/infographics/women-working-in-creative-roles.

18. Deborah Shepard, "Reframing Women: Gender and Film in Aotearoa New Zealand 1999–2014," *Diogenes* 62, no. 1 (2016): 7–23.

19. With regard to Canada, films from Quebec were not included in this study for the primary reason that Quebec has its own national identity, rooted in a Francophone Roman Catholic culture, with its own distinct folklore and legends. Quebec also has strong historical, cultural, and linguistic ties with France rather than Britain, even though Quebec was a colony of the British Empire. The Quebecois film industry also operates very separately from what is referred to in Canada as the English-Canadian cinema sector.

20. Raymond Williams, *Marxism and Literature* (Oxford: Oxford University Press, 1977), 115–16.

21. Richard Slotkin, *Gunfighter Nation: The Myth of the Frontier in Twentieth-Century America* (Norman: University of Oklahoma Press, 1998), 10.

22. Richard Slotkin, *The Fatal Environment: The Myth of the Frontier in the Age of Industrialization, 1800–1890* (Norman: University of Oklahoma Press, 1985), 19.

23. Elizabeth Furniss, "Pioneers, Progress, and the Myth of the Frontier: The Landscape of Public History in Rural British Columbia," *BC Studies*, no. 115/116 (Autumn/Winter, 1997/1998): 8.

24. Johnston, "Women's Cinema," 23.

25. Edward W. Said, *Culture and Imperialism* (New York: Vintage Books, 1994), xiii.

26. See Annette Blonski, Barbara Creed, and Freda Freiberg, eds., *Don't Shoot Darling! Women's Independent Filmmaking in Australia* (Richmond, S.A., Australia: Greenhouse, 1987); Barbara Creed, "Women's Cinema in Australia," in *Australia for Women: Travel and Culture*, ed. Susan Hawthorne and Renate Klein (Melbourne, Vic., Australia: Spinifex Press, 1994), 185–87; Lizzie Francke, "What Are You Girls Going to Do?," *Sight and Sound* 5, no. 4 (1995): 28–29; Jocelyn Robson, *Girls' Own Stories: Australian and New Zealand Women's Films* (London: Scarlet Press, 1997); Lisa French, "On Their Own Merits: Women and the Moving Image in Australia," in *Womenvision: Women and the Moving Image in Australia* (Melbourne, Vic., Australia: Damned, 2003), 11–30; and Ina Bertrand, "'Woman's Voice': The Autobiographical Form in Three Australian Filmed Novels," *Literature/Film Quarterly* 21, no. 2 (1993): 130–38.

27. See D. Bruno Starrs, "Unlike Mainstream: Towards a Definition of the Australian Art Film," in *Creative Nation: Australian Cinema and Cultural Studies Reader*, ed. Amit Sarwal and Reema Sarwal (Delhi, India: SSS, 2009), 54–72; Susan Dermody and Elizabeth Jacka, *The Screening of Australia: Anatomy of a National Cinema*, vol. 2 (Sydney, N.S.W., Australia: Currency Press, 1988); and Nicholas Adrian Prescott, "'All We See and All We Seem . . .'—Australian Cinema and National Landscape," paper presented at the Understanding Cultural Landscapes Symposium, Flinders University, July 11–15, 2005.

28. Women Make Movies, "*Bedevil*: A Film by Tracey Moffat," accessed December 7, 2019, https://www.wmm.com/catalog/film/bedevil/.

29. Liz McNiven, "A Short History of Indigenous Filmmaking," Australian Screen, December 7, 2019, http://aso.gov.au/titles/collections/indigenous-filmmaking/.

30. The film won six awards at the 1986 Canadian Genie Awards, now called the Canadian Screen Awards. See "My American Cousin," IMDb Pro, accessed December 9, 2019; and *The Canadian Women Film Directors Database*, accessed December 9, 2019, http://femfilm.ca/film_search.php?film=wilson-my&lang=e.

31. Adam Gaudry, "Métis," *Canadian Encyclopedia*, accessed December 9, 2019, https://www.thecanadianencyclopedia.ca/en/article/Métis/.

32. The film also garnered awards from various film festivals, such as the Yorkton Film Festival, the Festival of Films and Videos by Women, and the American Indian Film Festival. See "*The Wake*," Our Collection, National Film Board of

Canada, accessed December 9, 2019, http://onf-nfb.gc.ca/en/our-collection/?idfilm=16800#nav-prix.

33. Marc Gervais, "Cannes 86—The Year of Revelation," *Cinema Canada*, July/August 1986, 7: "Well crafted, superb in its handling of acting, and rich in its human (feminist) insights, *Loyalties* captures life at Lac La Biche in Northern Alberta and the complexities of cultural adaptation. It may well be the best dramatic portrayal of contemporary Canadian Indians yet seen." *Loyalties* won multiple awards and was instrumental in establishing Wheeler as one of Canada's most important women filmmakers. Wheeler has been awarded six honorary doctorates and the Order of Canada for her contributions to Canadian filmmaking. *Canadian Film Encyclopedia*, s.v. "Anne Wheeler," accessed December 9, 2019, https://thecanadianencyclopedia.ca/en/article/wheeler-anne.

34. NZ On Screen, "Merata Mita," accessed December 7, 2019, http://www.nzonscreen.com/person/merata-mita/biography. See also Emiel Martens, "Maori on the Silver Screen: The Evolution of Indigenous Feature Filmmaking in Aotearoa/New Zealand," *International Journal of Critical Indigenous Studies* 5, no. 1 (2012): 4.

35. Martens, "Maori on the Silver Screen," 4.

36. Hepi Mita, *Merata: How Mum Decolonized the Screen*, documentary film by Arama Pictures, 2019.

37. "Jane Campion," Overview, NZ On Screen, accessed December 7, 2019, http://www.nzonscreen.com/person/jane-campion.

38. Kate Muir, "Jane Campion: 'Capitalism is such a macho force. I felt run over,'" *Guardian*, May 20, 2018, https://www.theguardian.com/film/2018/may/20/jane-campion-unconventional-film-maker-macho-force.

39. "Jane Campion," Biography, NZ On Screen, accessed December 9, 2019, https://www.nzonscreen.com/profile/jane-campion/biography. *The Piano* has been included alongside such world cinema classics as *Citizen Kane*, *The Godfather*, and *Casablanca*.

40. "Julie Dash," Women Make Movies, accessed December 7, 2019, https://www.wmm.com/filmmaker/Julie+Dash/.

41. "Librarian of Congress Adds 25 Films to National Film Registry," Library of Congress, National Film Registry, December 28, 2004, https://www.loc.gov/item/prn-04-215/films-added-to-national-film-registry-for-2004/2004-12-28/. "*O* Magazine included *Daughters of the Dust* among its 50 Greatest 'Chick Flicks,' and in 1999, the twenty-fifth Annual Newark Black Film Festival honored Julie and her film *Daughters of the Dust* as being one of the most important cinematic achievements in Black Cinema in the 20th century." African Film Festival, "Daughters of the Dust," accessed December 9, 2019, https://www.africanfilmny.org/2012/daughters-of-the-dust/.

42. Michael Wilmington, "Movie Review: Valuable View of Old West in 'Gold," *Los Angeles Times*, June 26, 1991, https://www.latimes.com/archives/la-xpm-1991-06-26-ca-1138-story.html.

43. "Rosalind Chao's performance is a wonder—the sort that, in a conventional Hollywood epic, would inspire Oscar speculation." Roger Ebert, "Thousand Pieces of Gold," RogerEbert.com, November 8, 1991, https://www.rogerebert.com/reviews/thousand-pieces-of-gold-1991.

44. Tania Modleski and Maggie Greenwald, "Our Heroes Have Sometimes Been Cowgirls: An Interview with Maggie Greenwald," *Film Quarterly* 49, no. 2 (Winter 1995–1996): 2.

45. Stephen Holden, "Review/Film: A Feminist Cross-Dresser in the Old West," *New York Times*, August 20, 1993, https://www.nytimes.com/1993/08/20/movies/review-film-a-feminist-cross-dresser-in-the-old-west.html.

46. Annette Kuhn, *Women's Pictures: Feminism and Cinema* (London: Verso, 1993), 173.

47. The Sydney Women's Film Group was formed "with the aim of training women filmmakers and making and distributing films on subject matter ignored by mainstream media." The activities of the SWFG were instrumental in raising the skills, confidence, and participation of women in Australian filmmaking. "The SWFG's first project, *Film for Discussion*, directed by Martha Ansara, Jeni Thornley and others, was commenced in 1971 and released in 1973. One of the first projects screened was *Woman's Day 20C* (1972), directed by Margot Knox, Virginia Coventry, Kaye Martyn and Robynne Murphy, a portrait of a housebound mother addicted to barbiturates." Australian Screen, "Australian Film and Television Chronology: The 1970s," accessed December 7, 2019, http://aso.gov.au/chronology/1970s/.

48. The National Film and Sound Archive of Australia, "Feminist Filmmakers," accessed December 9, 2019, https://www.nfsa.gov.au/latest/feminist-filmmakers.

49. Armstrong "was one of twelve, along with Phillip Noyce and Chris Noonan, selected for the inaugural year of the AFTRS. Her graduation films *Satdee Night*, *Gretel*, and *100 A Day* won numerous awards and were selected for the Sydney Film Festival and Grenoble International Festival of Short Films in 1974." "Gillian Armstrong," *The Big Screen Symposium*, accessed December 7, 2019, https://bigscreensymposium.com/speakers-2012/.

50. The Australian Film Commission has been replaced by Screen Australia. Screen Australia is the key federal government direct funding body for the Australian screen production industry. Its functions are to support and promote the development of a highly creative, innovative, and commercially sustainable Australian screen production industry. Screen Australia was created under the Screen Australia Act 2008 and from July 1, 2008, took over the functions and appropriations of its predecessor agencies: the Australian Film Commission (AFC), the Film Finance Corporation Australia (FFC), and Film Australia Limited. Screen Australia, "Who We Are," accessed December 7, 2019, https://www.screenaustralia.gov.au/about-us/who-we-are.

51. Lisa French, "An Analysis of *Nice Coloured Girls*," *Senses of Cinema*, *Australian Cinema*, no. 5 (April 2000), http://sensesofcinema.com/2000/5/nice/.

52. The same year that the Australian Film Commission established the Women's Film Fund (1975), the Whitlam Government implemented human rights legislation in the form of the Racial Discrimination Act 1975. "These legislative and policy changes were brought about by growing pressures from Aboriginal activists to abolish racist segregation policies, which had become unpopular on the global stage. This act helped create new opportunities for Aboriginal and Torres Strait Islander peoples. This was the real beginning for Indigenous self-representation and self-empowerment in the arts." McNiven, "Short History of Indigenous Filmmaking."

53. "In the early 1980s, the Film Unit of the Australian Institute of Aboriginal Studies (AIAS, now the Australian Institute of Aboriginal and Torres Strait Islander Studies) employed a number of trainees. . . . With a background in commercial television, Ralph Rigby, AIAS Video Fellow in the 1980s, facilitated rural and remote Aboriginal community access to video technology. In doing so, he enabled Indigenous peoples to tell their stories in their own way." McNiven, "Short History of Indigenous Filmmaking."

54. "CAAMA aimed to utilise audiovisual technology for cultural maintenance, self-expression and empowerment. Soon after, CAAMA moved into television broadcasting with Imparja Television. As a result CAAMA became the first Indigenous organisation in the world to own a television station. In 1987, Aboriginal people in remote areas of central Australia voiced their concerns about the influence of mass media on their cultures. The Australian satellite Aussat was being launched and Aboriginal people requested resources to enable them to broadcast local material in their own languages. They also sought to control the content broadcast within their communities. In response, the federal government introduced the Broadcasting for Remote Aboriginal Communities Scheme to deliver radio and television to rural and remote Aboriginal and Torres Strait Islander communities." McNiven, "Short History of Indigenous Filmmaking."

55. "The Royal Commission into Aboriginal Deaths in Custody outlined in its final report (1991) a number of recommendations with direct reference to public and commercial media organisations and their treatment of Indigenous people. The commission recommended that media bodies develop codes and policies for the presentation of Indigenous issues and establish training for Indigenous people. These recommendations marked a turning point in the television industry. They supported Indigenous peoples having influence over their own representation and increased their access to employment within the film and television industry." McNiven, "Short History of Indigenous Filmmaking."

56. The New Zealand Film Commission is a Crown entity: "We support a diverse range of New Zealand and international stories to be told here, and seen everywhere. We promote our talented individuals and our industry's reputation for creativity, innovation and superb production values. We balance cultural and economic objectives to achieve successful outcomes for our industry and our

people." New Zealand Film Commission, "What We Do," accessed December 9, 2019, https://www.nzfilm.co.nz/new-zealand/about-us/what-we-do. Regarding Maori filmmaking, the New Zealand Film Commission states, "He Ara is a development fund committed to presenting more Māori and Pacific Island stories on screen. In 2018 the NZFC introduced its Te Rautaki Māori (Māori Screen Strategy) and hired a Pou Whakahaere to deliver on its aims. A range of development and production funding programmes to support Māori filmmakers have been introduced, with   more being developed." New Zealand Film Commission, "Supporting Diverse Voices," accessed Dec. 9, 2019, https://www.nzfilm.co.nz/new-zealand/about-us/what-we-do/supporting-diverse-voices.

57. Martens, "Maori on the Silver Screen," 4.

58. Mita's documentaries made through the Auckland Co-op Alternative Cinema also included *The Hammer and the Anvil* (1979), about the trade union movement, and *Karanga, Hokianga ki o Tamariki*, about the Hokianga Catholic Maori community. NZ On Screen, "Merata Mita," accessed December 7, 2019, http://www.nzonscreen.com/person/merata-mita/biography.

59. Alistair Fox, *Jane Campion: Authorship and Personal Cinema* (Bloomington: Indiana University Press, 2011), 241.

60. Alistair Fox has traced the connections between Mander's story and *The Piano*, concluding that though there are indeed many similarities between the two texts, Campion diverted enough from the original material to make it her own. Fox, *Jane Campion: Authorship*, 108–9.

61. See Alistair Fox, "Puritanism and the Erotics of Transgression: The New Zealand Influence in Jane Campion's Thematic Imaginary," in *Jane Campion: Cinema, Nation, Identity*, ed. Hilary Radner, Alistair Fox, and Irène Bessière (Detroit, Mich.: Wayne State University Press, 2009), 103–22. See also Anna Neill, "A Land Without a Past: Dreamtime and Nation in *The Piano*," in *Piano Lessons: Approaches to* The Piano, ed. Felicity Coombs and Suzanne Gemmell (London: Libbey, 1999), 136–47.

62. Hilary Radner, "Screening Women's Histories: Jane Campion and the New Zealand Heritage Film, from the Biopic to the Female Gothic," in *New Zealand Cinema: Interpreting the Past*, ed. Alistair Fox, Barry Keith Grant, and Hilary Radner (Bristol, U.K.: Intellect, 2011), 259–75.

63. Sandy Wilson directed the NFB documentary *Pen-Hi Grad* (1975). National Film Board of Canada, "*Pen-Hi Grad*," accessed December 7, 2019, http://www.nfb.ca/film/pen_hi_grad/. Anne Wheeler directed the award-winning Studio D documentary *Great Grand Mother*. Bailey's NFB documentary *Nose and Tina* (1980) tells of the troubled relationship between an indigenous sex worker and her alcoholic white boyfriend. Bailey's real-life documentary subject "Tina" was later cast as Cora in *The Wake*, a character who also earns her living through sex work. Wheeler's earlier work was also financed and distributed by Studio D. Many of Wheeler's NFB films received acclaim, particularly her documentaries *Great Grand Mother* (1975), *Happily Unmarried* (1977), and *Augusta* (1976), which

profiled an elderly indigenous woman struggling to maintain her dignity and identity in a racist system. Wheeler's other films with the NFB were *Teach Me to Dance* (1978), *One's a Heifer* (1984), *A Change of Heart* (1984), and the docudrama *A War Story* (1981), which explored her father's prisoner of war camp experiences during World War II. National Film Board of Canada, "Anne Wheeler," accessed December 7, 2019, https://www.nfb.ca/directors/anne-wheeler/. Norma Bailey directed numerous documentaries for the NFB, including *The Performers* (1980), which won the Jury Prize for Short Film at the Cannes Film Festival. IMDb—International Movie Database, "Norma Bailey," accessed December 7, 2019, http://www.imdb.com/name/nm0047425/.

64. Studio D operated from 1974 to 1996. Spearheaded by Kathleen Shannon, Studio D was dedicated to making films for, about, and by women. Because of government funding cuts, Studio D closed its doors in 1996. See Gail Vanstone, *D Is for Daring: The Women Behind the Films of Studio D* (Toronto, Ont., Canada: Sumach Press, 2007), 11–12.

65. The NFB "is a federal cultural agency within the portfolio of the Canadian Heritage Department. Initially known as the National Film Commission, it was created by an act of Parliament in 1939. Its mandate, as set forth in the *National Film Act*, 1950, is 'to produce and distribute and to promote the production and distribution of films designed to interpret Canada to Canadians and to other nations.'" National Film Board of Canada, "About the NFB: Mission and Highlights," accessed December 7, 2019, http://onf-nfb.gc.ca/en/about-the-nfb/organization/mandate/.

66. "In 1981, the Alberta Motion Picture Development Corporation, the first provincial film-funding agency in English-speaking Canada, opened its doors for business. Headed by entertainment lawyer Lorne MacPherson, the AMPDC started as a development lending bank, expanded into partial equity financing, and in its 15 year existence, invested $16-million in Alberta projects." Linda Kupecek, "Alberta Onscreen: Why Fight for an Indigenous Film Industry?," *Alberta Views*, January/February 2000, 18.

67. The Government of Canada established the Canadian Film Development Corporation in 1967. It would be renamed Telefilm Canada in 1984, "to better reflect the full range of its activities in film and television." In 1986 the Feature Film Fund was created, "aimed at supporting works by Canadian filmmakers. This fund is to play a decisive role in the growth of Canadian cinema." Its mandate is "to foster and promote the development of the audiovisual industry in Canada." Telefilm Canada, accessed December 7, 2019, http://www.telefilm.ca/en/?q=en.

68. Colin Hoskins and Stuart McFadyen, "The Canadian Broadcast Program Development Fund: An Evaluation and Some Recommendations," *Canadian Public Policy/Analyse de Politiques* 12, no. 1 (March 1986): 227–35.

69. *Encyclopedia Britannica*, s.v. "National Endowment for the Arts," accessed December 7, 2019, https://www.britannica.com/topic/National-Endowment-for

-the-Arts. "Subsequent opposition to the NEA in the U.S. Congress, however, resulted in a decrease in funding from a high of nearly $176 million in 1992 to less than $100 million in 1996."

70. Dave Lewis, "A Brief History of the National Endowment for the Arts," *Los Angeles Times*, March 16, 2017, http://www.latimes.com/entertainment/la-et -entertainment-news-updates-march-a-brief-history-of-the-1489686723 -htmlstory.html. "The endowment has especially encouraged culturally diverse American arts, providing National Heritage Fellowship Awards to [many artists] who embody Native American, Latin American, Asian, and other ethnic arts traditions in American communities." *Britannica Academic, Encyclopædia Britannica*, s.v. "National Endowment for the Arts (NEA)," last modified July 3, 2015, academic-eb-com.library.sheridanc.on.ca/levels/collegiate/article/National-Endowment-for-the-Arts/2438.

71. Julie Dash, Toni Cade Bambara, and bell hooks, *Daughters of the Dust: The Making of an African American Woman's Film* (New York: New Press, 1992), 7–9.

72. Dash, Bambara, and hooks, *Daughters*, 9.

73. Judith Michaelson, "PBS's *Playhouse* Faces Prospect of Fading Role," *Los Angeles Times*, May 12, 1994.

74. Michaelson, "PBS's *Playhouse*." The themes and issues featured across this series ranged from racial tension and inequity in the public school system (*Stand and Deliver*), gay rights (*Longtime Companion*), African American working-class struggles (*The Killing Floor*), and AIDS (*Angels in America*). The films released theatrically were *Stand and Deliver, Longtime Companion, El Norte, Testament*, and the documentary *The Thin Blue Line*.

75. American Film Institute, "History of AFI," accessed December 7, 2019, http://www.afi.com/about/history. The AFI "grew from the seeds planted in the White House Rose Garden by President Lyndon B. Johnson in 1965 to a fully rounded Institute that has defined American film for more than half a century."

76. Patrice Apodaca, "Screen Play: PolyGram Hopes to Bolster Its Hollywood Presence with Purchase of Once-Venerable ITC Entertainment," *Los Angeles Times*, February 21, 1995. In 1991, Michael Kuhn was dispatched to Los Angeles as president of PolyGram Filmed Entertainment with the job of spending $200 million to expand the company's filmmaking activities. PolyGram films included *Notting Hill, The Usual Suspects, Lock Stock and Two Smoking Barrels, Elizabeth, Trainspotting*, and *Priscilla, Queen of the Desert*. UK Jewish Film, "Board Member: Michael Kuhn," accessed December 7, 2019, http://ukjewishfilm.org/people /michael-kuhn/.

77. Andreas Furler, "Structure Is Essential/Absolutely Crucial/One of the Most Important Things," in *Jane Campion: Interviews*, ed. Virginia Wright Wexman (Jackson: University Press of Mississippi, 1999), 93.

78. Denise Riley, *"Am I That Name?" Feminism and the Category of Women in History* (Minneapolis: University of Minnesota Press, 1988). Using poststructuralism, Riley traced the changes in the notion of womanhood and the shifting historical

constructions of the category of "women" in relation to other categories central to concepts of personhood: the soul, mind, the body, nature, and the social.

79. Elsa Barkley Brown, "'What Has Happened Here?' The Politics of Difference in Women's History and Feminist Politics," *Feminist Studies* 18, no. 2 (Summer 1992): 295–312.

80. Barkley Brown, "What Has Happened Here?," 297.

81. Karen Gocsik, Richard Barsam, and Dave Monahan, *Writing About Movies*, 4th ed. (New York: Norton, 2016), 36.

82. Elizabeth Thompson, *The Pioneer Woman: A Canadian Character Type* (Montreal, Que., Canada: McGill-Queen's University Press, 1991).

1. WOMEN'S STORYTELLING

1. Raymond Williams, *Marxism and Literature* (Oxford: Oxford University Press, 1977), 115–16.

2. Carroll Smith-Rosenberg, "The Female World of Love and Ritual: Relations Between Women in Nineteenth-Century America," in *Disorderly Conduct: Visions of Gender in Victorian America* (New York: Oxford University Press, 1985), 53–76. Smith-Rosenberg examined unpublished women's love letters and diaries focused on same-sex relations between Victorian American middle-class women, reconstructing a homosocial female world in which men played a secondary role. These voices contradicted assumptions about repressed female Victorian sexuality. See also Christine Stansell, *City of Women: Sex and Class in New York, 1789–1860* (Chicago: University of Illinois Press, 1987). Stansell also foregrounded female desires from Victorian urban America, but those of popular-class (working-class, under-class) women who left no written records. Stansell focused on women's negotiation of urban spaces, such as the Bowery Girl, who straddled the good girl/bad girl dichotomy. The Bowery Girl boldly crossed into (and invaded) male spaces such as the street and the workplace (i.e., the factory), engendering fear and moral panic in the minds and discourses of her middle-class reformers.

3. Natalie Zemon Davis, *The Return of Martin Guerre* (Cambridge, Mass.: Harvard University Press, 1983). Davis retold the popular story of Pansette, a sixteenth-century French peasant accused of identity theft. In her narrative, Davis imagined the voice of Bertrande de Rolls, Martin Guerre's illiterate peasant wife, a woman who would have left no official written accounts. Davis advocated for the role of subjective stories in reconstructing the past.

4. Joan Wallach Scott, "Gender: A Useful Category of Analysis," in *Gender and the Politics of History* (New York: Columbia University Press, 1988), 28–50. "It assumes a consistent or inherent meaning for the human body—outside the social or cultural construction—and thus the ahistoricity of gender itself. History

becomes, in a sense, epiphenomenal, providing endless variations on the unchanging theme of fixed inequality" (34).

5. Adrienne Rich, "When We Dead Awaken: Writing as Re-vision," *College English* 34, no. 1 (1972): 18–30.

6. Gayle Rubin, "The Traffic in Women: Notes on the 'Political Economy' of Sex," in *The Second Wave: A Reader in Feminist Theory*, ed. Linda Nicholson (New York: Routledge, 1997), 27–62. Rubin analyzed the ritual of the interfamily exchange, or traffic, of women, engaging with the anthropological work of Claude Lévi-Strauss, the field of psychoanalysis (Sigmund Freud and Jacques Lacan), and the theories of Karl Marx and Friedrich Engels.

7. Adrienne Rich, "Compulsory Heterosexuality and Lesbian Existence," in *Feminism and Sexuality*, ed. Stevi Jackson and Sue Scott (New York: Columbia University Press, 1996), 135.

8. Rich, "Compulsory Heterosexuality," 136.

9. Hélène Cixous, "The Laugh of the Medusa," trans. Keith Cohen and Paula Cohen, *Signs: Journal of Women and Culture* 1, no. 4 (Summer 1976): 875–93.

10. Luce Irigaray, "This Sex Which Is Not One" (1977), in Nicholson, *The Second Wave*, 323–30.

11. Julia Kristeva, "Approaching Abjection" (1982), in *The Feminism and Visual Culture Reader*, ed. Amelia Jones (New York: Routledge, 2003), 389–92.

12. Monique Wittig, "The Straight Mind" (1980), in Jones, *Feminism and Visual Culture Reader*, 130–35.

13. Julia Creet, "Monique Wittig," in *Encyclopedia of Feminist Theories*, ed. Lorraine Code (London: Routledge, 2000), 492.

14. Wittig, "Straight Mind," 133.

15. Judith Butler, "Performative Acts and Gender Constitution: An Essay in Phenomenology and Feminist Theory" (1988), in Jones, *Feminism and Visual Culture Reader*, 392–401.

16. Many of these feminists came out of the British Film Institute's *Screen* journal collective, rooted in poststructuralist, psychoanalytic, and Marxist methods of analysis.

17. Laura Mulvey, "Visual Pleasure and Narrative Cinema" (1975), in *Feminism and Film*, ed. E. Ann Kaplan (Oxford: Oxford University Press, 2000), 34–47. Mulvey argued that male subjectivity is produced through a masculine logic of the narrative and the erotic gaze, which enables, privileges, and projects male desire through the pleasures of voyeurism (looking), fetishism (fragmentation), and a return to the pleasures of infancy's mirror phase through a screen surrogate, his own more perfect mirror image, in order to imagine himself whole and powerful.

18. Mulvey, "Visual Pleasure." The male's ability to control events in the narrative "coincides with the active power of the erotic look, both giving a satisfying sense of omnipotence" (63). These subjective processes are dependent upon

reducing the woman to a silent sign by constructing her as an erotic and threatening fragmented object of the male's desire and fear. The woman as erotic
spectacle and castrated other (due to her lack of the phallus) occludes her power
of vision and dramatic agency in the narrative.

19. Teresa de Lauretis, "Rethinking Women's Cinema: Aesthetics and Feminist
    Theory," in *Technologies of Gender: Essays on Theory, Film, and Fiction* (Bloom-
    ington: Indiana University Press, 1987), 127–46.

20. See Sandy Flitterman-Lewis, *To Desire Differently: Feminism and the French
    Cinema*, Expanded ed. (New York: Columbia University Press, 1996); and Mary
    Ann Doane, *The Desire to Desire: The Woman's Film of the 1940s* (Indianapolis:
    Indiana University Press, 1987). Doane argued that the heroine's identifica-
    tion is not, however, with an eroticized female or with the male image as spec-
    tacle, but with herself as image, placing herself in a masochistic position of
    identification. Rather than investing the female gaze with desire, the film's
    visual and sound regimes imbue it with anxiety and fear, compromising female
    pleasure. Interestingly, this process involves dissolution of the distinction
    between the subject of the gaze and its object, identifying the potential for
    female subjectivity (117).

21. Claire Johnston, "Women's Cinema as Counter-Cinema" (1973), in Kaplan, *Fem-
    inism and Film*, 32.

22. bell hooks, *Black Looks: Race and Representation* (Boston: South End Press, 1992).
    "Feminist film theory rooted in an ahistorical psychoanalytic framework that
    privileges sexual difference actively suppresses recognition of race, reenacting
    and mirroring the erasure of black womanhood that occurs in films, silencing
    any discussion of racial difference—of racialized difference" (123).

23. Jane Gaines, "White Privilege and Looking Relations: Race and Gender in Fem-
    inist Film Theory" (1988), in Kaplan, *Feminism and Film*, 337.

24. Patricia Hill Collins, *Black Feminist Thought: Knowledge, Consciousness, and the
    Politics of Empowerment*, 10th anniversary ed. (New York: Routledge, 2000). Col-
    lins looked at antislave activism (Sojourner Truth), women's literature and
    poetry (Zora Neale Hurston), and jazz (Billie Holiday), as well as the ordinary
    testimonies (wisdoms) of working-class and enslaved women, including
    mothers. The voices of black mothers, as heads of families or community lead-
    ers and caregivers, were of particular importance to Collins's work. Part of Col-
    lins's interdisciplinary project involved (re)constructing a genealogy of African
    American women's intellectual tradition by recuperating black women's voices
    from the past, both published (literary and popular) and ordinary speech acts.

25. Gayatri Chakravorty Spivak, "Can the Subaltern Speak?," in *Marxism and the
    Interpretation of Culture*, ed. Cary Nelson and Lawrence Grossberg (Urbana: Uni-
    versity of Illinois Press, 1988), 66–111.

26. Andrew Tudor, "Genre," in *Film Genre Reader*, ed. Barry Keith Grant (Austin:
    University of Texas Press, 1991), 7.

27. Barry Keith Grant, introduction to Grant, *Film Genre Reader*, xi.

28. Patrick Phillips, "Genre, Star and Auteur," in *An Introduction to Film Studies*, 2nd ed., ed. Jill Nelmes (London: Routledge, 1999), 169.

29. R. L. Wilson, *Buffalo Bill's Wild West: An American Legend* (New York: Random House, 1998), 316.

30. Susan Hayward, "Westerns," in *Key Concepts in Cinema Studies* (London: Routledge, 1996), 411.

31. Douglas Pye, "Introduction: Criticism and the Western," in *The Book of Westerns*, ed. Ian Cameron and Douglas Pye (New York: Continuum, 1996), 10.

32. J. Hoberman, "How the West Was Lost," in *The Western Reader*, ed. Jim Kitses and Gregg Rickman (New York: Limelight, 1998). "But baseball is all form; the Western is heavy, heavy on content. That the national pastime was successfully integrated after World War II while the demographics of the Western remained overwhelmingly white up until the eve of the genre's demise—despite the fact that at least a quarter of the working cowboys in the late nineteenth century were of African descent—should alert us to the possibility that the Western was as concerned with concealing as enacting historical truth" (86).

33. David Lusted, "Social Class and the Western as Male Melodrama," in Cameron and Pye, *Book of Westerns*, 65–66.

34. Jane Tompkins, *West of Everything: The Inner Life of Westerns* (New York: Oxford University Press, 1992), 45.

35. Richard Slotkin, *Gunfighter Nation: The Myth of the Frontier in Twentieth-Century America* (Norman: University of Oklahoma Press, 1998), 10.

36. Joanna Hearne, *Native Recognition: Indigenous Cinema and the Western*, The SUNY Series: Horizons of Cinema (Albany: State University of New York Press, 2012).

37. Hayward, "Westerns," 412.

38. Michael Coyne, *The Crowded Prairie: American National Identity in the Hollywood Western* (London: Tauris, 1998), 62.

39. Tompkins, *West of Everything*, 43.

40. Pye, "Introduction," in Cameron and Pye, *Book of Westerns*, 14.

41. Tompkins, *West of Everything*, 44.

42. Hayward, "Westerns." Writing on the introduction of sex to the Western, focusing on Howard Hughes's *The Outlaw* (1943–1946), Hayward argued, "Jane Russell was the first of a number of actresses to play the role of a 'smouldering', sexy, décolleté Mexican woman. Sex was launched, but it had to be with stereotypes. Plenty of hot-blooded foreign womanhood but not 'nice, nice Ms. American pie'—she had to be kept virginal at all costs. Until the eruption of sex the characterization of women was fairly peripheral. The Western is a man's movie. A man with a horse, a man in action, a loner who leaves the woman behind rather than staying. His lust for adventure far outweighs his lust for women" (418).

43. Barbara Welter, "The Cult of True Womanhood: 1820–1860," *American Quarterly* 18, no. 2, part 1 (Summer 1966): 151–74.

44. African American men were also largely absent from the Western but started to make an appearance in the 1970s and 1980s, particularly in the sympathetic Westerns of the 1970s through the 1990s. Because of this absence, very little critical attention has been paid to the representation of African Americans in Hollywood Western films.

45. Pam Cook, "Women and the Western" (1988), in *Screening the Past: Memory and Nostalgia in Cinema* (London: Routledge, 2005), 34–41. Cook highlighted Mae West's Klondike Annie in Raoul Walsh's *Klondike Annie* (1936), Doris Day's Calamity Jane in *Calamity Jane* (1953), Joan Crawford's Vienna in Nicholas Ray's *Johnny Guitar* (1954), and Barbara Stanwyck's Jessica Drummond Cook in Samuel Fuller's *Forty Guns*. Cook argued that these feisty heroines dressed as men, carried guns, consumed alcohol, had sexual relations outside marriage, and found ways to support themselves financially in order to survive in a hostile masculine space.

46. Cook, "Women and the Western," 40–41.

47. Cook, "Women and the Western," 34.

48. Maryann Oshana, "Native American Women in Westerns: Reality and Myth," in *Frontiers: A Journal of Women Studies* 6, no. 3 (Autumn 1981): 46–50. In her analysis, Oshana highlighted the important leadership and advisory roles indigenous American women played in their communities, a stark contrast to the simplistic, one-dimensional, and degrading depictions seen in Hollywood Westerns.

49. Rayna Green, "The Pocahontas Perplex: The Image of Indian Women in American Culture," *Massachusetts Review* 16, no. 4 (Autumn 1975): 698–714.

50. Green, "Pocahontas Perplex," 698–99.

51. Annette Kolodny, *The Lay of the Land: Metaphor as Experience and History in American Life and Letters* (Chapel Hill: University of North Carolina Press, 1975), 5.

52. M. Elise Marubbio. *Killing the Indian Maiden: Images of Native American Women in Film* (Lexington: University Press of Kentucky, 2006), 21. Marubbio traced the Indian Maiden figure across nearly one hundred years of cinema, focusing on thirty-four films, primarily Westerns.

53. Hayward, "Westerns." "The hero's 'job' is to make the west safe for the virgins to come out and reproduce, but not with him, that is the job for the rest of the community" (418).

54. Pye, "Introduction," in Cameron and Pye, *Book of Westerns*. "It is as though the ending on the frontier as a clear line of settlement in the late nineteenth century and the consequent end of the unsettled West to feed the imagination meant that the twentieth century Western story must finally be about the integration into society that had become inevitable" (14).

55. Hayward, "Westerns," 419–20.

56. Hayward, "Westerns," 421.

57. Hearne, *Native Recognition*.

58. Oshana, "Native American," 48.

59. It should also be noted that the Japanese Samurai film is often deemed to be the origin for many of these international Westerns, which, it could be argued, are a hybrid of Japanese and Hollywood traditions.

60. Red Westerns were also known as Soviet Westerns. *White Sun of the Desert* (1969) is perhaps the best known of the Red Westerns made during the Soviet era. Vincent Bohlinger, "'The East Is a Delicate Matter': *White Sun of the Desert* and the Soviet Western," in *International Westerns: Re-Locating the Frontier*, ed. Cynthia J. Miller and A. Bowdoin Van Riper (Plymouth, Mass.: Scarecrow Press, 2014), 373–93.

61. Madhuja Mukherjee, "The Singing Cowboys: *Sholay* and the Significance of (Indian) Curry Westerns Within Post-Colonial Narratives," *Transformations: Journal of Media & Culture*, no. 24 (2014), http://www.transformationsjournal.org /journal/24/02.shtml.

62. Tassilo Schneider, "Finding a New *Heimat* in the Wild West: Karl May and the German Western of the 1960s," in *Back in the Saddle Again: New Essays on the Western*, ed. Edward Buscombe and Roberta E. Pearson (London: British Film Institute, 1998), 142.

63. See Christopher Frayling, *Spaghetti Westerns: Cowboys and Europeans from Karl May to Sergio Leone* (London: Tauris, 1998). Frayling argued that Leone's hugely successful spaghetti Westerns were rooted in a "'critical cinema,' utilizing the internal conventions of the genre (and extending them), in order critically to examine not so much the mythology of the frontier itself, as a later cinematic mythology, debased but still producing 'infatuated tributes.' A form of 'cinema about cinema'—but one with the potential to 'comment' as well" (40).

64. Marcia Landy, "He Went Thataway: The Form and Style of Leone's Italian Westerns," in Kitses and Rickman, *Western Reader*, 215.

65. Hayward, "Westerns," 418.

66. Pam Cook, "No Fixed Address: The Women's Picture—from *Outrage* to *Blue Steel*," in *Gender Meets Genre in Postwar Cinemas*, ed. Christine Gledhill (Champaign: University of Illinois Press, 2012), 31.

67. Susan Hayward, "Melodrama and the Woman's Film," in *Key Concepts in Cinema Studies* (London: Routledge, 1996), 200.

68. Thomas Elsaesser, "Tales of Sound and Fury: Observations on the Family Melodrama," in *Imitations of Life: A Reader on Film and Television Melodrama*, ed. Marcia Landy (Detroit, Mich.: Wayne State University, 1991), 68.

69. Elsaesser, "Tales of Sound and Fury," 69.

70. Elsaesser, "Tales of Sound and Fury," 69.

71. Elsaesser, "Tales of Sound and Fury," 77.

72. Peter Brooks, "The Melodramatic Imagination," in Landy, *Imitations of Life*. "That the term covers and, in common usage, most often refers to a cheap and banal melodrama—to soap opera—need not decrease its usefulness: there is a range from high to low examples in any literary field, and the most successful

melodrama belongs to a coherent mode that rewards attention, in its literal as well as in its 'extrapolated' forms. What I will say about melodrama in general will, I think, be relevant to the low examples as well as in the high, with the difference that, as in all art, the low is attempting less, risking less, is more conventional and less self-conscious. At its most ambitious, the melodramatic mode of conception and representation may appear to be the very process of reaching a fundamental drama of the moral life and finding the terms to express it" (58).

73. Hayward, "Melodrama," 202.

74. Peter Brooks, *The Melodramatic Imagination: Balzac, Henry James, Melodrama, and the Mode of Excess* (New Haven, Conn.: Yale University Press, 1976), 80. Brooks deployed Freud's theories of the "moral occult," the domain of the operative spiritual values, which are both indicated within and masked by the surface of reality.

75. Brooks, *Melodramatic Imagination*, 4.

76. Hayward, "Melodrama," 204.

77. Hayward, "Melodrama," 208.

78. Marcia Landy, introduction to Landy, *Imitations of Life*, 14.

79. See Pam Cook and Claire Johnston, "The Place of Women in the Cinema of Raoul Walsh" (1974), in *Issues in Feminist Film Criticism*, ed. Patricia Erens (Bloomington: Indiana University Press, 1990), 19–27; Mary Ann Doane, "Film and the Masquerade: Theorizing the Female Spectator" (1982), in Kaplan, *Feminism and Film*, 418–36; E. Ann Kaplan, "The Case of the Missing Mother: Maternal Issues in Vidor's *Stella Dallas*" (1983), in Kaplan, *Feminism and Film*, 466–78; and Annette Kuhn, "Women's Genres" (1984), in Kaplan, *Feminism and Film*, 437–49.

80. Doane, *Desire to Desire*, 117.

81. *Christopher Strong* (1933) is about Christopher Strong, "a middle-aged nobleman and politician, happily married with a grown daughter." He falls in love with Lady Cynthia Darrington (Hepburn), "a dedicated aviatrix so consumed by flying that she has no time for romance. The two fall in love, and their affair threatens Strong's marriage and career." Turner Classic Movies, "*Christopher Strong*," accessed December 10, 2019, http://www.tcm.com/this-month/article .html?isPreview=&id=158602%7C311&name=Christopher-Strong.

82. *Craig's Wife* (1936) is about "a domineering woman [who] marries a wealthy man for his money, and then uses her position to further her own ambitions for money and power." IMDb—International Movie Database, "*Craig's Wife* (1936)," accessed December 10, 2019, http://www.imdb.com/title/tt0027474/.

83. *Dance, Girl, Dance* (1940) is about two ambitious burlesque dancers, the wisecracking, worldly Bubbles (Lucille Ball) and the naïve, innocent Judy (Maureen O'Hara). In contrast to Judy's artistic aspirations to become a ballerina, Bubbles wants to marry a rich man, and uses her sexuality to get what she wants in life. Though the women have their differences and compete with one another, they are never truly enemies. Feminist film theorist Alison Butler writes, "Arzner

uses dance dialectically to represent the women's economic and sexual dilemmas: Bubbles dances to attract men, performing stereotypical female sexuality; Judy dances for artistic self-expression, attracting a man incidentally (insofar as such a thing could be incidental in a Hollywood film). Both are ultimately in pursuit of money and social mobility." Alison Butler, *Women's Cinema: The Contested Screen* (London: Wallflower, 2002), 36.

84. Claire Johnston, "Dorothy Arzner: Critical Strategies" (1975), in Kaplan, *Feminism and Film*, 142.

85. E. Ann Kaplan, *Women and Film: Both Sides of the Camera* (New York: Routledge, 1988).

86. The Hays Code is the unofficial name for "the motion Pictures Producers and Distributors of America (later the Motion Pictures Association of America), derived from the name of its president, Will H. Hays. The MPPDA was formed in 1922 by the film industry in response to public indignation over apparent sex scandals in Hollywood. Hays had considerable political influence and a strong moral reputation. His job, and the organization's, was mainly to prevent censorship by state and federal governments. Hays and the MPPDA did so by applying pressure on the studios to control the sexual contents of films and the private lives of their stars." Ira Konigsberg, *The Complete Film Dictionary*, 2nd ed. (Toronto, Ont., Canada: Penguin Reference, 1997), 172.

87. Judith Mayne, "Lesbian Looks: Dorothy Arzner and Female Authorship" (1991), in Kaplan, *Feminism and Film*, 170.

88. Patricia White, *Uninvited: Classical Hollywood Cinema and Lesbian Representability* (Bloomington: Indiana University Press, 1999), 2.

89. hooks, *Black Looks*, 135.

90. hooks, *Black Looks*, 135.

91. Jane Gaines, "Fire and Desire: Race, Melodrama and Oscar Micheaux," in *Melodrama: Stage, Picture, Screen*, ed. Jacky Bratton, Jim Cook, and Christine Gledhill (London: British Film Institute, 1994), 235.

92. Chuck Kleinhans, "Realist Melodrama and the African-American Family: Billy Woodbury's *Bless Their Little Hearts*," in Bratton, Cook, and Gledhill, *Melodrama: Stage, Picture, Screen*, 163.

93. Jane Shattuc, "Having a Good Cry Over *The Color Purple*: The Problem of Affect and Imperialism in Feminist Theory," in Bratton, Cook, and Gledhill, *Melodrama: Stage, Picture, Screen*, 147.

94. Shattuc, "Having a Good Cry," 148.

95. Hayward, "Horror/Gothic," in *Key Concepts in Cinema Studies*, 174.

96. Hayward, "Melodrama," 210.

97. Barry Keith Grant, introduction to *The Dread of Difference: Gender and the Horror Film* (Austin: University of Texas Press, 1996), 5.

98. Grant, introduction to *Dread of Difference*, 1.

99. Linda Williams, "When the Woman Looks" (1983), in Grant, *Dread of Difference*, 15–34.

100. Barbara Creed, "Horror and the Monstrous-Feminine: An Imaginary Abjection" (1986), in Grant, *Dread of Difference*, 35–65.

101. Carol J. Clover, "Her Body, Himself: Gender in the Slasher Film" (1987), in Grant, *Dread of Difference*, 66–113.

102. Barry Barclay, "Celebrating the Fourth Cinema," *Illusions: New Zealand Moving Images and Performing Arts Criticism*, no. 35 (July 2003): 7.

103. hooks, *Black Looks*, 116.

104. "The griot profession is hereditary and has long been a part of West African culture. The griots' role has traditionally been to preserve the genealogies, historical narratives, and oral traditions of their people; praise songs are also part of the griot's repertoire." *Encyclopedia Britannica*, s.v. "Griot: African Troubador-Historian," accessed December 10, 2019, http://www.britannica.com /EBchecked/topic/246348/griot.

105. Karen Alexander, "*Daughters of the Dust*—Julie Dash, Director," *Sight and Sound* 3, no. 9 (1991): 20–23.

106. Julie Dash, Toni Cade Bambara, and bell hooks, *Daughters of the Dust: The Making of an African American Woman's Film* (New York: New Press, 1992), 32.

107. Dash, Bambara, and hooks, *Daughters*, 5.

108. Pascale Lamche, "Interview with Merata Mita," *Framework* 25 (Autumn 1984): 3.

109. Rickard (1925–December 6, 1997) was an activist for Maori land rights and women's rights. "She is perhaps best known for leading the Raglan golf course protest in the 1970s. The Raglan protest, and others at Bastion Point in central Auckland, helped to change land legislation. If land taken for public works is no longer needed, the government is now required to return it to the original owners." New Zealand Ministry for Culture and Heritage, "Eva Rickard: Biography," New Zealand History, accessed December 10, 2019, http://www.nzhistory .net.nz/people/eva-rickard.

110. "McLean and Orbell distinguished three kinds of waiata (songs): waiata tangi (laments—for the dead, but also for other kinds of loss or misfortune), waiata aroha (songs about the nature of love—not only sexual love but also love of place or kin), and waiata whaiaaipo (songs of courtship or praise of the beloved). In addition, there are pao (gossip songs), poi (songs accompanying a dance performed with balls attached to flax strings, swung rhythmically), oriori (songs composed for young children of chiefly or warrior descent, to help them learn their heritage), and karanga (somewhere between song and chant, performed by women welcoming or farewelling visitors on the marae). Some chants are recited rather than sung. These include karakia (forms of incantation invoking a power to protect or to assist the chanter), paatere (chants by women in rebuttal of gossip or slander, asserting the performer's high lineage and threatening her detractors), kaioraora (expressions of hatred and abuse of an enemy, promising terrible revenge), and the haka (a chant accompanied by rhythmic movements, stamping, and fierce gestures, the most famous of these being war dances that incorporate stylized violence)." *Britannica*

Academic, s.v. "New Zealand Literature," accessed December 10, 2019, https://academic-eb-com.library.sheridanc.on.ca/levels/collegiate/article/New-Zealand-literature/109391#33319.toc.

111. Daniel Mudie Cunningham, "Something More from a Distance," *Sturgeon: Australian Art, Culture, etc.*, no. 6 (February 5, 2017), http://sturgeonmagazine.com.au/something-more-from-a-distance/.

112. Bill Nichols, *Representing Reality: Issues and Concepts in Documentary* (Bloomington: Indiana University Press, 1991), 225.

113. Creed, "Horror and the Monstrous-Feminine," 40.

114. Robert Holden and Nicolas Holden, *Bunyips: Australia's Folklore of Fear* (Canberra, A.C.T.: National Library of Australia, 2001), 11.

115. Kaja Silverman, *The Acoustic Mirror: The Female Voice in Psychoanalysis and Cinema* (Bloomington: Indiana University Press, 1988), 164.

116. Vincent Osteria and Thierry Jousee, "*The Piano*: An Interview with Jane Campion," in *Jane Campion: Interviews*, ed. Virginia Wright Wexman (Jackson: University Press of Mississippi, 1999), 125.

117. "Bluebeard, murderous husband in the story *La Barbe bleue*, in Charles Perrault's collection of fairy tales, *Contes de ma mère l'oye* (1697; *Tales of Mother Goose*). In the tale, Bluebeard is a wealthy man of rank who, soon after his marriage, goes away, leaving his wife the keys to all the doors in his castle but forbidding her to open one of them. She disobeys and finds in the locked room the bodies of his former wives. On his return, Bluebeard discovers on one of the keys a telltale spot of blood and threatens to cut off her head as a punishment for disobedience. The wife is saved by her brothers just as Bluebeard is about to strike the final blow." *Britannica Academic*, s.v. "Bluebeard," accessed December 10, 2019, https://academic-eb-com.library.sheridanc.on.ca/levels/collegiate/article/Bluebeard/15767.

118. See Maria Tatar, *Secrets Beyond the Door: "Bluebeard" in Folklore, Fiction, and Film* (Princeton, N.J.: Princeton University Press, 2006). Abstract: "The tale of Bluebeard's Wife—the story of a young woman who discovers that her mysterious blue-bearded husband has murdered his former spouses—no longer squares with what most parents consider good bedtime reading for their children. But the story has remained alive for adults, allowing it to lead a rich subterranean existence in novels ranging from *Jane Eyre* to *Lolita* and in films as diverse as Hitchcock's *Notorious* and Jane Campion's *The Piano*. In this fascinating work, Maria Tatar analyzes the many forms the tale of Bluebeard's Wife has taken over time, particularly in Anglo-European popular culture." See Christina Bacchilega, *Postmodern Fairy Tales: Gender and Narrative Strategies* (Philadelphia: University of Pennsylvania Press, 2011). Abstract: "*Postmodern Fairy Tales* seeks to understand the fairy tale not as children's literature but within the broader context of folklore and literary studies. It focuses on the narrative strategies through which women are portrayed in four classic stories: 'Snow White,' 'Little Red Riding Hood,' 'Beauty and the Beast,' and 'Bluebeard.'

Bacchilega traces the oral sources of each tale, offers a provocative interpretation of contemporary versions by Angela Carter, Robert Coover, Donald Barthelme, Margaret Atwood, and Tanith Lee, and explores the ways in which the tales are transformed in film, television, and musicals."

119. Kari E. Lokke, "'Bluebeard' and 'The Bloody Chamber': The Grotesque of Self-Parody and Self-Assertion," *Frontiers: A Journal of Women Studies* 10, no. 1 (1988): 7.

120. Feona Attwood, "Weird Lullaby: Jane Campion's *The Piano*," *Feminist Review* 58, no. 1 (1998): 85–101. Abstract: "The article examines the construction of woman's voice, gaze and desire in Jane Campion's Oscar-winning film *The Piano*, 1993, with particular reference to the film's central character, Ada, and to the traditional female figures which her character suggests—siren, mermaid, Little Red Riding Hood, Bluebeard's wife. It investigates the ways in which *The Piano* interrogates and disturbs traditional patriarchal narratives, ways of speaking and seeing, and patriarchal constructions of bodily pleasure and desire; revealing these as partial, hard of hearing, short sighted and incapable of pleasure" (85).

121. Jaime Bihlmeyer, "Bluebeard in Jane Campion's *The Piano*: A Case Study in Intertextuality as an Enunciation of Femininity in Mainstream Movies," *International Journal of the Humanities* 8, no. 7 (2010): 183–90. Abstract: "The Bluebeard folktale is (re)produced in Jane Campion's *The Piano* (1993) as the featured performance in a pageant that a minister organizes for his colonial New Zealand/Aotearoa congregation. This construction-en-abyme is representative of intertextuality in terms of Julia Kristeva's 'affirmative negativity.' The paper explores intertextuality in *The Piano* as an agent of a multiplex and extra-lingual dialogism linked to femininity and the female gaze" (183).

122. Ruth Barcan and Madeleine Fogarty, "Performing *The Piano*," in *Piano Lessons: Approaches to* The Piano, ed. Felicity Coombs and Suzanne Gemmell (London: Libbey, 1999), 3–18. "In August, 1993, the Coalition Against Sexual Violence Propaganda newsletter carried a two paragraph review of *The Piano*, with the first paragraph condemning it as sexist and the second declaring it to be racist. The writer lamented what she saw as the film's shift away from a depiction of two strong women towards a focus on aggressive and coercive male sexuality" (7). See also Lisa Sarmas, "What Rape Is," Letter to the Editor, *Arena Magazine*, no. 8 (1993–1994): 14.

123. Peter Britos, "A Conversation with Merata Mita," *Spectator* 23, no. 1 (Spring 2003): 53–62.

124. Leonie Pihama, "Are Films Dangerous? A Māori Woman's Perspective on *The Piano*," *Hecate: Special Aotearoa/New Zealand Issue* 20, no. 2 (1994): 239–42. "The Maori characters are the background against which images of white are positioned. We remain the 'natives' who provide the backdrop for the 'civilised.' Our dialogue is centred upon sexual service which is 'raw' and 'crude' as opposed to what is (supposedly) 'erotic.' The images presented in *The Piano* say much about colonial perceptions of the indigenous people, as these perceptions have

endured to the 1990s. They also say much about the colonisers themselves as they position themselves in opposition to Maori people as 'Other'" (240).

125. Reshela DuPuis, "Romanticizing Colonialism: Power and Pleasure in Jane Campion's *The Piano*," *Contemporary Pacific* 8, 1 (Spring 1996): 52.

126. Harriet Margolis, introduction to *Jane Campion's* The Piano, ed. Harriet Margolis (Cambridge: Cambridge University Press, 2000), 19.

127. Harriet Margolis summarizes the debate around Campion's deployment and depiction of the Maori in her introduction to *Jane Campion's* The Piano.

128. Modleski and Greenwald, "Our Heroes Have Sometimes Been Cowgirls." "The only thing that's known is what was published in the newspaper article when she died, which gave me the information for the beginning and the end of the story. She was a society girl who had a child out of wedlock. It's believed her sister cared for the child, or someone else may have adopted him. Her family threw her out, and somewhere between the time she left the Northeast and arrived in the West she assumed the identity of a man and lived her whole life that way" (7).

129. Doane, *Desire to Desire*, 112.

130. Doane argued, "There is, however, a more 'old fashioned' means of articulating the effects of such a presence-in-absence: letters. The number of film titles which invoke this method of communication testifies to its significance: *Love Letters* (1945), *Letter from an Unknown Woman* (1948), *The Letter, A Letter to Three Wives* (1948). The letter is first and foremost evidence of a crime: the crime of one man assuming another's identity (*Love Letters*); the crime of a man's failure to recognize the woman who bore his son (*Letter From an Unknown Woman*); adultery and murder (*The Letter*); or just adultery (*A Letter to Three Wives*)" (113).

131. Spivak, "Can the Subaltern Speak?"

132. Hayward, "Melodrama," in *Key Concepts in Cinema Studies*, 206.

133. Elsaesser, "Tales of Sound and Fury," 86–87.

134. Laura Hyun-Yi Kang, "The Desiring of Asian Female Bodies: Interracial Romance and Cinematic Subjection," *Visual Anthropology Review* 9, no. 1 (March 1993): 5–21.

135. Gillian Armstrong interview, *My Brilliant Career* Special Edition DVD (2005), Blue Underground.

136. Janis Cole and Holly Dale, *Calling the Shots: Profiles of Women Filmmakers* (Toronto, Ont., Canada: Quarry Press, 1993), 252.

137. Trinh T. Minh-ha and Nancy N. Chen, "Speaking Nearby," in Kaplan, *Feminism and Film*, 327.

138. Linda Kupecek, "*Loyalties*: Anne Wheeler's Film Family," *Cinema Canada*, no. 123 (October 1985): 6.

139. "The long take or sequence shot is a lengthy shot. André Bazin, the French film critic and theoretician, has drawn attention to the related techniques of the long take and deep focus. For Bazin both the long take and deep focus opened up

the image for the spectator and involved him or her more deeply in its 'reality.'" Konigsberg, *Complete Film Dictionary*, 221–22.

140. Spivak, "Can the Subaltern Speak?"

141. Judith Doyle, "Norma Bailey," in *In a Different Voice: Conversations with Women Artists and Filmmakers* (Toronto, Ont., Canada: Funnel Experimental Film Theatre, 1986), 22. Exhibition catalogue.

142. National Film Board of Canada, "Our Collection: Daughters of the Country Series," accessed December 10, 2019, http://onf-nfb.gc.ca/en/our-collection/?idfilm=32975. "The stories that comprise *Daughters of the Country 1 and 2*. *Ikwe*: In 1770, a young Ojibway woman marries a Scottish fur trader. The union promises prosperity for her tribe, but hardship for Ikwe (57 min.). *Mistress Madeleine*: In the 1850s, a Métis woman is torn between loyalty to her people and loyalty to her 'husband,' a Hudson's Bay clerk. Her life is shattered when he returns from England with a legal wife (57 min. 1 sec.). *Places Not Our Own*: By 1929, the Métis had become a forgotten people, relegated to eking out a living as best they could. Rose L'Espérance is determined that her children will have a better life (57 min. 10 sec.). *The Wake*: Set in contemporary Alberta, this is the story of a love affair between a Royal Canadian Mounted Police officer and a feisty Métis woman. Their lives are changed by the death of some young Métis on a frozen lake (57 min.)."

143. hooks, *Black Looks*, 116.

144. Spivak, "Can the Subaltern Speak?"

145. Elsa Barkley Brown, "'What Has Happened Here?' The Politics of Difference in Women's History and Feminist Politics," *Feminist Studies* 18, no. 2 (Summer 1992): 295–312.

146. Faye Ginsburg, "Breaking the Law with Two Laws: Reflections on a Paradigm Shift," *Studies in Documentary Film* 2, no. 2 (2008): 172.

147. Michael Ray, "Alison Bechdel: American Cartoonist and Graphic Novelist," *Encyclopedia Britannica*, accessed December 10, 2019, https://www.britannica.com/biography/Alison-Bechdel.

148. Adrienne Rich, "Compulsory Heterosexuality," 135.

149. Silverman, *Acoustic Mirror*, 164.

2. DEBUNKING THE CULT OF TRUE WOMANHOOD

1. Sue Mathews, *35mm Dreams: Conversations with Five Directors About the Australian Film Revival* (Ringwood, Vic., Australia: Penguin Books, 1984), 163.

2. Marilyn Lake, "Australian Frontier Feminism and the Marauding White Man," in *Gender and Imperialism*, ed. Claire Midgley (Manchester, U.K.: Manchester University Press, 1998), 126.

3. Collins quoted African American writer Zora Neale Hurston's *Their Eyes Were Watching God* (1937). Patricia Hill Collins, *Black Feminist Thought: Knowledge,*

Consciousness, and the Politics of Empowerment, 10th anniversary ed. (New York: Routledge, 2000), 51.

4. Jane Tompkins, *West of Everything: The Inner Life of Westerns* (New York: Oxford University Press, 1992), 44. "For the most of the 19th century the two places that women could call their own in the social structure were the church and the home. The Western contains neither. It is set in a period and in an environment where few women are to be found and where conditions are the worst possible for acquiring any social power: a technology and a code of justice both of which required physical strength in order to survive" (44).

5. Barbara Welter, "The Cult of True Womanhood: 1820–1860," *American Quarterly* 18, no. 2, part 1 (Summer 1966): 152.

6. Welter, "Cult of True Womanhood," 154.

7. Virginia Woolf, "Professions for Women," in *The Moth and Other Essays* (San Diego: Harcourt, Brace & Company, 1974. First published 1942), 237. "She was intensely sympathetic. She was immensely charming. She was utterly unselfish. She excelled in the difficult arts of family life. She sacrificed herself daily. If there was chicken, she took the leg; if there was a draught, she sat in it—in short she was so constituted that she never had a mind or a wish of her own, but preferred to sympathize always with the minds and wishes of others" (237).

8. See Betty Friedan, *The Feminine Mystique* (New York: Dell, 1963); Ann Oakley, *Sex, Gender, and Society* (London: Gower, 1985); Adrienne Rich, *Of Woman Born: Motherhood as Experience and Institution* (New York: Bantam, 1976); Dorothy Dinnerstein, *The Mermaid and the Minotaur: Sexual Arrangements and Human Malaise* (New York: Other Press, 1999); Nancy Chodorow, *The Reproduction of Mothering: Psychoanalysis and the Sociology of Gender* (Berkeley: University of California Press, 1978); Jane Lazarre, *The Mother Knot* (Durham, N.C.: Duke University Press, 1997); Gayle Rubin, "The Traffic in Women: Notes on the 'Political Economy' of Sex," in *The Second Wave: A Reader in Feminist Theory*, ed. Linda Nicholson (New York: Routledge, 1997), 27–62; and Shulamith Firestone, *The Dialectic of Sex: The Case for Feminist Revolution* (New York: Farrar, Straus and Giroux, 2003).

9. Meg Luxton, *More Than a Labour of Love: Three Generations of Women's Work in the Home* (Toronto, Ont., Canada: Women's Press, 1980).

10. Luxton, *More Than a Labour*, 11–12.

11. Waring is quoted in the documentary *Who's Counting? Marilyn Waring on Sex, Lies and Global Economics*, directed by Terre Nash (National Film Board of Canada, 1995), https://www.nfb.ca/film/whos_counting.

12. Marilyn Waring, *If Women Counted: A New Feminist Economics* (San Francisco: HarperCollins, 1989).

13. Elizabeth Thompson, *The Pioneer Woman: A Canadian Character Type* (Montreal, Que., Canada: McGill-Queen's University Press, 1991).

14. Ann Romines, *Constructing the Little House: Gender, Culture, and Laura Ingalls Wilder* (Amherst: University of Massachusetts Press, 1997). "[Rose Wilder] Lane's

heir Roger MacBride (until his death in 1995) proposed to extend the Little House series forward in time, by fictionalizing Lane's childhood in his "Little House in the Ozarks" books, which are available through the Book of the Month Club. Another author has begun a project that takes the series backward, fictionalizing Ma's childhood (7)." The Little House franchise is ongoing; the books have never gone out of print since their first date of publication in 1932, and a number of prequels and projects continue to keep the history-myth of the Ingalls family, ever westbound, as part of frontier lore.

15. Robin Morgan, "Theory and Practice: Pornography and Rape," in *Going Too Far: The Personal Chronicle of a Feminist—Kindle Edition* (New York: Open Road Integrated Media, 2014), Kindle location 83.

16. Andrea Dworkin, *Pornography: Men Possessing Women* (New York: Plume, 1989).

17. Catharine A. MacKinnon, "Sexuality," in *The Feminist Philosophy Reader*, ed. Alison Bailey and Chris Cuomo (Boston: McGraw-Hill, 2008), 204–21. "Dominance eroticized defines the imperatives of its masculinity, submission eroticized defines its femininity. So many distinctive features of women's status as second class—the restriction and constraint and contrition, the servility and the display, the self-mutilation and requisite presentation of self as a beautiful thing, the enforced passivity, the humiliation—are made into the content of sex for women. Being a thing for sexual use is fundamental to it" (206).

18. Marysia Zalewiski, "Andrea Dworkin," in *Encyclopedia of Feminist Theories*, ed. Lorraine Code (London: Routledge, 2000), 147.

19. Gayle Rubin, "Thinking Sex: Notes for a Radical Theory of the Politics of Sexuality," in *Pleasure and Danger: Exploring Female Sexuality*, ed. Carole S. Vance (Boston: Routledge and Keagan Paul, 1985), 267–319. "According to this system, sexuality that is 'good,' 'normal,' and 'natural' should be ideally heterosexual, marital, monogamous, reproductive, and non-commercial. It should be coupled, relational, within the same generation, and occur at home. It should not involve pornography, fetish objects, sex toys of any sort, or roles other than male and female. Any sex that violates these rules is 'bad,' 'abnormal,' or 'unnatural.' Bad sex may be homosexual, unmarried, promiscuous, non-procreative, or commercial" (286).

20. Rubin, "Thinking Sex," 150.

21. Luce Irigaray, "This Sex Which Is Not One," in *The Second Wave: A Reader in Feminist Theory*, ed. Linda Nicholson (New York: Routledge, 1997), 326. "Even without speaking of the hysterization of her entire body, one can say that the geography of her pleasure is much more diversified, more multiple in its differences, more complex, more subtle, than is imagined—in an imaginary centered a bit too much on one and the same."

22. Vron Ware, *Beyond the Pale: White Women, Racism, and History* (London: Verso, 1992), Kindle location 987.

23. Enakshi Dua, "Canadian Anti-Racist Feminist Thought: Scratching the Surface of Racism," in *Scratching the Surface: Canadian Anti-racist Feminist Thought*, ed.

Enakshi Dua and Angela Robertson (Toronto, Ont., Canada: Women's Press, 1999), 7–34.

24. Collins, *Black Feminist Thought*, 57.

25. Collins, *Black Feminist Thought*. "Efforts to control Black women's sexuality were tied directly to slave owners' efforts to increase the number of children their female slaves produced. Techniques such as assigning pregnant women lighter workloads, giving pregnant women more attention and rations, and rewarding prolific women with bonuses were all used to increase Black women's reproduction. Punitive measures were also used" (57–58).

26. Sojourner Truth was a well-known freed slave who became an antislavery activist. She is famous for her speech later titled "Ain't I a Woman?," which was delivered at the Women's Convention in Akron, Ohio, on May 29, 1851. See Carleton Mabee and Susan Mabee Newhouse, *Sojourner Truth: Slave, Prophet, Legend* (New York: New York University Press, 1995).

27. bell hooks, *Ain't I a Woman: Black Women and Feminism* (Boston: South End Press, 1981), 32.

28. hooks, *Ain't I a Woman*, 52.

29. Evelynn M. Hammonds, "Toward a Genealogy of Black Female Sexuality: The Problematic of Silence," in Bailey and Cuomo, *Feminist Philosophy Reader*, 249–60. "Thus, the black female became the antithesis of European sexual mores and beauty and was relegated to the lowest position on the scale of human development. The image of the black female constructed in this period reflected everything the white female was not" (250–51).

30. Evelyn Brooks Higginbotham, *Righteous Discontent: The Women's Movement in the Black Baptist Church, 1880–1920* (Cambridge, Mass.: Harvard University Press, 1993), 14.

31. Michele Wallace, *Black Macho and the Myth of the Superwoman* (London: Verso, 1979).

32. Collins, *Black Feminist Thought*. "In a climate where one's sexuality is on public display, holding fast to privacy and trying to shut the closet door becomes paramount. [Darlene Clark] Hine refers to this strategy as a culture of dissemblance, one where Black women appeared to be outgoing and public, while using this façade to hide a secret world within. In contexts of violence where internal self-censorship was seen as protection, silence made sense" (135).

33. Collins, *Black Feminist Thought*, 70.

34. Rayna Green, "The Pocahontas Perplex: The Image of Indian Women in American Culture," *Massachusetts Review* 16, no. 4 (Autumn 1975): 698–714.

35. The essential idea behind this infamous quote was, in Duncan Campbell Scott's words, "to solve the Indian problem." "Writer Mark Abley argues that Scott is often misquoted as having said that the goal of residential schools was to 'kill the Indian in the child.' Abley instead credits this line to an American military officer. While Scott may not have uttered those words, he did say something similar in 1920, before the amendment to the Indian Act became law that same

year." Robert L. McDougall, "Duncan Campbell Scott," in *The Canadian Ency-clopedia*, August 11, 2008, last edited September 10, 2018, https://www.the canadianencyclopedia.ca/en/article/duncan-campbell-scott.

36. J. R. Miller, "Residential Schools in Canada," in *The Canadian Encyclopedia*, accessed December 12, 2019, http://www.thecanadianencyclopedia.ca/en/article /residential-schools/.

37. Sam Grey, "Decolonising Feminism: Aboriginal Women and the Global 'Sister-hood,'" *Enweyin: The Ways We Speak* 8 (January 2004): 9–22. "Institutionalization and adoption into non-Native households has had an immeasurable impact on gender dynamics in Aboriginal societies" (13).

38. Australians Together, "The Stolen Generations: The Forcible Removal of Indig-enous Children from Their Families," accessed December 12, 2019, https://www .australianstogether.org.au/discover/australian-history/stolen-generations.

39. Aileen Moreton-Robinson, "Tiddas Speakin' Strong: Indigenous Women's Self-Preservation Within White Australian Feminism," in Bailey and Cuomo, *Femi-nist Philosophy Reader*, 366. "Indigenous women are positioned as being either primitive or exotic sexual objects. As primitive sexual objects they are seen to be closer to animals than white women and therefore naturally predisposed to sex in any form, which is one reason why Indigenous women find it difficult to report rape."

40. Hélène Cixous, "The Laugh of the Medusa," trans. Keith Cohen and Paula Cohen, *Signs: Journal of Women and Culture* 1, no. 4 (Summer 1976): 875–93. Cixous argued, "My text is written in white and black, in 'milk' and 'night.' . . . A woman is never far from 'mother.' . . . There is always within her at least a little of that good mother's milk. She writes in white ink" (881–82).

41. Julia Kristeva, "Motherhood According to Giovanni Bellini," in *Desire in Lan-guage: A Semiotic Approach to Literature and Art*, ed. Leon S. Roudiez, trans. Thomas Gora, Alice Jardine, and Leon S. Roudiez (New York: Columbia Univer-sity Press, 1980), 305. This maternal space is where mother first bonds with child, before the child sees sexual difference, but this bond is created through the child's connection with the maternal reproductive body; it's a corporeal language. Kristeva in general rejected all forms of authority, hierarchy, and rules and embraced a structure that is rooted in fluidity. Kristeva presented motherhood and pregnancy as metaphors rather than experiences.

42. Directed by Michael Curtiz, *Mildred Pierce*, about a single mother, Mildred (Joan Crawford), "hell-bent on freeing her children from the stigma of economic hardship, solidified Crawford's career comeback and gave the actor her only Oscar. But as Mildred pulls herself up by the bootstraps, first as an unflappa-ble waitress and eventually as the well-heeled owner of a successful restaurant chain, the ingratitude of her materialistic firstborn (a diabolical Ann Blyth) becomes a venomous serpent's tooth, setting in motion an endless cycle of des-perate overtures and heartless recriminations." "Mildred Pierce," Criterion

Collection, accessed December 12, 2019, https://www.criterion.com/films/29025
-mildred-pierce.

43. Directed by King Vidor, *Stella Dallas* (1937) "is an adaptation of Olive Higgins
Prouty's novel. Barbara Stanwyck essayed the role of an uncouth mother who
sacrifices her own happiness for that of her class-conscious daughter (Anne
Shirley)." *Britannica Academic*, s.v. "King Vidor," accessed December 12, 2019,
https://academic-eb-com.library.sheridanc.on.ca/levels/collegiate/article
/King-Vidor/75287. The film is one of the most well-known Hollywood maternal
melodramas from the 1930s.

44. Lucy Fischer, *Cinematernity: Film, Motherhood, Genre* (Princeton, N.J.: Princeton University Press, 1996), 12.

45. Molly Haskell, *From Reverence to Rape: The Treatment of Women in the Movies*
(Baltimore, Md.: Penguin Books, 1974), 169.

46. Linda Williams, "'Something Else Besides a Mother': *Stella Dallas* and the
Maternal Melodrama," in *Feminism and Film*, ed. E. Ann Kaplan (Oxford: Oxford
University Press, 2000), 479.

47. Mary Ann Doane, *The Desire to Desire: The Woman's Film of the 1940s* (Indianapolis: Indiana University Press, 1987), 74.

48. E. Ann Kaplan, "The Case of the Missing Mother: Maternal Issues in Vidor's
Stella Dallas," in *Feminism and Film*, ed. E. Ann Kaplan (Oxford: Oxford University Press, 2000), 466.

49. Sandy Flitterman-Lewis, *To Desire Differently: Feminism and the French Cinema*,
expanded ed. (New York: Columbia University Press, 1996), 188–214.

50. Flitterman-Lewis, *To Desire Differently*, 33.

51. Ginette Vincendeau, "Alice Guy," in *The Woman's Companion to International
Film*, ed. Annette Kuhn and Susannah Radstone (Berkeley: University of California Press, 1990), 184–85.

52. Fischer, *Cinematernity*. "Given this basic fear of imagined female powers, it is
not surprising to find the iconography of theatrical and cinematic magic
plagued by a rampant *hostility* toward the female subject—an animosity that
we might read as directed at motherhood. In fact, it is this very aggression that
makes the theory of masculine fear most plausible. If the male magician only
wished to 'play' with the female subject, why has he devised for her such a
chamber of horrors?" (46).

53. Fischer, *Cinematernity*, 47.

54. One-reel films were typically fifteen minutes in length.

55. Vincendeau, "Alice Guy," 185.

56. *Britannica Academic*, s.v. "Alice Guy-Blaché," accessed December 12, 2019, https://
academic-eb-com.library.sheridanc.on.ca/levels/collegiate/article/Alice-Guy
-Blach%C3%A9/106409.

57. Woolf, "Professions for Women," 237.

58. Collins, *Black Feminist Thought*, 131–32.

59. "Hoodoo is the indigenous, herbal, healing, and supernatural-controlling spiritual folk tradition of the African American in the United States. Hoodoo has endured numerous labels, among them black magic, witchcraft, devil's work, and superstition, though other less pejorative names include spirit work, root work, conjure, spiritualism, psychic work, or simply 'the work.'" Katrina Hazzard-Donald, *Mojo Workin': The Old African American Hoodoo System* (Urbana: University of Illinois Press, 2013), 4, http://search.ebscohost.com.library .sheridanc.on.ca/login.aspx?direct=true&db=nlebk&AN=569512&site=ehost -live&scope=site.

60. Hazzard-Donald, *Mojo Workin'*, 4.

61. "From the practical to the sacred, woven items were prized and often given as precious gifts or traded. These taonga (treasures) include *kākahu* (prized cloaks), piupiu (flax skirts), pākē or hīeke (rain capes), whāriki (floor mats), kete (woven baskets), and tūrapa or tukutuku (panels placed into the carved meeting house)." "Weaving People and Communities Together," Te Puia: The Centre For New Zealand's Maori Culture and Geothermal Wonders, December 12, 2019, https://tepuia.com/news/weaving-people-and-communities-together/.

62. Janis Cole and Holly Dale, *Calling the Shots: Profiles of Women Filmmakers* (Toronto, Ont., Canada: Quarry Press, 1993), 246.

63. Barbara Creed, "Horror and the Monstrous-Feminine: An Imaginary Abjection" (1986), in *The Dread of Difference: Gender and the Horror Film*, ed. Barry Keith Grant (Austin: University of Texas Press, 1996), 36.

64. "The loss of the daughter to the mother, mother to daughter, is the essential female tragedy. We acknowledge Lear (father-daughter split), Hamlet (son and mother), and Oedipus (son and mother) as great embodiments of the human tragedy, but there is no presently enduring recognition of the mother-daughter passion and rapture." Rich, *Of Woman Born*, 240.

65. E. Ann Kaplan, *Motherhood and Representation: The Mother in Popular Culture and Melodrama* (New York: Routledge, 1992), 48.

66. Quoted in Katie Pickles, "The Old and New on Parade: Mimesis, Queen Victoria, and Carnival Queens on Victoria Day in Interwar Victoria," in *Contact Zones: Aboriginal and Settler Women in Canada's Colonial Past*, ed. Katie Pickles and Myra Rutherdale (Vancouver, B.C., Canada: UBC Press, 2005), 277–78.

67. Joan Templeton, *Ibsen's Women* (Cambridge: Cambridge University Press, 2000), 229.

68. See Rose Lovell-Smith, "Anti-Housewives and Ogres' Housekeepers: The Roles of Bluebeard's Female Helper," *Folklore* 113, no. 2 (October 2002): 197–214.

69. The fairy godmother figure, whose roots are in the figures of the Fates, uses her magic to help or otherwise support a prince or princess in achieving his or her goals and desires. See John Clute and John Grant, eds., *The Encyclopedia of Fantasy* (New York: St. Martin's Griffin, 1997), 330.

70. In English folklore Queen Mab, queen of the fairies, is a mischievous but basically benevolent figure. Queen Mab's place was eventually taken over by Titania,

who bears some resemblance to Hera, the Greek goddess of marriage and of the life of women. *Encyclopedia Britannica*, s.v. "Hera," November 25, 2010, http://www.britannica.com/EBchecked/topic/262402/Hera.

71. Translated into the Maori language for *The Piano* by Selwyn Mum.

72. Tania Modleski and Maggie Greenwald, "Our Heroes Have Sometimes Been Cowgirls: An Interview with Maggie Greenwald," *Film Quarterly* 49, no. 2 (Winter 1995–1996): 9.

73. Joanna Hearne, *Native Recognition: Indigenous Cinema and the Western*, The SUNY Series: Horizons of Cinema (Albany: State University of New York Press, 2012).

74. Hearne, *Native Recognition*, 33.

3. FEMINIST SYMBOLIC FRONTIER LANDSCAPES

1. Tania Modleski and Maggie Greenwald, "Our Heroes Have Sometimes Been Cowgirls: An Interview with Maggie Greenwald," *Film Quarterly* 49, no. 2 (Winter 1995–1996): 7.

2. Anne McClintock, *Imperial Leather: Race, Gender and Sexuality in the Colonial Contest* (New York: Routledge, 1995), 30.

3. Elizabeth Furniss, "Pioneers, Progress, and the Myth of the Frontier: The Landscape of Public History in Rural British Columbia," *BC Studies*, no. 115/116 (Autumn/Winter 1997/1998): 8.

4. Raymond Williams, *Marxism and Literature* (Oxford: Oxford University Press, 1977), 115–16.

5. There is a long history of the Western's relationship with wide-angle big-screen cinematography. This goes back to one of the first films, *The Great Train Robbery*. During the advent of television, Hollywood developed wide-screen technologies in order to lure audiences back to the cinema. *How the West Was Won* is an epic Western that introduced audiences to technologies such as Cinerama. Westerns were particularly suited to wide-screen aesthetics because of the prevalence of landscapes and high levels of action.

6. Douglas Pye, "The Western (Genre and Movies)," in *Film Genre Reader*, ed. Barry Keith Grant (Austin: University of Texas Press, 1986), 148.

7. Pye, "The Western," 148.

8. Jim Kitses, *Horizons West: Anthony Mann, Budd Boetticher, Sam Peckinpah: Studies of Authorship Within the Western* (London: Thames and Hudson, 1969).

9. Frederick Jackson Turner, *The Significance of the Frontier in American History* (New York: Henry Holt, 1920), 9.

10. J. Hoberman, "How the West Was Lost," in *The Western Reader*, ed. Jim Kitses and Gregg Rickman (New York: Limelight Editions), 86.

11. Richard Slotkin, *Gunfighter Nation: The Myth of the Frontier in Twentieth-Century America* (Norman: University of Oklahoma Press, 1998), 3.

12. D. J. Mulvaney, "Thomas, William (1793–1867)," *Australian Dictionary of Biography*, National Centre of Biography, Australian National University, accessed December 13, 2019, http://adb.anu.edu.au/biography/thomas-william -2727/text3845.

13. Nathan Wolski, "All's Not Quiet on the Western Front—Rethinking Resistance and Frontiers in Aboriginal Historiography," in *Colonial Frontiers: Indigenous-European Encounters in Settler Societies*, ed. Lynette Russell (Manchester, U.K.: Manchester University Press, 2001), 217.

14. Wolski, "All's Not Quiet," 219.

15. Judith Kleinfeld, *The Frontier Romance: Environment, Culture, and Alaska Identity* (Fairbanks: University of Alaska Press, 2012), ix.

16. Turner, *The Significance of the Frontier*, 9.

17. Tompkins, *West of Everything: The Inner Life of Westerns* (New York: Oxford University Press, 1992), 44.

18. Kleinfeld, *Frontier Romance*, ix.

19. Britannica Academic, s.v. "Gullah," accessed December 12, 2019, https:// academic-eb-com.library.sheridanc.on.ca/levels/collegiate/article/Gullah /38490. "Gullah, also called Sea Island Creole or Geechee, English-based creole vernacular spoken primarily by African Americans living on the seaboard of South Carolina and Georgia (U.S.), who are also culturally identified as Gullahs or Geechees. Gullah developed in rice fields during the 18th century as a result of contact between colonial varieties of English and the languages of African slaves."

20. Julie Dash, Toni Cade Bambara, and bell hooks, *Daughters of the Dust: The Making of an African American Woman's Film* (New York: New Press, 1992), 31.

21. Caroline Brown, "The Representation of the Indigenous Other in *Daughters of the Dust* and *The Piano*," *NWSA Journal* 15, no. 1 (Spring 2003): 1–19. Brown argued that both *Daughters of the Dust* and Campion's *The Piano* silence indigenous characters "in order to permit non-native women the right to speak and affirm themselves and their embattled identities" (1).

22. Janis Cole and Holly Dale, *Calling the Shots: Profiles of Women Filmmakers* (Toronto, Ont., Canada: Quarry Press, 1993), 247.

23. "Snow confesses there was some initial hostility toward her on the part of the Metis because she, a white actress, has been cast in the film's central role, 'and I have to agree . . . I mean, I think if there was a native Indian who could have been cast, she should have been cast'" (80). L. Slack, "Driven Snow," *Star Week*, *The Toronto Star*, March 26, 1988, 80, http://search.proquest.com.ezproxy .torontopubliclibrary.ca/docview/1366921068?accountid=14369.

24. Green, "The Pocahontas Perplex: The Image of Indian Women in American Culture," *Massachusetts Review* 16, no. 4 (Autumn 1975): 703.

25. An angled perspective of the camera that suggests a specific character's point of view (e.g., an extreme high-angle shot suggesting a character's view from the

top of a building). Ira Konigsberg, *The Complete Film Dictionary*, 2nd ed. (Toronto: Penguin Reference, 1997), 400.

26. "Shallow space involves staging the action in relatively few planes of depth. It is the opposite of *deep space* [481]. Deep space is an arrangement of *mise-en-scène* elements so that there is considerable distance between the place closest to the camera and the one farthest away. Any or all of these planes may be in focus [478]." David Bordwell and Kristen Thompson, *Film Art: An Introduction*, 5th ed. (New York: McGraw-Hill, 1997).

27. Bill Nichols, *Representing Reality: Issues and Concepts in Documentary* (Bloomington: Indiana University Press, 1991), 225.

28. Woolf argued that "a woman must have money and a room of her own if she is to write fiction" (3). In the introduction to Virginia Woolf's *A Room of One's Own*, feminist literary theorist Michèle Barrett claims that the book (which is actually a published series of lectures) "is often regarded as the twentieth century's most important statement on the question of women and writing" (xix). Virginia Woolf, *A Room of One's Own/Three Guineas*, ed. Michèle Barrett (London: Penguin Books, 1993).

29. Turner, *The Significance of the Frontier*, 9.

30. "The first colonists saw in America an opportunity to regenerate their fortunes, their spirits, and the power of their church and nation; but the means to that regeneration ultimately became the means of violence, and the myth of regeneration through violence became the structuring metaphor of the American experience." Richard Slotkin, *Regeneration Through Violence: The Mythology of the American Frontier, 1600–1860* (Middletown, Conn.: Wesleyan University Press, 1973), 5.

31. Turner, *Significance of the Frontier*. "The United States lies like a huge page in the history of society. Line by line as we read this continental page from West to East we find the record of social evolution. It begins with the Indian and the hunter; it goes on to tell of the disintegration of savagery by the entrance of the trader, the pathfinder of civilization; we read the annals of the pastoral stage in ranch life; the exploitation of the soil by the raising of unrotated crops of corn and wheat in sparsely settled farming communities; the intensive culture of the denser farm settlement; and finally the manufacturing organization with city and factory system" (11).

32. *The Piano* is set during a time when there were a number of battles between Maori people and the settler government. "In the 1840s and 1860s conflict over sovereignty and land led to battles between government forces and some Māori tribes. The largest campaign was the clash between the Māori king and the Crown. Land confiscations to punish tribes that fought against the Crown have left a long legacy of grievances." Danny Keenan, "Story: New Zealand Wars," *Teara: The Encyclopedia of New Zealand*, accessed December 13, 2019, https://teara.govt.nz/en/new-zealand-wars.

33. Estella Tincknell, "The Time and the Place: Music and Costume and the 'Affect' of History in the New Zealand Films of Jane Campion," in *New Zealand Cinema: Interpreting the Past*, ed. Alistair Fox, Barry Keith Grant, and Hilary Radner (Bristol, U.K.: Intellect, 2011), 279–89.

34. Wolski, "All's Not Quiet," 219.

35. Pye, "The Western," 148.

36. Collins, *Black Feminist Thought: Knowledge, Consciousness, and the Politics of Empowerment*. 10th anniversary ed. (New York: Routledge, 2000), 140.

37. McClintock, *Imperial Leather*, 30.

CONCLUSION

1. Pascale Lamche, "Interview with Merata Mita," *Framework* 25 (Autumn 1984): 4.

2. Sue Mathews, *35mm Dreams: Conversations with Five Directors About the Australian Film Revival* (Ringwood, Vic., Australia: Penguin Books), 160–61.

3. Lamche, "Interview with Merata Mita," 4.

4. Jane Tompkins, *West of Everything: The Inner Life of Westerns* (New York: Oxford University Press, 1992), 43.

5. Catherine Summerhayes, "Haunting Secrets: Tracey Moffatt's *Bedevil*," *Film Quarterly* 58, no. 1 (Fall 2004): 14–24. "One (apocryphal?) story of *Bedevil*'s first screening tells how a famous figure in the Australian film industry argued quite publicly and vehemently with her husband, an equally famous film critic, long into the opening night party and over the next couple of days. Their argument proceeded along these lines: 'That was positively the worst film I have ever seen.'—'Darling, don't be silly, it's a work of art . . . It should be in an art gallery.' This anecdote indicates the deep disquiet that people still feel when trying to understand any manifestation of Moffatt's artistic practice—a practice that continues to stretch the boundaries of form and genre" (14).

6. Many (male) international filmmakers, such as Ingmar Bergman, Robert Altman, David Lynch, Quentin Tarantino, Lars von Trier, Alejandro González Iñárritu, and Charlie Kaufman, all deemed important film auteurs who have made significant contributions to world cinema, have worked with nonlinear or highly stylized storytelling structures.

7. Claire Johnston, "Women's Cinema as Counter-Cinema" (1973), in *Feminism & Film*, ed. E. Ann Kaplan (Oxford: Oxford University Press, 2001), 23.

8. See Kathleen Anne McHugh, "*The Piano*: Surrealism, Melodrama, and Mimetic Infection," in *Jane Campion* (Urbana: University of Illinois Press, 2007), 79–92; Hilary Radner, "'In Extremis': Jane Campion and the Woman's Film," in *Jane Campion: Cinema, Nation, Identity*, ed. Hilary Radner, Alistair Fox, and Irène Bessière (Detroit, Mich.: Wayne State University Press, 2009), 3–24; Ann Hardy, "Jane Campion and the Moral Occult," in Radner, Fox, and Bessière, *Jane Campion*, 251–76; Sue Gillett, "'The Piano Is Mine. It's *Mine*.' My (Free Association

with) Jane Campion, or, the Child in the Spectator," in Radner, Fox, and Bessière, *Jane Campion*, 233–48.

9. Ruth Barcan and Madeleine Fogarty, "Performing *The Piano*," in *Piano Lessons: Approaches to* The Piano, ed. Felicity Coombs and Suzanne Gemmell (London: Libbey, 1999), 3–18. See also Lisa Sarmas, "What Rape Is," *Arena Magazine*, no. 8 (1993–1994): 14. "In August, 1993, the Coalition Against Sexual Violence Propaganda newsletter carried a two paragraph review of *The Piano*, with the first paragraph condemning it as sexist and the second declaring it to be racist. The writer lamented what she saw as the film's shift away from a depiction of two strong women towards a focus on aggressive and coercive male sexuality" (7).

10. Harriet Margolis, ed., *Jane Campion's* The Piano (Cambridge: Cambridge University Press, 2000). Margolis summarizes the debate around Campion's deployment and depiction of the Maori in her introduction.

11. Sandra M. Gilbert and Susan Gubar, *The Madwoman in the Attic: The Woman Writer and the Nineteenth-Century Imagination* (New Haven, Conn.: Yale University Press, 1979).

APPENDIX

1. Jill Roe, "Franklin, Stella Maria Sarah Miles," Australian Dictionary of Biography, accessed December 8, 2019, http://adb.anu.edu.au/biography/franklin -stella-maria-sarah-miles-6235.

SELECTED BIBLIOGRAPHY

Armatage, Kay, Kass Banning, Brenda Longfellow, and Janine Marchessault, eds. *Gendering the Nation: Canadian Women's Cinema.* Toronto, Ont., Canada: University of Toronto Press, 1999.

Attwood, Feona. "Weird Lullaby: Jane Campion's *The Piano.*" *Feminist Review* 58, no. 1 (1998): 85–101.

Bacchilega, Cristina. *Postmodern Fairy Tales: Gender and Narrative Strategies.* Philadelphia: University of Pennsylvania Press, 2011.

Backstein, Karen. *"The Ballad of Little Jo."* *Cinéaste* 20, no. 2 (1993): 45–47.

——. "The Cinematic Jazz of Julie Dash." *Cinéaste* 19, no. 4 (1993): 88.

Barcan, Ruth, and Madeleine Fogarty. "Performing *The Piano.*" In *Piano Lessons: Approaches to* The Piano, ed. Felicity Coombs and Suzanne Gemmell, 3–18. London: Libbey, 1999.

Barclay, Barry. "Celebrating the Fourth Cinema." *Illusions: New Zealand Moving Images and Performing Arts Criticism*, no. 35 (July 2003): 7–11.

Barkley Brown, Elsa. "'What Has Happened Here?' The Politics of Difference in Women's History and Feminist Politics." *Feminist Studies* 18, no. 2 (Summer 1992): 295–312.

Bentley, Greg. "Mothers, Daughters, and (Absent) Fathers in Jane Campion's *The Piano.*" *Literature/Film Quarterly* 30, no. 1 (2002): 46–58.

Bertrand, Ina. "'Woman's Voice': The Autobiographical Form in Three Australian Filmed Novels." *Literature/Film Quarterly* 21, no. 2 (1993): 130–38.

Bessière, Jean. "Jane Campion and the International Theme: From *The Portrait of a Lady* to *An Angel at My Table.*" In *Jane Campion: Cinema, Nation, Identity*, ed. Hilary Radner, Alistair Fox, and Irène Bessière, 157–73. Detroit, Mich.: Wayne State University Press, 2009.

Bihlmeyer, Jaime. "Bluebeard in Jane Campion's *The Piano*: A Case Study in Intertextuality as an Enunciation of Femininity in Mainstream Movies." *International Journal of the Humanities* 8, no. 7 (2010): 183–90.

——. "The (Un)Speakable Femininity in Mainstream Movies: Jane Campion's *The Piano*." *Cinema Journal* 44, no. 2 (Winter 2005): 68–88.

Blonski, Annette, Barbara Creed, and Freda Freiberg, eds. *Don't Shoot Darling! Women's Independent Filmmaking in Australia*. Richmond, S.A., Australia: Greenhouse, 1987.

Bobo, Jacqueline, ed. *Black Women Film and Video Artists*. New York: Routledge, 1998.

Bovenschen, Silvia, and Beth Weckmueller. "Is There a Feminine Aesthetic?" *New German Critique*, no. 10 (Winter 1977): 111–37.

Bratton, Jacky, Jim Cook, and Christine Gledhill, eds. *Melodrama: Stage, Picture, Screen*. London: British Film Institute, 1994.

Britos, Peter. "A Conversation with Merata Mita." *Spectator* 23, no. 1 (Spring 2003): 53–62.

Brooks, Peter. "The Melodramatic Imagination." In *Imitations of Life: A Reader on Film and Television Melodrama*, ed. Marcia Landy, 50–67. Detroit, Mich.: Wayne State University Press, 1991.

——. *The Melodramatic Imagination: Balzac, Henry James, Melodrama, and the Mode of Excess*. New Haven, Conn.: Yale University Press, 1976.

Brower, Sue. "'They'd Kill Us if They Knew': Transgression and the Western." *Journal of Film and Video* 62, no. 4 (Winter 2010): 47–57.

Brown, Caroline. "The Representation of the Indigenous Other in *Daughters of the Dust* and *The Piano*." *NWSA Journal* 15, no. 1 (Spring 2003): 1–19.

Brownlie, Robin Jarvis. "Intimate Surveillance: Indian Affairs, Colonization, and the Regulation of Aboriginal Women's Sexuality." In *Contact Zones: Aboriginal and Settler Women in Canada's Colonial Past*, ed. Katie Pickles and Myra Rutherdale, 160–78. Vancouver, B.C., Canada: UBC Press, 2005.

Buscombe, Edward, and Roberta E. Pearson, eds. *Back in the Saddle Again: New Essays on the Western*. London: British Film Institute, 1998.

Butler, Alison. *Women's Cinema: The Contested Screen*. London: Wallflower Press, 2002.

Butler, Judith. "Performative Acts and Gender Constitution: An Essay in Phenomenology and Feminist Theory" (1988). In *The Feminism and Visual Culture Reader*, ed. Amelia Jones, 392–401. New York: Routledge, 2003.

Cameron, Ian, and Douglas Pye, eds. *The Book of Westerns*. New York: Continuum, 1996.

Caputo, Raffaele, and Geoff Burton. *Second Take: Australian Filmmakers Talk*. St. Leonards, N.S.W., Australia: Allen and Unwin, 1999.

Carter, Sarah, Lesley Erickson, and Patricia Roome. Introduction to *Unsettled Pasts: Reconceiving the West Through Women's History*, ed. Sarah Carter, Lesley Erickson, and Patricia Roome, 1–13. Calgary, Alta., Canada: University of Calgary Press, 2005.

Chen, Chiung Hwang. "Feminization of Asian (American) Men in the U.S. Mass Media: An Analysis of *The Ballad of Little Jo.*" *Journal of Communication Inquiry* 20, no. 2 (1996): 57–71.

Cheshire, Ellen. *Jane Campion.* Harpenden, U.K.: Pocket Essentials, 2000.

Chodorow, Nancy. *The Reproduction of Mothering: Psychoanalysis and the Sociology of Gender.* Berkeley: University of California Press, 1978.

Chu, Janet H. "Film and Multiculturalism: Erasing Race in Nancy Kelly's *Thousand Pieces of Gold.*" In *Changing Representations of Minorities, East and West: Selected Essays,* ed. Larry E. Smith and John Rieder, 75–97. Honolulu: University of Hawaii Press, 1996.

Chumo, Peter N. II. "Keys to the Imagination: Jane Campion's *The Piano.*" *Literature/Film Quarterly* 25, no. 3 (1997): 173–77.

Cixous, Hélène. "The Laugh of the Medusa." Trans. Keith Cohen and Paula Cohen. *Signs: Journal of Women and Culture* 1, no. 4 (Summer 1976): 875–93.

Clover, Carol J. "Her Body, Himself: Gender in the Slasher Film" (1987). In *The Dread of Difference: Gender and the Horror Film,* ed. Barry Keith Grant, 66–113. Austin: University of Texas Press, 1996.

Cole, Janis, and Holly Dale. *Calling the Shots: Profiles of Women Filmmakers.* Toronto, Ont., Canada: Quarry Press, 1993.

Collins, Patricia Hill. *Black Feminist Thought: Knowledge, Consciousness, and the Politics of Empowerment.* 10th anniversary ed. New York: Routledge, 2000.

Columpar, Corinn. "At the Limits of Visual Representation: Tracey Moffatt's Still and Moving Images." In *There She Goes: Feminist Filmmaking and Beyond,* ed. Corinn Columpar and Sophie Mayer, 146–59. Detroit, Mich.: Wayne State University Press, 2009.

Cook, Pam. "No Fixed Address: The Women's Picture from *Outrage* to *Blue Steel,*" in *Gender Meets Genre in Postwar Cinemas,* ed. Christine Gledhill, 29–40. Champaign: University of Illinois Press, 2012.

——. "Women and the Western" (1988). In *Screening the Past: Memory and Nostalgia in Cinema.* London: Routledge, 2005.

Coombs, Felicity, and Suzanne Gemmell, eds. *Piano Lessons: Approaches to* The Piano. London: Libbey, 1999.

Cooper, Annabel. "On Viewing Jane Campion as an Antipodean." In *Jane Campion: Cinema, Nation, Identity,* ed. Hilary Radner, Alistair Fox, and Irène Bessière, 279–304. Detroit, Mich.: Wayne State University Press, 2009.

Coyne, Michael. *The Crowded Prairie: American National Identity in the Hollywood Western.* London: Tauris, 1998.

Creed, Barbara. "Horror and the Monstrous-Feminine: An Imaginary Abjection" (1986). In *The Dread of Difference: Gender and the Horror Film,* ed. Barry Keith Grant, 35–65. Austin: University of Texas Press, 1996.

——. "Women's Cinema in Australia." In *Australia for Women: Travel and Culture,* ed. Susan Hawthorne and Renate Klein, 185–87. Melbourne, Vic., Australia: Spinifex Press, 1994.

Crofts, Stephen. "Foreign Tunes? Gender and Nationality in Four Countries' Reception of *The Piano*." In *Jane Campion's* The Piano, ed. Harriet Margolis, 135–162. Cambridge: Cambridge University Press, 2000.

Dapkus, Jeanne R. "Sloughing Off the Burdens: Ada's and Isabel's Parallel/Antithetical Quests for Self-Actualization in Jane Campion's Film *The Piano* and Henry James's Novel *The Portrait of a Lady*." *Literature/Film Quarterly* 25, no. 3 (1997): 177–87.

Dash, Julie, Toni Cade Bambara, and bell hooks. *Daughters of the Dust: The Making of an African American Woman's Film*. New York: New Press, 1992.

Davis, Natalie Zemon. *The Return of Martin Guerre*. Cambridge, Mass.: Harvard University Press, 1983.

De Lauretis, Teresa. "Rethinking Women's Cinema: Aesthetics and Feminist Theory." In *Technologies of Gender: Essays on Theory, Film, and Fiction*, 127–46. Bloomington: Indiana University Press, 1987.

Dinnerstein, Dorothy. *The Mermaid and the Minotaur: Sexual Arrangements and Human Malaise*. New York: Other Press, 1999.

Doane, Mary Ann. *The Desire to Desire: The Woman's Film of the 1940s*. Indianapolis: Indiana University Press, 1987.

Dowell, Kristen. "Indigenous Media Gone Global: Strengthening Indigenous Identity On- and Offscreen at the First Nations/First Features Film Showcase." *American Anthropologist* 108, no. 2 (June 2006): 376–84.

Dua, Enakshi. "Canadian Anti-Racist Feminist Thought: Scratching the Surface of Racism." In *Scratching the Surface: Canadian Anti-racist Feminist Thought*, ed. Enakshi Dua and Angela Robertson, 7–34. Toronto, Ont., Canada: Women's Press, 1999.

Dworkin, Andrea. *Pornography: Men Possessing Women*. New York: Plume, 1989.

Elsaesser, Thomas. "Tales of Sound and Fury: Observations on the Family Melodrama." In *Imitations of Life: A Reader on Film and Television Melodrama*, ed. Marcia Landy, 68–91. Detroit, Mich.: Wayne State University Press, 1991.

Emberley, Julia V. "Gender, History and Imperialism: Anne Wheeler's *Loyalties*." In *Feminism/Postmodernism/Development*, ed. Marianne H. Marchand and Jane L. Parpart, 94–109. London: Routledge, 1995.

Feng, Peter X. *Identities in Motion: Asian American Film and Video*. Durham, N.C.: Duke University Press, 2002.

Firestone, Shulamith. *The Dialectic of Sex: The Case for Feminist Revolution*. New York: Farrar, Straus and Giroux, 2003.

Fischer, Lucy. *Cinematernity: Film, Motherhood, Genre*. Princeton, N.J.: Princeton University Press, 1996.

Flitterman-Lewis, Sandy. *To Desire Differently: Feminism and the French Cinema*. Expanded ed. New York: Columbia University Press, 1996.

Foster, Gwendolyn Audrey. *Women Filmmakers of the African and Asian Diaspora: Decolonizing the Gaze, Locating Subjectivity*. Carbondale: Southern Illinois University Press, 1997.

Fox, Alistair. *Jane Campion: Authorship and Personal Cinema*. Bloomington: Indiana University Press, 2011.

——. "Puritanism and the Erotics of Transgression: The New Zealand Influence in Jane Campion's Thematic Imaginary." In *Jane Campion: Cinema, Nation, Identity*, ed. Hilary Radner, Alistair Fox, and Irène Bessière, 103–22. Detroit, Mich.: Wayne State University Press, 2009.

Francke, Lizzie. "An Interview with Jane Campion." In *Jane Campion*, ed. Kathleen Anne McHugh, 147–62. Urbana: University of Illinois Press, 2007.

——. "What Are You Girls Going to Do?" *Sight and Sound* 5, no. 4 (1995): 28–29.

Frayling, Christopher. *Spaghetti Westerns: Cowboys and Europeans from Karl May to Sergio Leone*. London: Tauris, 1998.

French, Lisa, ed. *Womenvision: Women and the Moving Image in Australia*. Melbourne, Vic., Australia: Damned, 2003.

Gaines, Jane. "Fire and Desire: Race, Melodrama and Oscar Micheaux." In *Melodrama: Stage, Picture, Screen*, ed. Jacky Bratton, Jim Cook, and Christine Gledhill, 231–45. London: British Film Institute, 1994.

——. "White Privilege and Looking Relations: Race and Gender in Feminist Film Theory" (1988). In *Feminism and Film*, ed. E. Ann Kaplan, 336–55. Oxford: Oxford University Press, 2000.

Gilbert, Sandra M., and Susan Gubar. *The Madwoman in the Attic: The Woman Writer and the Nineteenth-Century Imagination*. New Haven, Conn.: Yale University Press, 1979.

Gillett, Sue. "Lips and Fingers: Jane Campion's *The Piano*." *Screen* 36, no. 3 (Autumn 1995): 286–87.

——. "'The Piano Is Mine. It's *Mine*.' My (Free Association with) Jane Campion, or, the Child in the Spectator." In *Jane Campion: Cinema, Nation, Identity*, ed. Hilary Radner, Alistair Fox, and Irène Bessière, 233–48. Detroit, Mich.: Wayne State University Press, 2009.

——. "Views from Beyond the Mirror: The Films of Jane Campion." *Australian Screen Education*, no. 36 (2004): 177. https://link-gale-com.library.sheridanc.on.ca/apps/doc/A135216703/AONE?u=ko_acd_shc&sid=AONE&xid=eeaf8671.

Ginsburg, Faye. "Breaking the Law with Two Laws: Reflections on a Paradigm Shift." *Studies in Documentary Film* 2, no. 2 (2008): 169–74.

Gittings, Christopher E. *Canadian National Cinema: Ideology, Difference and Representation*. London: Routledge, 2002.

Goldwon, Annie. "Piano Recital." *Screen* 38, no. 3 (Autumn 1997): 275–81.

Gordon, Suzy. "'I Clipped Your Wing, That's All': Auto-Eroticism and the Female Spectator in *The Piano* Debate." *Screen* 37, no. 2 (Summer 1996): 193–205.

Grant, Barry Keith, ed. *The Dread of Difference: Gender and the Horror Film*. Austin: University of Texas Press, 1996.

——. Introduction to *Film Genre Reader*, ed. Barry Keith Grant, xi–xvi. Austin: University of Texas Press, 1996.

Green, Rayna. "The Pocahontas Perplex: The Image of Indian Women in American Culture." *Massachusetts Review* 16, no. 4 (Autumn 1975): 698–714.

Grey, Sam. "Decolonising Feminism: Aboriginal Women and the Global 'Sister-hood.'" *Enweyin: The Ways We Speak* 8 (January 2004): 9–22.

Hammonds, Evelynn M. "Toward a Genealogy of Black Female Sexuality: The Problematic of Silence." In *The Feminist Philosophy Reader*, ed. Alison Bailey and Chris Cuomo, 249–60. Boston: McGraw-Hill, 2008.

Harding, Bruce. "'The Donations of History': *Mauri* and the Transfigured 'Mauri Gaze': Towards a Bi-national Cinema." In *New Zealand Cinema: Interpreting the Past*, ed. Alistair Fox, Barry Keith Grant, and Hilary Radner, 219–37. Bristol, U.K.: Intellect, 2011.

Hardy, Ann. "Jane Campion and the Moral Occult." In *Jane Campion: Cinema, Nation, Identity*, ed. Hilary Radner, Alistair Fox, and Irène Bessière, 251–76. Detroit, Mich.: Wayne State University Press, 2009.

Haskell, Molly. *From Reverence to Rape: The Treatment of Women in the Movies*. Baltimore, Md.: Penguin Books, 1974.

Hearne, Joanna. *Native Recognition: Indigenous Cinema and the Western*. The SUNY Series: Horizons of Cinema. Albany: State University of New York Press, 2012.

Higginbotham, Evelyn Brooks. "African-American Women's History and the Meta-language of Race." *Signs* 17, no. 2 (Winter 1992): 251–74.

——. *Righteous Discontent: The Women's Movement in the Black Baptist Church, 1880–1920*. Cambridge, Mass.: Harvard University Press, 1993.

Hoeveler, Diane Long. "Silence, Sex, and Feminism: An Examination of *The Piano*'s Unacknowledged Sources." *Literature/Film Quarterly* 26, no. 2 (1998): 109–16.

Hollows, Joanne. *Feminism, Femininity and Popular Culture*. Manchester: Manchester University Press, 2000.

hooks, bell. *Ain't I a Woman: Black Women and Feminism*. Boston: South End Press, 1981.

——. *Black Looks: Race and Representation*. Boston: South End Press, 1992.

Irigaray, Luce. "This Sex Which Is Not One" (1977). In *The Second Wave: A Reader in Feminist Theory*, ed. Linda Nicholson, 323–30. New York: Routledge, 1997.

Jackson, Beth. "Self-Inscription in the Work of Doppio Teatro, Tracey Moffatt and Linda Dement: An Interpretation of Feminist Use of Technology According to Deleuze's Writings on Masochism." *Continuum* 8, no. 1 (1994): 226–39.

Jacobs, Carol. "Playing Jane Campion's *Piano*: Politically." *MLN* 109, no. 5 (December 1994): 757–85.

James-Guerrero, M. A., "Native Women, Civil Rights, and Sovereignty." In *Encyclopedia of Feminist Theories*, ed. Lorraine Code, 360. London: Routledge, 2000.

Johnston, Claire. "Dorothy Arzner: Critical Strategies" (1975). In *Feminism and Film Theory*, ed. Constance Penley, 36–45. New York: Routledge, 1988.

——. "Women's Cinema as Counter-Cinema" (1973). In *Feminism and Film*, ed. E. Ann Kaplan, 22–33. Oxford: Oxford University Press, 2000.

Jolly, Margaret. "Looking Back? Gender, Sexuality, and Race in *The Piano*." *Australian Feminist Studies* 24, no. 59 (March 2009): 99–121.

Kang, Laura Hyun-Yi. *Compositional Subjects: Enfiguring Asian/American Women*. Durham, N.C.: Duke University Press, 2002.

——. "The Desiring of Asian Female Bodies: Interracial Romance and Cinematic Subjection." *Visual Anthropology Review* 9, no. 1 (March 1993): 5–21.

Kaplan, E. Ann. "The Case of the Missing Mother: Maternal Issues in Vidor's *Stella Dallas*" (1986). In *Feminism and Film*, ed. E. Ann Kaplan, 466–78. Oxford: Oxford University Press, 2000.

——. "Women, Film, Resistance: Changing Paradigms." In *Women Filmmakers: Refocusing*, ed. Jacqueline Levitin, Judith Plessis, and Valerie Raoul, 15–28. New York: Routledge, 2003.

Kilpatrick, Jacquelyn. *Celluloid Indians: Native Americans and Film*. Lincoln: University of Nebraska Press, 1999.

King, Wilma. "'Suffer with Them Till Death': Slave Women and Their Children in Nineteenth-Century America." In *More Than Chattel: Black Women and Slavery in the Americas*, ed. David Barry Gaspar and Darlene Clark Hine, 147–68. Bloomington: Indiana University Press, 1996.

Kitses, Jim. *Horizons West: Anthony Mann, Budd Boetticher, Sam Peckinpah: Studies of Authorship Within the Western*. London: Thames and Hudson, 1969.

Kitses, Jim, and Gregg Rickman, eds. *The Western Reader*. New York: Limelight, 1998.

Kleinfeld, Judith. *The Frontier Romance: Environment, Culture, and Alaska Identity*. Fairbanks: University of Alaska Press, 2012.

Kleinhans, Chuck. "Realist Melodrama and the African-American Family: Billy Woodbury's *Bless Their Little Hearts*." In *Melodrama: Stage, Picture, Screen*, ed. Jacky Bratton, Jim Cook, and Christine Gledhill, 157–66. London: British Film Institute, 1994.

Knight, Christine. "Ada's Piano Playing in Jane Campion's *The Piano*: Genteel Accomplishment or Romantic Self-Expression?" *Australian Feminist Studies* 21, no. 49 (March 2006): 23–34.

Kolodny, Annette. *The Lay of the Land: Metaphor as Experience and History in American Life and Letters*. Chapel Hill: University of North Carolina Press, 1975.

Kristeva, Julia. "Approaching Abjection" (1982). In *The Feminism and Visual Culture Reader*, ed. Amelia Jones, 389–92. New York: Routledge, 2003.

——. *Desire in Language: A Semiotic Approach to Literature and Art*. Ed. Leon S. Roudiez. Trans. Thomas Gora, Alice Jardine, and Leon S. Roudiez. New York: Columbia University Press, 1980.

Kuhn, Annette. "Women's Genres" (1984). In *Feminism and Film*, ed. E. Ann Kaplan, 447–48. Oxford: Oxford University Press, 2000.

——. *Women's Pictures: Feminism and Cinema*. London: Verso, 1993.

Lake, Marilyn. "Australian Frontier Feminism and the Marauding White Man." In *Gender and Imperialism*, ed. Claire Midgley, 123–36. Manchester, U.K.: Manchester University Press, 1998.

Lamche, Pascale. "Interview with Merata Mita." *Framework* 25 (Autumn 1984): 2–11.

Landy, Marcia, ed. *Imitations of Life: A Reader on Film and Television Melodrama*. Detroit, Mich.: Wayne State University Press, 1991.

Lane, Christina. *Feminist Hollywood: From* Born in Flames *to* Point Break. Detroit, Mich.: Wayne State University Press, 2000.

Lauzen, Martha M. "The Celluloid Ceiling: Behind-the-Scenes Employment of Women on the Top 100, 250, and 500 Films of 2018." San Diego, Calif.: San Diego State University, Center for the Study of Women in Television and Film, 2019. Accessed December 9, 2019. https://womenintvfilm.sdsu.edu/wp-content/uploads/2019/01/2018_Celluloid_Ceiling_Report.pdf.

Lazarre, Jane. *The Mother Knot.* Durham, N.C.: Duke University Press, 1997.

Leotta, Alfio. "Framing the Beach: A Tourist Reading of *The Piano.*" *Studies in Australasian Cinema* 3, no. 3 (2009): 229–38.

Levitin, Jacqueline, Judith Plessis, and Valerie Raoul, eds. *Women Filmmakers: Refocusing.* New York: Routledge, 2003.

Lokke, Kari E. "'Bluebeard' and 'The Bloody Chamber': The Grotesque of Self-Parody and Self-Assertion." *Frontiers: A Journal of Women Studies* 10, no. 1 (1988): 7–12.

Longfellow, Brenda. "Gender, Landscape, and Colonial Allegories in *The Far Shore*, *Loyalties*, and *Mouvements du désir.*" In *Gendering the Nation: Canadian Women's Cinema*, ed. Kay Armatage, Kass Banning, Brenda Longfellow, and Janine Marchessault, 165–82. Toronto, Ont., Canada: University of Toronto Press, 1999.

Lord, Susan. "Canadian Gothic: Multiculturalism, Indigeneity, and Gender in Prairie Cinema." In *Canadian Cultural Poesis: Essays on Canadian Culture*, ed. Garry Sherbert, Annie Gérin, and Sheila Petty, 399–420. Waterloo, Ont., Canada: Wilfrid Laurier University Press, 2006.

——. "States of Emergency in the Films of Anne Wheeler." In *North of Everything: English-Canadian Cinema Since 1980*, ed. William Beard and Jerry White, 312–26. Edmonton, Alta, Canada: University of Alberta Press, 2002.

Lusted, David. "Social Class and the Western as Male Melodrama." In *The Book of Westerns*, ed. Ian Cameron and Douglas Pye, 65–66. New York: Continuum, 1996.

Luxton, Meg. *More Than a Labour of Love: Three Generations of Women's Work in the Home.* Toronto, Ont., Canada: Women's Press, 1980.

Lyotard, Jean-François. *The Postmodern Condition.* Trans. Geoff Bennington and Brian Massumi. Minneapolis: University of Minnesota Press, 1984.

Mabee, Carleton, and Susan Mabee Newhouse. *Sojourner Truth: Slave, Prophet, Legend.* New York: New York University Press, 1995.

Mackinnon, Catherine A. "Sexuality." In *The Feminist Philosophy Reader*, ed. Alison Bailey and Chris Cuomo, 204–21. Boston: McGraw-Hill, 2008.

Margolis, Harriet, ed. *Jane Campion's* The Piano. Cambridge: Cambridge University Press, 2000.

Margoroni, Maria. "Jane Campion's Selling of the Mother/Land: Restaging the Crisis of the Postcolonial Subject." *Camera Obscura* 18, no. 2 (2003): 93–123.

Marsh, Selina Tusitala. "Migrating Feminisms: Maligned Overstayer or Model Citizen?" *Women's Studies International Forum* 21, no. 6 (1998): 665–80.

Martens, Emiel. "Maori on the Silver Screen: The Evolution of Indigenous Feature Filmmaking in Aotearoa/New Zealand." *International Journal of Critical Indigenous Studies* 5, no. 1 (2012): 2–30.

Marubbio, M. Elise. *Killing the Indian Maiden: Images of Native American Women in Film*. Lexington: University Press of Kentucky, 2006.

Mathews, Sue. *35mm Dreams: Conversations with Five Directors About the Australian Film Revival*. Ringwood, Vic., Australia: Penguin Books, 1984.

Mayer, Sophie. Political Animals: The New Feminist Cinema. London: Tauris, 2015.

Mayne, Judith. "Lesbian Looks: Dorothy Arzner and Female Authorship" (1991). In *Feminism and Film*, ed. E. Ann Kaplan, 159–80. Oxford: Oxford University Press, 2000.

——. *The Woman at the Keyhole: Feminism and Women's Cinema*. Bloomington: Indiana University Press, 1990.

McClintock, Anne. *Imperial Leather: Race, Gender, and Sexuality in the Colonial Contest*. New York: Routledge, 1995.

McHugh, Kathleen Anne. *Jane Campion*. Urbana: University of Illinois Press, 2007.

McPherson, Kathryn. "Was the 'Frontier' Good for Women? Historical Approaches to Women and Agricultural Settlement in the Prairie West, 1870–1925." *Atlantis* 25, no. 1 (Fall/Winter 2000): 75–86.

Mellencamp, Patricia. "An Empirical Avant-Garde: Laleen Jayamanne and Tracey Moffatt." In *Fugitive Images: From Photography to Video*, ed. Patrice Petro, 173–95. Bloomington: Indiana University Press, 1995.

Mikula, Maja. "Narrative." In *Key Concepts in Cultural Studies*, 133–34. New York: Palgrave Macmillan, 2008.

Minh-ha, Trinh T. "Difference: 'A Special Third World Woman Issue'" (1989). In *The Feminism and Visual Culture Reader*, ed. Amelia Jones, 151–73. New York: Routledge, 2003.

Minh-ha, Trinh T., and Nancy N. Chen. "Speaking Nearby." In *Feminism and Film*, ed. E. Ann Kaplan, 317–35. Oxford: Oxford University Press, 2000.

Modleski, Tania. *Old Wives' Tales and Other Women's Stories*. New York: New York University Press, 1998.

——. "A Woman's Gotta Do . . . What a Man's Gotta Do? Cross-Dressing in the Western." *Signs: Journal of Women in Culture and Society* 22, no. 3 (Spring 1997): 519–44.

Modleski, Tania, and Maggie Greenwald. "Our Heroes Have Sometimes Been Cowgirls: An Interview with Maggie Greenwald." *Film Quarterly* 49, no. 2 (Winter 1995–1996): 2–11.

Mohanty, Chandra Talpade. "Under Western Eyes: Feminist Scholarship and Colonial Discourses" (1991) and "Cartographies of Struggle: Third World Women and the Politics of Feminism." In *Feminism Without Borders: Decolonizing Theory, Practicing Solidarity*, 17–42. Durham, N.C.: Duke University Press, 2003.

Moine, Raphaëlle. "From Antipodean Cinema to International Art Cinema." In *Jane Campion: Cinema, Nation, Identity*, ed. Hilary Radner, Alistair Fox, and Irène Bessière, 189–204. Detroit, Mich.: Wayne State University Press, 2009.

Moreton-Robinson, Aileen. "Tiddas Speakin' Strong: Indigenous Women's Self-Preservation Within White Australian Feminism." In *The Feminist Philosophy Reader*, ed. Alison Bailey and Chris Cuomo, 355–72. Boston: McGraw-Hill, 2008.

Morgan, Robin. "Theory and Practice: Pornography and Rape." In *Going Too Far: The Personal Chronicle of a Feminist*. New York: Random House, 1977.

Muir, Kate. "Jane Campion: 'Capitalism is such a macho force. I felt run over.'" *Guardian*, May 20, 2018. https://www.theguardian.com/film/2018/may/20/jane-campion-unconventional-film-maker-macho-force.

Mulvey, Laura. "Visual Pleasure and Narrative Cinema" (1975). In *Feminism and Film*, ed. E. Ann Kaplan, 34–47. Oxford: Oxford University Press, 2000.

Natharius, David, and Bethami A. Dobkin. "Feminist Visions of Transformation in *The Ballad of Little Jo, The Piano*, and *Orlando*." *Women and Language* 25, no. 1 (Spring 2002): 9–17.

Neill, Anna. "A Land Without a Past: Dreamtime and Nation in *The Piano*." In *Piano Lessons: Approaches to* The Piano, ed. Felicity Coombs and Suzanne Gemmell, 136–47. London: Libbey, 1999.

Nichols, Bill. *Representing Reality: Issues and Concepts in Documentary*. Bloomington: Indiana University Press, 1991.

Nochlin, Linda. "Why Have There Been No Great Women Artists?" In *Women, Art, and Power and Other Essays*, 147–58. Boulder, Colo.: Westview Press, 1988.

Oakley, Ann. *Sex, Gender, and Society*. London: Gower, 1985.

Oshana, Maryann. "Native American Women in Westerns: Reality and Myth." *Frontiers: A Journal of Women Studies* 6, no. 3 (Autumn 1981): 46–50.

Phillips, Patrick. "Genre, Star and Auteur." In *An Introduction to Film Studies*, 2nd ed., ed. Jill Nelmes, 162–208. London: Routledge, 1999.

Pickles, Katie. "The Old and New on Parade: Mimesis, Queen Victoria, and Carnival Queens on Victoria Day in Interwar Victoria." In *Contact Zones: Aboriginal and Settler Women in Canada's Colonial Past*, ed. Katie Pickles and Myra Rutherdale, 277–78. Vancouver, B.C., Canada: UBC Press, 2005.

Pihama, Leonie. "Are Films Dangerous? A Māori Woman's Perspective on *The Piano*." *Hecate: Special Aotearoa/New Zealand Issue* 20, no. 2 (1994): 239–42.

Pipes McAdoo, Harriett. "African-American Families." In *Encyclopedia of Feminist Theories*, ed. Lorraine Code, 9. London: Routledge, 2000.

Polan, Dana B. *Jane Campion*. London: British Film Institute, 2001.

Pye, Douglas. "Introduction: Criticism and the Western." In *The Book of Westerns*, ed. Ian Cameron and Douglas Pye, 9–21. New York: Continuum, 1996.

——. "The Western (Genre and Movies)." In *Film Genre Reader*, ed. Barry Keith Grant, 143–58. Austin: University of Texas Press, 1986.

Radner, Hilary. "'In Extremis': Jane Campion and the Woman's Film." In *Jane Campion: Cinema, Nation, Identity*, ed. Hilary Radner, Alistair Fox, and Irène Bessière, 3–24. Detroit, Mich.: Wayne State University Press, 2009.

——. "Screening Women's Histories: Jane Campion and the New Zealand Heritage Film, from the Biopic to the Female Gothic." In *New Zealand Cinema: Interpreting the Past*, ed. Alistair Fox, Barry Keith Grant, and Hilary Radner, 259–75. Bristol, U.K.: Intellect, 2011.

Ramanathan, Geetha. *Feminist Auteurs: Reading Women's Films*. London: Wallflower, 2006.

Ramsey-Kurz, Helga. "Tokens or Totems? Eccentric Props in Postcolonial Re-enactments of Colonial Consecration." *Literature and Theology* 21, no. 3 (September 2007): 302–16.

Redding, Judith M., and Victoria A. Brownworth. "Jane Campion: A Girl's Own Story." In *Film Fatales: Independent Women Directors*, 179–84. Seattle: Seal Press, 1997.

Rich, Adrienne. "Compulsory Heterosexuality and Lesbian Existence." In *Feminism and Sexuality*, ed. Stevi Jackson and Sue Scott, 130–43. New York: Columbia University Press, 1996.

——. "When We Dead Awaken: Writing as Re-vision." *College English* 34, no. 1 (1972): 18–30.

Riley, Denise. *"Am I That Name?" Feminism and the Category of Women in History*. Minneapolis: University of Minnesota Press, 1988.

Robson, Jocelyn. *Girls' Own Stories: Australian and New Zealand Women's Films*. London: Scarlet Press, 1997.

Roe, Jill. *"My Brilliant Career."* In *Making Film and Television Histories: Australia and New Zealand*, ed. James E. Bennett and Rebecca Beirne, 220–30. London: Tauris, 2011.

Romines, Ann. *Constructing the Little House: Gender, Culture, and Laura Ingalls Wilder*. Amherst: University of Massachusetts Press, 1997.

Rubin, Gayle. "The Traffic in Women: Notes on the 'Political Economy' of Sex." In *The Second Wave: A Reader in Feminist Theory*, ed. Linda Nicholson, 27–62. New York: Routledge, 1997.

Rutherford, Anna. "Changing Images: An Interview with Tracey Moffatt." In *Aboriginal Culture Today*, ed. Anna Rutherford, 146–57. Sydney, N.S.W., Australia: Dangaroo Press, 1988.

Said, Edward W. *Culture and Imperialism*. New York: Knopf, 1993.

Sarmas, Lisa. "What Rape Is?" *Arena Magazine*, no. 8 (1993–1994): 14.

Schneider, Tassilo. "Finding a New *Heimat* in the Wild West: Karl May and the German Western of the 1960s." In *Back in the Saddle Again: New Essays on the Western*, ed. Edward Buscombe and Roberta E. Pearson, 143–59. London: British Film Institute, 1998.

Scott, Joan Wallach. "Gender: A Useful Category of Analysis." In *Gender and the Politics of History*, 28–50. New York: Columbia University Press, 1988.

Shattuc, Jane. "Having a Good Cry Over *The Color Purple*: The Problem of Affect and Imperialism in Feminist Theory." In *Melodrama: Stage, Picture, Screen*, ed. Jacky Bratton, Jim Cook, and Christine Gledhill, 147–56. London: British Film Institute, 1994.

Silverman, Kaja. *The Acoustic Mirror: The Female Voice in Psychoanalysis and Cinema*. Bloomington: Indiana University Press, 1988.

Slotkin, Richard. *The Fatal Environment: The Myth of the Frontier in the Age of Industrialization (1800–1890)*. Norman: University of Oklahoma Press, 1985.

——. *Gunfighter Nation: The Myth of the Frontier in Twentieth-Century America*. Norman: University of Oklahoma Press, 1998.

Smith, Linda Tuhiwai. *Decolonizing Methodologies: Research and Indigenous Peoples*. London: Zed Books, 2012.

Smith-Rosenberg, Carroll. "The Female World of Love and Ritual: Relations Between Women in Nineteenth-Century America." In *Disorderly Conduct: Visions of Gender in Victorian America*, 53–76. New York: Oxford University Press, 1985.

Spivak, Gayatri Chakravorty. "Can the Subaltern Speak?" In *Marxism and the Interpretation of Culture*, ed. Cary Nelson and Lawrence Grossberg, 66–111. Urbana: University of Illinois Press, 1988.

Staiger, Janet. "The Politics of Film Canons." *Cinema Journal* 24, no. 3 (Spring 1985): 4–23.

Stansell, Christine. *City of Women: Sex and Class in New York, 1789–1860*. Chicago: University of Illinois Press, 1987.

Starrs, D. Bruno. "Unlike Mainstream: Towards a Definition of the Australian Art Film." In *Creative Nation: Australian Cinema and Cultural Studies Reader*, ed. Amit Sarwal and Reema Sarwal, 54–72. Delhi, India: SSS, 2009.

Summerhayes, Catherine. *The Moving Images of Tracey Moffatt*. Milano: Charta, 2007.

Tatar, Maria. *Secrets Beyond the Door: "Bluebeard" in Folklore, Fiction, and Film*. Princeton, N.J.: Princeton University Press, 2006.

Templeton, Joan. *Ibsen's Women*. Cambridge: Cambridge University Press, 2000.

Terry, Patricia. "A Chinese Woman in the West: *Thousand Pieces of Gold* and the Revision of the Heroic Frontier." *Literature/Film Quarterly* 22, no. 4 (October 1994): 222–26.

Thompson, Elizabeth. *The Pioneer Woman: A Canadian Character Type*. Montreal, Que., Canada: McGill-Queen's University Press, 1991.

Thornley, Davinia. "Duel or Duet? Gendered Nationalism in *The Piano*." *Film Criticism* 24, no. 3 (Spring 2000): 61–76.

Tincknell, Estella. "The Time and the Place: Music and Costume and the 'Affect' of History in the New Zealand Films of Jane Campion." In *New Zealand Cinema: Interpreting the Past*, ed. Alistair Fox, Barry Keith Grant, and Hilary Radner, 279–89. Bristol, U.K.: Intellect, 2011.

Tompkins, Jane. *West of Everything: The Inner Life of Westerns*. New York: Oxford University Press, 1992.

Tudor, Andrew. "Genre." In *Film Genre Reader*, ed. Barry Keith Grant, 3–10. Austin: University of Texas Press, 1991.

Turner, Frederick Jackson. *The Significance of the Frontier in American History*. Marlborough, U.K.: Adam Matthew Digital, 2007. Electronic reproduction. Originally published in *Annual Report of the American Historical Association*, 1894.

Udel, Lisa J. "Revision and Resistance: The Politics of Native Women's Motherwork." *Frontiers* 22, no. 2 (2001): 43–62.

Van Kirk, Silvia. "The Role of Native Women in the Fur Trade Society of Western Canada, 1670–1830." *Frontiers: A Journal of Women Studies* 7, no. 3 (1984): 9–13.

Vanstone, Gail. *D Is for Daring: The Women Behind the Films of Studio D.* Toronto, Ont., Canada: Sumach Press, 2007.

Verhoeven, Deb. *Jane Campion.* New York: Routledge, 2009.

Wallace, Michele. *Black Macho and the Myth of the Superwoman.* London: Verso, 1979.

Ware, Vron. *Beyond the Pale: White Women, Racism, and History.* London: Verso, 1992.

Waring, Marilyn. *If Women Counted: A New Feminist Economics.* San Francisco: HarperCollins, 1989.

Welter, Barbara. "The Cult of True Womanhood: 1820–1860." *American Quarterly* 18, no. 2, part 1 (Summer 1966): 151–74.

Wexman, Virginia Wright, ed. *Jane Campion: Interviews.* Jackson: University Press of Mississippi, 1999.

White, Patricia. *Uninvited: Classical Hollywood Cinema and Lesbian Representability.* Bloomington: Indiana University Press, 1999.

——. *Women's Cinema, World Cinema: Protecting Contemporary Feminisms.* Durham, N.C.: Duke University Press, 2015.

Williams, Linda. "'Something Else Besides a Mother': *Stella Dallas* and the Maternal Melodrama" (1984). In *Issues in Feminist Film Criticism*, ed. Patricia Erens, 137–62. Bloomington: Indiana University Press, 1990.

——. "When the Woman Looks" (1983). In *The Dread of Difference: Gender and the Horror Film*, ed. Barry Keith Grant, 15–34. Austin: University of Texas Press, 1996.

Williams, Raymond. *Marxism and Literature.* Oxford: Oxford University Press, 1977.

Wilson, R. L. *Buffalo Bill's Wild West: An American Legend.* New York: Random House, 1998.

Wittig, Monique. "The Straight Mind." In *The Feminism and Visual Culture Reader*, ed. Amelia Jones, 130–35. New York: Routledge, 2003. First published in *Feminist Issues* 1, no. 1 (Summer 1980): 103–11.

Wolski, Nathan. "All's Not Quiet on the Western Front—Rethinking Resistance and Frontiers in Aboriginal Historiography." In *Colonial Frontiers: Indigenous-European Encounters in Settler Societies*, ed. Lynette Russell, 216–36. Manchester, U.K.: Manchester University Press, 2001.

Woolf, Virginia. "Professions for Women." In *The Moth and Other Essays.* San Diego, Calif.: Harcourt, Brace, 1974.

Young, Lola. *Fear of the Dark: 'Race,' Gender and Sexuality in the Cinema.* New York: Routledge, 1996.

INDEX

"Compulsory Heterosexuality and Lesbian Experience" (Rich), 21–22
Rickard, Eva, 53, 274n109
Rigby, Ralph, 262n53
Riis, Sharon, 84, 86, 88–89, 91, 93, 253
Riley, Denise, 15, 265n78
riot grrrls, 23
Rogers, Alva, 48
romance, tragic, 79
romanticism, 97
Room of One's Own, A (Woolf), 287n28
Royal Commission into Aboriginal Deaths in Custody (1991), 12, 262n55
Rubin, Gayle, 21, 22, 23, 96, 243, 267n6; on angel-in-the-house figure, 99; on sex negativity, 102, 280n19
Russell, Jane, 269n42
Russell, Rosalind, 40

Said, Edward, 7–8, 186
saloon girl, 30, 74
Sarah and Son (Arzner, 1930), 109
Sarris, Andrew, 3
Satdee Night (Armstrong, 1973), 261n49
savage squaw figure, 106, 208
Schatz im Silberseel, Der [*Treasure of Silver Lake*] (May novel), 35
Scott, Duncan Campbell, 107
Scott, Joan, 21, 56
Screen (BFI journal), 267n16
Screen Australia, 5, 261n50. *See also* Australian Film Commission
Second Sex, The (Beauvoir), 23
selective tradition, 6, 7, 184, 185, 242
sexism, 45, 100, 129, 172, 276n122; heterosexist colonialism, 216; heterosexist gaze, 24, 41, 76; heterosexist patriarchy, 101; in pro-Indian Westerns, 34; stereotypes and, 31
sexuality, 2, 14, 56, 72, 161; active and desiring female sexuality, 151–53;

Australian identities and, 57; of Black women under slavery, 281n25; concept of difference and, 10; construction of, 23; divisions within feminist movement and, 101; feminism and, 15; good/normal versus bad/abnormal, 102, 280n19; heterosexual desire and women's voice, 221; masculine, 149; outside of marriage, 171, 173; sex negativity, 102; subaltern mothers and, 179; symbolic frontier landscapes and, 221, *221*; Victorian, 266n2; in white-settler communities, 216
sex work, 91, 101, 103, 133, 263n63
Sham, John, 255
Shannon, Kathleen, 264n64
Shattue, Jane, 43
Shelley, Mary, 43
Shepard, Deborah, 5
Sholay (1975), 35
shot/reverse-shot technique, 86, 159, 171
Silverman, Kaja, 63, 97
Sirk, Douglas, 36–37, 42, 237
slavery, 10, 47, 49, 50–51, 52, 103, 120; abolition of, 166; in China, 73, 74, 225; maternal bonds and, 104, 281n25; rape of black women and, 104
Slotkin, Richard, 6, 29, 185, 228
Smith, John, 32
Smith-Rosenberg, Carroll, 21, 266n2
Snow, Victoria, 8, 91, 203, 286n23
social realism, 17, 26, 84
Sojourner Truth, 104, 281n26
Sotweed Factor (Barth), 106
sound regimes, 16, 96–97, 110, 181; of *Daughters of the Dust*, 194; of Hollywood, 63; of *My American Cousin*, 83; of *My Brilliant Career*, 80; of *The Piano*, 67
Soviet Union, 34